THE
HOT
HOUSE

Books by Pete Earley

FAMILY OF SPIES
PROPHET OF DEATH
THE HOT HOUSE

THE
HOT
HOUSE

Life Inside Leavenworth Prison

PETE
EARLEY

BANTAM BOOKS
NEW YORK · TORONTO · LONDON · SYDNEY · AUCKLAND

THE HOT HOUSE

A Bantam Book / March 1992

Library of Congress Cataloging-in-Publication Data

Earley, Pete.
   The hot house : life inside Leavenworth Prison / Pete Earley.
      p.   cm.
   ISBN 0-553-07573-X
   1. United States Penitentiary in Leavenworth, Kansas.
2. Prisons—Kansas—Leavenworth.   I. Title.
HV9474.L5E22 1992
365'.978138—dc20   91-25400
                                                          CIP

Published simultaneously in the United States and Canada

---

*Bantam Books are published by Bantam Books, a division of
Bantam Doubleday Dell Publishing Group, Inc. Its trademark,
consisting of the words "Bantam Books" and the portrayal of a
rooster, is Registered in U.S. Patent and Trademark Office and in
other countries. Marca Registrada. Bantam Books, 666 Fifth Avenue, New York, New York 10103.*

PRINTED IN THE UNITED STATES OF AMERICA

RRH   0 9 8 7 6 5 4 3 2 1

For Elmer and Jean,
my parents

"Fancy thinking the beast was something you could hunt and kill! . . . You knew, didn't you? I'm part of you? Close, close, close! I'm the reason why it's no go. Why things are what they are."

WILLIAM GOLDING
Lord of the Flies

This book is an eyewitness account of day-to-day life inside the United States penitentiary in Leavenworth, Kansas, the oldest federal prison and one of the most dangerous in the nation. I was the first writer ever to have been given unlimited access by the federal Bureau of Prisons to one of its maximum-security prisons. The events that follow took place between July 1987 and July 1989. The names of a handful of persons have been changed to protect them from physical harm or from further criminal prosecution, but all the characters are real and the events are described exactly as they happened.

PETE EARLEY

CONTENTS

MAJOR PLAYERS

CARL BOWLES: **The Predator**

WILLIAM POST: **The Catman**

ROBERT MATTHEWS: **The New Warden**

THOMAS LITTLE: **The Newcomer**

DALLAS SCOTT: **The Gang Member**

THOMAS SILVERSTEIN: **The Killer**

NORMAN BUCKLEW: **The Savage**

EDWARD GEOUGE: **The Tough Cop**

BILL SLACK: **The Humanitarian**

PART ONE

"Toto, I've a feeling we're not in Kansas anymore!"

DOROTHY
FROM THE MOVIE
THE WIZARD OF OZ

CHAPTER ONE

CARL BOWLES

Jeffrey Joe Hicks was a snitch. Carl Bowles was certain of it. But Bowles needed proof. Convicts at the U.S. penitentiary in Leavenworth, Kansas, hated informants even more than they hated guards. A "hack," as guards at the maximum-security prison were called, was simply doing his job. But an inmate snitch was a Judas, and the best way to deal with a rat, as far as Bowles was concerned, was to kill it.

Bowles had been suspicious of Hicks from the moment they met eight months earlier, when Hicks was still being held in an area of the ancient prison reserved for new inmates not yet assigned permanent cells. Hicks had stood out among the "fish," prison slang for newcomers. At twenty-eight, he had a small build and pubescent appearance, but it was his demeanor that everyone noticed. Hicks was terrified. "Guys were damn near fighting each other over him," Bowles recalled later. "They said, 'Oh, we got to protect this poor kid! Why, he's white and he doesn't want anything to do with the niggers and he is afraid they are going to take him and fuck him. Somebody's got to do something.' "

Bowles had been the first to actually meet Hicks. At the time, he claimed he simply wanted to give Hicks some advice, but guards suspected that the forty-seven-year-old Bowles had a different motive. The federal Bureau of Prisons identified Bowles in its files as a sexual predator, a convict who forced weaker inmates to satisfy his sexual needs. "It wasn't the goodness of his

3

heart that caused Carl Bowles to search out Jeffrey Hicks," a guard remarked. "It was a lower section of his anatomy."

Except for a short stint when he was free after an escape, Bowles had spent twenty-three consecutive years in prison. A convicted cop killer, kidnapper, and triple murderer, he had been taken into custody for the first time at age twelve. Bowles had literally grown up in jail, and few inmates knew their way as well around a prison or had better jailhouse instincts.

At Leavenworth, all convicts are released from their cells at six A.M., and are free to roam the large prison compound relatively unrestricted until ten P.M., when they are locked up for the night. Bowles had gone to the "fish tier" to meet Hicks within days after he arrived.

"First time in a penitentiary?" Bowles had asked.

"Yeah."

"It can be pretty scary until a man figures out what is going on," Bowles had said, shaking a cigarette out of a pack for himself and then offering one to Hicks. "Where you from?"

"A state joint in Michigan," Hicks had answered.

"Oh yeah?" Bowles had remarked with interest. "Well, what they got you for?"

"Uh, I can't say," Hicks had answered. "I got an appeal, you know, still in court."

"Sure, kid," Bowles had replied, his mood noticeably colder. He had dropped his cigarette, stomped it on the prison's tile floor, and left.

Months later when he recalled that meeting, Bowles explained: "When Hicks told me he was a state prisoner from Michigan and then refused to tell me his crime, I knew there was something spooky about him. You see, there are only two reasons why the feds accept state prisoners. The guy is either such a mean son of a bitch that the state joint can't handle him or the state has to get rid of him because he'll be killed by convicts if they put him in a state joint.

"Now, even an idiot can see that Hicks ain't no ruthless motherfucker, so I figured there was something wrong with him. I figured he was a snitch."

Just because Bowles had suddenly lost interest in Hicks didn't mean others had. It took prison officials two weeks to process Hicks's paperwork, and by that time another convicted killer and alleged sexual predator had invited Hicks to move into his cell. Guards and inmates assumed Hicks was the inmate's "punk"—serving as the convict's sexual partner in return for protection. But a few months after Hicks moved into the inmate's cell, something strange had happened. Hicks and his cellmate were accused of plotting an elaborate helicopter escape. Lieutenant Edward Gallegos, who exposed the plot, said Hicks's cellmate had tried to hire a helicopter pilot to swoop into the prison yard and rescue them.

As punishment, Hicks was moved into an isolation cell in the prison's Hole. His cellmate received a worse punishment. He was sent to the federal penitentiary in Marion, Illinois, the harshest prison operated by the federal government. At Marion, prisoners were kept locked in one-man cells twenty-three hours a day and denied nearly all privileges.

"The only way guards find out anything in here is when someone snitches," Bowles complained. "Someone had tipped off the cops to that helicopter plot, and it sure as hell wasn't the guy who got shipped to Marion. After that I was certain Hicks was a snitch."

When Hicks was released from the Hole, another white inmate took him in as his cell partner and sexual punk. Bowles knew this inmate. They were friends and Bowles was worried about him. He figured that Hicks was going to do something to get the inmate into trouble. Bowles decided to investigate Hicks's background and he began by visiting Harold Gooden.

Every prison has its oddballs, and at Leavenworth, Gooden was one of them. A convicted counterfeiter, he was the only inmate in the penitentiary who subscribed to *Architectural Digest*. Gooden was college-educated, an honorably discharged navy veteran, and a bearded, pipe-smoking, self-proclaimed prison philosopher who passed his time by writing what he claimed was an epic novel. He also had the largest magazine collection at Leavenworth, much of it not the convicts' typical reading materials—*Penthouse* and *Hustler*—but old copies of the Sunday edition of *The New York Times*, *The New Yorker*, *The Atlantic*, and *Harper's*. But these were not what Bowles had come looking for when he paused outside Gooden's open cell door, knocked, and waited to be invited in, a sign of respect between convicts in prison.

"I need to borrow a few magazines," Bowles explained.

"Help yourself, Carl," Gooden told him. "Anything in particular?"

"True crime," Bowles replied.

Besides his rows of highbrow publications, Gooden also kept a large collection of sleazy detective magazines. He subscribed to them, not because he enjoyed reading them, but to identify inmates who had committed particularly heinous sex crimes. After snitches, the most despised inmates in Leavenworth were child molesters, rapists, and other sexual deviants. Sex offenders gave criminals a bad name, convicts claimed. Most inmates either were married or had been, and many were fathers. Like men outside prison, they didn't want their mothers, wives, and children to be victims of a deviant.

Bowles took a few magazines and returned to his cell, where he scanned them, but he found nothing of interest and returned to Gooden's cell.

"Carl, I think you should check out this one," Gooden volunteered, handing Bowles a copy of *Inside Detective*. Page thirty-six was folded down, so Bowles turned to it. He saw a two-column, black-and-white photograph of a freckle-faced boy grinning into the camera. Above it was a headline: STOP THE SEXUAL SADIST FROM ABDUCTING BOYS! The story below said that the thirteen-year-old boy in the picture had been forced off a road while riding his bicycle on October 19, 1986, in Green Oak Township, Michigan. The driver had jumped from his Jeep, dragged the boy inside the vehicle, and sped away. A few days later, the youngster's naked body was found abandoned in a forest. He had been sexually molested and strangled. When Bowles turned the page, the baby face of Jeffrey Joe Hicks stared up at him. The caption underneath the photograph read, "Hicks has a long history of molesting children sexually."

Bowles closed the magazine, said "Thanks," and took it back to his cell. There he read the entire story. It reported that Hicks had first gotten into trouble in January 1975, when he was sixteen, and abducted a twelve-year-old boy at knife-point, forced him to swallow several tranquilizers, and molested him. Despite the seriousness of the crime, Hicks was put on five years' probation. Seven years later, he sexually assaulted two other youngsters, but was released on probation again. Only after he was accused of kidnapping and murder was he finally jailed. At his trial, Hicks's attorneys admitted their client was guilty, but said he shouldn't be sent to prison because he was himself a victim. Hicks had been raped as a child by a psychiatrist who was supposed to be treating him for deviant behavior, they said, and it was that molestation that caused him to attack young boys. Hicks testified in his own defense, describing how he had held his victim's hands down and strangled the cyclist with his belt after abusing him. A jury ignored Hicks's plea for mercy and sentenced him to life in prison, plus sixty-five to one hundred years.

Now Bowles knew why state officials in Michigan had arranged for Hicks to serve his sentence in a federal prison rather than in a state institution. His crime was so monstrous and had attracted such wide publicity that Hicks would have been instantly recognized in a state prison and most likely would have been physically attacked or even murdered by other inmates. In the federal prison system, however, Hicks would be safe because he would be just another anonymous convict—unless, of course, someone put out word about his crime.

Clutching the magazine in his hand, Bowles walked toward the prison law library where he planned to photocopy the article. He would post copies on the bulletin boards in each cellblock. But before he reached the copying machine, he decided to tell Hicks's cell partner about his discovery. He walked directly to the cell, entered without knocking, and tossed the magazine to Hicks's cellmate. Hicks wasn't there.

"Why, that little fucker!" the inmate snapped when he saw the photograph.

Bowles took back the magazine and started back toward the library. Midway down the tier, he spotted Jeffrey Hicks coming toward him. Hicks had been doing his cellmate's laundry and was carrying several carefully folded items. Bowles grinned and kept walking until Hicks was close, then lifted the magazine so that Hicks was suddenly face-to-face with his own photograph.

"You little bastard!" a voice yelled from behind Bowles. It was Hicks's cellmate, who had come charging out on the tier.

Terrified, Hicks dropped the laundry, spun around, and bolted toward the two guards stationed near the tier stairwell. They hustled him out of the cellblock.

There was no longer any need for Bowles to make copies of the story, but he made one for himself anyway. "I spread the word about Hicks because I wanted everyone to see how the cops in here work," he said. It wasn't the fact that Hicks was a sexual deviant that bothered Bowles. It was the fact that he was a snitch. "The guards will deny it, but I know exactly what happened," Bowles said later. "Some hack from Michigan called up a lieutenant here and said, 'Hey, I got a prisoner and I got to get him out of my state institution before someone kills him.' Now a lieutenant here says, 'Well, why should we take him? Does he cooperate?' and the guy in Michigan says, 'Fuck yes, he'll cooperate, because if he don't we'll tell everyone he's a baby-raper and they'll kill his ass.'

"When Hicks gets down here, the lieutenant says, 'Hey, boy, we will put you in population, but at the same time you got to come to us every once in a while and tell us things, because if you don't, then someone might just slip up and let folks know your past.' Don't you see what happens next? Suddenly, some lieutenant is breaking up a big helicopter escape."

Lieutenant Gallegos discounted Bowles's scenario. "He's telling how he operates, how he thinks, how he manipulates people," said Gallegos. "We don't do that. No one forced Hicks to say or do anything. Believe me, we don't have to do anything to force these guys to snitch. Most will tell on each other in a second."

Prison officials acknowledged that they had accepted Hicks from state officials in Michigan because he would have been harmed in a state prison. But they denied that Hicks had been planted in Leavenworth or coerced into providing Gallegos information. "This prisoner was sent to Leavenworth because of the length of his sentence," a prison spokesman said. "We felt he needed to be placed in a high-security environment." A few days after Bowles exposed Hicks, however, the young inmate was quietly transferred to a lower-security federal prison in another state. "The prison grapevine is such that we had to move this prisoner to a much lower security prison," an official explained. "Otherwise his past would have been exposed and he would have been in danger."

Bowles saw things differently. "I don't care what they say, they used Hicks and now they are rewarding him by moving him to an easier joint. That's how both sides work in this place. When someone weak like Hicks comes in, then each side preys on him."

A short time after Hicks had gone, Bowles heard through the grapevine that another fish was coming to Leavenworth, and that he, like Hicks, was scared. No one knew why prison officials were sending Thomas Edgar Little to a maximum-security penitentiary. Little had never been to prison before and he was young and weak.

Bowles figured Thomas Little was someone he wanted to meet.

CHAPTER TWO

DALLAS SCOTT

Dallas Earl Scott sounded mean as he spoke into the telephone. "Now this has already gone on for a week and a half," the forty-two-year-old convict complained. "The position you're putting people in, particularly your boyfriend, Bill, you're putting a lot of pressure on him . . . and a lot of people are beginning to get upset."

Scott had emphasized the word *upset*. He was trying to make it clear to the woman on the other end of the line that her boyfriend, Bill, was going to be hurt if she didn't do what Scott had asked. Scott didn't want to come right out and say this, because he knew all prison telephone calls were recorded. A card posted above the phone warned: ATTENTION: ALL INMATE TELE-PHONE CALLS ARE MONITORED AND TAPE RECORDED.

The woman that Scott was trying to frighten had promised to bring 2.73 grams of heroin into Leavenworth. Scott had paid $500 to buy the drug from his contacts in Sacramento, California, and had paid another $500 to the woman's boyfriend, Bill Hutchinson, an inmate who claimed that he could get the drug smuggled safely inside. Hutchinson had seemed so confident that his girlfriend would agree to be a "mule" that Scott had arranged for the drug to be mailed directly to her from California, assuring his financial backers in prison that the heroin was on its way.

But Hutchinson's girlfriend balked. She was refusing to bring in the heroin, and Scott was indeed upset. Earlier that morning, he had confronted Hutchinson, and it had been Hutchinson's idea to use the telephone located inside the cellhouse to call his girlfriend and then put Scott on the line to intimidate her. Inmates at Leavenworth are allowed to use cellhouse telephones whenever they wish without first asking for permission from a guard. But they can only dial collect calls, and a prison computer automatically logs the number and records the entire conversation. Hutchinson had told his girlfriend that he was in trouble and then handed Scott the telephone receiver.

"Pressure is being put on Bill, you see," Scott said carefully. "You got him, ah, well . . . he's in a spot, because you said yes from jump street and that triggered a lot of things. That leaves him holding the bag . . . and now you got cold feet."

Scott had sounded threatening at first. Now, his voice became sympathetic. "Look, I can understand why you are scared and I appreciate that, but we got to get this thing resolved. . . . If you just do what Bill asks you, it's not going to be near as bad as you think. . . . In your mind, you got pictures of being beaten with rubber hoses and being dragged off. That's not gonna happen. . . ."

Hutchinson had explained the procedure to her. The heroin was delivered inside a balloon, no different from those used at children's birthday parties. She was supposed to hide it in her vagina, like a tampon. Once inside the prison visiting room, she would step into the women's bathroom, remove the balloon, and conceal it in her mouth. Visitors were allowed to kiss an inmate once when a visit began and once when it ended. The balloon would be exchanged during the first kiss. Hutchinson would swallow it and either regurgitate it later when he was alone in his cell or reclaim it after it passed through his system.

"It's just a simple matter of boom, boom, and that's it," Scott continued. "Believe me, this thing happens a thousand times a year. Don't make monsters in your mind."

Scott decided he had said enough, but before he handed the phone back to Hutchinson, Scott decided to remind the woman that her boyfriend was in trouble.

"Now, I'm sure you understand what goes on in here," Scott said firmly. "You know, this place, well, it's dangerous. . . ."

Had Scott been talking to the girlfriend in person, there

wouldn't have been any need for him to make thinly disguised verbal threats. Scott was intimidating even when he didn't intend to be. A bank teller had once described him during a trial as being "really mean-looking," and it fit. Scott had been in prison off and on for twenty-four years, and his body language sent out a signal as clear as a diamondback's rattle. He was built like a pit bull. Short, with massive shoulders made hard by weight lifting, Scott wore his ink-black hair combed back in the greasy pompadour style popular among bikers in the 1950s when Scott was a teenager. A nearly fatal heroin habit acquired in prison and an incurable liver disease brought on by hepatitis had left his skin jaundiced, his face gaunt. There were dark circles under his eyes, and when he became angry, his black eyes shone with rage.

Ironically, among his convict pals Scott was considered easygoing, funny, street-smart, and, as much as an inmate could be, devoted to his wife, son, and daughter. But even his closest friends knew better than to double-cross Scott. There was no question in anyone's mind that he was deadly.

The collection of tattoos that adorned Scott's arms, chest, legs, and even his hands was a sign that he was a professional convict. Daggers dripping blood, half-naked women, even Donald Duck's laughing face, were cut into his yellowish skin. These were not parlor tattoos, applied from patterns in rainbow colors. They were convict tattoos, carved freehand by cumbersome tattoo guns made from melted-down toothbrushes, sewing machine needles, and motors stolen from portable tape players. Even though they had been drawn by different inmates in different prisons at different times, each tattoo was done in the identical color: a bluish-green ink—the standard ink used for printing forms in prisons. In the outside world the tattoos would have made Scott look like a circus sideshow freak, but in Leavenworth they were badges of honor, particularly one tattoo cut directly over his heart. It was a cloverleaf with the numbers 6–6–6 printed over it. Even fish knew what that tattoo represented. It was the insignia of the Aryan Brotherhood, the most savage white prison gang ever formed. The three sixes referred to a mark given by "the beast"—the antichrist, or son of Satan—to the wicked as explained in the Book of Revelation, chapter 13, verses 16–18. The cloverleaf was a symbol of white supremacy.

The fact that Scott's chest bore the "triple sixes" was evidence that he was one of the gang's earliest members, because it had abandoned the use of tattoos shortly after it was formed, when it realized that guards and the police used the tattoos to track gang members.

The bureau's Special Investigative Service (SIS), which operated much like the FBI inside prisons, had a thick file of alleged gang activity by Scott. The most damning was an affidavit given by a former AB gang member who had turned against his former friends in exchange for an early release and a new identity through the Justice Department's witness-protection program. He had identified Scott as a top gang member and had implied that he had once been a gang "hit man," although there was absolutely no proof that he was linked to any murders.

Scott denied the hit-man charge and pointed out that his entire criminal career consisted of only two felonies: a 1966 armed robbery and a 1975 bank robbery. That was it, yet the government had managed to keep him in jail for nearly three decades by tacking on extra time for various violations that it said Scott had committed while in prison.

"My criminal record ain't shit," Scott complained, "but if you look at how they treat me, you'd think I was some sort of Jesse James or Godfather!"

As a matter of fact, that is exactly how the bureau viewed him, and without apology. "He is definitely Aryan Brotherhood and once a convict becomes an AB, he is an AB for life," the bureau's gang expert, Craig Trout, explained. "What we are dealing with is a professional, lifelong criminal. . . . An AB member like Dallas Scott is actually doing a life sentence—only he's doing it on the installment plan, serving a few years at a time."

After Scott had finished speaking to Hutchinson's girlfriend, he had gone to wait outside Hutchinson's cell.

"She's gonna do it," Hutchinson announced when he returned from the phone call. "This week sometime."

Scott didn't know whether or not to believe him, nor was he confident that the girlfriend really understood the seriousness of what was happening. Scott hadn't been bluffing on the telephone. If she didn't bring in the heroin, Hutchinson was going to be hurt. Scott couldn't afford to let word leak out that he had paid $500 to the man and then simply let him off the hook when his girlfriend didn't deliver. Every convict in Leavenworth would think that Scott was either getting soft or was afraid, in convict slang, to "make a move on Hutchinson" for fear of being punished by the guards. Either way, Scott would look weak and other convicts would quickly take advantage of him. If Hutchinson didn't deliver, why should the inmates who gambled at the nightly poker game that Scott operated in the cellblock television room pay their debts? If Scott was reluctant to punish Hutchinson for fear of getting caught by the guards, wouldn't he be equally afraid of attacking someone who came into his cell and took his radio, shoes, mattress? Scott didn't really have any choice. For Hutchinson's sake, he hoped the girlfriend delivered.

The next afternoon, Scott was standing inside his cell near the front bars as required for the daily four o'clock head count. At Leavenworth, every inmate is counted at least five times a day to make certain no one has escaped. These counts are held at ten P.M., when inmates are locked in their cells for the night, and at midnight, three A.M., and five-thirty A.M., before the cells are unlocked for the day. Each afternoon at exactly four o'clock, inmates are required to return to their cells for the most important count of the day. It differs from the others because convicts are required to be standing up when guards pass by and count them. By making them stand, guards can be certain that they are counting a breathing human being, not a papier-mâché dummy tucked under the bedclothes. Because the inmates are locked in their cells for the four o'clock count, it is the easiest time during the day for guards to make arrests. Not only do they know where every convict is inside the prison, but they can also arrest an inmate without worrying about his friends jumping into the fray.

When Scott looked through his cell door, he spotted a group of guards coming down the tier. Instinctively, he lowered one shoulder and slightly bent his knees. Scott was no stranger to fistfights with guards. In the 1970s, he had beaten an associate warden in the prison yard. He was charged with assault by the bureau and given additional time to serve for that attack, but what wasn't mentioned, Scott claimed later, was that after he was wrestled down and handcuffed, he was taken to the Hole and beaten by guards in retaliation. The officers at Leavenworth didn't doubt his claim. It used to be common within the bureau for guards to give inmates an "ass-whipping" if they struck a staff member. If anything, the beating made Scott more resolute. The only way for convicts to avoid being picked on was to fight back. "There are two sides in prison and only two. If one side gives an inch, the other side tries to grab two inches. That's just how it is; you never willingly give up ground."

When it came to guards, Scott said he followed a simple philosophy. "If they are respectful, I return respect. If they speak in a courteous manner, I will speak in a courteous manner, but if they want to start that silly shit, then I'm going to push back—hard."

When the cell door popped open, Scott took a deep breath and made fists. But the lieutenant in charge of the guards said matter-of-factly, "We need you to come with us."

If the guards had wanted to fight, they would have rushed him. Scott stuck out his hands to be handcuffed. He was marched down the tier as other inmates pressed their faces to the bars and watched. Scott strutted along, holding his head up proudly.

"You are being charged with attempting to smuggle contraband inside a federal penitentiary, to wit, two point seven three grams of heroin," the lieutenant on duty explained once Scott was downstairs inside the lieutenant's office, a room that serves the same role inside the prison as a police headquarters. "Got anything to say?"

"This is bullshit," Scott replied. "I didn't do a fucking thing and I don't know anything about any heroin."

The lieutenant didn't bother asking any further questions. Guards escorted Scott to the Hole, where he continued to fume.

"This is a bum beef," he told the guards there. "Total bullshit." For days he complained, and then one morning he got some news from a friendly guard. The FBI had a copy of the tape-recorded telephone conversation of Scott threatening Bill Hutchinson's girlfriend, the guard told him.

"No one has my voice on tape," Scott insisted. "They may have someone's voice on tape, but they will never be able to prove it is mine."

They might not have to, the guard said. The word circulating among the guards was that inmate Bill Hutchinson had been whisked out of Leavenworth during the night and taken to another prison so that Scott couldn't get to him. Hutchinson and his girlfriend had cut some sort of deal with the FBI, according to the guard. They had agreed to testify against Scott in return for a plea bargain.

If the guard was waiting for Scott to react, he was disappointed.

"Fuck the government," Scott said. "This is a bullshit charge. I don't know nothing about any heroin."

CHAPTER
THREE

WILLIAM POST

As he walked briskly around the blacktop track in the prison yard, William Post felt hopeful. The federal Parole Commission was reviewing his request for leniency and Post was optimistic about his chances. After all, he had served fifteen years of his forty-five-year sentence for bank robbery, and most parole boards turned a criminal loose after he completed one-third of his prison term. Post also had an exemplary record while in prison. He had earned a college degree in psychology, participated in thirty-four psychotherapy group sessions (a prison psychologist had described Post as "a highly motivated and cooperative individual who has made a positive contribution to the group"), and he had kept out of trouble. A prison counselor had even congratulated the forty-two-year-old convict for "gaining significant insight into his behavior" and "making an excellent institutional adjustment." Surely with that kind of record, the Parole Commission would grant him his freedom.

As a rule, Post didn't think about the outside world. "You got to cut yourself off from such thoughts," he explained. "You have to deal with the reality of where you physically are, not daydream about the streets."

But as he strode along the outdoor track that July 1987 day, Post let his mind wander. He thought about what he would do when he was freed, where he would go, and then, in a flash, he recalled the crime that had landed him in Leavenworth.

It was supposed to be an easy heist. At least, that is what

Post and his partner, Gary Tanksley, thought when they burst through the doors of a bank in Dearborn, Michigan, waving pistols and screaming at the tellers and customers to get down on the floor. At most, the robbers figured, it would take five minutes to grab the cash and escape. It was not the first time they had robbed banks together and they had perfected their technique.

Leaping over the counter, Tanksley scooped bills from the tellers' drawers while Post hustled the bank manager into the vault and ordered him to open the safe. But during the excitement neither robber had taken time to check behind a door near the front entrance. It looked as if it were a storage closet, but it actually opened onto stairs that led to an employee lounge in the basement. Seconds before Tanksley and Post had entered the bank, a security guard had gone down the stairway into the lounge for a cup of coffee, and now he was on his way up. As soon as he opened the door and saw the customers on the floor, he realized a robbery was under way. Pulling the door closed, he put down his coffee and slipped out his revolver. But Tanksley had spotted him. When the guard opened the door for a second time, Tanksley was waiting, and leveled his pistol at the guard's head.

For some reason, he didn't fire. The guard did. His bullet ripped into Tanksley's shoulder, ricocheted off a bone, and severed his aorta. Blood spurted from the exit wound in his chest as he fell dying. Hearing gunfire, Post dashed from the vault just in time to see the guard swing around. Post ducked behind a counter and began firing. The guard dived back into the stairwell and pulled the door shut. Post riddled the door with rounds from his .357 Magnum handgun. The metal-piercing slugs splintered the wood as the guard raced down the steps to safety.

Post ran over to Tanksley. "Blood was squirting out of his chest like a spigot," Post recalled. "I mean, blood is everywhere, and I swear he's got a big red halo around him."

Post had taken $21,000 from the vault and Tanksley was still clutching a bag of cash from the teller drawers. But as Post reached for it, he suddenly jerked back his hand. "It was crazy but I thought, 'Man, I'm not reaching down in all that blood.'" Instead, he dashed outside to a waiting getaway car.

A few hours later, Post was captured, and on April 24, 1973, he was turned over to the bureau. Had the bank robbery been his only crime, he might have received a lighter sentence than forty-five years, one month, and seventeen days. But his criminal record dated back to 1953, when, only eight years old, he stole a car and ran away from home. As he grew older, he was arrested for robbery, burglary, assault, car theft, and assorted petty crimes. By fifteen, Post was described by a court psychologist as a "psychopathic delinquent with highly destructive impulses and no apparent motivation for altering his behavior." Over the next twenty-seven years, Post only spent a combined total of one year as a free man. That was it—*one year*—between the ages of fifteen and forty-two. Every other moment was spent in some sort of incarceration.

At Leavenworth, Post was known simply as the "Catman" because he took care of six cats that lived inside the prison. No one knows exactly when the cats arrived. Probably they were brought in to catch mice, but before long there were so many cats running around the cellhouses that they had become a nuisance, and guards began talking about getting rid of them. The inmates protested. There were rumors that for every cat killed, a guard would be slain. A compromise was reached. As long as an inmate took care of the cats and the feline population was kept to a reasonable number, they could stay.

Post was the prison's second catman. He fed the cats each morning and night, paid their veterinary bills out of his meager earnings from his prison job, and badgered guards into taking kittens home as pets. Since Post had taken over the job in 1982, he had found homes for more than one hundred kittens. His entire day revolved around the cats. In the mornings, he worked at the trash dumpster behind the kitchen, one of the filthiest jobs at the prison, but the best for collecting meat scraps. In the afternoon, he played with the cats in the yard. His antics were so lighthearted that other convicts often gawked as Post chased the cats, mimicking their shrill meows, or lay on his back on the ball field tossing a kitten in the air above his chest like a father playing with a toddler. His favorite cat was Tiger. When asked why he bothered with the cats, Post replied, "Because I'm a militant heterosexual. I love pussy!" Most guards—and inmates—figured he was nuts.

He did little to discourage that opinion. He was the scruffiest inmate in Leavenworth. Most days, the rail-thin Post wore faded army dungarees, tattered black tennis shoes, a soiled T-shirt, and a light purple jogging jacket with gaping holes in the elbows. A bright red cowboy bandanna was wrapped around his unwashed, shoulder-length brown hair and he wore a full unkempt beard and sunglasses with mirror lenses that hid his bright blue eyes. His nose was flat, as if it had been smashed several times and rebuilt with fewer and fewer pieces.

Post lived in a one-man cell that was as unkempt as he was. Washed and filthy clothes were strewn together on his unmade bed. Old issues of *Guns & Ammo* lay on the floor. Used yellow legal pads peeked from cardboard boxes crammed with envelopes, crumpled papers, and tattered paperback books. Guards were always getting after Post to clean up his cell; some even threatened to assign him extra work around the cellhouse if he didn't straighten up the mess. Such threats would usually prompt him to pick up a few things, but within minutes after guards had checked his cell, it was as messy as it had been before.

While Post was seen as dimwitted by some at Leavenworth, he had actually scored higher on intelligence tests than most of his peers, and, unlike nearly all of them, he came from a stable, middle-class family. His father was a naval officer cited for heroism in the Pacific theater during World War II. His mother was a housewife and devoted mother. None of Post's siblings had gotten into trouble.

Why had he been different?

Post himself had spent much of his time in prison trying to answer the puzzle. The experts hadn't helped. Numerous prison psychologists had examined Post since his first arrest, and each had issued a diagnosis that mirrored the latest fad. When society felt criminals were being coddled, the psychologist wrote that Post had not received adequate discipline in his home as a child. Whenever a more liberal attitude prevailed, psychologists reasoned that Post had turned to crime because he was "rebelling against the rigidity of the family setting—a military father who ran his home like he ran his ship." After Post earned his bachelor's degree in psychology while in prison, he read the information in his prison file more judiciously. He understood what a psychologist meant in 1968 when he had written that Post exhibited "a sociopathic personality disturbance, anti-social reaction personality trait disturbance, and emotionally unstable personality." Not only did Post understand the terms, he could remember the interview with the psychologist.

"He began by reading me my rights, which I thought was odd," Post recalled, "and then he turned on his tape recorder and started questioning me about my crime like a prosecutor looking for information. I said to him, 'You dickhead, you faggot motherfucker, why are you asking me about my crimes? I've got nothing to say to you.' That is all he heard—and from that, he wrote that description which has been part of my file for nearly twenty years!"

Post had drawn up his own diagnosis: he had always identified with losers. "I was always an outsider," he explained. "When my family lived at the naval base in the Philippines, I used to tag along with Filipino kids, not Americans. We would sit on the roofs of the whorehouses near the navy base yelling 'Americans are pigs!' When my family came back to the States, my brother and sisters and parents didn't have any problem fitting in, but I did. I used to look at pictures in magazines, you know, of the Chevy commercial with the dad and mom and kids all sitting in the car in suburbia, and it gave me vertigo. I didn't want it."

His relationship with his father played some role in his rejection of society, although Post wasn't certain how or why. "I was raised by a genuine war hero. He won the Silver Star, Bronze Star, Purple Heart. People were used to looking up to him," Post recalled. "No one looked up to me."

When Post went to Saturday matinees as a child, he found himself cheering for the outlaws. "I could identify with James Cagney, Humphrey Bogart, guys who didn't fit in, because that is how I always felt."

There was one evaluation in his prison file that Post liked. On June 14, 1973, a prison psychologist wrote:

"It must be noted that Post has spent most of his entire life incarcerated. Yet, he has not become an institutionalized individual. . . ."

That someone in authority had written that he had not become "an institutionalized individual" was momentous to him. "After all these years, they still think I can make it in the outside world," Post said as he walked around the prison track. "That's significant."

Privately, Post said he sometimes wondered if he could. "It's getting to the point where I can't even picture myself on the streets anymore. I look at children on television and they no longer look real to me. After fifteen straight years, they look like cartoon characters.

"Lately, I've been having scary thoughts," he continued. "Being in here gets to you, day after day after day. Sometimes, I think about what it would be like to just go into a bank and blow the head off the first teller I see. I know that I am capable of that; I mean, any criminal is capable of that, and long-term prisoners can kill easier than most people, because you are around the dregs so much and for so long that you forget the worth of a human life. You think all humans are dregs. The guards are no different. They are dregs, broken by the same system."

That is why the cats are so important to him. "I don't want to be a mass murderer, a killer. The cats keep me feeling some warmth, some kind of feeling connected to something other than 'those' dregs or 'us' dregs. The cats are what I need to remind me that I still have some standards and have not yet gone to the bottom, where you are capable of anything."

Post knew convicts at Leavenworth who, he said, were institutionalized and happy about it. "The truth is, some of these guys really like it here. It's their home! But it's not mine. That's why I don't clean my cell. I want to remind myself that it isn't my cell. Guys in here refer to their cell as being their 'house.' This isn't my 'house.' It's theirs, and if they want it clean, then they can clean it."

Post had dealt with parole boards several times, he knew his long criminal past was going to be difficult to overcome, but he had been gathering newspaper clippings about other criminals who had been successful at getting paroles. He found the stories encouraging. The case of Lawrence Singleton had caught his attention. Convicted in 1978 of raping a fifteen-year-old hitch-hiker, hacking off her forearms with an ax, and leaving her for dead along a rural California road, Singleton had been paroled after serving nine years. "If a guy like that can get a parole after nine years and I can't get one for a simple bank robbery after serving fifteen years, then I got to wonder what kind of message they are trying to send me," Post said. "Does that mean I'm worse than Lawrence Singleton? If the parole board makes me stay here for twenty-five years, are they telling me I am twice as bad as a guy like him? *Twice as bad!* And if that's the case, what am I allowed to do? Am I missing out on not taking advantage?

"The next time I rob a bank," Post continued, "why not rape the teller or shoot everyone, since society already has said to me that I am *twice* as bad as someone who rapes a little kid and chops off her arms? Where is the justice in turning him loose and keeping me in prison?"

In his appeal to the parole commission, Post had tried to differentiate between himself and the likes of a Singleton:

> I committed none of the mindless random violence of the terrorist or airplane hijacker. None of my crimes was designed specifically to harm people as is the murderer; and none of my crimes had the countless victims as has the large scale heroin dealers. . . .

As he turned toward the main penitentiary building and completed his last lap around the track, Post explained: "Perhaps it's rationalization on my part, but I have always tried to think of my crimes in terms of permanent damage, and I don't think that bank robbery causes permanent damage. Maybe a teller gets so scared she wets her pants, but it's not a crime like rape."

As soon as Post entered his cellblock, a guard told him that a prison counselor wanted to see him. There could be only one explanation. The federal Parole Commission had written him an answer. Post hurried to the counselor's office and took the envelope from his outstretched hand. He removed the neatly typed letter.

> In response to your plea for a more lenient decision, you provide no significant mitigating circumstances sufficient to merit a different decision. . . . Your institutional behavior and achievements have been considered by the commission, but are not deemed sufficient

to warrant a more lenient decision. . . . Your plea is therefore denied.

Post walked back into the prison yard and tracked down Tiger. He was angry, not at the commission, he said, but at himself for actually believing that the college degree and his good behavior while in prison would sway the board.

"How can I take these people seriously," he asked, stroking Tiger, "when they tell me I'm worse than a guy who rapes a girl, chops off her arms, and throws her out on the side of a road?"

CHAPTER FOUR

THE PENITENTIARY

There is no air-conditioning in C cellhouse, and until a man sits inside a cell on the top tier during a scorching Kansas summer, he does not really understand sweat. The brown metal fans turning sluggishly outside the cells do not cool the air, they simply move it back and forth as if to make certain no corner is untouched by the heat. The design of the cellhouse contributes to the misery. It is actually two independent structures, one within the other—a great stone building dropped like a cake dish over a rectangular, five-story-tall row of human cages. The cells are stacked in the center of the building like a giant honeycomb: side by side, one row atop the other and back to back, so that each cell facing north has an identical cell behind it facing south. There is a twenty-foot open space between the cells and the exterior walls. Because of this, you can stand on the bottom floor and look down the entire length of the shoebox-shaped cellhouse. You can look up, too, and see each of the five tiers bounded by steel balconies. But if you try to count the cells you will eventually lose track, because the five-and-a-half-by-nine-foot cubicles are indistinguishable from one another, and counting them is as difficult as keeping track of boxcars on a mile-long freight train.

On most afternoons the sun filters through the cellhouse's cathedral-size windows, casting a grid of shadows on the white tile floor. It is then that the cellhouse's double-structure design works like a greenhouse, capturing the warmth inside. Some convicts claim that the bottom tier is the coolest when they are locked in their cells at night because it is closest to the ground. But others argue the middle floors are the best because they are nearest the few windows that actually open. No one disagrees about the fifth tier. It is agony. The air is thick, hot to the tongue. Convicts sit on mattresses at night on the top tier as if in a narcotic stupor, naked except for sweat-soaked boxer shorts. They keep their cells dark, afraid that the heat generated by the single 100-watt bulb above the metal sink will make the cell even more unbearable. Their bodies are covered with a thin layer of sweat that gleams even in the blackness when illuminated by the red glow of a half-spent cigarette. When you walk along the fifth tier you can smell the sweat and stale smoke. Sometimes, a face will loom forward from a darkened cell, appearing a ghostly white behind the inch-thick steel bars before disappearing moments later into the blackness.

Little wonder that years ago a gang of convicts called the federal penitentiary in Leavenworth "the Hot House."

The twelve hundred men imprisoned there are considered to be among the most dangerous criminals in the United States. Years ago, the Bureau of Prisons learned that mixing first-time offenders with hard-core criminals was disastrous, so it created a stepladder system. Nonviolent and white-collar felons, as well as inmates in their twenties and thirties serving short prison sentences, are supposed to be sent to level-one prison camps, where they live in college-style dormitories and attend therapeutic rap sessions and drug-treatment classes. Some of these camps don't even have walls or fences, and in recent years they have been dubbed "Club Feds" by the media because the inmates, including the Watergate conspirators in the 1970s and Wall Street inside traders in the 1980s, often spend their afternoons playing tennis or sunbathing. At the Hot House, level-one camps are called "kiddie joints" because they are considered the kindergarten of prisons.

On the next rung of the bureau's ladder are the medium-security prisons, officially labeled "level-two, -three, and -four federal correctional institutions." These prisons are progressively more secure, and most have perimeter fences and guards stationed in gun towers, but the emphasis remains on educational and vocational training. The Hot House convicts call these prisons "gladiator schools," because they are where an inmate gets his first taste of real prison life.

At the top of the ladder are the level-five penitentiaries, the true colleges of crime. The Hot House is the Harvard of them all. It is the oldest, the most infamous.

There is only one federal penitentiary with a higher ranking than Leavenworth and that is the much-dreaded prison in Marion, Illinois, the bureau's only level-six penitentiary. It is considered the end of the line for the "worst of the worst convicts." But Marion's reputation as being the nation's most dangerous prison is deceiving. Marion houses only four hundred inmates, and since 1983, when two guards were murdered there, the inmates have been locked in one-man cells for twenty-three hours of each day. Whenever an inmate at Marion is taken from his cell, his hands are cuffed, his legs are chained, and he is surrounded by three guards, each armed with a nightstick.

The federal penitentiary at Leavenworth holds three times as many inmates as Marion and they roam the compound relatively unchecked during the day. Hot House guards are not permitted to carry nightsticks or any weapons without special authorization. On any given day, Leavenworth holds a minimum of two hundred men whose records are filled with just as much violence as anyone at Marion. In fact, these men would have been sent to Marion if there had been room for them. So while Marion reigns as the bureau's "toughest prison," it is, in many ways, a safer place for both guards and inmates than is the Hot House.

According to bureau statistics, the average Leavenworth convict is a 39.5-year-old bank robber serving a 35-year prison sentence. But statistics cannot convey the horror of these men's pasts. Most have spent more than half of their lives in institutions, beginning with reform schools, graduating later to county jails and state prisons. Some (like William Post) started on the treadmill as young as eight years old. They often come from abusive, alcoholic, and violent homes. Many are drug addicts. Through the years, some have been raped in prison, others beaten. A few have been taught job skills, earned high school diplomas, even college degrees. Nearly all have been psychologically analyzed up, down, over, and under, and have participated in some "revolutionary" new program that the public was assured would rehabilitate them. Yet, regardless of whether the latest fad in corrections was mind-altering drugs or group therapy sessions, virtually all the convicts at the Hot House have proved to be resolute, intractable, irredeemable outlaws. Crime is their *chosen* occupation, violence their tool of choice. A popular saying within the Bureau of Prisons goes like this:

"No criminal is sent directly to Leavenworth. He must earn his way there."

How does a criminal achieve that?

"He fucks up everywhere else."

Leavenworth is an enormous warehouse of the most loathsome, a prison where society isolates men for whom it no longer has any hope—only fear.

The bureau requires each penitentiary to keep a "Posted Picture File" of prisoners within its walls who are classified as life-threatening or extreme escape risks. The red-covered log at Leavenworth has two hundred entries—more than any other level-five penitentiary. These are typical:

> This inmate was a member of the Westies, violent criminals who controlled, exploited and terrorized the West Side of Manhattan for 20 years through extortion, murder, drug dealing, auto theft, burglary, blackmail, and a variety of other criminal enterprises. The gang caused eight murders including the dismemberment of at least three bodies.

> This inmate was a member of a South Carolina drug and prostitution ring involved in 22 murders and the kidnapping of young girls who were later forced into white slavery.

> This inmate assassinated three CBS employees in 1982, stole five million in jewelry from a New York store, and is worth an estimated $17 million, making him a prime escape risk.

> This inmate took a mother and 14-month-old baby hostage during a bank robbery. When the mother broke loose and escaped, he stabbed the baby to death.

This inmate operated a major Colombian drug-trafficking ring and is known to have plotted a prison escape by means of an assault with rocket-firing helicopters and paramilitary mercenaries.

Leavenworth was the first federal prison ever built. Always before, Congress had paid state prisons and county jails a fee in return for housing criminals convicted of federal crimes such as bank robbery, kidnapping, and counterfeiting. But after the Civil War most of these prisons became badly overcrowded, and states started to turn away federal prisoners. Congress responded in 1891 by ordering the construction of two federal penitentiaries and the acquisition of a third.

Actual construction at Leavenworth began in 1898, and from all accounts, conditions were cruel. Convict laborers, marched daily from the army stockade at nearby Fort Leavenworth, worked twelve straight hours with only a short break for lunch. Rations were meager and there were complaints that the food was little better than garbage. Discipline was crushing. Anyone disobeying an order was forced to "carry the baby," a form of punishment in which prisoners were chained for months to a twenty-five-pound ball which they had to lift in order to walk. Even the guards were affected by the harsh conditions. According to local newspaper accounts, many quit, saying only "the wall got me," a reference to the great stone wall being built around the penitentiary compound.

On February 1, 1906, Leavenworth received its first inmate, John Grindstone, a Native American convicted of murder. He was paroled a few years later, but returned to the Hot House within months for killing another man. He eventually died of tuberculosis at the prison and achieved another first by being buried in the first plot of a new pauper cemetery on a hill a half mile from the penitentiary. Officially called Mount Hope, the prison's cemetery is still used today, although it is better known as Peckerwood Hill, the tag given it by convicts and guards.

By the early 1900s, the government had outgrown Leavenworth and its sister institution in Atlanta, Georgia, as well as a former territorial jail at McNeil Island, Washington. It built four more federal prisons. All were supposed to be overseen by the Justice Department, but each operated independently. In 1930,

Congress created the federal Bureau of Prisons to make them conform to uniform standards.

From the start, the Hot House was designed to intimidate, and when you turn into the horseshoe-shaped driveway that leads to the entrance, you suddenly understand what a convict meant in 1929 when he described the penitentiary in a letter to his mother as a "giant mausoleum adrift in a great sea of nothingness." The prison dominates the Kansas countryside. It juts abruptly from the gentle grassland north of the town of Leavenworth (population 33,700), piercing the hard blue sky and clear air. Most old prisons are surrounded by high walls that hide them from public sight. At the Hot House, the penitentiary's two largest cellhouses *are* the front wall. Each is seven stories high and longer than a football field. These great stone giants are joined in the center by a rotunda capped by a grand silvery dome that rises more than 150 feet above the ground.

The prison's architects patterned Leavenworth after the majestic United States Capitol building in Washington, D.C., with its two cellhouses replicating the chambers of the Senate and House of Representatives and its rotunda serving as a smaller version of the Capitol dome.

At the time, the design was not meant ironically; it reflected the boundless optimism that even the worst criminals could be rehabilitated in so authoritative and exalted an environment. But the prison has none of the grandeur of the marble-clad Capitol. Its facade, made of rough ashlar limestone cut from a nearby quarry, is a faded yellow and has a stark, impermeable look that makes it foreboding.

A red brick wall is connected to the cellhouses and it encloses the penitentiary's twenty-two acres. Built entirely by convicts' hands, the wall is unlike any other in the bureau. Four feet thick in spots, it rises thirty-five feet above the ground and sinks another thirty-five feet below to prevent ingenious or diligent convicts from burrowing to freedom.

Because of the wall, it is impossible to see inside the prison grounds from Metropolitan Avenue, the street that runs parallel to the prison, and it is just as impossible for a convict inside the prison yard to see the outside world.

This isolation was intentional.

When drawings of the prison were unveiled on March 21,

1897, architect William S. Eames proclaimed that the new penitentiary was the first in the world to be entirely self-contained. It would have its own power plant, water supply, maintenance shop, hospital, and the first school ever built inside a penitentiary. It would be a "city within a city," he said, where convicts could be safely tucked away and forgotten by the outside world.

The Hot House has lived up to Eames's promises. When asked, prison officials often describe themselves in municipal terms. The warden explains that he is "like a mayor" overseeing a $17 million annual budget, nearly 500 employees, and a walled city that would cost several hundred million dollars to construct today. His executive staff, known as associate wardens, compare themselves to city commissioners. There is a commissioner of public works (associate warden for maintenance and operations), a commissioner of parks and recreation (associate warden for programs), a police commissioner (associate warden for custody), and a police chief (the prison's captain). Even convicts lapse into municipal jargon, calling their cells "my house," the guards "the police," the Hole "the jail." When it first opened, the prison needed next to nothing from the Leavenworth community. It used convict labor to grow its own food at a prison-owned farm, and chose its meat from its own herd of beef cattle. It produced what clothing, furniture, and other goods it needed at plants inside the walls. The only commodity that it couldn't produce was the guard force.

The farm and cattle are gone now, but Leavenworth still remains set apart from the outside community. It doesn't allow "civilians" inside its claustrophobic world. Relatives and friends can visit convicts, but these sessions take place in a special visiting room that is not part of the prison's interior. Public tours of the main penitentiary compound ended on June 26, 1910. "We are short of help during the hot season," Warden R. W. McClaughry told a reporter for *The Leavenworth Times*. "If anything should happen, such as a woman or child fainting under the intense heat while passing through, there would be much liability of panic and injury to visitors." McClaughry's attitude prevailed through the decades, although the reason for excluding the public changed. Most wardens simply didn't want to be bothered.

The Bureau of Prisons had never before given a journalist

unlimited access to one of its six maximum-security penitentiaries, and I did not know what to expect when I first arrived. If I had not received special permission from the bureau's director, J. Michael Quinlan, I would have been turned away.

Most journalists only flock to a penitentiary when there is trouble, usually an inmate riot. From outside the walls they watch as the flames lick up from burning buildings, they listen to the angry demands of convicts and wait until officials have regained control, and then they move on to some other calamity. I wondered what everyday life was like inside a prison.

We are all affected by crime, even those who are never directly victims. We avoid walking the streets of major cities at night for fear of attack. We are not permitted to board an airplane without first walking through a metal detector. We awaken in the middle of the night startled by a noise and lie paralyzed with fear that an intruder is lurking in the shadows. Who are these criminals who terrorize us?

By observing the routine rather than the aberrant events in a prison, I hoped to understand the inmates, the men who guarded them, the institution itself. Everyday happenings rarely reflect extremes; rather, they spring from multiple factors—institutional constraints and demands, coincidence, self-interest, and individual efforts, noble and selfish. In the ordinary we are likelier to see the real person, not some mask worn for the glare of television lights.

At first, Quinlan was enthusiastic about my project, but when I mentioned that I wanted to focus on Leavenworth, he politely suggested an alternative. Newer institutions are more efficient because they are better designed, he explained, and rehabilitative programs that are effective in many of the bureau's other forty-seven facilities simply don't work at Leavenworth because its inmates are too hardened, too hopeless. Quinlan said he was worried I would get an unfair view of the entire system by studying the Hot House.

I understood, but disagreed. There is a permanence about the penitentiary at Leavenworth that transcends the latest psychotherapeutic rehabilitation program or whizbang architecture that makes prisons look like suburban shopping malls. Almost ninety years have passed since Leavenworth first opened, and during that time society's views about prisons have

swayed like Kansas wheat in a spring breeze. Yet, it is a penitentiary like Leavenworth that society always has sought as a last
resort.

While I could not actually live inside the prison, Quinlan
agreed to let me come and go as I pleased at any hour. I could
speak to any inmate or guard who wished to speak to me. There
would be no guards standing at my side to monitor conversations. Nor would they be there to protect me if I got into trouble.
Inside the Hot House, I would be on my own.

When you enter the horseshoe drive at the prison, a sign
directs you to stop at a brick-encased intercom under a
lighthouse-shaped gun tower at the front of the prison. A mono-
tone voice asks your name and why you wish to go inside. As a
matter of routine, you are asked if you have any contraband,
such as illegal drugs or firearms. No one expects a visitor to
admit that he is smuggling. The question is a Miranda-style
warning to prevent anyone from pleading ignorance if caught
later.

The only way into the front of the prison is through the
double doors of the administration building, a square structure
that stands four stories high and juts out from the prison rotunda. A heavy steel gate protects this outside entrance, and a
large wooden sign is posted next to the doorway bearing the
Leavenworth employee motto:

LEAVENWORTH PRIDE

Proud of where we have been
Proud of where we are
Proud of where we are going
Pride in a job well done

The electronic gate makes a low-pitched hum as it slowly
opens. The administration building lobby is as far as most visitors ever get. Those coming to see inmates are directed left
through a series of steel gates into the prison's oblong visiting
room. The warden's office is on the right side of the lobby,
protected by an electronically locked glass door that must be
buzzed open by a guard. Straight ahead, barely visible through
a grid of steel bars, is the prison rotunda.

The prison's control center sits in the middle of the lobby. It looks like a drive-in window at a bank. Guards within stand behind waist-high bulletproof glass and the walls are protected by armor plates hidden from view by pine paneling and red bricks. Inside the center are four thousand keys, which unlock every door within the penitentiary. They are kept on a numbered pegboard that reaches from the tile floor almost to the ceiling. Each time a guard takes a key, a quarter-size brass chit with his name engraved on it is placed on the pegboard where that key usually hangs. This way, guards can tell instantly who has which keys.

Because Director Quinlan had given me permission to enter Leavenworth, the control center issued me a special laminated pass containing my photograph, name, and a coded magnetic strip. The guards also posted my picture inside the center, because they are required to be able to visually identify everyone who enters or leaves the interior of the prison. Once I was given my pass, I could walk through the second steel gate that led toward the rotunda. Like the gate at the front door, this second gate was eight feet tall, five feet wide, and made of reinforced, one-inch round steel bars. I stepped through it and was now standing in a twelve-foot-wide "sally port," a holding area between the outside world and the Hot House. I slipped my identification badge across a scanner and my name was automatically added to a computerized list of "non-inmates" inside the prison. In case of a riot, the control center would know my name, as well as the name of every guard inside.

The final gate, or grille, as it is called by guards, was opened and shut by a guard stationed inside the rotunda, not by a guard in the control center. This was a security precaution. If someone from outside the prison stormed the control center and somehow seized control of it, he would still not be able to open this final gate. Conversely, if inmates rioted and took the guard's key, they would only be able to get through one gate. The control center would keep the other two gates closed. The bureau always wanted at least two gates between convicts and their freedom.

On my first day, the guard in the rotunda had been warned by his peers in the control center that I was coming, so I didn't have to wait long for him to walk over and let me in. As I stepped into the rotunda and heard the gate shut behind me, I felt that awful sensation everyone describes the first time he is actually locked inside a prison. I later learned that most convicts felt that same initial dread when they first entered the Hot House.

If Leavenworth is an isolated community, then the rotunda is its town square. All the prison's cellhouses join at the rotunda. There are four. In addition to the two large cellhouses that make up the front of the prison, there are two smaller cellblocks that can't be seen from the street. From the sky, these four cellblocks look like spokes on a wagon wheel with the rotunda serving as the hub. In keeping with the dehumanized starkness of penitentiary life, none of the cellhouses has a name. They are identified by the first letters of the alphabet. A and B cellhouses are the two largest; C and D are the others.

Each cellhouse, I noticed, had only one doorway, and it led into the rotunda. Each of these four doors had a steel gate across it. The guard showed me how he could open and close these gates electronically by pushing various red and green buttons at his desk.

"I can push one button and close all four gates at the same time," he explained. "Each cellhouse would be sealed off from the rest of the penitentiary."

The only furniture in the rotunda is the guard's wooden desk, which sits directly in the center of the room. At night, after the warden has gone home and the convicts are locked in their cells, guards sometimes heave tennis balls at the crown of the dome. It looks as if it would be easy to hit, but no one has ever been able to hurl a ball straight up 150 feet to the center.

Besides the four cellhouses, there is a fifth spoke connected to the rotunda. It is a long hallway that leads to the rest of the penitentiary compound. Guards call it center hall and the floor there is covered with red and white tiles. Until the 1960s, convicts were only permitted to walk on the red tiles. If they stepped over onto the white, the guards knocked them back.

The lieutenant's office is located about halfway down this center hall. It does not belong to a single lieutenant, but is used by the eleven lieutenants who actually run the day-to-day operations of the prison. They report to the prison captain, who technically is in charge of every guard within the prison. Few supervisors in the outside world have as much authority and responsibility as a Leavenworth lieutenant, and the men who earn that rank are quick to remind guards of that fact. A plaque in the office reads: IF YOU AIN'T A LIEUTENANT AT LEAVENWORTH, YOU AIN'T SHIT. The slogan can be read two ways, but few guards are foolish enough to mention the double entendre.

There are always at least three lieutenants on duty, and they make the countless decisions that must be resolved each day if the prison is to run smoothly.

Across from the lieutenant's office is the prison commissary, where inmates can buy snacks, greeting cards, a limited amount of clothing, and toilet items. On the day that I arrived, a red neon sign outside the door flashed: ATTENTION SHOPPERS: LAST SHIP-MENT OF MOONPIES. $2.05 PER BOX!!!! The commissary is no little operation. Sales to prisoners in fiscal 1987 totaled $1.75 million. They could have been much higher, but the bureau limits each convict to $105 in spending money per month. The money is deposited in the inmate's account by family or friends outside prison or by direct deposit from wages he earns working at prison jobs. Each inmate can have twenty dollars in change, but not a cent more, for use in the vending machines in the cell-houses. The amount is limited to reduce extortion, theft, and gambling inside the prison. All paper money is prohibited.

Beyond the lieutenant's office, at the end of center hallway, is another steel gate that leads to the prison dining hall, kitchen, employee cafeteria, auditorium, and chapel. There are two out-side exits at the end of the rear corridor that open into the prison yard.

When the penitentiary first opened, a railroad track ran across the yard, passing through two big iron gates and holes punched into the perimeter wall. A special government train, used exclusively to ferry convicts between federal prisons, was the only vehicle ever permitted on the track. But the track was torn up and removed after six convicts commandeered the train on April 21, 1910, and crashed the steam locomotive through the gates as the guards in the gun towers tried to shoot them. The convicts abandoned the locomotive a few miles from the peni-tentiary and fled on foot, but only one made his way to Canada and freedom. He remains the *only* convict ever to escape from the Hot House and never be recaptured.

The yard is also where Kansas performed its first legal hanging on September 5, 1930, when it executed Carl Panzram for the murder of a Leavenworth guard. Panzram was the first known serial killer in the United States, having killed twenty-two persons. When they put the noose around his neck, he spit in his executioner's face and declared, "I wish all mankind had one neck so I could choke it!"

Today, the prison yard is crisscrossed by chain-link fences that slice it into crooked pieces. To an untrained eye there seems to be no purpose to the zigzag design, but the fences are positioned to divide the yard into compartments. During emergencies, guards can quickly separate inmates by opening and shutting gates much like the wooden chutes in a cattle yard.

The yard contains some buildings, a much-used baseball diamond, concrete tennis courts, an outdoor weight-lifting pit, running track, unfinished miniature-golf course, and several basketball courts. Convicts also play handball and racquetball by using the penitentiary wall as a backstop. The buildings in the prison yard include the "butcher shop" (the prison hospital), the "Hole" (the disciplinary housing unit), and a sprawling four-story building known as "UNICOR"—an acronym for the federal prison industry program. Inside UNICOR, Leavenworth inmates produced $27 million worth of goods in 1986, netting the bureau a tidy $5 million profit that was paid into the national UNICOR coffers to help keep less profitable prison factories solvent. There is a printing plant, a textile shop, and a furniture factory located in the industry building. The most famous product made there was John F. Kennedy's rocking chair.

Six gun towers protect the Hot House, and every employee, including clerical workers, prison counselors, and even the prison psychologists, is expected to spend time in them at some point during his or her career. Only the chaplains are exempt. When people apply for a job at Leavenworth, they are asked what they would do if they saw an inmate climbing the wall. The correct answer is "shoot to maim." Any who say they are not willing to shoot an inmate are not hired.

All new employees, even those who aren't guards, undergo a week of familiarization at the Hot House during which they are taught how to search a cell, frisk an inmate, identify contraband, and avoid being conned by inmates. Leavenworth's training officer Bob Lawrence also gives newcomers this advice: "Scrape the mud and cow manure off your boots before coming to work, otherwise inmates will snicker and say to themselves, 'Hell, he can't even dress right and he is going to tell me what to do.' " All employees are sent for three additional weeks of training at the bureau's academy in Glynco, Georgia, where they are taught self-defense, bureau regulations and policies, and how to fire various weapons.

Penitentiaries are the most expensive form of confinement because they must be manned by guards around-the-clock. In fiscal 1987, the Hot House had a budget of $17 million, of which $12 million went for salaries. It cost $35.62 per day to keep an inmate in Leavenworth. In 1989, that figure had risen to $39.72 per day, in comparison to $28.32 to house a prisoner in a less secure, level-one camp. The $11.40 difference is due to having fewer guards.

When convicts arrive at the Hot House, they receive a twenty-two-page book that lists the rules and what punishments they can expect for violating them. After a short processing period, they are assigned cells. The majority are put in two-man cells; only about thirty percent of the men in the Hot House live in single-man cells. The bureau is supposed to assign these much-desired cells based on inmate seniority. The longer a prisoner stays at Leavenworth and keeps out of trouble, the better his chances of living alone. At least, that is how the system is supposed to work. In actuality, the least deserving inmates are often assigned to single-man cells simply because prison officials know that their violence is a real threat to a cellmate. Regardless of how many occupants there are in a cell, each has identical furnishings: a single bed or a two-man bunk, a lidless steel toilet, a metal counter (for use as a desk) with an attached swing-out stool, a locker with a combination lock, a metal sink, a single light bulb, a mirror. The mirrors are sheets of polished steel bolted onto the wall.

Most convicts, I soon learned, try to avoid trouble and simply do their time as easily as possible. But about twenty percent of the inmates operate inside the prison much the same as they did on the streets. They deal drugs, extort money, bankroll card and dice games, pimp, and run scams on other inmates. These inmates are known as predators. Their victims are called lops. The line between the two groups shifts daily.

"There are no nice guys in Leavenworth," explained Craig H. Trout, the bureau's gang expert. "They are all sharks, and when you put sharks together the stronger ones feed on the rest."

The 487 employees at the Hot House are broken into groups, too. Guards who needlessly harass inmates are called super cops. Those who simply do their jobs are hacks. Besides the 239-man guard force, there are 248 other staff members. These include nineteen hospital workers, thirty-five maintenance men, three psychologists, two ministers, and seventy supervisors at the prison's UNICOR operations. The remaining 119 employees are secretaries, food stewards who oversee inmate cooks, teachers, counselors, and administrators. Many of these employees earn higher salaries than the guards, whose entry-level annual starting pay is $16,851. But few have as much clout. It is the guards who control all movement inside the prison. They issue commands, make "arrests," and keep order. As far as the guards are concerned, all other employees are "weak sisters," especially those whose jobs require them to help inmates.

Unlike Hollywood scripts in which guards and convicts share a mutual respect and, at times, even become friends, in the real world of the Hot House the hostility between convicts and guards is palpable and enduring. It permeates every aspect of prison life—even the jargon. Guards get angry when anyone calls them that: they are correctional officers. For their part, they never refer to prisoners by any word except inmate. This is an insult to the prisoners, who claim the word is better suited to a patient in a mental ward than it is to them. Using the proper title is a matter of unbelievable significance inside the Hot House. When you are a prisoner and are stripped of all your possessions, the term you are called by becomes important. The same holds true for officers. Without weapons, the only authority that a guard has comes from respect and fear. Titles play a role in establishing both. In this book, all these terms are used interchangeably.

Getting the language straight was not the only problem I encountered. The dual society inside a prison is not used to outside observers. For instance, I did not feel comfortable carrying a portable emergency alarm or two-way radio like those carried by employees, because I felt inmates would view me as a staff member and think that I was afraid of them (I often was).

So I walked around the Hot House unprotected. The first time I went into the penitentiary yard and found myself in the midst of several hundred convicts, I wondered if I had made a mistake. The bureau had warned me about two inmates. Bruce Carroll Pierce, the second-in-command of The Order, a neo-Nazi paramilitary group that had murdered Denver talk-show host Alan Berg, was considered a potential threat to me because I had worked at *The Washington Post* and, while not Jewish, was seen as a member of the "liberal Eastern Establishment press." Already serving a 250-year sentence, Pierce had little to lose by killing me, bureau officials said. Convicted spy Jerry Whitworth was considered dangerous because he was disgruntled about what I had written about him in my book, *Family of Spies: Inside the John Walker Spy Ring.* But I never spoke to Pierce, and Whitworth never did anything but complain to me. Nor did I ask the bureau to take any special precautions on my behalf. In fact, I asked for the reverse, because I felt convicts at the Hot House would misinterpret such protection and be reluctant to speak frankly.

When I first arrived, only a few convicts spoke to me. Some wanted to be mentioned in a book because it made them feel important. A few hoped that I would use my access to Quinlan to help them. I discovered that these inmates were of little help. They simply told me what they thought I wanted to hear. As the weeks passed, however, I was able to identify inmates and guards who played strong roles within the prison society. I began to focus on six inmates: Carl Bowles, William Post, Dallas Scott, Norman Bucklew, Thomas Little, and Thomas Silverstein. Only Norman Bucklew is a pseudonym. I chose these men because their lives, values, and attitudes were representative, I felt, of other convicts I met. At first, I spoke to them without a tape recorder or notepad and pencil. They were suspicious of me and these tools would have made them even more so. Why had the bureau let me inside? Obviously, the fact that it had given me access made them suspect me. In the beginning I did not ask too many questions; I simply listened. Some inmates tested me. They would commit a minor rule infraction, such as smuggling a sandwich back to their cell from the prison mess hall, knowing that I had seen them tuck it into their trousers. They wanted to see if I would snitch on them. I never did. After weeks of watching me, one by one these men began to open up. I found them to be amazingly frank, naively so at times. I am certain that some decided to speak to me out of boredom. Monotony is every inmate's curse, and being able to speak to a writer broke the routine. But as I got to know these six men, I became convinced that for five of them there was a deeper motivation. Buried inside the federal system for years, cut off from the outside world, they wanted to explain their actions, not because they were seeking forgiveness from society, but because they felt they had achieved something in their strange prison world that they had never been credited with when living outside prison. They each considered themselves honorable men—at least by jailhouse standards.

It was not easy to walk the line that separates convicts and guards at the Hot House. Even small matters had to be handled delicately. One afternoon I was invited to a routine target-practice session outside the prison. I found guards firing at targets that contained life-size silhouettes of a man. Several referred to the targets as inmates, in some cases calling them by specific names. I was offered a pistol, but declined. The next night, I visited a convict who was drinking homemade hooch in his cell. "You are always asking what this shit tastes like," he said. "Well, come have some." I refused. I felt accepting either offer would make me suspect. I do not know how long I could have continued this balancing act. Knowing a convict is drinking hooch is of little consequence. Knowing that he has a homemade knife hidden in his cell is another matter, particularly if he uses it a few days later to stab an inmate or guard. The same is true about guards. Shooting a convict target is insignificant, but having a guard tell you how he gave a belligerent convict some "thump therapy," a euphemism for hitting an inmate, makes you squirm.

When you are inside the Hot House for a long period, even as an outsider, you soon forget what it is like to be anywhere else. Steel doors clanging closed behind you, hostile guards yapping orders, television rooms dominated by hollering blacks watching sports, white toughs in polka-dot gang bandannas pumping iron, mirror-polished tile floors, drab walls painted an unvarying chocolate brown and tan, naked white flesh adorned with obscene tattoos, dainty men with shaven legs dressed in scanty shorts that expose panties made from Jockey shorts dyed pink in red Kool-Aid, old drunks high on homemade mash, neurotics, addicts, sexual deviants, fat bikers with acne-like bullet scars—this is the Hot House community.

In the Leavenworth penitentiary, a carton of cigarettes is worth stabbing for, masturbation—"pulling your choke"—becomes something to brag about, a man's ass gradually seems less repugnant. Events that would be insignificant anywhere else become momentous. While talking with a convicted murderer one night in his cell, I suddenly heard the country singing of Hank Williams, Jr., blaring from a radio in the cell next door. As I watched, the murderer excused himself and walked down the tier. The music stopped. Later, the murderer explained that he had retrieved a "shank" from a nearby hiding place and, after tucking it under his shirt, had confronted his noisy neighbor. "You're disrespecting me," he said. There is little doubt that if the inmate had refused to turn down the radio, the murderer would have, as he said later, "run the gears"—a reference to the most effective method of stabbing another human being, as in "You slam a shank into his chest and then pull up and over and then down and over, just like shifting gears in a car."

It is difficult to peer into such blackness without eventually being sucked inside.

While this book focuses on the lives of six convicts and a handful of prison officials during a two-year span from July 1987 until July 1989, numerous other guards and inmates were also interviewed. Many of their comments and stories are significant. Each day, hundreds of chaotic episodes were played out in the prison, many of them unrelated to the major events and characters in this book. Yet these incidents are the heart of prison life. A fistfight breaks out in the dining hall because one inmate has cut in front of another in the serving line. Someone sets a cell on fire because the inmate living there has failed to pay a gambling debt. A guard discovers a shank hidden inside a candy machine. Interspersed throughout the book are short vignettes under the rubric of "the lieutenant's office" or, in the case of interviews, "voices." Most of the people mentioned in these episodes play no role in the full-length chapters. They simply appear and then vanish, just as they do in daily life at the Hot House. Some readers may find this disjointedness to be confusing. It is meant to be. The Hot House is an erratic place. Convicts arrive, others are transferred. The inmate who lived in the cell next door for twelve years is gone one morning without explanation. Guards are promoted, they quit, they are fired. A new warden comes and changes all the rules. A new inmate moves onto the tier and decides to "move on you." In such a cauldron, it is often difficult for an observer to understand what he is seeing or to make sense of it. Rules are enforced to show who is the boss, not out of any sense of fairness. Respect can be worth more than freedom. Convicts do things that seem foolish at first yet months later make perfect sense. Watching events unfold at the Hot House is like trying to solve a puzzle. The answer is always right in front of your eyes, yet you don't—you can't—see it as long as you study it like a "Square John." In the Hot House, you must suspend much of what you know or have been taught in the outside world and simply let yourself feel the emotions, the tensions. Once you stop trying to understand, and simply watch, the solution to the puzzle suddenly becomes clear. The key to understanding the Hot House is that in an irrational world, irrationality makes sense.

Glenn Walters, a psychologist at Leavenworth, was the first to tell me that understanding events in prison is difficult because most of us do not think like criminals. "There are only two emotions in here," Walters said, "—fear and anger. Just remember that everything these inmates do revolves around those two emotions and nothing else."

A Voice: DRUG DEALER, AGE 32

The first day I was in prison, two dudes busted in on this guy in the cell next to mine and stuck him twenty-six times with shanks. He was sitting on the crapper when they killed him, and he couldn't fight back because his pants were wrapped around his legs. Stupid bastard. Anyone who don't know better than to take a leg out of his pants in prison before he sits down on a toilet deserves to die. Something you learn in here.

Another time, I saw a guy get stuck while he was walking out of the shower wearing those rubber thongs. Soon as they hit 'im, he fell over 'cause the floor was wet and he didn't have any footing. I always go to the shower barefoot.

Let me tell you another little secret. You know the best time to move on a Square John in the street? I used to do this in New York when I needed a few bucks. Go into a restaurant or bar and wait in the bathroom. You can always be washing your hands when some dude will come in to pee. As soon as he starts, you nail him against the urinal and grab his billfold.

Most folks don't know it, but it is physically impossible for a guy who is taking a piss to fight back. [Laughs] I'm not bullshitting. I never met anyone who can piss and fight at the same time. It just can't be done.

CHAPTER FIVE

ROBERT MATTEWS

On the morning of July 13, 1987, Robert L. Matthews pulled his beige Toyota into the space marked WARDEN in the parking lot outside the Hot House. He sprinted up the front stone steps that led to the administration building, counting them automatically. When he reached the top—number forty-three—Matthews paused, pleased. He was not the least bit winded. At age thirty-nine, the new warden was in top physical shape. He ran three miles each morning, six miles on Saturdays, lifted weights three times a week, and kept his weight at exactly 195 pounds, the same as it had been when the six-foot two-inch Matthews was a freshman in college. Bolting up stairs was a habit, a way for Matthews to check himself. That was the sort of compulsive man he was. Robert Matthews was always looking for challenges.

From the moment he had joined the bureau in 1973, he had pushed himself to excel. Being good didn't cut it; he had to be the best. He had told his wife that he intended to be a warden by thirty-five, a seemingly impossible goal given the fact that wardens were almost invariably men seasoned by decades of experience. A mere eight years later, Matthews was chosen to be warden at the prison in Ashland, Kentucky. He was only thirty-three, the youngest warden in bureau history. Now, six years later, he was setting another precedent. He was entering his new job as the first black ever put in charge of the Hot House. This was no small matter in the summer of 1987. While race relations

45

outside federal prisons had improved in many ways over the decades, the fires of racial hatred still burned as intensely as ever in the prisons. In Leavenworth, black and white convicts segregated themselves in the inmate dining hall and prison officials never housed blacks and whites in the same cell. At least a dozen white convicts had large swastikas or the words WHITE POWER boldly tattooed on their arms. At the Hot House, the numbers of black and white inmates were intentionally kept equal to prevent either side from gaining an advantage. In the summer of 1987, 51 percent of its convicts were white, 45 percent were black, the rest were other minority races.

Of course, convicts were not the only racists in prison. The staff that Matthews had come to supervise was overwhelmingly white, and many were frank about their racial hatred. Of the 487 full-time employees, 63 were blacks (13 percent), 24 were Hispanic (5 percent), and one was Native American. The other 399 (82 percent) were white, and all but 40 of them were men.

At the local watering hole for guards, a tiny bar called Benny's located a few blocks from the Hot House, it was not uncommon to hear racial slurs between sips of beer and during dart games. A white guard would later recall a conversation that took place before Matthews reported to work. "There is nothing wrong with niggers," one guard said. "In fact, I think everyone should own a few of them!" When the laughing ended, he added, "But work for a nigger warden? Holy shit, what's the bureau coming to?"

After Matthews, Charles Carter was the highest-ranking black at the Hot House, and he knew firsthand how racist white guards could be. When Carter joined the bureau in 1974 at the federal prison in El Reno, Oklahoma, he was snubbed by white guards, one referring to him behind his back as the "new nigger." Carter complained to his lieutenant when he learned of the ongoing slur, but he was told that he would have to solve his own problems. Carter did just that. He confronted the guard in the prison parking lot after work.

"Don't ever call me nigger again," Carter demanded. "If you can't talk to me with respect, then stay away from me. Otherwise, I'll whip your ass."

"Fuck you, nigger," the guard replied.

"When he said that, the fight was on," Carter later recalled, "and I ended up beating his ass, which is what I should have done in the first place."

Over the years, Carter had risen through the ranks until now he was a unit manager, which meant he was in charge of the day-to-day operation of B cellhouse. Because he was now an executive, white guards at the Hot House watched what they said, but Carter could tell from his conversations with young black guards that racial hatred still ran deep in the guard force.

Racism was only one of the problems that the new warden would have to overcome. Matthews also had to please his new boss. On the surface, the decision to send Matthews to Leavenworth was unanimous. The bureau's five regional directors meeting in Washington, D.C., at the bureau's headquarters had approved the transfer during their last meeting under the leadership of Director Norman Carlson. Carlson, who retired July 1, had run the bureau for seventeen years and Matthews had been one of his favorites. Carlson's handpicked successor, J. Michael Quinlan, did nothing to stop Matthews's promotion, but privately he admitted that he had some reservations about him. Quinlan didn't know Matthews well, and the new warden was not on the list of managers that he had chosen as up-and-coming leaders.

Neither Carlson nor Quinlan had ever said anything to Matthews, but he understood through the grapevine that he had to convince Quinlan of his abilities. He also realized that Carlson had given him an opportune spot to show them. Leavenworth was considered a make-or-break institution for wardens. "If a warden can run Leavenworth successfully, then the feeling in the bureau is that he can run any prison in the world," Matthews explained later. The Hot House guards put it more bluntly. "This is where the bureau finds out if a man clangs when he walks." In other words, a Leavenworth warden had to "have two brass balls" and both had to be "awfully damn big."

Nearly all of the bureau's top managers had spent some time at Leavenworth. Carlson had worked there early in his career; so had Quinlan. It had also played a key role in the life of James V. Bennett, who, more than any other man, was responsible for the creation of the bureau.

The son of an Episcopal minister, Bennett was a lawyer in Washington, D.C., during the mid-1920s when he was first asked

if he would investigate the seven prisons then owned by the
federal government. At the time, Bennett worked for the U.S.
Bureau of Efficiency, a now-defunct agency that was responsible
for finding ways to make the federal bureaucracy more effective.
Bennett had never been in a prison and he immediately left to
tour the federal ones and several state institutions. What he
found sickened him. He later wrote:

> Within prisons, men are routinely strung up by the
> thumbs, handcuffed to high bars, kept for weeks in soli-
> tary confinement on bread and water, are whipped,
> paddled, and spanked, spread-eagled in the hot sun,
> locked up in sweatboxes, confined in tiny spaces where
> they can neither lie nor sit nor stand.

Although the federal prisons were part of the Justice Department, each was run independently by a warden appointed
by the U.S. Senate. Most wardens were political hacks. Some
knew nothing about running a prison. Bennett described the
federal prisons as "vast, idle houses filled with a horde of de-
spairing, discouraged, disgruntled men, milling aimlessly about
in overcrowded yards."

During his tour of Leavenworth, Bennett paused in the
prison yard and looked up at the dome that was still under
construction even though work on the penitentiary had started
two decades earlier. The warden had just bragged about how the
dome would be second in size only to the U.S. Capitol dome
when finished. Just then, an inmate walked up to Bennett,
pointed to the dome, and asked him if he was really serious
about prison reform or if he was simply going to perpetuate a
system that was more interested in building "that preposterous
dome" than in actually helping inmates. Bennett would later
recall that incident in his autobiography, *I Chose Prison*, and
state that his exchange with the inmate made him realize that
the purpose of a federal prison was not to punish inmates or
warehouse them, but to *rehabilitate* them.

A deeply religious man, Bennett returned to Washington
and drafted legislation for the Hoover administration that
called for the creation of a federal Bureau of Prisons. This new
bureau, he wrote, would not only bring uniformity to the seven

federal prisons, but also "humanize prison life." On May 14, 1930, President Herbert Hoover signed a bill creating the bureau and appointed Sanford Bates, the head of the Massachusetts prison system and a dedicated reformer himself, as its first director. Although Bennett was not put in charge, he was named Bates's chief assistant and was asked to set up the structure of the bureau and define its goals. Seven years later, when Bates resigned to run the Boys Clubs of America, Bennett officially took charge.

"I struck first and hardest at what would now be called the 'gut issue' of prison reform—brutality," he later wrote. "I made it plain to all the wardens that there was to be no lashing, no use of the strap, no handcuffing men to the bars, no improper solitary confinement."

During the next *twenty-seven years* as director, Bennett built the bureau into the most progressive prison system in the country. He got Congress to approve funds so that educational and vocational classes could be taught in prisons. He put inmates to work by creating UNICOR, which enabled them to earn money for themselves and their families. He built separate prisons for mentally ill inmates, for those addicted to narcotics, and for offenders under age twenty-two. He got Congress to force the U.S. Public Health Service to provide medical and psychiatric care at federal prisons because he knew its doctors would do a better job than the local physicians whom wardens hired part-time or whenever there were emergencies.

But his biggest priority remained finding a way to rehabilitate convicts, and in 1958, he felt the bureau had finally found a "cure" for crime. It was called the "medical model of rehabilitation" and it soon became the hottest treatment program in both federal and state prisons. The concept was simple. A criminal committed a crime because he was "sick" and, just like a person who was physically ill, he could be "cured" if the cause of his "sickness" was diagnosed and treated. In the early 1960s, criminologists claimed that crime was caused by a lack of education, a bad environment, no job skills, poor self-image. The bureau responded by giving each inmate a battery of tests and then prescribing a treatment program for each man that listed exactly how many hours of education, vocational training, and psychotherapy an inmate would have to complete to be "cured."

The "medical model" was supposed to make penitentiaries such as Leavenworth obsolete. There was talk of closing the Hot House. Construction of all federal prisons stopped.

Bennett retired in 1964, confident that he had found the cure for crime. His replacement, Myrl E. Alexander, a former assistant director under Bennett, continued to push Bennett's programs until poor health forced his retirement six years later.

If Bennett had been the bureau's impassioned reformer, its next director, Norman Carlson, was its pragmatic administrator. Carlson, who was only thirty-six when he became director, had started his career working part-time as a prison guard while earning a master's degree in criminology in the early 1950s. As he rose through the ranks at the bureau, he implemented many of Bennett's reforms, and when he became director in 1970, he was fairly certain that most of them didn't work. He ordered his staff to investigate and monitor inmates to see how many returned to prison after being pronounced "cured." The reports showed that recidivism had not dropped significantly.

Based on these studies, the bureau officially abandoned the medical model in 1975. "None of the programs in themselves was a failure," said Carlson. "The failure was that we assumed there would be a magical cure for crime and delinquency. We have to divorce ourselves from the notion that we can change human behavior, that we have the power to change inmates. We don't. All we can do is provide opportunities for inmates who want to change."

Bennett's vision that prisons could heal "sick" inmates had been replaced by Carlson's belief that only men who wanted to be cured could be.

Between 1970 and 1987, Carlson shifted emphasis and focused on modernizing the bureau, changing it from Bennett's one-man dynasty into a solidly run and effective bureaucracy. He divided it into five regions and delegated much of his authority to regional directors who then formed his executive staff. Despite tremendous opposition, he launched an aggressive construction program that added twenty new prisons, nearly doubling the existing number, to ease overcrowding. Stressing professionalism, he implemented better training and higher standards for guards. He set up the bureau's stepladder system, which ranks prisons from one to six based on the caliber of their inmates. And he guided the bureau through a decade of turbulence during the 1970s when federal judges gave prisoners a cluster of expanded rights.

Carlson could have remained the bureau's director longer than seventeen years, but he had always required his wardens to retire at age fifty-five, and he wasn't going to grant himself an exemption. That created a problem for him, however, because he would turn fifty-five during the 1988 presidential election, and he was worried that if he retired then, the new president would appoint a political hack as director. So Carlson decided to retire two years early so his successor would be firmly in place by election time. The Reagan administration asked Carlson to reconsider this unselfish act and offered to let him pick his own successor in return. Carlson agreed to stay one more year. That would give the new director twelve months to become entrenched. He spent his final year with Quinlan at his side.

Quinlan had joined the bureau in 1971 as an attorney at Washington headquarters, but Carlson had sent him to Leavenworth almost immediately after arrival for on-the-job training. It was the first of a variety of jobs aimed at preparing Quinlan. Carlson knew that his successor was not only going to have to understand prisons, but also Washington politics. In 1987, the bureau had a staff of 13,000, and operated 47 prisons holding more than 44,000 inmates. It had become a big bureaucracy inside the Justice Department and it was destined to grow even larger. Because of tougher federal sentencing guidelines taking shape in Congress, more money for law enforcement, and the booming drug-trafficking business, the bureau expected the number of inmates to increase to at least 85,000—possibly as many as 125,000—by 1995. To meet this need, the bureau estimated it would have to construct at least seventeen new prisons, and budget analysts were predicting the new director would have to send Congress a $1.4 billion budget request for fiscal 1988—the biggest ever, more than double the previous year's.

"The fact that Mike was a lawyer was a factor in my choice," said Carlson, who did not have a legal degree. "I had learned early on that being a lawyer means something in the Justice Department because lawyers like to talk to other lawyers."

When Quinlan took charge on July 1, 1987, the bureau had completely reversed its philosophy. Six decades had passed since James Bennett had stood in the Leavenworth yard, stared at the giant dome, and decided that the purpose of federal prisons was to rehabilitate inmates. Now the word *rehabilitation* was considered passé, replaced by a new buzz word: *expansion.*

All of this growth, of course, meant that Quinlan would have to hire more employees, who, in turn, would require more managers. He would need a larger executive staff to oversee his mushrooming empire, and this made the spotlight on Warden Robert Matthews burn even brighter.

Matthews did not wish to be left behind or see his soaring career stall. He intended to prove himself by becoming the master of the Hot House.

When it was announced that Matthews was coming to Leavenworth, guards began calling friends who had worked for him in other prisons to learn what he was like. What they heard made them nervous. Matthews was described as a perfectionist, a physical-fitness zealot, and a stickler for rules and procedure. The new warden emphasized appearances. He wanted his institutions to sparkle and he expected guards to keep their shirts tucked in, shoes shined, to answer with snappy "Yes sirs." Matthews himself wore tailored suits and crisply ironed shirts, and whenever his wing-tips got dirty, he immediately cleaned them, with his handkerchief if necessary. According to those who had worked with him at other prisons, Matthews was such a stickler for neatness that he never left anything on his desk. If papers needed to be signed, he signed them and put them out of sight. If reports needed to be read, he read them and gave them to his secretary to file. He didn't even keep his phone on his desk at one prison. He put it in a drawer.

It was the stories about Matthews's note-taking, however, that most upset the Hot House guards. Within the bureau, Matthews was something of a legend for being the warden who always carried a small notepad in his coat pocket so he could jot down inmate complaints as he walked through a prison. It didn't matter how minor the gripe, how trivial it might seem to the guards. Matthews investigated every complaint. "Inmates are really our customers," he had been fond of saying in his previous posts as a warden, "and it is our job to respond to their needs. They aren't always right, but they still are our customers."

The staff at Leavenworth had never looked upon inmates as customers, nor were the guards there eager to have a warden question them about some picayune incident. "The rap about Matthews was that he cared more about clean floors and inmate gripes than he did about the staff," one guard recalled. "Believe me, everyone was watching when Matthews came up those front steps that first day as warden. We all wanted to see what he was made of."

No one had to wait long.

CHAPTER
SIX

THOMAS LITTLE

The 727 jetliner taxied to an out-of-the-way runway near the cargo buildings at Kansas City International Airport and stopped near a waiting passenger bus and a white van parked on the concrete airstrip. Inside the airplane cabin, a U.S. marshal called out the names of the federal prisoners who were supposed to disembark. Thomas Edgar Little stood up when he heard his name, and shuffled toward the exit. At the bottom of the stairs, another marshal and two guards from Leavenworth were waiting.

"Little?" one guard yelled. The pilot had not turned off the engines and the noise made it difficult to hear.

"Yeah," Little replied.

One guard checked off his name on a list while the other frisked him and made certain that he had not unlocked the handcuffs or somehow slipped out of the chains on his ankles.

"In there," came the order, and Little fell in line behind another inmate, whose name had been called before his, and walked to the bus. He chose a window seat and looked outside through the bars that covered the green-tinted pane. Little would later describe his feelings that morning: "I was upset—no, it was more than that, I was scared shitless. I couldn't believe I was being sent to Leavenworth."

Little was twenty-six years old and had been convicted of two armed bank robberies in his home state of Florida. He had never been to prison before, and when he discovered that the bureau had elected to send him to the Hot House, he had been dazed. Little had assumed, as had his attorney, that a first-time felon would be sent to a minimum-security institution, probably one of the camps. They were wrong.

When the last Leavenworth prisoner was finally off the federal marshal's jet and inside the bus, the white van that Little had seen parked nearby pulled forward and preceded the bus off the airstrip. It was a chase car. The armed guards inside it were responsible for protecting the bus from attack. Besides the twenty or so prisoners, the bus held three guards. One sat in a metal cage at the rear of the bus with a pump shotgun cradled in his lap; another stood with a shotgun at the front of the bus, outside a wire-mesh screen that enclosed the convicts. The third guard, who wore a pistol, drove the bus.

As Little watched, the 727 taxied down the runway. Every day the marshal's plane flew cross-country picking up and discharging prisoners at key cities. The Hot House guards jokingly called it Convict Airlines.

"Hey, white boy," a black inmate sitting in the seat across from Little whispered, "they gonna love your ass in prison." He laughed. Little ignored him.

When he was first arrested, Little had actually relished the idea of going to prison. All his life, the slightly built inmate had wanted to be a tough guy. A short stint in jail would be just like going to college, he figured. "I liked stealing things, but I wasn't very good at it because my mama had raised me to think like a Square John," he explained later.

While Little was being held for trial in a county jail, he discovered there were drawbacks to being a thief. Three inmates demanded he have sex with them, and when he refused, they attacked. Little had held them off with a mop handle until a jailer separated him from the group. When he learned that he was being sent to the Hot House, he began having nightmares. "I figured if this shit happens in a county jail, then imagine what Leavenworth is going to be like."

Another young inmate, who introduced himself as Gary, had sat next to Little on the airplane and had offered him some advice. Gary had done time in Leavenworth before and was quick to tell Little that young, good-looking convicts had a difficult time. There is a saying in the Hot House that goes like this,

Gary had explained: "Every convict has three choices, but only three. He can fight [kill someone], he can hit the fence [escape], or he can fuck [submit]."

"You're gonna need someone to show you around," Gary said. "Ask for Carl Bowles. No one fucks with him."

How, Little asked, could he find Bowles?

Gary had laughed. "Don't worry, Carl will find you," he said.

When the bus stopped outside the prison's front entrance, a guard yelled, "Everybody out!"

The guards from the chase car had already formed a gauntlet on each side of the stone steps. The inmates hustled off the bus and climbed the steps single-file. They were directed through the rotunda and downstairs, where they were ordered to strip and stand next to each other in a line.

"Run your fingers briskly through your hair," a lieutenant yelled.

"Open your mouth, stick out your tongue."

A guard walked along the row of naked men peering into each gaping mouth.

"Lift up your dick and balls."

The inmates complied and the same guard looked to see if they were concealing anything.

"Turn around, bend over, and spread your cheeks."

Little would learn later that this last order was done simply to humiliate inmates, although bureau officials would argue differently. The most common spot for prisoners to hide keys, drugs, and even hacksaw blades was inside metal cigar tubes—called "butt plugs"—inserted in the rectum. But the only way a guard could tell if an inmate had something hidden there was by conducting what the bureau referred to as technically as a "digital examination." Convicts called it a "finger wave." There was no way for a guard to look at a man's anus and learn anything other than whether he had hemorrhoids. But the bureau still insisted on performing the visual check.

Satisfied that the fish were not hiding anything, the guards issued them a set of clothing and took them one by one to have their prison mug shots made and fingerprints taken. Finally each was taken to a cell.

By this time it was late afternoon, and Little tried to rest but couldn't. "All I wanted to do was get a piece of pipe and crawl into some corner," he said later. "I just wanted to be left alone."

The next morning, a short muscular convict in his late forties paused outside Little's cell. His brown hair was cut military-short, revealing a scalp freckled by the sun.

"Thomas," the convict said, "I'm Carl Bowles."

This is how both men later recalled their conversation.

"Look," Bowles told Little, "you're in prison now. You need to keep your mouth shut, stay out of people's way, and don't cultivate friends. I don't care how nice they are, don't take nothing from anybody, 'cause you don't know the man's intent. You don't know whether he is a good person or not. Any man can walk up to you and tell you anything. You might be impressed by the way he looks. He might be a weight lifter. He might be clean and neat. He might have books under his arms, but you don't know his real intent."

Then Bowles gave a warning about himself. "I'm like every other asshole in here," he said. "You don't know me any better than anyone else. But I work out in the east yard with flowers. You come out there some day and look at those flowers if that's what you want to do. You come out there and look around, and I'll be out there and I'll make sure you can go to the yard anytime you want. I'll make sure no one fucks with you."

Little nodded and Bowles left.

"You know, I wanted to go out there the very next day—out to the yard and look at the flowers," Little recalled later, "but I didn't want to be caught dead in prison looking at flowers. There was no fucking way that I was going near him and flowers, 'cause you think, 'O-o-o-h-h-h flowers, there's the pretty boy looking at the flowers.'"

The next morning, Bowles stopped outside Little's cell again.

"You okay? Need anything?"

"I'm okay," responded Little. "Thanks."

Bowles left.

"I was scared to leave my cell," Little recalled. "Guys were coming by acting friendly, offering to do things for me, bring me stuff from the commissary. It was just like Carl had said it would be. I was ready to snap."

The next morning when Bowles stopped by, Little asked if

they could talk. Bowles suggested that they take a walk, and he
boldly led Little past the guards in the fish tier back to his own
cell. "Carl sat on the bunk and I sat in a chair," Little recalled.
"He asked me what was wrong and I told him I felt like I was on
the moon and didn't know what to do."

"Well, what do you want to do?" asked Bowles.

"I'd like to draw. I want to study mathematics. I want to
work out with weights and I want people to leave me alone. I just
want to be left alone."

"Okay," replied Bowles, "you can do those things."

"But how?" asked Little.

"Just breathe," Bowles replied.

"What?"

"Just do 'em, that's all."

"Wait," said Little, "it ain't that simple. I just can't go out
there in the yard and do those things."

"Sure you can," Bowles replied. "Why can't you?"

" 'Cause I . . . uh . . . just can't."

"You can if you want to. I'll show you how you can," Bowles
replied. "Look at me. I'm not some big, beefed-up motherfucker,
but I haven't had to stab anyone in twenty-three years. It's how
you carry yourself in here that matters, and how you think. You
can learn those things. I can teach you."

"What do you want?" Little asked.

"I'm just looking for a friend," said Bowles. "That's all. Just
a friend."

Lieutenant Michael Sandels had seen Little go into Bowles's
cell. There were no regulations against Bowles showing a fish
around, but Sandels was suspicious. He made a point of talking
to Little in private after the two convicts' meeting. Sandels came
right to the point. "You are young and you probably will get a lot
of sexual pressure. Do you know what Carl is about?"

Little didn't answer.

"Hey, man," Sandels said, "Carl Bowles is a homosexual
predator and he's looking to make you his wife. He'll have you
waiting on him, having sex with him, doing whatever he demands. You'll be a slave, and when he's tired of you, he'll sell you
to someone else."

"I know people think he is a homosexual, but we are *not*
homosexuals," Little answered. "Everyone thinks he is pres-

suring me, but he is not, and if you want to believe that he is, then that's fine, but we aren't doing anything. That stuff about Carl is bullshit!"

"Well," said Sandels, "if you have any problems, I know the situation you are in, and you can just come by and see me and I will take care of you."

Sandels said later that he was sincere in offering to help Little. "I wanted to help, because when you are young, something like this could fuck you up for the rest of your life, but the truth is, I really couldn't do anything for him if he had asked."

Dr. Thomas White, the chief psychologist at the Hot House, had also noticed Bowles and Little, but he too felt there was nothing that he could do. "Most of us are never pushed into a corner during our lives," White explained later. "When you are small and need help, you run to your parents. When you get older, you run to a priest, a minister, a psychologist. If you have a legal problem, you hire an attorney. If someone threatens you, you call a cop. In prison there is no one to turn to, no one to solve your problems for you. If you go to the guards, you will be known as a snitch and that can get you killed. So you are on your own, perhaps for the first time in your life, and you are forced to deal with your own problems. Believe me, the guy demanding that you drop your drawers isn't going to be a good sport and simply let you walk away. You must either be willing to fight or you must give in."

Little returned to Bowles's cell after his conversation with Sandels.

"He told me to stay away from you," Little reported.

"Look here," Bowles replied, "the cops have a category in prison for everything. If more than three people get together in a prison, then they're members of a gang. If there are two people, you're both homosexuals, and if you hang by yourself, you're antisocial. That's just how cops are. Now, here's the thing, Thomas. You are in here twenty-four hours a day. The cop is here eight hours. The cop is not suffering the same thing you are suffering. The cop is not here to see you going through these mind changes. I have little faith in having them protect me in here. Why, I can't even find a lieutenant when I want to find him. If I was getting stabbed right now and went looking for Lieutenant Sandels, I probably couldn't even find him. You got to deal with the reality of this place. Who means more to a guy in here? Who is in here twenty-four hours a day with him? Who is here to talk to him, help him through difficult times? It's very simple. Don't you understand that trust and reliance are built on very little things?

"Okay, when I don't get my mail, I go up to the officer and I ask him if he knows where it is. 'I don't know where the fuck your mail is! Check with the fucking mailroom!' he says. Now listen to me, if this cop is not concerned about my mail, does he really care about me? Or when I go to the chow hall and the doors are being closed and I tell the officer there that I'm late but I have a reason, and he says, 'Fuck your reason, you're out a dinner!' Now, when those things happen, those little things, why the fuck do you think that Sandels or any other cop is going to give a shit about you and whether you are being preyed upon? He isn't in here twenty-four hours a day. I am. He says he is going to protect you? Well, what are you going to do the sixteen hours that he's off duty?"

Little nodded. Bowles was making sense.

"The reason that Sandels wants to help you," Bowles continued, "is because he really wants to use you. He's gonna tell you, 'Hey, a guy in here, he pretty much makes his own bed. If you want to help us, then we can help you. These convicts, they don't give a fuck about you, but I can help you, and all you have to do is help me. Give me a little bit of information here and there, and I can help you get a transfer or help keep those predators away. It doesn't have to be anything really serious, why, just tell us who was drinking the other night up on your tier. That's all, something small like that.'

"I've seen guys fall in that trap. See, it doesn't matter what you tell them, 'cause once you've crossed that line you're a snitch, and they know it and they got you. It's just a fucking trap. Everyone in the world is trying to use everyone else in here. That's how life is, and that's what it is all about in this joint.

"Now you go back to your cell and you think about what I just told you," said Bowles, "and if you are afraid of me and afraid I'm going to fuck you, then you just tell me and we will go our separate ways. I told you, Thomas, all I'm looking for is a friend."

Little left.

"I didn't want to have to kill someone in prison," Little said later, recalling his thoughts. "I didn't come here to get a life sentence, but I didn't want to have guys fucking me, either."

Little knew he had to make a choice—move in with Bowles or try to make it on his own in the general population. Although he had never been in the Hot House before, Little had heard stories about some of its most notorious residents, including Cyclops, a convicted murderer from Washington, D.C., who had a glass eye and was known for turning young inmates into "fuck boys," a term used to describe a prisoner who is not a homosexual but is forced to work as a prostitute in prison by a pimp. The idea of being raped and forced into being a fuck boy terrified Little. The idea of being forced into trying to kill someone as deadly and cold-blooded as Cyclops was just as terrifying. He didn't see any other choices.

Little didn't have much of a criminal past to fall back on. His parents were upper-middle-class and well-educated, and he was raised in a nonviolent, suburban home. Little was twelve when his parents were divorced and he moved from Florida to Nebraska with his mother. "My mama is the most wonderful woman to ever walk the face of this vile earth," Little recalled. "My father is some sort of genius. He runs his own company. We cannot understand one another. I do not like him. He does not like me. So be it."

As a teenager, Little yearned for adventure and liked to consider himself somewhat of a rebel. He told everyone in high school that he was going to join the navy and become a member of SEAL, the navy's elite underwater demolition-and-attack team, as soon as he turned seventeen. Few of his classmates took him seriously. After graduation, Little returned to Florida and enlisted, but he washed out. Afraid to return home a failure, he got a job as a bartender in a club near the base frequented by SEALs. He began smoking marijuana and using uppers and downers. Soon he was selling them. "I would do anything for money. I sold dope, and began pimping, pushing pussy at the bar. I started robbing left and right, too." At first, he hit mom-and-pop grocery stores and all-night gasoline stations. He tried banks next, but didn't know any of the secrets that most felons learn from older thieves—the simple things, like the best day to rob a bank being a Friday because that's when banks have money on hand to cash paychecks. His first bank robbery was in Orlando. He got caught doing his second one, in Lakeland, Florida. The conviction was his first and he hadn't hurt anyone during the two robberies. Little couldn't understand why the bureau had decided to put him in the Hot House. It just didn't make sense.

When it came time for Little to move into the general population, he asked for permission to live with Bowles. "I decided to use Carl," Little said. "I sure did. I figured, 'Okay, Thomas, you're in Leavenworth. Carl Bowles is the best thing you got going for you. You'd better grab onto this guy and do what's necessary to be his friend.'"

Little's request was sent to Edward Geouge, who was in charge of the cellhouse where Bowles lived. Geouge was a highly decorated Vietnam combat grunt, former marine drill sergeant, and an eighteen-year bureau veteran with a reputation for being as scrappy as any convict in the Hot House. He was forty-seven, with receding red hair and a chain-smoker's raspy voice. When Geouge saw Little's request, he knew what was happening. Geouge didn't approve of any convict preying on a weaker convict, but if Little wanted to cell with Bowles, it was okay by him. "The truth is that Bowles is doing everyone a favor," Geouge candidly admitted later. "Little is the sort of guy who can't take care of himself in here, and if we tell him he can't live with Bowles, then Bowles won't be able to protect him from other convicts. There will be heaps of problems for everyone, particularly Little. As long as Bowles and Little don't do anything out of line, then it's really no one's business."

As soon as Little was released from the fish tier, he moved into Bowles's cell. From that moment on, word spread through the penitentiary that anyone who messed with Little had to answer to Carl Bowles. That was something that no one wanted to risk. But behind both men's backs, inmates and guards alike began making fun of Little. They called him "the new Mrs. Bowles."

CHAPTER
SEVEN

CARL BOWLES

Carl Bowles's criminal record took up two thick files in the Hot House record room. The paper trail gave a step-by-step account of Bowles's development into a cold, calculating killer.

Born in Lubbock, Texas, in 1940, Bowles was only eight years old when he first got into trouble. At the time, a social worker theorized that he was acting out because his parents' marriage was disintegrating and he wanted attention. His father, according to prison files, was a drunk, a womanizer, and frequently out of work. Bowles's mother was beaten by her husband. They fought constantly and Bowles had basically raised himself. He had done a poor job. "I was on my own, you know, hanging around the streets." At age eleven, he was declared a habitual truant; at twelve, he was declared incorrigible by the juvenile court; and at fifteen, Bowles was sent by a Texas judge to the Gatesville State Training School for Boys. A court psychologist who examined him wrote this when he entered the reformatory:

> The source of this boy's trouble is his deep feelings of rejection by his parents, plus resentment of his unstable homelife. He is very anxious for love and stability. He seems to have developed a hostile identification with his mother, yet is very dependent on her. There is some sexual disturbance in this boy. Homosexuality is quite possible. It is likely it would be covert.

If Bowles was looking for love and acceptance, he certainly didn't find it at Gatesville. Like most Texas reformatories at the time, the program was designed to break a boy's bad habits with brutal punishment and slave labor. Every boy, regardless of his age, worked ten hours in the fields, usually picking cotton. Troublemakers were put in the "bull pen"—a tiny isolation box. Bowles would later recall that he arrived at Gatesville on a Sunday, the only day when the boys didn't work, and was told to report to a counselor in the school's recreation room. When he opened the screen door and looked inside, all fifty or so of the boys stopped what they were doing. An older boy twice his size came up to him.

"Hey, what size shoes do you wear?" the boy asked.

"Don't know," said Bowles.

"Let me see one of 'em, will ya?" the boy asked politely.

Bowles sat down on the floor and removed a shoe. The older boy took off one of his own shoes and put on Bowles's.

"How 'bout lettin' me see the other one?"

"I took off my other shoe and handed it to him," Bowles remembered, "and he puts it on and ties it and then walks over to this table and every boy in the place starts laughing at me. That's when I realized I am the butt of the joke."

Bowles grabbed a cue stick from a pool table nearby and attacked. The boy who had taken his shoes started to run, but Bowles reached him first and smacked him in the head so hard that the cue stick snapped in two pieces. Still holding the jagged end, Bowles lunged forward at another boy, but before he could stab his target, Bowles was knocked to the floor by a fist.

He looked up just in time to see another fist smash into his face. It was the adult counselor. For the next seven days, Bowles worked his regular ten-hour shift cutting cotton and then four more hours as punishment. He worked barefoot—just as he had been when the counselor found him—and he didn't say a word to anyone. At night, he was locked in the sweltering bull pen, which wasn't big enough for him to lie down in.

When his punishment ended, Bowles was assigned a housing unit. "As I am walking up the steps, the guy who took my shoes steps out of the door and puts my shoes down and says, 'Here are your shoes, man. Thanks for not snitching, you know.' I sat down and put on my shoes and went in."

When a new youngster arrived later that week at the school, he too was confronted by a boy who demanded his shoes. Only this time, it was Carl Bowles who was taking advantage of the new kid. "It was my turn to dish it out," he recalled. "I had earned that right."

For nine months, Bowles worked at Gatesville, and during that time he learned his lessons well. He became one of the worst bullies in the school. "The kid who was the toughest did whatever he wanted, got whatever he wanted. He was respected, admired, even by the adults," Bowles recalled. "If they had a problem, they came to me to help solve it."

Bowles was sent back to his parents, but they couldn't control him. Within four weeks, he had shot another boy during an argument. Luckily, the boy didn't die, but a judge sentenced Bowles to four years in the federal youth facility at Englewood, Colorado. Bowles was sixteen when he arrived, and this is how the prison psychologist described him:

> I do not see him as a psychopathic personality, but I fear that he has formed some sort of *criminal identification* . . .

The psychologist recommended a treatment program for Bowles that included counseling and schooling, but Bowles would have none of it. He preferred running with the tougher, older inmates. Because he was good with his fists, he soon won grudging respect from his peers. It was at Englewood that prison officials claimed Bowles started to show signs of sexual aggression toward weaker inmates.

One year after Bowles arrived in Englewood, another psychologist examined him. He wrote that Bowles exhibited a "great deal of childish frustrated rage" at being in prison. The psychologist also added, with surprise and irritation, that Bowles had developed for unclear reasons "a chip on his shoulder" and had decided that "no one can really be trusted."

Bowles served two years at Englewood before he was paroled. Without friends, a job, or any skills, he washed dishes in a cheap hotel for two months before he stole a car and headed to Oregon on a "vacation." Arrested and taken to jail, Bowles feigned illness and then overpowered the jailer when he came to investigate. Captured a few hours later, he was taken to a different jail where he repeated his ploy, this time beating up the jailer and escaping again. Within days he was arrested and sentenced to eight years in the Oregon State Penitentiary. The prison psychologist who examined him this time warned in Bowles's file that the nineteen-year-old was about to pass the point where he could be rehabilitated.

> He seems to live for the moment, shows no guilt, regrets, or remorse because he simply does not dwell on the past or concern himself with consequences . . . He has an exaggerated concern with power and physical toughness . . . This man verbalizes considerable bitterness and resentment concerning his parents and their faults of infidelity, incompatibility and his father's inebriety . . .

For six years, Bowles remained in the state prison. He wasted no time getting into trouble again as soon as he was paroled in the summer of 1965. He teamed up with a pal from the prison who also was on parole, and together they went on a multi-state crime spree. By the time they were caught a week later, Bowles and his partner had robbed a bank, kidnapped the California state comptroller general, his wife, and their small child, stolen several cars, held six other people as hostages, and murdered an Oregon policeman. Bowles wrote a short confession when he was taken to jail. Because he had dropped out of school at age eleven, the note was filled with grammatical and spelling errors. Amazingly, a copy of it was still in his prison file more than twenty years later.

> I felt poeple just realy didn't give a dam. Well, if they don't I don't so to hell with it all. Ill just do as I please but I know that is not right. I know I'll go right back to the joint, this time for good, besides what difference does it make anyway who cares. I want to believe in people, do right and live happy but how? Why? I just hung it up again . . . I still feel there is something mentialy wrong with me because I can't be like other people on the street. I don't think I am crazy I know right from

wrong, good and bad, but I cannot control myself. I am split up between the two—believe and not believing, caring and not giving a damn.

This time, the prison psychologist who examined Bowles reported that there was little chance he could be reformed. At age twenty-five, Bowles was declared hopeless.

He appears to have been thoroughly conditioned by his many years of incarceration.... Treatment, as such, may not ever have any effect on this young man who has been a social problem for years and who now must be classified as a major social problem. The only known solution is long term confinement. This is a drastic technique, but it is the only known way to preserve community safety.

Because he had been found guilty of the federal crimes of bank robbery and kidnapping, Bowles was initially sent to the prison at McNeil Island near Tacoma, Washington, but he was later transferred to the Oregon State Penitentiary to begin serving a life prison term for murdering the policeman. Incredibly, on May 17, 1974, nine years after his crime spree, Bowles was issued a four-hour "social pass" to visit a girlfriend in a local motel. A social worker drove Bowles to the motel where he met his date. While the social worker sat in the parking lot waiting, Bowles slipped out a bathroom window in the rear of the building.

The fact that a convicted cop killer had been issued a social pass made front-page headlines and sparked community outrage. Police organized a massive manhunt, and after several days, two FBI agents thought they spotted him walking down a street in Eugene, Oregon; but because he was wearing a beard, they weren't certain. One of them approached Bowles on foot while the other stayed behind in his car. "He asked me for identification," Bowles recalled, "so I reached around like I was getting my billfold, but instead I pulled out my gun and started shooting." The agent reached for his gun too, but he had a hole in the lining of his jacket, and when he pulled the weapon from its holster, it got caught and fell harmlessly to the sidewalk. The agent jumped for cover. "I fired every shot, and you know what? I missed him. It still cracks me up today when I see these guys in movies shoot each other with one shot across a football field. Hell, we were standing five feet from each other and I missed him." Bowles grabbed the agent's gun and ran. A few blocks away from the shooting, he broke into a home owned by Earl C. and Viola Hunter, an elderly couple, whom he took hostage. Forcing them into their car, Bowles managed to elude some one hundred police officers who had flooded the neighborhood. Once he was safely out of Eugene, he pulled into a field and ordered the Hunters outside.

"I told them that I was going to kill them," Bowles remembered without a glint of emotion, "but it wasn't anything personal, you know. I wanted them to know that I didn't have no hard feelings against them and I hoped they didn't have no hard feelings toward me. Hell, I didn't even know them. They just happened to be in the wrong place at the wrong time and so I killed them." Bowles shot Viola, age 61, first. "I told her to make her peace with God and then I shot her in the head." Earl, age 63, was next. "He went to pieces so I shot him in the head and then shot both of them in the heart to make certain they were dead."

Two days later, Bowles was captured after a wild chase that ended when he was shot in the stomach while trying to ford a river. He was sentenced to two additional life sentences for the Hunter murders. This time, no prison psychologist bothered to evaluate Bowles, but an anonymous prison official did make this notation in his file:

> This man is ruthless, has no conscience, shows no sign of regret or remorse . . . He should *never* be released again in society.

In prison, Bowles had proved to be as uncontrollable as he was on the streets. Over the years he had violated just about every prison rule. At one point, he was arrested by guards for placing an advertisement in the *National Enquirer* posing as a psychic with "72 years experience." For three dollars, he offered to tell the future. He also was caught trying to hide a homemade listening device in the room used by the guards so he could overhear when they planned to search his cell. His record included reprimands for possessing drugs, strong-arming, sexual misconduct, gambling, carrying a knife. But Bowles was best known at the Hot House for successfully bribing a guard in 1981. The incident began innocently enough when a guard stopped outside his cell one afternoon and complimented him on a painting that he was doing. Two days later, the artwork was delivered by mail to the guard's house. Rather than returning the picture and reporting Bowles, the guard kept it. A week later, Bowles offered the guard $100 in return for bringing $400 in cash inside the prison. The money would be delivered to the guard by a friend of Bowles's outside the prison. Inmates were not permitted to have any cash at that time and the guard knew he could be fired if caught. But when he hesitated, Bowles reminded him that he was already guilty of accepting a bribe—the painting. The guard was soon working as Bowles's mule, smuggling in money, marijuana, and pills. Other guards became suspicious when they noticed the two men spending so much time together. When the guard reported to work one morning, he was frisked. He was carrying several .22 caliber bullets in his pockets destined for Bowles. He planned to bring in a pistol the next day. Bowles was sent to Marion as punishment. The guard was allowed to resign.

"Carl Bowles doesn't give a damn about anything or anybody but himself," said Edward Geouge, the veteran cellhouse manager who had agreed to let Little move in with Bowles. "He's a real cold-blooded piece of work."

CHAPTER
EIGHT

ROBERT MATTHEWS

Warden Robert Matthews had only been at work in his new office for a few hours when there was a knock at the door. He waved in Richard Smith, Leavenworth's associate warden for custody, the de facto second-in-command at the Hot House.

"We've gotten a death threat against you," said Smith. An inmate informant, who had provided reliable tips in the past, claimed that he had overheard members of the Aryan Brotherhood plotting to kill the "new nigger warden." According to the snitch, a black guard in the California state prison system had shot and killed an AB member. Matthews was to be murdered in retaliation.

"We don't know how real the threat is," Smith explained. "It probably is just talk, but we can't be certain." Both men knew there were plenty of inmates at Leavenworth capable of carrying out such a threat.

Matthews didn't react, Smith said later. "If it was intimidating to him, it never did show."

Killing a warden was something that inmates simply didn't do. In the entire history of the bureau, Matthews had never heard of a warden being murdered. The last time a warden had been attacked was fifty-six years ago and it had happened at the Hot House. On December 11, 1931, seven inmates appeared at the front gate armed with several revolvers which they had smuggled into the prison.

"Open it or we'll kill you!" one of the inmates yelled at a

guard named Oscar Dempsey, according to newspaper accounts. At the time, the front gate was opened and closed by a single guard stationed outside.

"Go ahead and shoot!" Dempsey was quoted as saying. "I'm an old man, so it don't matter. I'm not opening the gate for you!"

Frustrated, the inmates had grabbed Warden Thomas B. White who happened to be inside the compound. When the guard saw White, he opened the gate and the convicts commandeered a car and fled, still holding White as hostage. The police chased them into a farmhouse a few hours later, and in the gun battle that followed, three convicts were killed. The others eventually surrendered but not before shooting the warden. White recovered and eventually returned to his post, but after that incident the bureau adopted a regulation for all of its prisons that ordered guards never to open a gate for anyone holding a hostage, regardless of who it was.

Matthews didn't believe the AB death threat was legitimate. Later, he said that it was probably just inmates bragging among themselves. But he knew that his reaction to the rumor was important. There are no secrets in a prison, and convicts and guards would be watching to see his response.

"No warden can sit around fretting and saying, 'Jesus Christ, they might kill me today! I'd better not make any convicts angry!'" Matthews explained. "You've got to show everyone that you aren't afraid. If I ever get to the point where I am afraid to walk inside the institution, then I'd better resign."

Under previous director Norman Carlson, the bureau had adopted a practice in all its prisons that was called "standing mainline." Each day during the noon meal, all the prison's senior officials stood in the dining hall while inmates ate. The main reason for doing this was to provide inmates with an opportunity to talk to staff members without being accused of being a snitch. In the old days, convicts always went in pairs to speak to prison officials. This enabled them to vouch for each other when they returned to the cellhouse, thus assuring other inmates that neither had snitched. Now because convicts could walk up to a prison official in the dining hall and talk in full sight of everyone, there was no need for a witness. If other inmates thought someone was snitching, they could walk up beside him and overhear what he was saying to the staff.

There was also a more subtle but equally important reason for standing mainline. Having the top officials stand in front of the inmates at mealtime was a reminder that despite the fact that the staff was vastly outnumbered and completely unarmed, they were in charge. "Image is a thousand times more important in a prison than on the street," explained psychologist Dr. Thomas White. "The fact that the top leaders of this institution are standing before them at mealtime sends an important psychological message."

Some wardens hated standing mainline; they felt it encouraged sniveling over inconsequential matters. But Matthews, with his ever-present notepad, was a mainline junkie.

The dining hall began serving lunch shortly after 10 A.M. Matthews hurried there seconds before the first convicts were scheduled to arrive.

Most officials stood along a wall away from the doors, out of the way of the serving line where each inmate collected a tray, plate, and plastic eating utensils before proceeding down a food line. Matthews positioned himself directly in front of the tray area. It was impossible for a convict to eat lunch without first walking past the new warden. There were no guards near him. No one was protecting him. With his arms folded across his chest, rocking back and forth on his heels, Matthews waited.

You could hear the rush of convicts coming before they appeared in the doorway. Like children scurrying out of school, they raced through the double doors and came face-to-face with the new warden. Immediately, the wave stopped. No one, it seemed, knew exactly what to do. The inmates at the front of the pack simply stared, and then moved forward cautiously, each grabbing a tray and walking past Matthews. Some ignored him, a few glared at him, some whites acted as if he weren't there. Not a single convict spoke to him. After the meal, Matthews walked back to his office. But just before the evening meal, he returned to the dining hall and once again positioned himself by the entrance. Again, no one approached him.

Smith met with Matthews the next morning and told him informants were still claiming that the AB intended to kill him.

"Let's take a walk," Matthews replied. With the warden taking the lead, the two men went directly into the west yard and into a two-story, brick building—the Hole. There was a time when going to the Hole at Leavenworth meant exactly that. Inmates were stripped and put into a windowless, dark cell that was completely bare. A hole in the floor served as a latrine. If the inmate's behavior still didn't improve, guards reduced his rations until he only received enough food to stay alive. Such cells were supposed to be used only in the most drastic cases. Other inmates sent to the Hole were assigned to isolation cells, where they were locked up twenty-three hours a day. Even though the majority had never been put in a windowless cell, it was those cells that the inmates recalled, and the tag, the Hole, stuck.

While the Hole was no longer so gruesome, it still contained two types of cells. Inmates were locked in isolation cells that were not much different from any other cells in the prison. The solitary confinement was supposed to be their punishment. But because Leavenworth's inmates were constantly getting into trouble, the Hole was always overcrowded and there weren't enough single-man cells to keep the prisoners apart. Most shared cells with three or four other inmates. They passed their time by playing cards. The only real discomfort for them was being locked up for all but two hours a day.

If a convict caused trouble in the Hole, he was moved to a punishment cell. These were known as "sidepocket" cells because they were off to the side of the building, away from other inmates. Each cell contained only a bed bolted to the wall, a sink, and a toilet. The men in these cells were isolated from everyone else. They were not given cards, books, or anything to occupy their time. If a convict continued to be disruptive, guards could spread-eagle him on the bunk in what the bureau called a "four-point position" and chain each limb to a corner. This was supposed to be the harshest punishment allowed, and could only be done if one of the Hot House's lieutenants supervised the chaining. The bureau prohibited inmates from being intentionally deprived of food or being kept for hours in total darkness.

The Hot House's Hole was notorious because it is where the most famous prisoner in the bureau's history had been kept for twenty-six years. Robert Franklin Stroud, better known as the "Birdman of Alcatraz," was put into the Leavenworth Hole in 1916 after he murdered a guard in the dining hall. After several days in the punishment cell, he was moved into an isolation cell.

One day while Stroud was outside in an exercise area, he found a sparrow lying on the ground near death. He nursed the bird back to health in his cell and eventually trained it to do tricks. That experience sparked an interest that eventually led Stroud to become a self-trained expert on birds and to write a book about bird diseases. At one time, he had more than twenty birds in his single-man cell. He remained in Leavenworth's Hole until 1942, when the bureau decided to silence him. At the time, Stroud was receiving national and international acclaim and had become a vocal critic of the bureau through his correspondence with the media. Without warning, the bureau moved Stroud to its penitentiary at Alcatraz where he wasn't permitted to have a single bird. Despite this, Hollywood's 1962 hit movie about Stroud centered the story in Alcatraz because the "Rock" was better known than Leavenworth. Stroud eventually died of old age in an isolation cell in the bureau's medical center.

Matthews decided to go to the Hole because Aryan Brotherhood gang member Dallas Scott was confined there along with other gang members. The warden wanted them to know that he wasn't afraid of any gang threats. Inside, he walked from cell to cell, asking prisoners if they had any complaints. Scott and the other white inmates in his cell ignored him. When Matthews reached the sidepocket, a white racist peered up from his bed. "Nigger," he snarled.

"If Matthews had any sensitivity to racial remarks, it was unknown to me," Smith recalled later. "If he heard him at all, he didn't react, and the incident didn't faze him."

After visiting the Hole, Matthews returned to the main penitentiary and positioned himself, as always, near the entrance of the dining hall for lunch. Nothing happened. The evening meal found him at his post without incident once again.

When Smith met with the new warden the next morning, he told him that rumors about an AB hit had stopped. Smith figured Matthews would be relieved, but he wasn't. "The inmates weren't talking to me," Matthews explained. How could he jot down inmate complaints on his notepad if no one spoke to him?

At lunch that day, he searched the face of each inmate, looking for someone he knew from his previous jobs. He recognized a black inmate and flashed a smile. The convict grinned, and walked over to talk. By the time they finished, another black stepped forward to complain that the guards were not delivering his mail promptly. Matthews pulled out his pad and wrote down the inmate's name, number, and complaint. When he looked up, two other inmates had lined up. Later that day, Matthews ordered his associate wardens to investigate each of the complaints. "I want word to spread that I take inmates' complaints seriously and get them an answer even if it isn't what they want to hear," he said. Soon a line of convicts waited for Matthews each day in the dining room. But Matthews was still not satisfied. Every convict who had come forward was black. Whites were still boycotting him.

Twice each day, Matthews took up his post. Each day, blacks came forward. Each day, he returned to his office without talking to a single white inmate. By week's end, he was thoroughly discouraged. He stood his ground during the Friday lunch and shortly after twelve o'clock, he started back toward his office.

"Excuse me, uh, Warden, can I have a moment of your time?"

Matthews turned around. At the time, he didn't know the inmate's name. All he saw was that he was white.

"What's the problem?" Matthews asked, pulling out his notepad.

Carl Bowles told the new warden that he needed some supplies for the flower beds that he took care of outside the prison hospital. Matthews made a note.

That night, Matthews stepped outside the front grille of the administration building and smiled. "I was happy," he said later. "I had broken through the barrier."

Now there was only one other group that he still had to deal with, and that was Leavenworth's staff. Being accepted by them would prove to be much harder.

CHAPTER
NINE

DALLAS SCOTT

When I asked Dallas Scott if the Aryan Brotherhood had planned to kill Warden Matthews, he laughed and then became angry. "Snitches are always making up things," he explained. "If someone really wanted to kill the warden, do you think they would talk about it?" Leaning close to the bars that separated us, he added, "If the AB wanted someone dead, the first you'd know about it is when they found the body."

I spoke to Scott repeatedly for this book and he talked candidly about his crimes and his criminal lifestyle. But he always refused to admit that he was a member of the Aryan Brotherhood or even discuss the gang. I was not surprised. Of the prison gangs, the Aryan Brotherhood is one of the most secretive, and with good reason. Any member who betrays its secrets is automatically sentenced to die.

As we talked that morning, I noticed that Scott marked events in his life by prison incidents. "I hit the federal system the same year they executed the Red Light Bandit," he said. Seconds later, he added that something had happened "about the same time as the race wars at San Quentin." When this was called to his attention, Scott shrugged. "I've never really had much concept of life outside jail. I was twelve years old the first time I went in and I haven't really been out long enough since to know anything else but this life."

Scott claimed his childhood was ordinary. "Prisons are full of guys like me," he said. "You start out doing small things, you know, bucking authority, and the next thing you know you are in juvenile hall or jail, and that is where you form your basic personality. For me, it was in 1957 and 1958, when I was in various reform schools. I began smoking dope real big, and whenever I got out on the streets, I got myself into another beef and landed back in jail, and the next thing I knew, I was spending more time in than out. I suddenly found myself caught up in the lifestyle.

"As the years go by and you get older, you realize more and more that your life is considered a failure by society's standards," Scott continued. "You are a jailbird. You don't have any money, no house, no job, no status. In society's eyes you're a worthless piece of shit. Now, you can buy into what society says and decide you really are a piece of shit or you can say, 'Fuck society, I'll live by my own rules.' That's what I did. I decided to live by my own standards and rules. They aren't society's but they are mine and that's what I've done. In your society, I may not be anybody, but in here, I am."

There was a point in his early twenties when Scott tried to go straight. He married, had two children, and worked as a welder in the Texas oil fields. But it didn't last. Scott became addicted to heroin. In 1966, he robbed a bank in California, was caught, and was sentenced to San Quentin. At the time, San Quentin was in the midst of what prison officials now acknowledge was an all-out race war. The racial turmoil in the world outside prison, where fires were burning in Watts, Detroit, and Chicago, was magnified in San Quentin. Blacks and whites were stabbing one another, not because of anything anyone had done, but simply because of their skin color. "Your hate was at a peak," Scott recalled. "Your adrenaline was at a peak, everything was at peak level all the time. It was like a jungle. You'd get yourself fired up, so by the time that the cell doors opened, you'd be ready. You'd have a whole head of steam. You didn't have time to analyze and rationalize or philosophize, you just got strapped [got yourself a knife] and went out of your cell and did what you had to."

It was in this climate that the Aryan Brotherhood was born. Bureau officials claim that Dallas Scott was one of its founding members. I asked Scott if he recalled the birth of the AB, and without acknowledging that he was a member, he explained why the gang had formed at San Quentin. He didn't hide his racist attitude. "Whites are everyone's natural enemies," he said. "Minorities stick together, but the white man by nature walks alone. I've seen whites sit by and watch a bunch of niggers attack a white kid in a cell. These yahoos were sitting there thinking, 'Goddamn, I'm sure glad it's not me being fucked!' But if one white guy had the courage to say, 'Hey, leave that kid alone!' and he stepped forward, then there was a good chance that the pack will back off.

"See, people who herd together deep down are afraid of anyone who has the balls to stand up on his own. Now I ain't saying that the white man who stands up isn't going to get his ass kicked. But when he stands up, he's letting everyone know that he's willing to do what it takes, and get killed if necessary, because he don't like what's going down, and that is intimidating to someone who runs in a herd like blacks do.

"At San Quentin, the herds were getting out of hand and a bunch of old white bulls simply said 'Fuck this' and they decided to stand up, and you can be damn sure that when these old bulls formed the tip [Aryan Brotherhood], there were a bunch of white guys, who either weren't strong enough on their own or were just afraid, who were damn glad."

Scott's explanation, it turned out, was largely based in fact. The Aryan Brotherhood was originally formed to protect white inmates from being victimized by black and Hispanic prison gangs. The Black Guerrilla Family, a militant, black revolutionary gang with ties to the Black Panther party, was the first known prison gang, and was strong at San Quentin at the time. Chicanos were divided into two gangs: the Mexican Mafia, composed of urban Hispanics from the Maravilla section of East Los Angeles, and their hated rivals, the Nuestra Familia (Our Family), made up of rural Chicanos. The black and Hispanic gangs preyed on whites, as well as on members of their own races.

A study by the Criminal Intelligence Section of the Arizona Department of Public Safety later suggested that several outlaw bikers who called themselves the Diamond Tooth Gang were the forerunners of the Aryan Brotherhood. The gang members, each of whom had diamond-shaped pieces of glass embedded in his front teeth, tried to recruit other whites at San Quentin but failed to attract sufficient "soldiers." Next came the Blue Bird

Gang, so called because its members had bluebirds tattooed on their necks, but it too didn't last. The Aryan Brotherhood was born when remnants of the Blue Birds joined forces with several neo-Nazi groups. It is unlikely that it would have survived, either, except for an unusual tactic adopted by its original members. Black and Hispanic gangs had always relied on numbers for strength, and routinely pressured new inmates to join. The Aryan Brotherhood took the opposite tack. It based its membership on each member's physical strength and willingness to kill. Anyone who wished to join the AB had to meet a "blood in, blood out" rule.

" 'Blood in, blood out' simply means that to join the AB, an inmate had to 'earn his bones'—in other words, had to kill someone to get in," explained Craig Trout, the bureau's gang expert. "It also meant that there was only one way *out* of the gang. Death."

As soon as it was organized, the members of the AB put themselves under what they called "kill on sight" orders. When the cell doors at San Quentin opened each morning, AB members were required to hunt down and attack black inmates regardless of whether they belonged to a gang. The white gang was convinced that the best way to keep other gangs at bay was to prove that the Aryan Brotherhood was the most ruthless and savage gang in the prison.

California prison officials do not know the precise time when this kill on sight order went into effect. But in 1970, the California system began seeing a dramatic increase in gang-related violence. Seventy-nine gang-related assaults and eleven deaths were reported that year. In 1971, there were 123 assaults and nineteen deaths and in the following year, 186 assaults and thirty-four gang-related deaths. The Aryan Brotherhood was not wholly responsible for the increases, but among convicts at San Quentin it did earn a reputation for being bloodthirsty. Its founding members, estimated by prison officials to be one hundred men, tolerated "zero disrespect" from other inmates. Even a casual comment about the Brotherhood could result in a stabbing if members felt their "brothers" had been insulted.

Legend has it that the best and most respected AB warriors at San Quentin had tattoos of fierce Norsemen drawn on their arms.

Why would anyone join such a group? I asked Scott, after once again making it clear that the question was hypothetical and did not imply that he was a gang member. In his mind, personal honor drove white convicts with principles to join. "A few older white convicts still have principles. They don't let other convicts or the administration push them around," he said. I noticed that Scott had a Norseman tattoo, among many others, on his forearm.

When black militancy began to wane in the mid-1970s, the various gangs decided to sign a truce. This brought to a close what convicts call the California race wars, but none of the gangs dispersed. The politically motivated Black Guerrilla Family was eventually replaced by the 1980s drug-dealing Crips and Bloods. A 1982 study, by bureau employee Michael Lee Caltabiano, described the transformation of the AB thus:

> The Aryan Brotherhood developed during the 1970s into an organized predatorial gang [whose] main interest became protection, extortion, and narcotics in prison.

The white gang also began to specialize in contract murders for other gangs and individuals, Caltabiano wrote, maintaining its savage reputation.

In 1985, the bureau released a detailed study of what it described as the alarming problem of prison gangs. Investigators concluded that the Aryan Brotherhood was not a potent force in most lower-level federal institutions, but it continued to have strongholds in two penitentiaries: Leavenworth and Marion. In both, AB members played key roles in drug smuggling, extortion, and gambling, and were responsible for several contract murders.

Although the AB's power had diminished over the years, in the summer of 1987 it retained a certain status at the Hot House. There were only three or four actual members being housed in the prison and Scott was identified by the bureau as one of them. Had he not been sitting in the Hole, he would have had several "AB wanna-bes," younger convicts enamored of the gang, washing his laundry and performing other chores for him. Being a gang member gave an inmate an identity as well as protection.

The Aryan Brotherhood, in particular, liked to portray itself as family. At one point, bureau officials found a copy of the AB's secret creed.

An Aryan Brother is without a care,
He walks where the weak and heartless won't dare,
And if by chance he should stumble and lose control,
His brothers will be there, to help reach his goal.
For a worthy brother, no need is too great,
He need not but ask, fulfillment's his fate.

For an Aryan Brother, death holds no fear,
Vengeance will be his, through his brothers still here,
For the Brotherhood means just what it implies,
A brother's a brother, till that brother dies.
And if he is loyal, and never lost faith,
In each brother's heart, will always be a place.

So a brother am I and always will be,
Even after my life is taken from me.
I'll lie down content, knowing I stood,
Head held high, walking proud in the Brotherhood.

But while members might have rhapsodized about gang membership, the bureau claimed most members spent their time dealing and using drugs.

Although Scott would not admit he was a gang member, he did acknowledge that he was a career criminal. "It is how I make my living. It's a job. But that doesn't mean I don't have any ethics or code that I live by. Most Square Johns don't believe criminals live by any code or rules, but I do. You have to have standards, because they are the only things that set you apart from the real scumballs in here. You got to embrace something, some sort of principles, and if you keep those standards, you develop a reputation. Society may think you are a piece of shit, but in here, you are respected because everyone knows you are strong enough to stand by your own principles. . . . You see, in here, principles are the only things a man has. You are as good as your word."

An avid reader of the late western novelist Louis L'Amour,

Scott said he had patterned his conduct after that of the Old West. "I never rat. I don't tell on anyone. I don't say something to the weakest, smallest individual in here that I wouldn't say to the biggest motherfucker. If I give another convict my word, I'll keep it. I try to be professional when I do a job."

None of these principles applied to guards or Square Johns. "You can lie and steal and scam a Square John because he is not part of the criminal society. It's just like I am not really part of your society. Your society rejected me, doesn't want to have anything to do with me, so I owe you nothing. It's like there are two different worlds—your society and the criminal society—and those of us in the criminal world don't have to follow your rules, only our own, and the rules that I choose to follow may be different from another convict's.

"For example," Scott continued, "I don't rob mom-and-pop stores. I don't think it is right to take a workingman's money. That is bread out of his kid's mouth. But a Safeway or bank, hey, who's that really hurt? I don't kill innocent people or shoot the place full of holes. But if some teller tries to play hero when I'm pointing a shotgun in his face, sure I feel bad about that, but it really isn't my fault because I tried to be professional and plan the robbery and do a good job without anyone getting hurt. He's the one acting like a fool trying to stop me."

When I went to see Scott a few days later, he was unusually mellow. He had received an unexpected gift the night before, he whispered. A convict, later identified by guards as an AB wanna-be, had been sent to the Hole for arguing with a guard. What no one realized was that he had wanted to be arrested because he was carrying a package of marijuana in his rectum for Scott.

If anyone knew how difficult it was to get drugs into the Hot House, it was Scott. After all, he was in the Hole because of a botched heroin deal. The fact that his friends had sent him such a valuable present showed that he, as Scott put it, was "loved and respected." I later learned that Scott's use of those two words was no accident. They are the standard salutation that a member of the Aryan Brotherhood uses when he addresses another member. There was little question who had sent the package of marijuana.

A Voice: BANK ROBBER, AGE 45

They originally charged me with murder, kidnapping, and bank robbery, but I'm really just a bank robber with really bad luck. You see, my buddy and me were robbing this bank, and when we come outside there is a cop waiting across the street and he starts shooting. He shoots my buddy, but I don't know he's dead so I pull him into the car and drive away. When they bust me, they charge me with murder, kidnapping, and the robbery.

I ask my attorney, "How the hell can they do that? All I did was rob a bank."

He says the law says if you are committing a felony and someone dies, a bank teller has a heart attack or something, you can be charged with murder. He tells me they charged me with murder because my buddy got killed.

He says the law says when I pulled my buddy into the car and drove off, I kidnapped him because I was taking a body from the scene of a crime. That's how they got me for kidnapping.

He says the law says that I can be charged with all three even though I didn't kill nobody and I didn't kidnap nobody.

I say the law sucks.

CHAPTER
TEN

THE LIEUTENANT'S OFFICE

An anonymous letter was waiting in Lieutenant Bill Slack's mail slot when he came to work shortly before 7 A.M. one July 1987 day. As the operations lieutenant working the day shift, Slack was the equivalent of a desk sergeant in a police precinct. He poured himself some coffee and took his position behind the glass-topped desk, the biggest piece of furniture in the cramped lieutenant's office. Besides the desk, the room contained a bench, a typewriter, and a row of metal file cabinets. Slack lighted the first cigarette of what would be two packs that day and began reading the letter.

Although he was only in his early forties, Slack seemed older. He was nearly bald, had a smoker's hacking cough, and was no longer the trim-waisted marine he had been when he first joined the bureau direct from a combat tour in Vietnam. But it was his manner that set Slack apart. He was fatherly, always calm, slow to criticize. Many considered him the best desk lieutenant in the Hot House.

The anonymous letter contained one line: *Loook undur matress B-215*. The writer was either the world's worst speller or intentionally trying to appear dumb. Slack telephoned Steve Lacy, head of the prison's shakedown crew, and told him to search cell 215 in B cellhouse. Slack didn't mention anything about looking under the mattress. He figured he shouldn't have to.

Twenty minutes later, Lacy strutted into the lieutenant's

office with a "sissie shank," a knife made by melting a toothbrush around a razor blade. It wasn't much good for stabbing,
but it could be used to slice someone's face.

"Want me to bring in the shithead whose cell we found this
in?" asked Lacy, who nearly always called inmates shitheads.
Slack nodded, and a few minutes later, a white convict was led
into the office by Lacy and two other guards.

Slack lifted up the sissie shank so the convict could see it
and then dropped it safely in a desk drawer.

"Ever see that before?" asked Slack.

The inmate shook his head, and frowned.

"It was found under the mattress in your cell," Slack continued.

"Those fuckin' niggers!" the convict exclaimed. "They're
framin' me, settin' me up, I—"

"Watch your mouth," snapped Slack, who didn't tolerate
racial slurs.

The convict caught his breath. The arteries pulsing in his
neck looked like hot blue electric wires sheathed under skin
drawn as taut as a drumhead.

"It's a fuckin' frame, Lieutenant! Can't you see it?" he said.

Slack leaned back in his metal desk chair, which creaked
like a rusty schoolyard teeter-totter.

"So what's your version?"

The inmate glanced around. Two guards stood beside him.
Lacy was directly behind.

"Lieutenant, can we do this in private?"

Some inmates will fight when brought to the lieutenant's
office. It's a matter of pride to pop a guard before being dragged
to the Hole. But Slack didn't think the convict was looking to
better the odds by getting him alone. For one thing, he didn't
need to. It was going to be a struggle for the three guards and
Slack to handle him if he fought. The convict was a bulky body-
builder.

"Okay. C'mon," Slack replied, walking through a door at
the back of the office. It led into a room normally used by the
prison's captain, but the Hot House was temporarily without
one, so Slack slipped behind the desk and motioned the inmate
to begin talking.

"These niggers stole my watch, okay?" he explained. "I

didn't know at first who took it, but I let it be known I wanted it back. I had some friends put out word too, okay?"

"What friends?" Slack asked innocently.

"Don't bullshit me, Lieutenant! You know what I'm talking about."

Indeed, Slack knew. The convict ran numbers for a group of car thieves, pimps, extortionists, and bank robbers from the deep South known as the Georgia Boys. It was the Georgia Boys who put out word that the watch had better be returned or someone was going to get stabbed.

"The niggers who took my watch got a guy to bring it to me to apologize, you know. This guy, he says to me, 'Hey, no hard feelings, huh?' to see if I'm going to retaliate and I tell 'im 'No, everything is cool as long as I got my watch back.' "

Slack smirked.

"Hey, I'm serious. I'm a peaceful guy. I mean, I got my watch back, so what the fuck, who cares? But these niggers must've figured I was going to get even so they planted that shank in my cell and then tipped you off. Someone dropped a kite [letter] on me, didn't they?"

Slack didn't reply. He asked questions, he didn't answer them.

"Who were the guys who stole your watch?" Slack asked.

"Some niggers."

"Do these individuals have names?"

"Suspect so," the convict said.

"So what are they?" asked Slack.

The convict shrugged. "C'mon, Lieutenant, I'm no rat."

Slack asked a few more questions but didn't learn anything. He motioned the convict back into the outer office where Lacy and the others were waiting.

"As crazy as it sounds," Slack said, "I happen to believe you. But I still got to lock you up. If I let you go, how do I know you aren't going to leave this office and go stick one of these guys for trying to frame you?"

The inmate smiled.

"Now, let's say a man of your fine character decides that he's above all that," Slack continued. "Let's say I let you go and you don't seek revenge. What do you think the guys who tried to frame you are going to do? They're going to figure you are pissed, so they are going to try to stick you before you stick them. Either way, someone's going to get hurt, so I got to lock you up."

"Hey, don't do me no favors," the inmate snapped.

Lacy put handcuffs on the inmate and led him out.

"My gut feeling is he's telling the truth," Slack said. "But he could be lying. He might have written that letter to me himself. He might have put that shank under his own mattress because he wanted to go to the Hole."

Sometimes inmates get into debt or into an argument with another convict. They know that they are going to end up either stabbing someone or getting stabbed, so they set up their own arrest. That way they can be taken to the Hole, where they will be safe without losing face with their peers.

Whether or not the convict was framed or had planned his own arrest ultimately didn't matter, Slack said. Unless the inmate told the guards who had stolen his watch, he was going to be found guilty of having a weapon in his cell—a serious offense that would result in his spending an additional six months in prison and being transferred to Marion. But the inmate was caught in a catch-22. "He really can't say who framed him," Slack explained, "because if he tells, he'd be snitching, and he's not going to risk being labeled a rat. The truth is that we really don't know what is happening here," Slack admitted, "and there is no way to find out.

"The bottom line is that we come in here every day, do our jobs, and go home. These inmates are here twenty-four hours a day, and this is their home and their world. We only think we know what is happening, and most of the time we probably don't have any clue to what really is going on."

The remainder of the shift was uneventful, and at four o'clock, Slack turned over the operations desk to Lieutenant Edward Pierce. Slack still had an hour's worth of paperwork to complete before he went home, but Pierce was in charge. At age thirty-five, with a handlebar mustache and salt-and-pepper hair, Pierce had the sort of ruggedly handsome face seen in cigarette advertisements. Self-confident, some would say cocky, he ran his shift like a rooster overseeing the henhouse. Some guards never catch on to prison life. They lack the intuition that the best lieutenants have. Pierce had seemed to understand prisons from the first time he stepped into one. Yet, despite his abilities, he was not well-liked by supervisors. They said he lacked "polish." Pierce thought there was a different reason: because, in his words, "I don't kiss ass." His buddy, Lieutenant Sandels, had tried to school him in diplomacy, but it wasn't in his nature. "If a man is wrong, you got to call him no matter who he is," said Pierce. This sounded more gallant than it often was.

Pierce loved working the shift from four to midnight. "All you have to do is your job, not all the Mickey Mouse political bullshit that goes on when the brass are here."

At night, Pierce was literally in charge of the entire penitentiary and as soon as the mess hall finished serving dinner at six o'clock, the phones in the lieutenant's office began ringing.

"Hey, boss, I got two inmates here who want to swap mattresses," a guard in C cellhouse told him. "Can they do that?"

"As long as one ain't pressing the other out of his, it's okay with me," said Pierce, reminding the guard to make certain that both inmates really wished to swap.

Seconds later, another guard called. He had caught two inmates shooting craps in a cell, but when he tried to arrest them they had eaten the evidence.

"What evidence?" Pierce asked.

The inmates had made dice out of sugar cubes, the guard explained, which they swallowed when the guard caught them.

Pierce roared, and told the guard to assign them some extra chores around the cellhouse rather than take them to the Hole.

An alarm sounded: "Fight on B-cellhouse stairs!" Pierce bolted from his desk. Guards usually carry a two-way radio or a body alarm that emits a high-pitched squeal when punched. Whenever an alarm sounded, all guards were supposed to run to the source unless they were assigned to a job that couldn't be abandoned even in an emergency. Pierce ran down center hallway, into the rotunda, and up the B-cellhouse stairs, but both convicts had vanished by the time he got there. The guard who had sounded the alarm had gotten a glimpse of one of them but wasn't certain who it was. Naturally none of the inmates loitering in the stairwell had seen anything.

When Pierce got back to the lieutenant's office, a guard was waiting with a drunk convict. The inmate had been drinking a concoction made from bread, oranges, water, and sugar, left in a plastic bag for four days to ferment. Pierce gave him a breath test and sent him to the Hole. The phone rang. An inmate in C cellhouse had just ripped his sink from the wall and the entire tier was flooding. "Well, turn off the water," Pierce ordered. "Damn rookies," he said, hanging up the receiver. "They call me instead of turning off a valve." As Pierce poured himself a cup of coffee, he overheard two convicts yelling outside in the hall in front of the commissary.

"He's got my ice cream!" one complained when Pierce appeared.

"That's a fucking lie, Lieutenant! I don't owe you nothing, man," the other replied, grasping a half-eaten ice cream cone in his hand.

"Lieutenant, I'm telling you, if he takes another lick of that ice cream, I'm gonna break his face," the first inmate threatened.

The other inmate defiantly began to lift the cone to his mouth.

"Just hold it right there," Pierce ordered. The inmate lowered the cone. A few minutes later, Pierce had resolved the argument and both convicts walked away.

Fights, flooded cells, drunk inmates, the ice cream spat—no one would care the next morning that Pierce had handled each of these problems. They were trivial events, remembered only because he would have to file paperwork about them. Yet, even the most insignificant confrontation could swiftly escalate into violence at the Hot House. Convicts had killed over a pack of cigarettes.

"Some college-educated pencil-pusher making five times my salary in some big corporation fucks up and the only thing that happens is that the company loses some money," said Pierce. "I fuck up and there are bodies on the floor."

The threat of violence underlies every action and reaction in prison. Pierce liked to compare prison work to riding a motorcycle. Most rides were routine. But sometimes late on a sweltering summer night, a rider would find himself on one of those endless flat Kansas two-lanes with only the lights of a distant farmhouse pricking through the prairie blackness. Leaning forward, you could screw the throttle, ignore the red-and-green rpm gauge, let your instincts tell you when to shift gears. At 75 mph, the wind stings the naked face. At 95 mph, eyes squint, teeth clench. A rider must lean low, squeeze his thighs against the gas tank, keep the front tire on the white center stripe. At 105 mph, there is no time to think, no time to pause, only to react, and at 110 mph, there is not even time to do that. At that speed on a motorcycle, a rider simply shoots blindly ahead into the blackness. And then it happens, that strange feeling when pure elation and sheer terror join. Some call it pushing yourself to the edge, riding the lip of the envelope.

Being a lieutenant at the Hot House was like that, Pierce said. Routine, even boring, and then suddenly you were flying at 110 mph into the blackness never knowing for certain just where this ride would go or how it would end.

Pierce loved it.

Unlike Slack, he dreaded sitting behind a desk, and he looked for any excuse to leave the lieutenant's office. He could be reached by radio during emergencies. Tonight, he walked to the Hole, where a veteran convict was about to be escorted to the prison hospital. Some five years earlier, the inmate had gotten drunk, smeared his body with butter, broken a mop handle into two pieces, and screamed at guards until they finally rushed him. Pierce had been the first through the cell door that night and had been hit in the head with one of the sticks. They had not spoken since that fight.

"Old Thunderbird," Pierce said, calling the inmate by his nickname, "was just letting off steam. It wasn't personal on either of our parts."

Pierce fell in with the three young guards taking Thunderbird to the dentist, where he would be fitted with false teeth. At least once a week, the dentist stayed late into the evening to handle patients who were busy working in the prison factories during the day or who for some other reason couldn't come into the hospital during regular hours.

"What's Mama gonna say when you get home and pull those choppers out?" Pierce chided him.

"Shit, Lieutenant, her pussy ain't gonna taste no different."

Pierce left them at the hospital entrance and strolled into the prison yard, where he took a seat on the concrete bleachers. An after-dinner softball game was under way. He sat by himself midway between a group of black inmates perched along the top row and a cluster of Italians sitting on the bottom row.

The black inmates were from Washington, D.C., and were known simply as "D.C. Blacks." They were one of the most difficult groups at Leavenworth for guards to control. Because it has limited jail space of its own, the nation's capital sends a disproportionate number of inmates into the federal system, and most are black, a reflection of the city's predominantly black population. At the Hot House, D.C. Blacks were the largest single ethnic group from any single city, making up 10 percent of the overall population, and nearly all were well-schooled in violence. D.C. Blacks were especially notorious as "locker-knockers"—petty thieves who ransacked the personal lockers of other inmates—and for pressuring new inmates for sex.

The dozen Italians sitting below Pierce were Mafia "wise-guys." Each wore prison-issued white shorts and cotton shirts, but their clothing had been pressed and was brand-new. Some smoked William Penn cigars at fifty cents apiece, the highest-priced stogies in the commissary. Gold chains dangled from their necks, and a stack of graphite tennis rackets, the most expensive item a convict could special-order at the Hot House store, was nearby. Even though they were watching the ball game, each of the wiseguys was sitting so he could face and hear an older convict in the group. Anthony "Tony Ducks" Corallo didn't say much, but when he spoke, his comments either brought a solemn nod or a boisterous laugh, depending upon which was appropriate. Corallo was the boss of the New York–based Lucchese crime family, a real-life Mafia godfather, and no one at the Hot House bothered him. Not that anyone had reason to. He was a perfect gentleman. In prison, a Mafioso did his time as quietly as possible because it improved his chances for parole. There was only one time anyone could remember that a Mafia member got into trouble, and that had happened at the penitentiary in Lewisburg, Pennsylvania, where Mafia members are frequently housed because of its proximity to New York City. A guard, for some reason, began harassing a wiseguy. Every day the guard searched the inmate's cell, went through his mail, and frisked him as he walked the compound, until the wiseguy had simply had enough. One day a visitor from outside the prison came to see the wiseguy. The guard saw the visitor slip something into the wiseguy's hand.

"What you got there?" the guard demanded.

Without protest, the wiseguy opened his fingers, revealing a photograph of the guard's six-year-old daughter playing at her elementary school.

"See how easy it can be?" the Mafioso asked.

Whether or not the story was true was impossible to tell, but every guard and most inmates in the Hot House had heard it. The message was clear. The Mafia could "reach out into the streets," and that made guards and other convicts nervous.

Most of the black inmates sitting in the bleachers were dressed in "jams," long shorts made from gray and blue sweatpants chopped off at the knee. Each wore high-top Nike tennis shoes with the laces intentionally untied. A few had wool stocking caps on their heads despite the July heat. None wore a shirt. They were in their early twenties, loud, full of horseplay. They provided a running commentary on the game.

A batter slammed a pitch toward center field, a high, beautiful hit that forced the outfielder to race backward toward the prison wall. Just when it looked as if the hit was out of reach, the outfielder leaped backward and snagged the ball in his bare right hand since he didn't have time to raise his glove.

The black inmates cheered. Pierce did too. Even the wiseguys, who Pierce figured were wagering on the game in Italian, jumped up and applauded.

Minutes later another batter slammed the ball out into center field. There was a different outfielder playing now and he badly misjudged the ball, allowing it to fall several feet behind him.

"Stupid motherfucker!" a D.C. Black screamed.

"Your momma sucks!" another yelled, the end of his comment drowned by a chorus of boos and similar obscenities. Even the player's own teammates pelted him with vulgarities.

Except for a single guard standing across the yard, Pierce was the only officer out there among some four hundred inmates, many of them convicted killers. He leaned back in the evening sun, rested his black cowboy boots on the seat in front of him, and relaxed.

"Some officers come in here and try to act like trained killers," he said. "Hell, they ain't fooling nobody but themselves. These inmates are for real. They can smell fear, and they know who is for real and who is selling wolf tickets. Now, other officers will come in here and be real meek and mild, but if there's a shit storm, they're right there ready to do whatever is necessary.

"The secret is that there is no secret. You can't fake it in here. You either are the kind of person who can handle violence or you're not.

"People make this job harder than it is. If an inmate has something coming—his mail, a blanket, whatever—you give it to him. If he don't, you tell him. And most importantly, if an inmate ain't going over the fence or thumping somebody, then you just leave him the fuck alone."

Had you asked Pierce's classmates at Wiley High School in Terre Haute, Indiana, if they ever thought he would end up in prison, most would have quickly answered "Yes!" But as an inmate, not as a lieutenant. Pierce was, as he put it, "a hood, a problem child." Enough so that at age eighteen, he was taken before a judge who gave him a choice—jail or the military service. He chose the navy. "I decided to change my life. *I* decided. No one else gave a fuck, really. But I decided and I changed it."

Pierce said he was physically abused as a child. "I had the living shit beat out of me with belts, two-by-fours, fists—and that was by my own mother," he said. "Once I was beaten unconscious. That's why I'm not afraid of getting my ass whipped in here. There is nothing that these guys can bring to me that I've not already been through, and that is why it really pisses me off when some television program whips up a bunch of sympathy for these inmates by telling how they were abused children. That's bullshit. Their mama didn't drive them to the bank and force them to rob it."

Since he joined the bureau, Pierce's nose has been fractured twice, his upper lip sewed up more than a dozen times, and a piece of his ear chewed off during a scuffle. He paused, and looked at the inmates exercising in the yard. What kind of convict would he have been if he had not been able to turn his life around? I asked. The idea intrigued him, but only for a moment. He tried to picture himself out on the ball field staring back at the bleachers and the faceless lieutenant seated there. How would he have felt if he were on the other side? It didn't compute. "I'm not one of them," he said.

Pierce looked over at the prison industries buildings. In the summer, the yard stayed open until the shadow from the west prison wall reached the second-floor windows of the printing plant. When that moment arrived, a horn would sound and inmates would trudge back into the main penitentiary. The night before, the horn had sounded during the final inning of an electrifying ball game. The losing team was at bat, was only one run behind, had two men on base and its best hitter stepping to the plate. There were two outs. Before the pitcher could throw his first pitch, the horn sounded and the team that was ahead scrambled off the field declaring victory. Nine convicts had cornered Pierce. A few accused him of deliberately setting off the signal to throw the game. Pierce was sitting in the bleachers tonight to make certain that the horn sounded between innings. It didn't really matter, because tonight's game was lopsided. Still, he waited several minutes after the shadow reached the windows before giving his okay for the horn. He wanted the inmates to realize he had listened to them. The yard cleared peacefully and by ten o'clock all the inmates were locked in their cells and being counted.

Midnight approached, time for Pierce to go home. Lieutenant Bill Thomas, a lanky white-haired quiet man, arrived at the lieutenant's office on schedule and chatted with him. A few minutes later, Pierce stepped outside the prison and walked over to his black motorcycle. He revved the engine as the guard in the front tower looked down and waved, and then slowly rode down the horseshoe drive.

CHAPTER ELEVEN

THE CUBANS

In 1987, summer slipped quickly into fall at the Hot House, the weeks passing without incident, until Friday, November 20. Shortly after nine A.M., Associate Warden Richard Smith got a telephone call from the bureau's regional headquarters. Within seconds, he knew there was going to be trouble, big trouble, from an unlikely source.

Fidel Castro had just agreed to take back as many as 3,000 Cubans who were now sitting in federal prisons. These were Cubans who had sought political asylum in the United States in 1980 during the Mariel boatlift but had not qualified because they were either criminals or mentally ill. Getting rid of them after nearly eight years was great news to Smith. But when he was told that the State Department planned to announce their impending deportation at noon that same day, Smith was appalled. Cuban inmates would be enraged by the announcement. A few of them at the Hot House had told Smith that they would butcher a guard, if necessary, to keep from being sent back. They knew that such a murder would result in their spending their lives in prison. But it would be an American prison, not a Cuban one, and that was worth killing for.

The time of the State Department press conference gave Smith less than three hours to figure out what to do with the Hot House's thirty-five Cubans. They weren't really much of a threat, he decided. But as he put down the receiver he wondered what the wardens at the federal prisons in Atlanta, Georgia, and Oakdale, Louisiana, must have been thinking. Together, those two facilities held 3,000 Cubans.

What could they possibly do in so short a time to prepare for the violence that was sure to come? Smith also wondered how people at the State Department could be so reckless.

The so-called "Cuban problem" had actually begun in the spring of 1980, when thousands of Cubans swarmed the Peruvian embassy in Havana seeking to escape Cuba's crumbling economy. A furious Fidel Castro announced that any Cubans who wanted to desert their homeland could, but only if they left through the tiny port of Mariel. No Central American country would accept the refugees, however, so there was no place for them to go until then-President Jimmy Carter announced that the United States would welcome the Cuban refugees with "open arms and an open heart."

Virtually overnight, 125,000 Cubans made the ninety-mile journey from Mariel to Florida ports, where they completely overwhelmed immigration agents. To make matters worse, Castro thumbed his nose at the U.S. during the height of the boatlift by emptying his country's prisons and mental hospitals into Mariel. Months later, the Immigration and Naturalization Service would calculate that Castro had released 23,000 "undesirables," yet federal agents were only able to stop 210 of them at Florida ports. Many of the others were arrested during the months that followed, and were turned over to the INS for deportation. But Castro refused to take them back, so the INS had no choice but to house them in makeshift detention camps, mostly at old army bases. After numerous demonstrations and riots in the camps, the Justice Department forced the bureau to turn the penitentiary in Atlanta into a prison for Cubans.

In the beginning, Atlanta held only 1,844 men, but as the months passed, Cubans streamed into the badly dilapidated prison at an average of 100 new inmates per month. Worse, not all of the Cubans being sent to Atlanta were criminals or mentally ill. INS guidelines were so poorly written that even Mariel Cubans who had no criminal backgrounds were detained for deportation if they were stopped by police for *any* reason, even traffic violations. This contributed to even more overcrowding.

As the number of Cubans skyrocketed, the bureau became alarmed. Finally, a federal judge in Atlanta ordered the Justice Department to establish some sort of review process so that Cubans who were not dangerous could be released. On paper, the procedure sounded good, but it couldn't and didn't work. Presidential candidate Ronald Reagan had promised to slash the federal budget, and funds for halfway houses and other social programs that the Cubans needed were the first to go. A federal study would later reveal that only fifty Cubans out of two thousand declared ready for parole were actually released. A second setback for the Cubans and the bureau came when a federal appeals court ruled in 1983 that they were not protected by the U.S. Constitution because they were not U.S. citizens. That meant they could be held in prison indefinitely until Castro agreed to take them back, no matter what their crime.

Faced with drastic overcrowding at Atlanta, the bureau built a $17 million "Alien Detention Facility" in Oakdale in 1986. The only security at the forty-seven-acre camp was a twelve-foot-high chain-link fence, but the bureau said additional security wasn't needed because only Cubans who were about to be paroled would be confined there. Seven months later, the bureau reluctantly added a second twelve-foot fence to the camp, dropped razor wire between the two fences, and announced that overcrowding at Atlanta was so bad that violent Cubans were going to be shipped to Oakdale. The mood at the camp changed dramatically. When it opened, the camp had averaged one incident per month, usually a fistfight. By the fall of 1987, it was reporting thirty to thirty-five serious incidents each *week*, including attacks on guards.

When Richard Smith's telephone rang at the Hot House with news that Castro had suddenly agreed to begin taking back the Cubans, the Oakdale camp held 1,039 prisoners. It had been designed for a maximum of 574.

The bureau would later compare Oakdale to a pile of dry kindling drenched with gasoline. All that was missing was a match, and the State Department was about to strike one.

Normally, Warden Matthews would have received the telephone call about the Cubans, but he was out of town and had left

Smith in charge. Smith didn't shrink from the job. He ordered the lieutenants to round up every Cuban detainee in the prison and lock them up in separate cells so they couldn't cause any trouble. The real leader of the Cubans in Leavenworth, however, was an American. Osiris Morejon had been born in Cuba, but was a naturalized citizen and had lived in Florida for more than twenty years before he was arrested for drug trafficking and murder. In 1981, Morejon and nine other Cubans raided the hideout of another drug trafficker and seized more than two tons of marijuana. In the process, Morejon executed the two men who were supposed to be guarding the stash, and also shot an innocent passerby who happened upon the robbery. At the Hot House, Morejon had ingratiated himself with some guards because he was one of the few Cubans who spoke English well enough to be understood. But while he was jovial and friendly, guards suspected that he was extorting money from Cubans who didn't understand English and was casting himself in the role of a Cuban godfather.

Edward Geouge was in charge of Morejon's cellhouse, and when Smith told Geouge that five members of the prison's Special Operations Response Team (SORT) were being sent to round up Morejon, the crusty officer suggested an alternative.

"Hell, Dick, why don't I just go have a talk with Mr. Morejon?" he asked. "I figure the worst he can do is try to kill me."

Smith thought Geouge was kidding but he wasn't. Without waiting for any backup, Geouge walked down to Morejon's cell.

"Morejon, we got to lock you up," he said. "I don't know how long it's going to be for. It could be a day or it might be forever, but you are going to be locked up and that's not negotiable. Now, let's do it."

Geouge held up a pair of handcuffs. Morejon, who was sitting on his bunk, looked perplexed.

"What for?" he asked.

"Doesn't matter," Geouge replied. "Now, cuff up."

Morejon rose. He was taller than Geouge. His arms were three times as thick. For a few seconds, he glared at the smaller man.

"I said cuff up, and I don't aim to say it again," Geouge commanded.

Morejon stuck out his hands.

A few hours later, Smith got another frantic telephone call from the regional office. Inmates at Oakdale were rioting, the camp was burning, an unknown number of guards were being held hostage. How long would it take for Leavenworth to send its SORT team—some twenty men—to Louisiana?

"They're on their way," Smith replied.

The next question was tougher. How long would it take for the Hot House to be ready to house the Cubans from Oakdale once the riot ended?

Like Richard Smith, Oakdale Warden J. R. Johnson had been notified that the State Department was going to announce the deportation agreement. But unlike Smith, Johnson didn't have any way to lock up his Cuban prisoners. At Oakdale, inmates lived in dormitories, not individual cells. Johnson had ordered his staff to quiet the prisoners' fears by handing out a printed memorandum:

> Cubans at Oakdale can help their chances to gain community release through continued positive behavior and respect towards staff and other detainees.

Just in case the memo didn't work, Johnson ordered an additional fifty guards to stand by. All day Friday, he had walked through the camp reassuring the Cubans. None seemed to be alarmed, he later noted in his daily journal. But that night a drunk Cuban prisoner stumbled into the inmate dining room, and when guards tried to arrest him, other Cubans began overturning tables and smashing dishes. The guards retreated and let the drunk return to his dormitory.

A short time later, several guards decided to go after him. They marched to the dorm, but the Cuban prisoners intervened and the guards retreated again. Humiliated, they then covered up what really had happened by downplaying the incident in their nightly report.

A special task force appointed several months after the riot at Oakdale would later point to the dining-room and dormitory fracases as pivotal. The cover-up was the first error. The second error was retreating twice. "The Cuban detainees seemed to keep pushing the boundaries of bureau control and testing reactions," the task force wrote. "Evidently, staff were not perceived as taking a firm stand."

What happened the next day, Saturday, November 21, is hotly disputed by Warden Johnson and his own staff. Several guards told the task force after the riot that Johnson was warned repeatedly that between two hundred and three hundred Cubans were planning to crash the camp's front entrance at dinnertime to escape. The task force report noted that Cuban prisoners had started to prepare for trouble. Some began hoarding food, others were seen putting on several layers of clothing. A few even taped magazines to their abdomens, chests, and backs, a common device to help deflect blows from nightsticks or knives. The task force wrote:

> Information about these peculiar events was transmitted to the lieutenants and to the acting captain, who stated that he, in turn, informed the warden. The warden has no recall of these events being reported to him, although his log reflects he was contacted every half hour.

When the shift changed at four o'clock on that Saturday, the acting captain decided on his own to send all the women guards out of the camp. He also moved the fifty extra guards into the front entrance, but kept them out of sight. During the next two hours, nothing out of the ordinary was reported, but at 6:50 P.M., a mob of more than two hundred screaming Cubans rushed the entrance. The extra guards jumped into view and fired tear gas. Surprised, the prisoners retreated, giving guards trapped in the camp time to evacuate, but they regrouped within minutes and attacked again, this time hurling back the tear-gas canisters. Some Cubans swung broken mop handles. The guards were forced back. Now the only barrier between the Cubans and the outside world was a one-sixteenth-inch-thick sheet of Plexiglas.

Warden Johnson sent twenty officers armed with .12 gauge shotguns and .38 caliber revolvers into the entryway. They were less than four feet from the angry Cubans pounding on the Plexiglas. The guards waited nervously. They would be overrun if the Cubans broke through. A tiny crack appeared on the glass, and as the Cubans beat it, the crack inched its jagged way across the barrier in the shape of a lightning streak.

"If they break the glass," Johnson was later quoted by the task force as saying, "shoot until you have no ammunition left."

For several minutes the guards stood ready as the Cubans slammed against the barrier, but it did not give way.

Elsewhere in the compound prisoners tried to cut through the wire fences, but were stopped by guards wielding shotguns. Others lit fires or grabbed guards as hostages. Outside the camp, Lieutenant Charles Marmelejo donned an inmate's clothing and slipped inside. With the help of several American convicts who worked in the camp, Marmelejo led nine employees to safety before he was recognized by the Cubans and forced to stop his risky treks inside.

Guards Rick Nichols, Alvin Brandon, and Colton Duplechain weren't so lucky. Surrounded by angry Cubans, they took refuge in the camp's control center, which was located inside the compound, and watched helplessly as inmates set the building on fire. Dense smoke filled the booth. The three men gasped for air. When they could no longer stand it, Nichols punched the button that opened the electronic door. Nothing happened. He pushed it again and again, but it still refused to function. Nichols began slamming it with his fist. The smoke was so dense it was impossible for him to see his partners. Finally the door burst open and Duplechain stumbled outside armed with a stun gun, which shoots a nonlethal but hard-hitting beanbag. He aimed it at the Cubans, who backed away. Nichols came out next, but Brandon didn't appear. Still gagging, Nichols went back inside the smoldering center and found Brandon collapsed on the floor. He pulled him to safety, and with Duplechain's help, the three men made their way through the Cubans to the fence.

Fifty-four guards had been in the camp when the Cubans rioted. Twenty-six made it out. The others were hostages. As Johnson and his men watched, helpless, one of their coworkers was paraded through the compound in a laundry cart pushed along by whooping Cubans who beat on the side of the cart with sticks.

The Hot House was in the midst of a $13 million renovation of A cellhouse when the Oakdale riot started. This cellhouse was one of the two massive cellblocks at the front of the prison, and Smith estimated that it would take about three months for the renovations to be completed. They could begin moving Cuban prisoners in then, he told his superiors.

"I heard a big sigh on the telephone when I said that," Smith recalled, "so I suggested an alternative." If cost was no object, the bureau could kick out the private contractors, authorize around-the-clock overtime pay, and turn over the renovations to the Hot House's own staff of maintenance men. Those crews, plus workers flown in from nearby federal prisons, could finish the cellhouse in as little as three weeks, Smith predicted, but the cost to taxpayers would be horrendous. For several seconds the phone line was quiet, and then Smith got his answer.

"Go ahead and do it."

Then it was Smith's turn to sigh. "I was told the job would have to be done not in three weeks but three days!"

The bureau needed all the extra cells it could find. Not only was Oakdale burning, Smith was told, but the Cubans in Atlanta had started to riot.

When his Cuban prisoners first heard the State Department's announcement on Friday, Atlanta's warden, Joseph Petrovsky, was able to convince them that they wouldn't gain anything by causing problems. But on Saturday they learned from newscasts that Oakdale was in flames, and grew restless. On Monday morning, they rioted and took hostages. Then a Cuban armed with a large homemade knife attacked a guard in the prison yard. He was shot in the head and killed instantly by a guard firing from one of the gun towers. For the next ten minutes, guards shot down into the yard. Five Cubans were hit. The shooting stopped only when inmates inside the main penitentiary threatened to begin killing hostages. In only a matter of minutes, the Cubans had seized control of the Atlanta prison too and captured 106 employees.

Every available welder, locksmith, carpenter, and painter at the Hot House was put to work in A cellhouse. There were no breaks. Employees didn't go home to sleep. When a guard finished his shift, he reported to A cellhouse and was handed a paintbrush. Maintenance crews from other prisons were hustled in. Warden Matthews hurried back from his meeting in California to help supervise. He and Associate Warden Smith quickly decided it would be foolish to put Cubans in the cellhouse once the riots ended and the renovations were complete. Some of the locks hadn't been tested. More important, why should the Cubans be rewarded by getting the newest and nicest cellhouse at the Hot House?

Instead, the U.S. prisoners living in the hopelessly outdated C and D cellhouses would be moved. There was no question in Matthews's mind about whom he would put in charge of the refurbished cellhouse. That job would go to Edward Geouge, and the dangerous convicts that Geouge oversaw would have first priority when it came to cells.

"We told the American convicts that they were getting the best cellhouse in the prison," Smith recalled. "We also told them that we had planned to do a real thorough shakedown for weapons and other contraband but because of the Cuban riots we needed their cooperation." Smith offered the prisoners a deal. "If they were willing to move from C and D cellhouses into A cellhouse without causing any problems, then we were willing to ease up on the shakedown."

Overnight more than 550 convicts, as well as all of their private belongings, were moved into A cellhouse without a single incident. Without pausing, the work crews raced into the now-empty C and D cellhouses. Bunks were welded to the walls. All mirrors, wooden desks, and bulletin boards were stripped from the cells. Matthews and Smith didn't want anything left in a cell but a bunk, fireproof mattress, sink, and toilet.

Smith had learned that Cuban prisoners frequently crammed the locks in Atlanta with hundreds of match-heads. The sulfur from the matches reacted like dynamite when packed tightly in the locks and ignited. Other Cubans were skilled at picking locks. Smith had his guards bring in spools of heavy steel chain, which was cut into three-foot lengths. A piece of chain was brought to each cell, wrapped around the cell door and bars, and then padlocked, making it impossible for the door to be opened without first removing the chain.

Yards and yards of chain-link fence were hauled inside and welded onto the outside of each tier. Smith also had steel doors built at each end of every level—in effect, making each of the five floors into a separate cage. Still not satisfied, he ordered the crew to install a second door in the entrance of each cellhouse. This made it impossible for anyone to enter either C or D cellhouse without passing through two heavy metal gates.

After three days of nonstop work, the Hot House was ready to begin receiving Cuban prisoners. A weary but proud Smith called bureau headquarters in Washington to report that Leavenworth had completed the impossible. He expected to be congratulated. Instead he got another jolt. The bureau had originally told Smith that two hundred Cubans would be sent to Leavenworth. Now, that number was being changed. With both Oakdale and Atlanta still in flames, the bureau had decided that it needed a new permanent home for the rioting Cubans. Smith was told to expect at least seven hundred Cubans, perhaps even more.

At bureau headquarters in Washington, Director Quinlan made it clear that he would negotiate a peaceful end to the riots rather than launch a Rambo-style attack to rescue the hostages. This patient approach took time, and during the days that followed, Quinlan was in constant contact with a crew of FBI specialists brought in to negotiate with the Cubans.

There was one bureau official, however, who was more worried about an American inmate running loose in Atlanta than about the Cubans. Craig Trout, the bureau's gang expert, considered Thomas Silverstein a "deadly wild card." Of the 44,000 inmates in the federal system, none was more despised by prison officials than Silverstein. Nor was there an inmate more revered by white convicts.

"Terrible Tom" Silverstein was accused of committing four grisly murders, all in federal prisons. One of the inmates he killed was Raymond "Cadillac" Smith, at the time the most powerful D.C. Black in prison. That killing alone had made Silverstein, a member of the Aryan Brotherhood, into a celebrity among white gang members. But it was the savage stabbing of a guard, Merle E. Clutts, at Marion in 1983 that so infuriated the bureau that they put Silverstein under what was known as "no human contact," the harshest conditions permitted by law.

Since the Clutts slaying, Silverstein had been housed in a special isolation cell in Atlanta where he was completely sealed off from all other inmates. The lights in his cell were kept on twenty-four hours a day, and during the first nine months that he was in Atlanta, Silverstein was not permitted a television, radio, newspaper, magazine, book, or writing material. Provided only with meals and a single set of clothing, which he wore, Silverstein was given nothing else to help pass the time. He sat alone in an empty cell with two guards watching his every move. Out of respect to Officer Clutts, the guards refused to speak to him.

Over time, the bureau had eased the restrictions slightly and had given Silverstein drawing pencils and paper, but he remained totally cut off from other inmates and the outside world. Now, he was loose. The Cubans had broken into his hidden cell and freed him. Trout figured that Silverstein would seek revenge. "I was concerned that Silverstein would go on a kamikaze mission and simply start slaughtering hostages," recalled Trout. "He was certainly capable of it."

While others concentrated on the negotiations, Trout focused on locating Silverstein. There were plenty of reported sightings. A friendly Cuban told guards that Silverstein was building a motorized hang glider which he planned to use to soar over the penitentiary's walls at night. The bureau immediately instructed its guards to shoot anyone who came flying over the walls. Another story had Silverstein attempting to tunnel out under the walls. At one point, an FBI agent excitedly claimed that Silverstein was about to emerge from a tunnel. A heavily armed SWAT team raced to the spot, but he never surfaced. A few minutes later, an FBI sniper claimed that he had seen Silverstein on the roof of the prison hospital about to use his hang glider. Another agent interrupted. He had seen Silverstein at the prison's back gate. And so it went. The bureau's apprehensiveness about Silverstein can be seen in a confidential memo written by Warden Petrovsky on November 28, which told guards what to do once negotiators convinced the Cubans to surrender. The memo, made public now for the first time, read:

> Thomas Silverstein is a psychopathic killer and the most dangerous individual on the compound. It is not likely Silverstein will surrender and may hide out as long as he can. Once he is found, regardless of when and

where, any action on his part other than total submission and surrender should be interpreted as a maneuver to assault and he should be shot without hesitation.

At Trout's urging, FBI negotiators asked the Cubans to surrender Silverstein as a sign of good faith. It worked. On November 30, the Cubans poured chloral hydrate, stolen from the prison pharmacy, into Silverstein's morning coffee. When this failed to knock him out, more than a dozen Cubans surprised him and wrestled him to the ground. FBI Agent D. H. Rosario was monitoring radio broadcasts (the Cubans were using portable radios taken from hostages) when he heard an excited Cuban yell, "We got him! Come and get him, now, now, now!" Rosario rushed a team of U.S. marshals to the door that led into the prison yard. The Cubans had used a pair of handcuffs and leg irons taken from guards to restrain Silverstein. After the FBI dragged him away, a Cuban called Rosario on the radio and asked if the FBI would return the shackles. Rosario laughed. Later, he told reporters that the capture of Silverstein was a turning point in the negotiations. Each side had breathed a "sigh of relief" once Silverstein was in chains.

Craig Trout knew exactly where he wanted to put Silverstein. The day after his capture, the prisoner was hustled to Dobbins Air Force Base and taken by private flight to Kansas. A handpicked crew from the Hot House was waiting. Associate Warden Smith had never met Silverstein, but Smith had known Officer Merle Clutts personally and had attended Clutts's funeral. "As far as I am concerned, Silverstein is a cold-blooded, bloodthirsty, worthless killer," Smith said.

Even though he prided himself on being professional and objective, Smith was looking forward to seeing Silverstein's reaction when he was taken to the special isolation cell that had been prepared for him deep in the bowels of the Hot House. It had been constructed years ago as a concealed holding cell for "hot" prisoners whose location needed to be kept secret, usually because the Mafia had put out a contract on their lives. It was the worst cell in the penitentiary. Its walls and roof were made of one-inch-thick steel. The cell was buried underneath the rotunda in a section of the basement that hadn't been used for years. It was so isolated that you could not hear any of the familiar sounds of prison life—no human voices, toilets flushing, doors clanging shut, televisions blaring. Nothing.

The cell itself was just as desolate. There was no bed, only a platform of concrete blocks with a thin mattress on top. There was no mirror, only a metal sink, a shower stall, and a toilet without a lid.

There were no windows in the cell, no way of telling whether it was day or night or cold or hot outside, or spring, summer, fall, or winter. The only link to the world was a small black-and-white television set. It was not there out of kindness. Smith had installed the television to make Silverstein obey. If he refused to follow an order, the guards would shut it off.

Because Silverstein was considered a prime escape risk, Smith planned to have two guards sit outside his cell and watch him around the clock. Obviously, they wouldn't be able to see him unless the lights in his cell were left on. They would burn twenty-four hours a day.

In effect, Silverstein was being put into an empty fluorescent-lit cage. The lights would never be dimmed, the temperature would never change, the only sounds would come from the prisoner himself or the television.

On the night that the legendary killer arrived, Smith was waiting. Although Silverstein was six foot three inches tall, and weighed two hundred pounds, he did not seem as big as he had been portrayed. He was pale and apparently had been drugged before the flight. He didn't resist, wasn't belligerent, and didn't react to the cell as a horde of officers escorted him down into the Hot House basement. Without muttering a word, Silverstein stepped inside the cage, turned his back on Smith and the others gawking at him, curled up on the floor, and went to sleep.

The riots at Oakdale and Atlanta ended after thirteen days. In the Hot House, Smith's telephone rang again. The voice on the other end was concise.

"They're on their way."

CHAPTER
TWELVE

THOMAS LITTLE

As soon as Thomas Little moved in with Carl Bowles, the older man asked his new cellmate why he had been sent to the Hot House. Did Little have a secret hiding in his prison record as had Jeffrey Hicks? Putting a first-time bank robber in a maximum-security penitentiary just didn't make sense. Since 1985 the bureau had used a point system to determine where inmates were sent. The more violence in a criminal's background, the more points he received. Bowles knew all about the point system. He had received the highest total possible. But when he sat down with a pencil and legal pad and calculated the number Little should have received, Bowles always reached the same conclusion. Either Little was lying about his criminal record or someone in the bureau had made a big mistake.

Little clearly didn't belong at Leavenworth.

Little insisted that he wasn't hiding anything. There was only one possible explanation, he said. While he was being held in a Florida county jail awaiting trial, jailers had searched his cell and found that two of the bars were cut.

"They accused me of trying to escape," he explained.

"Well, did they ever charge you with escape?" Bowles asked.

"No," Little replied. "They blamed me for it, but they couldn't prove it."

With Little in tow, Bowles marched down the tier to see Little's case manager. Every inmate in Leavenworth was assigned a case manager who was responsible for keeping track of the multitudinous paperwork an inmate's presence generated. If a convict visited the prison doctor, asked to move to another cell, met with an outside visitor, or even bought a magazine subscription, a note was made in his prison file. Besides compiling all the paperwork, case managers kept tabs on when prisoners were to appear before the parole board or for other periodic reviews. If Little had been accused of trying to escape in Florida, there would be a record of it in his file and his case manager would know about it. And if a mistake had been made, then Little could appeal to him for help.

It was against the rules for one convict to examine another's records, but Bowles told Little exactly which forms to ask for, and sent him inside the case manager's cubbyhole office in A cellhouse. A few minutes after Little returned with copies of his records, Bowles knew why the first-time felon had been sent to a maximum-security penitentiary.

"Looky here," Bowles said, pointing at the paper, "they got you down as an extreme escape risk!"

Little's permanent police record listed him as being found guilty of attempted escape in Florida. As far as the bureau was concerned, Little had attempted to break out of the county jail, and that offense gave him enough points on the classification scale to merit his being held at the Hot House.

"But I was never even charged with escape," Little protested.

"This says you were," said Bowles. "C'mon."

This time, Bowles led the way into the case manager's office, where he explained his discovery. "You can't classify a guy on what you *think* he might have done," Bowles complained, "only what you can *prove* he did."

The case manager was not convinced. No staff members were going to take what Carl Bowles said as the truth. Besides, he pointed out, even if the bureau had screwed up, it had the authority to house a convict anywhere it wished regardless of the number of points that inmate had received. The points were merely a guideline, so the bureau was under no legal obligation to move Little.

"What if we get some written proof that shows Little don't belong here?" Bowles asked.

The case manager reluctantly agreed to take a look at any evidence that Bowles and Little could find. Until then, Little was going to be treated as an escape risk.

When they got back to their cell, Bowles told Little to write down the names of his attorney, the judge who sentenced him, the prosecuting attorney, the sheriff, even the guards who found the two cut bars. They would write a letter to each and ask for their help. Getting the evidence should be easy, Bowles said; the hard part would be getting someone at the Hot House—either the case manager or a prison counselor—to admit that the bureau had made a mistake.

"If we can get just one staff member to take your side, we can get you out of here," Bowles promised, "but getting one of these fat-ass bastards to stick out his neck is going to be fucking difficult."

Later Thomas Little recalled his feelings that morning. "No one in the system gave a damn about me. They all knew I didn't belong in a maximum-security prison. I stuck out, but none of the staff did anything to help and they all knew what would happen to me. But here is this supposedly mad-dog killer coming to my aid and he figures out how the bureau fucked up my case within a few days and he is writing letters trying to help me. Carl Bowles was the only person in Leavenworth who really gave a shit about me."

The two men became inseparable. On most days, they dressed alike in blue low-top sneakers, olive-green army trousers, white T-shirts, and white terry-cloth hats that looked like sailor caps with the rims pulled down. Most guards and inmates assumed Bowles was teaching "his wife" how to dress. Most didn't bother to learn Little's name. He was considered an extension of Bowles. Little knew about the whispers.

"I am not a homosexual," Little said one morning in a rare show of exasperation. "I am not Carl's kid or punk or wife or anything else, except for one thing: I am Carl's friend."

Little credited Bowles with literally saving his life. "In some ways, Carl and I are identical and in some ways we are so far fucking apart, but Carl and I have talked and talked and talked, probably for a thousand hours, and after I tell him something, he will say to me, 'You know, I've had those feelings before,' and I will say to him, 'You had those feelings?' I mean, he has felt just like I have and he has taught me that it is okay to think like I do, it's okay to feel like I do, and no one else has ever told me that. Everyone else told me my thoughts were wrong or bad or evil. I have never had any real friends, but Carl Bowles listens and he understands."

I had been warned by guards and convicts not to ask Bowles whether he and Little were homosexual lovers. "Carl is fucking crazy, man," an inmate warned. "You disrespect him like that and he'll rip out your throat before you know what's happening. Ever look in his eyes?—them is dead men's eyes, no emotion, nothing but blackness."

But when I finally brought up the rumors, Bowles said, "I wondered if you'd ever get around to that.

"Sex," Bowles explained, "is easy to get in prison. You don't have to prey on someone. This morning, an orderly who works in the lieutenant's office said to me, 'Hey, Carl, you sure are looking good. I'd like to suck your dick sometime.' Now, he is a homosexual, a known homosexual who enjoys it. Why would anyone have to be a sexual predator in here when it's that easy to get?

"See, sex is easy to find, but finding a friend is damn near impossible 'cause no one trusts anyone in here.

"Look, I've been in prison for twenty-three fucking years straight," Bowles continued. "You don't think I've not gotten lonely during that time? You don't think I don't need someone as a friend or someone to love me? Everyone is always worried about sex, okay, but there are different kinds of love. Just 'cause you love someone doesn't mean you want to fuck them. Goddamn, I mean, that's a perverted way of looking at things. Sex isn't everything. There is companionship, understanding, consideration, sharing tough times together, having a guy who knows exactly what you are talking about so when he says, 'Goddamn, that's fucked up,' you understand, 'cause you know it is fucked up too. Is that homosexual to have a friend like that? Or is that just being a human being?

"Of course my dick still gets hard," he said. "Sex drive is natural. Being in prison is what isn't natural. This whole society in here is perverted. Do you think I don't know the difference between a man and a woman? Bullshit. Sex with a man is a poor substitute, a poor substitute at best, but look around, do you see any women in here?

"So what do you do? What do you do? It drives you crazy. I've tried not to think about it, but there isn't a day in here when you don't look at television or look at a magazine and see something arousing. Some guys just try to kill it, pretend their sex drive is dead. Why? Because they are scared of becoming homosexuals. 'Oh my God, am I turning gay because I want someone to hold, to touch, to love me?' No one wants to be a homosexual in here because they are usually the weakest motherfuckers around and are considered as low as a snitch.

"But I've never met a motherfucker that is so fucking cold that he doesn't give a damn about another person. Never. I've never met another person who doesn't need some physical contact with another human being.

"Can you imagine not being able to touch another human being for twenty-three fucking years?

"So what do you do? What do you do? Do you run behind everyone's back and have some homosexual suck you off while you look around the whole time and don't enjoy it because you are worried that someone will see you? Or do you jack yourself crazy every night looking at fucking pictures? This is reality, man! *I ain't had no pussy in twenty-three fucking years.*

"What do you do? I'll tell you what you do. You recognize that sex is a strong desire, but there are different kinds of love, and if you lower your standard, then you destroy yourself. It's like food. If you start eating the slop that they throw into the trash compactor and you say, 'It's okay, this is still food,' then you have lowered your standard and it drops you down. You can't lower your standard, because once you do, all your standards drop. Every one of them. You got to cling to what is pure. You got to cling to what is good. And what is the purest thing? The purest relationship is one of *love*, not one based on sex, and that comes with friendship and caring about another human being and being there for that person just like he is there for you.

"The cops will tell you that I'm a predator, but you try to find one person in twenty-three fucking years who I've preyed on. There are fifteen or twenty cases, guys who I have helped through the years. Ask any one of them and they will tell you, 'Oh yeah, Carl, well, he'd probably fuck me if I let him, but he never pressed me out of anything. He's my friend. He cared about me and helped me.'

"That's what is pure.

"What do I want with Thomas Little? I want someone I can develop a friendship with. I want someone who will say, 'Hey, old Carl Bowles, society may think he's a piece of shit, but he's my friend. He is someone who I care about. He made a difference in my life.' "

Carl Bowles sounded sincere and he sounded convincing. At least Thomas Little thought so.

CHAPTER THIRTEEN

THE CUBANS

The Cuban prisoners, all 719 of them, arrived at Leavenworth in what seemed to be good spirits. Some flashed victory signs, others grinned. For thirteen days, the nightly news had broadcast footage about the riots and much of the coverage had been sympathetic toward the detainees. But their demeanor began to change as soon as they were placed in C and D cellhouses. "The Cubans had been babied and catered to in Oakdale and Atlanta," explained Lieutenant Steven Myhand, one of two lieutenants put in charge of the cellhouses, now known collectively as the Cuban units. "We intended to show them who was boss here and that is exactly what we did."

Always before, the Cubans had enjoyed the same privileges as U.S. inmates; in fact, they had often been treated better. Not at the Hot House. All visits between Cubans and their family members and friends were stopped. No nightly movies, no use of the prison gym or weight room, no educational classes, no jobs in the prison factories, no group religious services, no trips to the prison yard. The Cuban units were designed to be a miniature Marion. The inmates were locked in five-and-a-half-by-nine-foot cells, usually two men per cell, and were only allowed outside three times each week for exercise. Even then, they were simply moved to a larger screened cage the size of a two-car garage. Once a week, each Cuban got a shower. Once a month, he could place one collect telephone call, but if no one answered or the line was busy, the phone was passed to the next man. The only goodies were generic cigarettes and writing supplies. If a Cuban had enough money, he could buy a small transistor radio strong enough to pick up Kansas City radio stations. Otherwise, a few Spanish books and magazines passed up and down the tiers were his only entertainment.

If all that was not enough to make life inside C and D cellhouses miserable, there was the never-ending noise. The roar of hundreds of men yelling from cell to cell reverberated inside the old buildings. It was as loud at three A.M. as at noon. The babble of Spanish was unintelligible to most of the guards, making the racket even more maddening. Like the screech of fingernails across a blackboard, the clamor scraped the nerves. Tempers flared.

"I don't feel good about what we are doing here," Matthews admitted one morning as he inspected the Cuban units. "This is basically a jail and I have never wanted to run a jail. But we have no choice."

Not only had the Cubans caused $64.6 million in property damage and cost taxpayers another $48.8 million in funds spent to quell the riots, they had badly humiliated the bureau and committed an unforgivable sin. "These bastards took officers hostage," a Hot House guard explained, "and they had to be taught a lesson."

Warden Matthews and Associate Warden Smith stressed that all Cubans were to be treated as "humanely as possible." But when the two men chose Lieutenant Phillip Harden Shoats, Jr., to oversee the Cuban cellhouses, they sent the Hot House guards a subtle message. The thirty-eight-year-old Shoats, one of only two black lieutenants at the prison, was known as a "hardball lieutenant" with a reputation for being physical. "Shoats wasn't the kind of guy who tried to resolve conflicts by talking," recalled one guard. "He gave an inmate an order and he gave it only once. After that, he kicked butt."

Shoats resembled Santa Claus in appearance. He weighed more than three hundred pounds, at least one hundred pounds too much for his six-foot one-inch frame. He always seemed to be smiling, too, ready with some joke. But his easygoing manner could turn into anger in a flash, and when that happened Shoats became a bully. Warden Matthews would later explain that he had chosen Shoats because he wielded "an iron hand inside a velvet glove." "I needed someone who was cool under pressure, but firm," Matthews said. "I felt Shoats was that man."

Shoats's second-in-command, Lieutenant Myhand, was the youngest lieutenant at the Hot House at age twenty-nine. He had only worked for the bureau for seven years, but his father was a retired officer with thirty-one years of experience, including stints at the federal prisons at Alcatraz and Leavenworth. The younger Myhand had grown up living in the shadow of penitentiary walls. He knew the lingo, the legends, the procedures. At the Hot House, Myhand had a reputation as an energetic, likeable "cowboy" who, like Shoats, preferred action to talk.

Neither Shoats nor Myhand received any special training in how to deal with the Cubans. They did not understand Spanish. They did not know which Cubans were killers and which were petty crooks, because the inmates had destroyed their prison records during the riots. Worse, there were only five or six guards who could speak Spanish well enough to interpret.

"Every Cuban is a shithead until he proves otherwise," Shoats told the guards whom he handpicked to work with him, "and then he still is a shithead. Don't take any chances."

Trouble between guards and Cubans erupted very quickly. A few days after the Cubans arrived, an inmate in C cellhouse filled a plastic cup with his own urine and feces, let it curdle for several hours, and then screamed until a guard rushed to his cell. The Cuban threw the contents into the guard's face. Gagging, the guard backed away, trying to clear his burning eyes as the Cuban ducked into a corner of his cell to hide.

"You little bastard," the guard yelled. Other guards kept him from attacking the Cuban.

"It's time to show these shitheads we mean business," Shoats declared. "No one throws piss and shit on my officers without paying a price."

Shoats called in a SORT team of five specially trained guards who gathered outside the Cuban's cell. Word of the guard's "baptism" had spread through the cellhouse, sparking laughter and jeers from other Cubans. The guards unlocked the padlock, removed the chain draped through the door and bars, and slid open the heavy cell door. Inside, the Cuban had doused the floor with soapy water and smeared his body—naked except for undershorts—with soap. SORT attacked. The first guard hit the Cuban in the chest, knocking him onto the slippery concrete floor. Each of the other four grabbed a preassigned limb. Before the Cuban had time to react, he was lifted onto his bed and each arm and leg was shackled to rings on the bed frame. He remained chained down for eight hours.

"Getting shit and piss thrown on you became so common we called it 'getting slimed,' like in the movie *Ghostbusters*," one guard explained later. "At first, we put the little bastards in a four-point position when they slimed us, but after a while, they just laughed at you. They would lay there chained down for eight hours and then get up and piss in a cup and throw it on your face again. You just wanted to smack 'em 'cause they acted like little kids."

The bureau released an internal report after the riots that said the Cubans were the most unstable group of prisoners ever put under its care. "Their extremes can go from violent homicidal rage to crying, loneliness, and suicidal behavior," warned Dr. Bolivar P. Martineau, the report's author. "At various times, you will be talking to a reasonable twenty-six-year-old person. Suddenly, that same individual can become a sophisticated, manipulative forty-year-old con artist; or he can turn into a three-year-old child with a raging temper tantrum who just happens to be five foot ten inches tall, weighs 180 pounds, and who is physically threatening you."

But despite the slimings, the danger, and the dreadful working conditions, the Hot House guards were eager to work in the Cuban units. The reason was overtime. Warden Matthews was willing to pay any cost to keep the inmates under control. "I would rather pay for it now than have the Cubans burn down this institution like they did in Atlanta and Oakdale and pay for it later," he explained.

At first the bureau sent in guards from other institutions to help ease the staff shortage at Leavenworth, but the Hot House guards objected, treated the newcomers shabbily, and resented their cutting into the overtime pie. The bureau responded by pulling the outsiders and letting Leavenworth guards work double shifts. Most guards did their regular job and then an additional eight hours. Overtime expenses doubled by $2 million the first year. One veteran employee earned $50,000 in overtime pay—more than his yearly salary. A joke soon spread through the Hot House:

Question: How can you tell who works in the Cuban units?

Answer: He's the guy who is fucking nuts, but he's driving a brand-new Bronco.

Nobody questioned the wisdom of having exhausted guards working with such incendiary prisoners.

The choice of Shoats to run the volatile Cuban units didn't please everyone. When Lieutenant Torres Germany heard that Shoats had been put in charge, he grimaced. Germany had been Shoats's boss at the medium-security prison in La Tuna, Texas, before both men transferred to the Hot House. Another Leavenworth lieutenant, Charlie Hill, had also worked in La Tuna with Shoats and he, too, was worried.

But neither Germany nor Hill said anything, nor did they share their uneasiness with Warden Matthews. Shoats was well-liked at Leavenworth. He had done a good job there, and Germany and Hill said later that they really had no grounds to question his ability. Besides, the warden at La Tuna was fully aware of what Shoats had done there and Shoats had already been verbally disciplined for the mistakes he made. Both Germany and Hill knew that there was nothing written in Shoats's personnel file about his past errors. Both men felt they had no choice but to keep quiet.

When asked about Lieutenant Shoats's past, Don (D.J.) Southarland, the warden at La Tuna, said, "In this business, you are going to make mistakes. Everyone will. That's how you learn. Phillip had some weaknesses, but he always gave one hundred percent, was totally loyal to the bureau, and was a pretty dang good officer. I was proud to have him working for me."

The first time Southarland had to reprimand him verbally was in 1985 when Shoats lost his temper on a bus transporting convicts. He and two other guards were escorting thirty prisoners across the Texas desert late at night when one convict began stirring up the others. Within minutes, all thirty were rocking the bus back and forth. Shoats ordered the driver to pull off the road, and when the bus stopped, he opened the wire cage that separated him from the inmates, charged inside, grabbed the loudmouthed convict, and dragged him off the bus. Shoats took a .12 gauge shotgun with him. He later claimed that he merely "talked shit" to the inmate. The inmate claimed that Shoats threw him down and jammed the barrel of the shotgun into his mouth.

After several minutes, Shoats brought him back into the bus, chained him in his seat, and taped his mouth shut.

When Southarland heard what had happened, he called Shoats into his office. "You played right into the bastard's hands," Southarland later recalled saying. "No one in the world is going to believe you didn't threaten that guy. You violated security taking him off that bus. Even I believe you got him off the bus to threaten him."

"I came real close to busting Phillip for that stupid trick," Southarland said later. But he didn't.

A short time later, Shoats's thirteen-year-old daughter knocked on the door of the bureau-provided house where Torres Germany and his wife lived. They were neighbors of the Shoatses. The girl had a black eye and bruised face, and she claimed her father had beaten her. A county child-abuse investigator was called, and once again, Shoats ended up in front of Warden Southarland for a lecture.

"Phillip told me that he had gotten angry and slapped her around a bit," Southarland said later. Shoats had surprised his daughter kissing an older boy in his car. "I felt Phillip had a good reason to punish her, but I chewed his ass out for the way he did it and he told me that he was sorry," Southarland said. "He had just gotten carried away."

"I honestly believe his heart was in the right place," Southarland added. "Every day he dealt with inmates who had not been disciplined at home, and I think Phillip had a tendency to overreact. He didn't want his kids to end up like those inmates."

The county child-abuse investigator wasn't as understanding, particularly when other employees told her that there were rumors Shoats frequently hit his two sons. The investigator started asking questions, and when Warden Southarland heard that she was querying staff members, he became upset. "I told them that they couldn't just walk around on a federal prison reservation knocking on doors asking questions about Shoats's personal life," Southarland recalled. "In fact, we had a pretty heated discussion about what they could do and couldn't do on federal property." Southarland said later that he told the county investigator that he would have guards physically remove her from federal property if necessary. The county stopped its investigation.

Nonetheless Shoats's behavior sparked rumors among staff members. When his wife, Elke, and the children moved into a motel, the gossip increased. A few days later, they returned to the prison reservation. The Shoatses decided in the spring of 1987 to ask for a transfer to Leavenworth to start fresh.

At the time, the warden at the Hot House, Jerry O'Brien, needed a lieutenant. Still, he was suspicious because Shoats was willing to move laterally and that was unusual. O'Brien telephoned La Tuna. "The warden told me everything was hunkydory with Shoats and praised him highly, so I hired him," O'Brien said later. Shoats arrived on June 7, 1987, only one month before O'Brien retired and Warden Matthews took charge. The new warden knew absolutely nothing about what had happened in La Tuna, nor would he learn about Shoats's past—until it was too late.

CHAPTER
FOURTEEN

THOMAS SILVERSTEIN

The secret cell where Thomas Silverstein was kept was sealed off from the rest of the Hot House by three steel doors. Once you passed through them, you entered a large room with a cage in it like those in which large zoo animals are kept. There was a cage within a cage: Silverstein was locked behind a double row of bars, with a five-foot gap between the rows. He looked wild. His shoulder-length hair and beard were unkempt. I learned later that the bureau did not permit him to have a comb, brush, mirror, or razor. The guards opened the door to the outer cage and slipped a chair inside. I stepped in and the door was locked behind me. Silverstein sat on a hard metal stool directly across from me behind the second set of bars. I had been told before the interview not to wear a tie, unless it clipped onto my collar. "He might grab it through the bars and try to choke you," was the explanation. I didn't see how he could, because a heavy wire-mesh screen had been welded over the bars to prevent him from reaching through.

"Sometimes my words can't keep up with my thoughts," Silverstein said softly as we spoke. "I have trouble talking. I'm out of practice." Most of the Hot House guards, I learned, refused to speak to him out of respect for Merle Clutts, the guard he had killed in Marion. Most days, he had no one to speak to but himself.

Silverstein said he had been painting a picture in his cell at Atlanta when he heard banging on the metal door that separated him from the rest of the compound. A few minutes later, a gaggle of Cubans came bursting in and freed him. The first thing he did was hurry outside into the open air. Then he went directly to see the guards being held hostage. "If anyone deserved to take revenge," he said bitterly, "it was me, and when I saw this one guard who had told me once that if he had his way, I'd be dead, my first reaction was to slap him around a little. But he started whimpering, begging me not to hurt him. He started telling me about his family, cry, cry, cry, and I said, 'Hey, I got a family too, and you didn't care about tearing up my mail when I was behind bars and denying me pictures of them, and now you are crying for mercy.' It was sickening. I said, 'Why don't you be a man and take what you got coming?' And then I just walked away."

After the riots, the bureau said the Cubans had kept Silverstein under control, but that was nonsense. The hostages and Cubans both said later that he could have harmed the helpless guards if he wished. He didn't; in fact, he brought fruit to one lieutenant. There were several reasons why. If he had attacked the hostages, the FBI and the bureau would have tried to rescue them, and the last thing that Silverstein wanted was to have the riots end. He was trying to figure out how to escape, he explained, and that required time. He also hoped the bureau would drop its "no human contact" status. "I wanted to show that I could be with guards and not kill." That had been a mistake, he now said. "I should have taken my own set of hostages and negotiated my own peace."

The fact that the Cubans had surrendered him to the bureau was difficult for Silverstein to believe. "These people know what it is like to be locked up. I begged them to kill me. I said, 'Don't turn me over, just kill me right now. I'd rather be dead than to go back.' But they wouldn't do that."

I asked him about his childhood in Long Beach, California, and as we talked, I noticed that he continually mentioned his mother. Vivacious and tough, Virginia Silverstein herself had served time in prison for robbery as a teenager. She divorced her first husband in 1952 while pregnant with Silverstein and immediately married Thomas Conway, who Silverstein said was his natural father. Four years later, she divorced Conway and married Sid Silverstein, who legally adopted her son. Thomas

Silverstein remembered the marriage as rocky, fights as common, alcohol as a problem.

According to prison records, as well as his own recollections, Silverstein was timid, awkward, shy, and frequently bullied as a child in the tough working-class neighborhood where the family lived. Everyone assumed that he was Jewish, and that too made him an outcast.

One afternoon, a bully named Gary knocked Silverstein down as he was walking home from school. The next day, Virginia Silverstein was watching when Gary came past her house. She grabbed the bully by his shirt and marched him and her son into the backyard of her home.

"Hit him," she ordered her son. "You hit this boy as hard as you can or I'll take my belt to you."

"I took one look at my mom and her black belt and I took one look at Gary, and there wasn't any choice at all," Silverstein recalled. "I smacked him in the face as hard as I could."

The next day, when Silverstein left school, Gary's father was waiting. He escorted the boy to Gary's backyard.

"Hit him, Gary!" the man ordered. "Punch him in the face like he hit you."

But it seems that Gary, still recovering from yesterday's battle, was in no mood to fight. "His old man started yelling at him, and I broke loose and ran home and told my mom what had happened," Silverstein said. "She jumped in the car and drove over there and started yelling at this guy to come out of his house, but he was afraid to come to the front door, so my mom pulled these bricks from the flower bed in their front lawn and she threw them through their front window. Then she went home and called the cops and told them she wanted the guy arrested for kidnapping!"

When she hung up the telephone, Virginia Silverstein lectured her son. If he ever came home again crying because he had been beaten up by a bully, she would be waiting to give him a second licking. "That's how my mom was. She stood her mud. If someone came at you with a bat, you got your bat and you both went at it."

After his confrontation with Gary, Silverstein got into several fights at school and he made what to him was an amazing discovery. "I got beat up pretty bad and I discovered it wasn't the end of the world. The black eyes and bruises healed," he recalled. "I got over that fear of getting hit by someone." He realized something else at that moment too: some people never got over the fear of physical violence. "They would rather be a coward than fight."

At age fourteen, Silverstein stole a car. He began cutting school, running away from home, using drugs. A year later, he got into a fistfight with a police officer. "I hated authority, just like I hated bullies. What gives anyone the right to tell another person what to do?" he asked. Silverstein was sentenced to a California reformatory where, he said, his attitudes about violence were reinforced. "Anyone not willing to fight was abused." When he was released, he began experimenting with LSD, amphetamines, and heroin, and burglarized houses to get money for drugs.

In 1971, at age nineteen, Silverstein was sent to San Quentin for armed robbery. It was there, the bureau noted, that he first began associating with members of the Aryan Brotherhood. Four years later, he was paroled, but he was arrested soon after along with his father, Thomas Conway, and his uncle for three armed robberies. Their take was less than $1,400. A probation officer later blamed the older men for getting Silverstein, then age twenty-three, involved in the crimes. She wrote:

> The defendant may well have been led into his present circumstances by the codefendants. Individuals who have known him for long periods of time allude to the fact that he is easily led.

Bureau records show that Silverstein was sent to the Hot House for the first time in March 1977 to serve a fifteen-year sentence for armed robbery. For a year, he didn't get into any trouble, and then he moved into cell 410, with another inmate from California, Edward "Snail" Hevle, Jr. The bureau would later claim that Hevle was a hit man for the Aryan Brotherhood and was deeply involved in smuggling drugs into the Hot House.

Before long, Silverstein was running with other suspected white gang members, including Charles "Preacher" McEvoy, who was the alleged leader of the AB in Leavenworth. A prison counselor noted that:

Silverstein is rapidly establishing a pattern of being a management problem. He is displaying a predatory and assaultive behavior pattern and associating with known gang members. He seems to be easily influenced by these men and is eager to please them.

On February 17, 1979, a convict named Danny Edward Atwell stumbled from his cell and collapsed on the tier. Blood gushed from the stab wounds in his chest. He died within minutes. The next day, Silverstein and his prison buddies, Snail Hevle and Preacher McEvoy, were charged with murder.

Silverstein was brought to trial first, and the case against him is a classic example of the incredible difficulties that federal prosecutors face when they try to find out what really happened in a prison.

The government's chief witness was James Schell, an armed robber, who testified that McEvoy had told him all about the murder and had, in fact, admitted that he and Silverstein had both stabbed Atwell.

Schell claimed that the two of them had killed Atwell because he had balked at bringing heroin into the prison for the Aryan Brotherhood. The dead man had been smuggling drugs for the gang with the help of his girlfriend, but he had thought she was delivering marijuana, not heroin. According to Schell, Atwell didn't want his girlfriend mixed up with heroin, so he stopped cooperating. Schell also testified that Silverstein had volunteered to kill Atwell as a favor for the Aryan Brotherhood, which was worried that other mules would also quit smuggling drugs if Atwell wasn't punished.

The prosecution's second witness, Randolph Patrick Arnold, said he too knew all about the Atwell murder. He hadn't actually seen anything, but Arnold claimed that Silverstein himself had bragged about the killing one night while both men were in the Hole.

The only witness who wasn't an inmate was a guard nicknamed "Super Cop," who testified that Atwell had identified Silverstein as the killer while being carried on a stretcher to the prison hospital where he died.

David J. Phillips, the federal public defender representing Silverstein, challenged the witnesses one at a time.

Schell's testimony was inadmissible because it was hearsay, Phillips argued, but even if the judge allowed it (which he did), the jury shouldn't believe it. Under grilling from Attorney Phillips, Schell admitted that he originally offered to finger Silverstein as the murderer in return for a transfer to the jail in Fort Scott, Kansas. He claimed he was afraid to stay in Leavenworth, but the real reason he wanted to get to Fort Scott was because he had friends there willing to help him escape. The FBI transferred Schell, who in fact did escape. While loose, Schell told his girlfriend that Silverstein was innocent and that he had concocted the entire story as part of his escape plan. But when Schell was captured by the FBI, he once again offered his testimony as a bargaining chip. In return for the government's dropping the escape charges against him, Schell would claim that Silverstein was the killer. Prosecutors agreed.

By the time that Silverstein's attorney had extracted this information from Schell, jurors realized that he was capable of testifying to anything as long as it was to his advantage.

The prosecution's next witness, Randy Arnold, also had cut a sweet deal with prosecutors. In exchange for his testimony, the government had agreed to move him to a prison camp, drop a murder charge pending against him, and put in a good word for him with officials in Arkansas, where he was supposed to serve a twenty-five-year sentence for kidnapping once he was released by the bureau. Arnold also admitted that most inmates suspected him of being an informant, one of the last inmates whom Silverstein would trust.

At that point in the trial, Phillips felt confident. The only witness left was Super Cop, who had testified that Atwell identified Silverstein as the killer while being carried into the prison hospital. Phillips was able to shred his testimony too. Several other guards who had helped carry Atwell testified that Atwell had not said a word, and the prison doctor stated that Atwell was suffering from shock and couldn't speak.

"We had put on an extremely effective defense," Phillips recalled. "We had shown the two convicts were liars and shown that the guard's testimony was inconsistent with what everyone else saw."

But then Silverstein insisted on testifying. "He thought he could convince the jury of his innocence," said Phillips. It was a disaster. As soon as it was the prosecutor's turn to ask questions, he brought up the Aryan Brotherhood. Phillips jumped to his feet and objected, but the judge overruled him, and for the next several minutes Silverstein naively defended the prison gang. The prosecutor then called a long string of rebuttal witnesses who gave jurors a much grimmer picture of the AB, linking it with killings, prostitution, drug smuggling, and extortion. In effect, the prosecution had changed the focus of the trial from Silverstein to the Aryan Brotherhood.

The jury found Silverstein guilty and on March 3, 1980, he was sentenced to life in prison and transferred to the penitentiary at Marion.

"I was innocent," Silverstein later recalled. "I was being framed by these rats who had just flushed my life down the toilet. I knew I was going to Marion with a life sentence, and I had a real attitude problem because I was pissed. I figured I didn't have much to lose."

Five months later, Edward Hevle and Charles McEvoy both pleaded guilty to reduced charges. Once they were no longer under any legal jeopardy, they signed affidavits that cleared Silverstein of the Atwell killing. The murderer, they claimed, was none other than the prosecution's main witness, James Schell. Federal prosecutors were furious, and accused the two men of lying in revenge for Schell's testimony against their friend. But Schell himself signed a detailed confession that cleared Silverstein.

Phillips appealed Silverstein's conviction and, after studying the case, a three-judge panel of the U.S. Court of Appeals for the Tenth Circuit said it was appalled by the quagmire of conflicting testimony and recanted statements. "We do not view this as a case in which the evidence overwhelmingly points to the guilt of the defendant," the judges wrote. Schell's testimony was hearsay and should never have been admitted as evidence. Super Cop's testimony also should have been disregarded because it was "difficult to believe" and "ambiguous at best." The judges ordered federal prosecutors to either dismiss the murder charge against Silverstein or conduct a new trial.

Phillips was elated. He genuinely believed his client was innocent. But the appellate court's ruling had come too late for Silverstein. By the time the court ruled in his favor, Thomas Silverstein had already been convicted of two other murders at Marion. Phillips was told that his client had been given a new nickname in prison. Everyone called him "Terrible Tom."

CHAPTER
FIFTEEN

THE CUBANS

Stories about guards beating Cuban prisoners began to surface about one month after the Cubans arrived at Leavenworth. Lieutenant Torres Germany, who was responsible for investigating alleged staff brutality in the prison, decided to snoop around. The guards in C and D cellhouses quickly closed both their ranks and their lips. "We were pissed, really pissed," a guard recalled. "All of us had been pulling double shifts, working our butts off, and now Germany was looking over our shoulders." Another guard added, "You got to understand Cubans were throwing piss and shit on us. They were fucking animals. There wasn't any staff brutality. Sometimes a Cuban would give us a shot, a legitimate shot at him—for example, he would resist or he'd take a swing at an officer—and when that happened, you're damn right that Cuban got smacked around, but it was good for them and good for us. You got to understand these fucking Cubans only understand violence. Nobody was beating the shit out of them, but a guy might pull a Cuban's cuffs up between his shoulder blades when he was being taken somewhere just to give him a message: 'Hey, you fuck with us, we'll fuck with you!'

"Someone like Germany didn't understand that," the other guard continued, "but Germany wasn't in there every day. Lieutenant Shoats knew what was going on. He knew that what we were doing wasn't staff brutality. It was staff *survival*."

The relationship between Germany and Shoats turned icy

as Germany continued to probe. Most days they avoided each other. By the end of February 1988, Germany was able to document some minor incidents. He knew that guards in one cell-house had written "Hang the Cubans" on a wall. Someone had made hangman's nooses from string and left them dangling in front of several cells. The nooses were supposed to scare the Cubans by reminding them that guards could hang a prisoner in his cell and later claim he had committed suicide. But other than those two incidents, Germany hadn't really learned a thing.

On March 6, 1988, Germany and Shoats both happened to be working the day shift, and by chance met at the coffeepot in the lieutenant's office. Since it was a slow Sunday afternoon, they sat down together.

"Phil, I know you believe in the Holy Bible. Do you believe there is a heaven?" Germany asked at one point.

Shoats laughed. "I'm going to be one pissed-off mother-fucker if there's not."

The next time that Germany thought about Shoats was when he heard that Shoats had been murdered.

Elke Shoats was cooking hamburgers at Homer's, a local Leavenworth drive-in, when a prison guard called and asked her to come home immediately. It was just before 7 P.M. on March 7, a Monday, and as she hurried home, she figured something had happened to one of her two sons, who were ages fifteen and fourteen. Guards were clustered outside the brick house that the Shoatses rented from the bureau only a few hundred feet from the prison walls and refused to let her go inside. She was taken to a neighbor's.

"Are my sons okay?" she immediately asked when Warden Matthews came to get her.

Matthews nodded. Both boys were fine, he said, but her husband was dead.

Shoats's body had been found lying on the family room floor. He had been shot twice with a .12 gauge shotgun, once in the head.

Lieutenant Shoats was buried four days later at Belden Funeral Chapel in Leavenworth. Warden Matthews helped plan the funeral. The pallbearers included Torres Germany, Steven Myhand, Stephen Hobart, Edward Pierce, William Kindig, Monty Watkins, Billy Thomas, and William Blount, all Hot House lieutenants. A prison chaplain gave the eulogy. Everyone agreed afterward that the funeral had been a fitting tribute to a man whose life had revolved around the bureau. It wasn't until later that night at Benny's that guards began asking the one question on everyone's mind: What had Shoats done that would cause his own teenage sons to kill him?

Michael Harris, an assistant federal public defender, was filing papers at the courthouse in Topeka on March 8, 1988, when he was asked to represent two juveniles who had been arrested for shooting their father. "A twelve-gauge shotgun is a rather drastic way to deal with a problem," Harris said later, "but after talking to the boys, I realized this was a violent home, a very violent home."

Harris had represented victims of domestic violence before. This is how he later reconstructed the shooting. Shoats started arguing with his fifteen-year-old son and during a moment of rage slugged the boy in the chin, knocking him unconscious. Then Shoats turned toward his fourteen-year-old and reportedly snapped, "You're next!" The boy grabbed a double-barreled shotgun and fired both chambers at his father.

Harris immediately sent an investigator to Leavenworth to conduct interviews and take photographs of the murder scene, but the day after the shooting, the investigator called with disturbing news. "When he got to the Shoats house," Harris said, "the family's belongings had been moved out, the place had been scrubbed clean—even the bloodstains in the carpet had been cut out and the carpet repaired—all within forty-eight hours of the death. My suspicion was that the bureau didn't want Shoats's past to come out, and for a very good reason."

There was more at stake than embarrassment, Harris believed. "Every prison case that I've ever done usually comes down to who you believe: the guard or the inmate. When there is a fight, the guard says the inmate started it and the inmate says the guard started it. Those cases are always resolved in favor of the guards. In every one of those cases we try to get access to the guard's personnel file to see if he has gotten into trouble before, and the government always resists this to the maximum. The bureau doesn't want defense lawyers mucking around inside a guard's personnel file, and I think everyone knew that in a homicide case we were going to get inside Shoats's file. The bureau didn't want to set a precedent and it sure didn't want us peeking into Shoats's file."

Within a week, Harris had obtained copies of his juvenile clients' medical and school records. "They were replete with suspicions expressed by school personnel through the years," Harris said. "There were reports of the kids showing up at school with unexplained bruises, black eyes, and other injuries, yet no one did anything about it because Shoats always lived on a bureau reservation. No one wanted to interfere."

Harris got a call from the U.S. attorney's office a short time later. The complaint against the boys was dropped without explanation. "Someone had figured out what was going on in the Shoats house and they didn't want the case coming to light," said Harris. "It's only my suspicion, but I believe the bureau just made a decision early on that this case was more of a problem than it was worth." Both boys were released to their mother.

After her husband's funeral, Elke Shoats moved away from Leavenworth. "I was worried about my fourteen-year-old, how he'd take it. But he said he had a dream about his daddy and his daddy told him that it wasn't his fault and that he shouldn't feel bad about shooting him," said Mrs. Shoats, pausing long enough to wipe her eyes. "He said his daddy told him that he is very happy where he is now, very happy, and that helped."

When Elke and Phillip Shoats first met at a party in Wiesbaden, West Germany, back in August 1972, she was a single German mother raising three small children, two boys and a girl. He was a brash, street-smart U.S. serviceman stationed at the local base. "Phillip really could talk," she said. "He had me laughing and feeling good. He could have been a lawyer—the kind of lawyer you hired if you stole something—because he could have gone to court and gotten you off." Five months after they met, Phillip and Elke married. On their wedding night, Shoats said he didn't believe a husband and wife should keep

secrets from each other, but there was an incident in his past
that he had never told anyone, and even though he loved her, he
couldn't yet bring himself to reveal it.

"Why not, Phil?" she asked.

"I just can't tell anyone, baby," he replied. "Maybe on our
tenth anniversary, I'll tell you."

Elke Shoats quickly forgot about the secret, she said. "Phil
was super sweet and warm. He was a very loving and a gentle
man, particularly with my daughter. He was tender around her
and he was good with my two boys. I really didn't care what this
secret was." Within a year, Elke gave birth to a son.

When Phillip Shoats was discharged in 1975, the family
moved to his hometown of Kansas City and he scanned the
classified advertisements for work. Leavenworth was hiring and
Shoats signed on. "He didn't like it at first, but we needed the
money and Phil thought he could move up fast." For five years,
Shoats worked at the Hot House and it was during that time that
he changed, Elke Shoats later recalled. "He got harder, became
distant. Whenever the kids did something wrong, he got real
angry, I mean real, real angry. I'd say, 'Phil, kids will be kids.
They're going to make mistakes.' He'd say, 'Not mine. They ain't
never ending up in a place like Leavenworth.' "

If Shoats gave an order, he expected the children to jump. If
Elke interfered, he accused her of being "weak." It was the same
lingo, she noticed, that he used to describe guards who gave in to
convicts. "I found out later that he was beating the kids when I
was at work."

When Shoats was promoted to a medium-security prison in
Ray Brook, New York, Elke hoped things would improve. Her
husband was no longer working in such a hostile prison. But the
Shoatses' home life continued to deteriorate. "One day Phil was
playing cards with the kids, and he would get mad when he lost,
so he was cheating. Imagine, cheating your own kids, but he told
me that they wouldn't respect him if he lost. It was the same sort
of stuff I heard when he and his buddies from the prison got
together. Everyone had to respect you in prison. You couldn't let
anyone beat you at anything."

When Shoats was promoted to the rank of lieutenant at the
prison in La Tuna, Texas, a few miles north of El Paso, Elke
Shoats again hoped for the best. His new assignment was at a

level-two prison, a lower ranking than Ray Brook and much lower than the Hot House. Elke's oldest son had recently joined the military, leaving only three children at home to feed and clothe. "It got worse, not better," Elke said. "The prison just wouldn't leave him alone. The phone was always ringing and he was always having to choose between it and us.

"One night Phil accused me of having boyfriends, and I didn't have any boyfriends. The next night he apologized. The next morning, he'd accuse me again."

The turmoil inside the home became violent when Shoats found his stepdaughter kissing an older boy while both were in a parked car. Elke tried to intervene and Shoats slapped her as well as his stepdaughter. The next day Elke took the children and moved to a motel. Shoats begged them to return. She refused. Several days later, she received a long letter from her husband. In it, he revealed to her the secret that he had mentioned on their wedding night. After reading the letter, Elke Shoats moved back in with her husband. That is when they decided to get a fresh start by returning to Leavenworth.

"Phil promised to change, and he didn't hit the kids at first, but when they put him in charge of the Cubans, it was too much pressure," Elke Shoats said. "He couldn't keep all that anger bottled up inside at work and at home. He had to let it out and he took it out on us."

Shoats was having an especially tough time with his fifteen-year-old stepson. At Christmas, Shoats bought his stepdaughter an expensive stereo record player and gave his fourteen-year-old son a new bicycle. But Shoats gave his stepson one pair of white socks. That was all.

In January 1988, Elke Shoats won $500 playing bingo and sent her husband on a weekend trip to Las Vegas, Nevada, by himself, just to get him away from the Cuban units. "He had a blast, and when he arrived home, it was like I saw the old Phil, but then the phone rang and it was the prison and he left, and when he came back, he had changed back into that other person."

After the funeral, Elke Shoats called her children into her bedroom and read them the letter that her husband had sent her in La Tuna. She shared his secret. Now that he was dead, she said, he couldn't be embarrassed by what it revealed.

"When Phil was six years old he was raped by a boy named Willie, he's dead now, but he raped Phil five or six times until Phil threatened to tell," said Elke Shoats, who still has the letter. Shoats wrote that he had hated Willie and had felt guilty because he had never taken revenge by killing him. "It is difficult for me to understand, but the fact he was raped and working in prison did something to him. I don't know what, but it made him feel like he had to do something to make sure that bad people like Willie stayed locked up," Elke Shoats said. "I think the hate and anger just swallowed him up."

CHAPTER SIXTEEN

THE LIEUTENANT'S OFFICE

Associate Warden Smith was leaving the lieutenant's office when an alarm sounded in C cellhouse. Racing down center hallway, Smith hurried through the steel doors into the Cuban cellblock, where flames and thick smoke were pouring from cell 124.

John Streeter, the guard on duty, was dragging an unconscious Cuban prisoner from the cell. Another guard went inside with a fire extinguisher. Hundreds of arms thrust out between the bars as Cuban prisoners in the other cells tried to see down the tier, using the crystals on their wristwatches as mirrors.

Streeter used his fingers to clear the prisoner's mouth, then began pushing on his chest. A physician's assistant hurried into the cellblock and took over. He snapped an oxygen mask over the Cuban's face and turned on the nozzle of a portable green oxygen tank. The man gagged, his entire body trembled, his head swung from side to side.

The Cuban was dressed in badly wrinkled, filthy khaki trousers and a worn pair of blue nylon socks. His kinky hair was dirty. His face was unshaven. His chest was a canvas of tattoos. A haloed Madonna rose from his flabby belly, a red-tongued serpent wrapped around a naked woman with huge breasts and yellow hair decorated one arm, a dagger stabbed into a human skull adorned the other. The Cuban looked spent, as if his life had been sucked out from inside him, leaving only a limp torso behind.

As the oxygen slowly took effect, he began to moan through

the mask. More than a dozen guards had answered the alarm. Now they began to disperse. The medic said, "I got a pretty strong pulse. He's going to make it."

"What happened?" asked Smith.

"He's a porcelain termite," said Lieutenant Myhand, who was in charge. "He's destroyed the sinks and toilets in two cells since he's been here, but this is the first time he's started his cell on fire."

Myhand explained that the Cuban had placed his mattress against the front bars of his cell and put a match to the bed-sheets. Each cell has a vent at the back that pulls air through from the tier. When the Cuban set fire to the sheets the current fed the flames, causing them to erupt like needles from a dried Christmas tree.

Streeter lifted the prisoner at the waist and slipped a thin steel chain around him. He snapped on handcuffs and connected them to the chain, making it impossible for the Cuban to raise his hands more than five inches from his stomach. Then the guards lifted him onto a wire gurney so he could be transported to the prison hospital. Smith and Myhand followed.

"What's his story?" Smith asked.

"He's in love," Myhand replied. "He and his cellmate are homosexuals and had a fight, so we moved the cellmate. Now he wants him back."

In an examining room, a prison doctor flashed a tiny light in the inmate's pupils, removed one of his socks, and began tapping his foot. Even the right ankle had a tattoo. The Cuban yelled something in Spanish.

"He says he will kill himself unless you move his friend back into his cell," said one of the guards, a Hispanic.

There was another yell.

"He says he hates all guards. He says he will kill a guard if you don't move his friend back."

More yells.

"He says he started the fire and will keep starting fires until we move his friend back."

"Tell him we are going to take an X ray," the doctor said. "Tell him not to move."

The guard repeated the doctor's orders and the Cuban became rigid.

"Okay," the doctor said after taking the X ray. "Give me a few minutes and then I think you can take him back. He seems all right."

Smith turned to Myhand. "Better four-point him for a while. We can't have him starting fires."

The Cuban yelled. The guard interpreted.

"He says he will kill himself. He says he has been five years in American prisons, fifteen in Cuba. He will kill himself unless you move his lover back. He says he doesn't care about anything. We can do anything to him, but he will keep setting fires until we move his lover back."

Smith and Myhand ignored this.

The doctor announced that the prisoner could be returned to C cellhouse, and gave him a Dixie cup with a pill in it. Still in handcuffs, the inmate bent down and sucked the pill into his mouth. The doctor held a cup of water to his lips.

The Cuban walked back into the main penitentiary building on his own and was taken by guards to a cell in C cellhouse not far from cell 124. Other Cuban prisoners shouted to him but he didn't reply. The Spanish-speaking guard ordered him to lie on his back on the bed and the guards chained his feet, one foot at each corner, then unfastened the belly chain and pulled it from under him. One officer unlocked the handcuffs, another pinned the Cuban's arms against his chest. The two officers looked like cowboys about to release a Brahma bull from a rodeo chute. One swung the convict's right arm back and chained it in one swift motion to a ring welded onto the bed. The prisoner didn't resist. Then his other limp arm was pulled back and chained. Finally he yelled.

"He says he will kill a guard. He says he is very dangerous. He says that we should be afraid of him."

No one in the cell reacted. Instead, they filed out one by one, the last guard locking the door and padlocking the chain strung through the bars. From the corridor, you could see the Cuban's smoke-blackened face. Alone now, he began to cry. The tears washed through the black smudges, creating thin clear lines. For the next fifteen minutes, he sobbed unashamedly in the cell, and then he fell asleep.

PART TWO

Criminals cause crime—not bad neighborhoods, inadequate parents, television, schools, drugs, or unemployment. Crime resides within the minds of human beings and is not caused by social conditions . . . Despite a multitude of difference in their backgrounds and crime patterns, criminals are alike in one way: All regard the world as a chessboard over which they have total control, and they perceive people as pawns to be pushed around at will.

STANTON E. SAMENOW
Inside the Criminal Mind

A Voice: *ARMED ROBBER, AGE 35*

You can tell the rabbits, you know, the lops in here. They bring this guy in and he is doing time for some punk-ass white-collar rip-off, and right away I figure this guy's got no heart. He's a mark. One afternoon, I go into his cell and I steal some law books he's got. I wanted to make sure he's not connected, you know, 'cause some of these rabbits got friends, maybe in the Mafia or maybe he's a bookkeeper for one of the gangs, maybe his sister is married to the Godfather, who the fuck knows?

I wait a week and nothing happens. No one's put out word, you know, that the books better get returned or whoever took them is gonna get stuck. He obviously ain't connected.

Once I know this, I go up to him and I tell him, "Hey, man, I hear you lost some law books. I can get 'em back for three bills." Now this shithead knows I stole his books. Nobody is that stupid. But instead of jamming me right there, he just says, "I don't want no trouble, just leave me alone."

I mean, c'mon, a righteous motherfucker would have stuck me, 'cause he's gonna know that if he lets me take his law books, I'm coming back for his ass next. I'm no fool.

A few days later, I go up to this dude and tell 'im we are forming a partnership. He's gonna do my laundry for me and buy me whatever I want from the commissary and that's just how it's gonna be. If he's good, then I won't push too hard. But if he bucks, I'm gonna ride 'im. And you know what, I don't feel bad at all, 'cause this guy really wants to be a victim. I mean that. Otherwise he'd fight back.

You see, that's how it is with rabbits. You ever wonder what they are good for or why God made them? They're food.

141

CHAPTER SEVENTEEN

ROBERT MATTHEWS

Elke Shoats wanted her husband remembered. After his funeral she asked Warden Matthews if he would erect a memorial to Shoats at the prison. Matthews agreed at once. "Shoats was an excellent and outstanding lieutenant. His death is a big loss," he said. Later, after more details about Shoats's private life surfaced, Matthews adopted a "no comment" policy toward his former lieutenant.

When the Hot House guards learned Matthews was having inmates make a display case for some of Shoats's personal effects, they were furious. "We have had officers killed in the line of duty right here inside this penitentiary and the bureau has never done anything for them," the employee-union president griped. "And now the bureau is putting up a memorial for this guy who is killed by his own kids, kids he abused. Why, you bet we're angry!"

Rumors swept through the prison. Some claimed the bureau had known for years that Shoats beat his children. Others accused Matthews of honoring Shoats simply because both were black. Such gossip was untrue and unfair, but it didn't matter. The guards at the Hot House were furious. Shoats had embarrassed them. If there was one accusation that every guard hated, it was the age-old bugaboo that a guard really wasn't much different from an inmate. Former Bureau Director Norman Carlson had spent years trying to change the public's perception of guards as sadistic knuckle-draggers. Carlson had stressed professionalism, required intensive training, and fired guards suspected of brutality. It was Carlson who abandoned the bureau's police-style uniforms, replacing them with gray slacks, white shirts, red ties, and black blazers—the sort of look that a junior executive might adopt.

Suddenly Shoats's death seemed to cancel all that. Everyone was talking about the Hot House lieutenant whose kids had killed him. Of course, the worst razzing came from inmates.

Hey, I may be a thief but I don't beat my kids!

Now the new warden was compounding the problem. He was going to set up a memorial to Shoats, a daily reminder that every guard would see. But despite the complaints, Matthews would not change his mind. A special wooden case, for Shoats's cap, some of his papers, and the flag that had draped his coffin, was placed in the second-floor hallway of the administration building. A few days later, several employees shoved the case into a corner of an office where it was left to gather dust.

Matthews's decision to memorialize Shoats had strained his relations with the guard force. Rather than move to heal the wound, the new warden cut deeper. He continued to push his two priorities: better communication between staff and inmates, and improved sanitation. As Matthews stood in the dining room listening to inmates complain, a guard remarked, "Look at that fool listening to those crybabies." Later, when Matthews walked through A cellhouse and told guards there that he wanted several scuff marks removed from the floor, another guard grumbled, "He wants us to be maids, not officers."

Complaining about the warden became a normal pastime at Benny's after work, just like flirting with the blonde barmaid. The problem with Matthews, most agreed, was that he was nothing like his predecessor. Warden Jerry O'Brien had spent five years running the Hot House before he retired, and O'Brien had been popular. Within the bureau, he had been considered the last of the great dinosaur wardens, those hard, no-nonsense, bear-shaped wardens who had worked their way up from the guard force.

"He would bulldoze right over you if you didn't stand up for yourself," Associate Warden Richard Smith recalled, "but once you showed some backbone, you were okay. The staff called it becoming 'O'Brienized.' "

O'Brien had worked nearly every job there was in a prison, joining the bureau directly out of high school and gradually climbing the ladder to Washington headquarters, where he had served as Carlson's top troubleshooter. Whenever there were allegations of staff corruption or brutality, it was O'Brien who was sent to investigate. Whenever there was a riot, O'Brien was sent to clean up the mess. Being named warden of Leavenworth was O'Brien's payoff for fifteen years of dedicated service, and to him, there was no better job.

Guards at Leavenworth could watch O'Brien stroll through the rotunda and identify with him. O'Brien knew what it was like to wrestle an inmate to the floor. And his philosophy was similar to that of most guards: The Hot House didn't exist to rehabilitate inmates. Its purpose was "to keep the bastards locked up."

Guards had a tough time identifying with Matthews. He had never been a guard, had never wrestled down any inmates. Matthews had joined the bureau as a caseworker who helped prisoners with their family and legal problems, in guard parlance a "weak sister." He not only had been to college, but also had finished graduate school. Worst of all, he called inmates "our customers"!

The Hot House had never had a warden quite like him.

The fact that Matthews had never worked as a guard was significant at the Hot House, because guards held a special status not only inside the prison, but also in the community. It was the guards who made the prison function, and in the town of Leavenworth, federal guards were accorded the sort of respect common to lawyers and doctors. This had to do with the makeup and history of the community. Before there was even a state of Kansas, there was a prison in Leavenworth: the Oklahoma Territorial Jail, built just south of town. Wild West desperadoes from the Kansas-Oklahoma Indian Territories who were not gunned down at high noon or lynched were brought to the jail by frontier marshals. When Kansas was admitted to statehood in 1861, the territorial jail became the foundation for the Kansas State Penitentiary, a maximum-security prison that today holds nearly two thousand men. In 1874, Leavenworth got its second prison, another maximum-security penitentiary, this one at the army's Fort Leavenworth, north of the town. Today it holds

1,400 inmates, and is the only military prison in the nation. The Hot House, built between the fort and the town, was the community's third prison. It was followed in 1915 by yet another state penitentiary originally built for women. On any given day, some six thousand convicts are housed in the Leavenworth area.

Because prisons dominate the region's economy (the Hot House alone generates $15 million per year through purchases and staff salaries), it isn't uncommon for local boys to work as guards directly out of high school. Many of these youngsters plan never to leave Leavenworth, and this has created a hardship for them when they are hired at the Hot House. The bureau believes in transferring guards whenever they start getting promotions. That way they don't have to supervise their former buddies, and the bureau has an easier time rotating employees in and out of unpopular outposts. But while this seems like good management, it has created a tier system at the Hot House that has badly divided the staff.

The guards who don't want to leave town are forced to turn down promotions and remain on the bottom level of the payroll regardless of their years of experience. Guards who are willing to move every two years are regarded as transients, without ties to the Leavenworth community. This was also true of wardens. Warden Matthews was a transient and so were his associate wardens, and while no one would suggest that Matthews wasn't in charge, everyone knew that wardens came and went. It was the grunt guard force that gave the Hot House its continuity and personality. These were the men who lived in the community, who shared the prison's history, who grew old along with its convicts. These were the legend-keepers.

When you asked one of the veteran grunts about leadership in the Hot House, he would mention the names of Ralph Seever and John Drew, two Hot House lieutenants who still resided in Leavenworth and were idolized for their extraordinary skill at manipulating inmates. No one mentioned the twenty-three wardens who had passed through over the years. The same was true whenever guards got together at Benny's. They swapped tales about Fat Jack, a four-hundred-pound guard who called everyone "shitbird" and used to butt convicts up against the wall with his huge belly. They recalled the practical joker who, in 1973, when inmates were routinely referring to guards as pigs, wore a pig mask to work and passed by each cell oinking rather than calling out numbers during the four o'clock count. They remembered the time when lightning struck the prison power plant and the guards circled the Hot House with their cars and illuminated the walls with their headlights to prevent escapes.

The split between the grunts and transients had prompted a saying: "There are two ways to do every job—the bureau way and the Leavenworth way." Bureau Director Quinlan had worked at Leavenworth earlier in his career and he was familiar with the lasting power of "the Leavenworth way."

"We spend thousands of dollars each year sending each new employee to our training center in Glynco," Quinlan explained, "but when a correctional officer returns home, the first thing that happens is a lieutenant tells him, 'Well, that's all fine and dandy, but I'll teach you what you really need to know.' "

Even O'Brien had run into trouble with the grunts when he was warden. O'Brien was the creator of the bureau's first SORT team, the five-member squad specially trained in handling emergencies. "I outfitted them with their own helmets, vests, holsters, and even their own guns, and gave them special training. They were the best of the best," he recalled. "I was very, very proud of SORT and then it became a monster." Associate Warden Smith remembered that guards assigned to SORT "got to thinking that they didn't need us. The warden and the rest of us in management would be gone in a few years, but they were the real core of Leavenworth."

O'Brien began hearing rumors. If trouble broke out, the SORT team would handle it "the Leavenworth way" regardless of what O'Brien said. Finally, when a SORT member got into a fistfight in a bar after making several racial slurs, O'Brien disbanded the entire team. A year later, he formed a new SORT squad, but this time he put it under much tighter rein.

"At Leavenworth, either you are going to control the staff or they are going to take control," said Smith. "That's just how things are."

The institution that Warden Matthews inherited from O'Brien was a much different place from the one O'Brien had found when he arrived in 1982. Back then the Hot House was averaging three stabbings per month, three murders per year. "Inmates at Leavenworth didn't believe in fistfights," O'Brien recalled. "Their response to every problem was to pull out a knife." O'Brien took all metal grinders out of the inmate hobbycraft area, where they were being used to make knives. Overnight, he replaced all the stainless-steel flatware in the inmate dining room with plastic knives, forks, and spoons. "The Aryan Brotherhood tried to buck me by breaking all the plastic utensils after every meal," he recalled. "They figured it would cost so much to replace them that I'd be forced to go back to stainless steel. They were wrong."

O'Brien installed metal detectors, like the kind used in airports, in the east prison yard and required inmates to walk through them when going to and from work in the prison factories where most of the weapons were made. He distributed hand-held metal detectors and ordered guards to frisk inmates at random.

The number of stabbings began dropping dramatically and, for the first time in recent memory, Leavenworth went for one complete year without a murder.

Under O'Brien, security was always the number-one priority, and the Hot House soon led the bureau in developing and implementing various safeguards. It was the first federal penitentiary to develop a sophisticated telephone monitoring system to track inmate calls, the first to string steel wire across the yard to prevent helicopters from landing, the first to do mass urine testing of inmates to detect illegal drug use.

O'Brien began each morning by going directly to the lieutenant's office to confer with the lieutenants about the day's activities. Employees from other areas of the prison, such as recreation, education, religious, and psychological programs, were jealous. O'Brien didn't care. He had seen the bureau introduce dozens of rehabilitative programs and, as far as he was concerned, none had worked. "The only real thing that rehabilitates a convict in Leavenworth," O'Brien said, "is old age. When they get so old they can't run out of a bank, they retire."

Just before O'Brien stepped down as warden, he had outraged other wardens and proved himself just as independent as many of the Leavenworth grunts who worked for him. For years, convicts had been allowed to receive cookies and clothing from their families and friends at Christmastime, but in 1986 the warden at the Lewisburg penitentiary in Pennsylvaina claimed that the gifts were a threat to security. Cookies could be laced with illegal drugs, pieces of hacksaw blades might be concealed in clothing. Examining each Christmas gift would waste time and result in higher overtime pay. The argument made sense at bureau headquarters, but O'Brien would have none of it. "We have used an X-ray machine to check Christmas packages for years here in Leavenworth," O'Brien argued, "and we have never found any contraband nor spent a penny on staff overtime." O'Brien claimed the presents were important to maintaining good inmate morale, particularly in the Hot House, where convicts were serving long sentences. "Getting a sack of hard candy might not mean much to most people, but I'd seen these inmates' eyes when their kids sent one," he said, "and it meant a lot to them."

Because of O'Brien's resistance, the bureau decided to allow each warden to choose for himself whether or not his institution would accept packages, and the computer that links federal prisons soon was pouring forth bulletins as wardens announced their decisions. "Day after day, we were getting these messages over the computer that said no one was allowing Christmas packages anymore and it really irritated me," O'Brien recalled. He sat down and sent out his own response. "Leavenworth will accept all packages," he wrote, adding, "At Leavenworth, we *still* celebrate Christmas and have the Christmas spirit!" It was that last sentence that irked other wardens, particularly the one at Lewisburg. The regional director ordered O'Brien to apologize. "I never did," he recalled. "I figured the hell with it."

The guards at Leavenworth loved O'Brien's independence. His attitude, they said, was summed up on a plaque that he kept hanging behind his desk in the warden's office. It said: *"When rules and regulations are in conflict with common sense, common sense will prevail."*

Robert Matthews took down that plaque when he took charge of the Hot House and put up one of his own. It was entitled *Loyalty. "When you work for a man, don't complain behind his back . . ."* it read.

Under Matthews, Leavenworth stopped accepting Christmas packages for inmates. "I believe," Matthews explained, "in being conservative and following a strict chain of command. If the central office tells me to do something, we will do it—immediately."

Matthews did not give the guards preferential treatment as O'Brien had, nor did he begin his days by visiting the lieutenant's office. Adjusting to Matthews's style was difficult for many at the Hot House, particularly the associate wardens who had worked closely with O'Brien. The new warden had inherited all of O'Brien's top staff, except for one associate warden, Lee Connor, who had arrived at the prison on the same day as Matthews.

Soon stories about communication problems between Matthews and his inherited managers began to circulate. An incident involving manhole covers in the prison yard was typical. Matthews told his executives that he wanted the metal drain-covers painted. The next morning, he was shocked to find that the covers were all a gaudy bright green. Matthews said he wanted a less jarring color. The next day, he found that the covers had been painted fire-engine red. Once again Matthews complained, and the covers were painted again, this time stoplight yellow, the color of a child's rain slicker. Matthews gave up.

In the spring of 1988, the central office in Washington announced that all four of O'Brien's associate wardens were being transferred from the Hot House. Associate Warden Richard Smith was the only one being promoted. The other three were being shifted to what were perceived to be less glamorous jobs.

No one at the Hot House missed the significance of the transfers. In one swift move, all of O'Brien's men were gone. Like it or not, the prison had a new boss, and he was going to run things his way.

CHAPTER EIGHTEEN

CARL BOWLES

Carl Bowles hadn't paid much attention to the staff changes that Warden Matthews was making. Besides trying to help Thomas Little get documents that would prove he didn't belong in the Hot House, Bowles was busy with his prison job.

It was Associate Warden Richard Smith who had hired Bowles to look after a patch of grass outside the hospital about the size of a tennis court. Smith had known Bowles nearly twenty years and he had created the groundskeeping job just for him. "You got to treat someone who has been down as long as Carl differently from some kid fresh in from the streets," Smith explained. It was not just kindness that moved Smith to pay Bowles $50 per month from a special discretionary account in his office. Smith wanted the troublesome Bowles somewhere out in the open where he could be easily watched.

Much to Smith's delight, Bowles had always taken the job seriously. He was constantly pulling weeds and planting flowers. Bowles nursed his tulips and morning glories with such care that guards began calling the triple murderer a "flower child." Smith was so pleased that he allowed Bowles to plant a small garden in one corner of the lot just for himself. He also arranged for Little to work with Bowles.

A few weeks before Smith was scheduled to leave Leavenworth to take up his promotion, Bowles stopped him and Warden Matthews as they walked past the hospital. He needed wood chips for his flower beds, Bowles explained, and he needed them immediately.

Later that day Matthews mentioned Bowles's request during his daily afternoon meeting with his executive staff.

"Bowles is beginning to act like he's one of us," Matthews said good-naturedly. "The way he fusses about how the flowers look—we're going to have to start calling him Lieutenant Bowles."

Everyone in the room chuckled, but there was one associate warden who found the remark troubling. Lee Connor didn't like Carl Bowles and didn't think he should be getting special treatment. Nor did Connor get along well with Richard Smith. As soon as Smith left Leavenworth, Connor became the new associate warden for custody, and one of the first things that he did was visit the east yard where Bowles and Thomas Little were tending flowers.

"What is it?" Bowles asked, when he saw Connor approaching.

"I'm not happy," Connor replied coolly. "I'll send someone around to tell you about it." Lieutenant Tracy Johns appeared an hour later.

"The garden has to go," Johns said bluntly.

"*What?*" Bowles replied, but Johns simply shrugged. It was an order from Connor. "No more personal gardens. Period," Johns said.

Bowles and Little began ripping out the seedlings, tossing them into a trash container.

Four days later, Connor again strolled into the east yard to make certain the garden was gone. Bowles and Little scowled at him as they leaned against a wall of the hospital smoking cigarettes. An hour later, Lieutenant Johns appeared with another order from Connor.

"You both have been fired," said Johns.

Carl Bowles's face was blood-red as he stormed back to his cell. Before Bowles was notified of his firing a lieutenant had told me what was going on, and I was waiting near Bowles's cell when he and Little came up the tier. "The man didn't have the decency to fire me himself!" Bowles said, his voice filled with hatred. "I know what he's doing, he's pissing on me 'cause he and Dick Smith didn't get along."

Little scrambled to fix Bowles a Coca-Cola. He hurried down the tier to get ice, poured Bowles his drink, and climbed up onto the top bunk where he sat silently as Bowles continued to complain.

"I'm forty-seven years old," said Bowles, "and during all of my life, Dick Smith is the first person who ever gave me anything to be responsible for. Look around. The guards tell me when to eat, when to sleep, even when I can take a shit. What have I got to be responsible for in here? Not a damn thing. Do you know I've never lost a tool out there? In three years, I've never taken advantage of the trust that Dick Smith showed me. I worked my ass off 'cause I wanted to show that I could be responsible. Good old Carl Bowles, that worthless piece of shit, could actually be responsible. And what did all that hard work mean to these people? Nothing. Connor just blows in and fires me."

At that point, Bowles wanted a cigarette. Little hopped off the bunk. "I'll get 'em, Carl," he volunteered.

"I took human life and that was a bad thing, a terrible thing," Bowles said as he inhaled, somewhat calmer, "but I have spent twenty-three fucking years of my life in prison. Doesn't that count for something? Is there some redeemable value to me? If not, then what the fuck is the point of all this?

"If all of this is meaningless, then why not take me out to the city dump, hit me in the head with a hammer, and leave me there with the garbage? You could have done that, but, you see, society didn't. 'Oh my,' society said, 'all life is precious. Why, even Carl Bowles's life is worth rehabilitating.' So society put me in here under a 'correctional officer' who I assume is supposed to correct my behavior."

Little laughed. Bowles shot him an angry look. Little stopped chuckling.

"I'm the asshole in here, right?" Bowles continued. "You put me in this madhouse for twenty-three fucking years. You put me in here with a bunch of fools who are more demented than I am and then you send in even bigger fools to guard us. Every day I have to deal with society's scum. Every day I have to deal with guards who are complete idiots. There is a guard working right now on this tier who comes in here every day pissed off because his old lady is fucking some other guy. That's not my fault. I ain't fucking his old lady. But *I* have to deal with his anger. *I* have to adjust for his moods. *I* got no choice. Yet you expect me to respect this guy 'cause he's a 'correctional officer.' Bullshit!

"And then one day Dick Smith shows up and he is a halfway reasonable and intelligent man and he says, 'Carl, I want you to take care of these flowers. Keep it pretty.' It's not much. Listen, I know it's just a fucking flower bed, but it's *my* fucking flower bed! He gives me something to be responsible for, something I can do to prove that, yes, I may be a no-good motherfucker, but at least I can take care of flowers.

"And I don't care, quite frankly, if the fucking director of the Bureau of Prisons walks down here and says, 'Bowles, I took your flowers because I'm the director and I don't think we need flowers anymore.' I'd say, 'Well, there is no doubt in my mind that you can do that and you have done it, but it don't mean a fucking thing to me, not in my heart, because you can't make it right.' "

Bowles stopped talking. For several minutes we sat in silence. All you could hear were the noises outside the cell. An inmate shouted down the tier. "Hey, man, check that dryer. See if my laundry's done."

"Fuck you, man, check it yourself, think I'm your fucking maid?" came the reply.

Another inmate walked past reading a letter he had just received. Someone opened the door to the television room and for a few seconds the screams of Bon Jovi escaped from MTV.

Everywhere else, life inside the prison was going on as normal, but inside this cell time had stopped. Little looked down from his bunk at Bowles, but the older convict didn't respond. He sat on a metal chair in the center of the cell, drained of emotion. There was an uneasy silence. It was impossible to tell what Bowles was thinking.

The cell that Bowles and Little shared in the newly remodeled A cellhouse was unique because the afternoon sun actually fell inside it. On this particular day, the sunlight struck Bowles's stubbled face, giving it a jaundiced look. He appeared tired and old.

The cell was one of the neatest that I had seen. The magazines on the metal locker were not simply stacked together. They had each been turned face-up and their edges were flush. The sheets and blankets on the bunk beds had been pulled tight, military fashion. Both men's shoes and slippers were lined up as if they had been placed there by a maid. There were two bulletin boards on the wall and both contained the obligatory nude pinups, but Little's board was dominated by an intricate pencil drawing that, he explained later, was a diagram of a futuristic atomic fallout shelter that he had drawn. Bowles had a drawing too. It showed a man on his knees, his hands tied behind his back. The man's head had just been sliced off by a sword. Bowles had drawn blood dripping from the neck.

"See, the truth is that when society sent me here, it really *didn't* think my life was important," Bowles said. "The truth is, you bastards just didn't have the nuts to hit me in the head with that hammer and throw me in the dump. You put me in here and you wrote me off. You said, 'Don't ever let this motherfucker out,' and that ain't right.

"If you want to fuck me, come in here and say, 'Carl, we're going to fuck you and there's nothing you can do about it.' But don't lie to me. Don't tell me my life is worth saving. Don't tell me what I do in here matters when the truth is no one really gives a shit what I do.

"Whether I act good and take care of those flowers or fuck up and start stabbing people—the truth is no one really gives a fuck, 'cause to the outside world, I'm dead and you folks are never letting me out."

By the next morning, Bowles had cooled off. "Do you know how many wardens have come and gone since I've been here?" he asked. "Look, these people have caused me to bounce off the walls long enough. I'm never touching another flower again for these fuckers."

I asked Connor later that day about his decision to fire Bowles, and he quickly assured me that it had nothing to do with his personal clashes with Richard Smith. "No other inmates are allowed to have their own private gardens. Why should Carl Bowles get one? Maybe Dick Smith felt comfortable with that contradiction, but I don't."

Connor continued: "Bowles was referring to certain tools as 'my tools.' I was hearing people, including the warden, referring to Bowles as 'Lieutenant Bowles.' Comments like that mean something in here. Our environment dictates that an inmate and correctional officer will never be friends. We have to live on separate sides of the street. Even though people were joking about Bowles being a lieutenant, he was beginning to cross that street. Officers were letting down their guard."

I told Connor about Bowles's reaction, his speech about responsibility, how much he had enjoyed the garden. Connor chuckled. "What you got to realize about someone like Carl Bowles is that there is always an ulterior motive. The reason he had that garden was not because he liked gardening but because he was using it as part of some scheme. Maybe he was using it to hide dirt from a tunnel he is digging, maybe he was hiding a shank there, maybe he was simply growing himself a tomato to sell, I can't tell you, but I know Bowles, and I know he was up to something.

"The bottom line is that I decided it was time for Mr. Bowles's world to come crashing in on him," said Connor. "With someone like Bowles, it's good to shake them up every once in a while, and remind them of where they are and who is in charge."

Connor's statement sounded harsh. "What people from the outside world don't understand," he quickly added, "is that inside here, convicts put on their best face because they want you to feel sorry for them. You see them in a cell and you imagine yourself in that cell and you feel awful about it.

"But you got to remember that Carl Bowles killed three people simply because he wanted them dead, and you will never convince me that you can change a Carl Bowles. If I were the judge in the chair, I wouldn't care whether Carl could be rehabilitated, because what he did is so heinous that there is just one payment, either death or to keep him away from people forever. Period. You sure as hell aren't going to find me shedding tears because Carl Bowles lost his vegetable garden."

Now that Bowles and Little were out of work, they began spending more time in the recently remodeled Hot House exercise room. Warden Matthews had purchased several new stationary bicycles, weight benches, and other equipment for the inmates. Bowles had designed a weight-lifting program for Little. He was schooling him in other ways as well.

"Carl has opened my eyes to things I'd never seen and most people never see in here," Little explained one afternoon. "You look around, the guards look around, and everyone thinks they

see what is going on, but they really don't see shit. Believe me,
Carl sees things going on that you can't even imagine."

In the short time that they had been cellmates, Bowles had
already shown Little several scams. A few cells down the tier
from their cell was a convict-run store where inmates could
buy soft drinks, cigarettes, crackers, fruit, pornography, and
even jogging suits. It was against bureau regulations for convicts to stockpile goods from the prison commissary in their
cells and then barter or sell them to other inmates. But stores
like this could be found on nearly every tier at the Hot House.
They were frequented by inmates because the commissary was
only open a few hours each day, there was always a long line of
customers waiting to get in, and inmates were prohibited from
spending more than $105 per month. Moreover, the commis-
sary didn't give anyone credit. Convict-run stores were always
open, there were never lines, there was no limit on spending,
and most gladly offered credit. That was because the stores
charged one hundred percent interest. If an inmate took a can
of Coke on credit, he owed the store two cans of Coke the very
next day.

Most convict-run stores were run by "clerks" who worked
for a "backer." It was the backer's job to put up enough money to
stock the store and, more importantly, supply the muscle when
an inmate didn't pay. The clerk took the risk of getting arrested
by the guards for operating a business, although guards rarely
bothered them unless a convict got too greedy and stockpiled his
cell with so many items that it became obvious what he was
doing. In those cases, most guards would step in because they
didn't want to run the risk of being chastised by a lieutenant or
captain who happened by and noticed that an inmate's cell was
overflowing with goods.

Bowles had pointed out various prison bookies, explained
which gangs controlled the drugs, and told Little about the male
prostitutes who charged a carton of cigarettes for sex. These
were all small scams and most guards knew as much about them
as the inmates did. Occasionally, a guard would bust a convict
for some minor offense, but in Bowles's eyes, these routine, petty
crimes were inconsequential.

But extortion, contract murders, major drug smuggling,
and escape plots were serious, and Bowles prided himself on

being able to spot them long before other inmates or the guards did. One morning he pointed out a fish to Little and predicted that someone would soon make a move on the fat white middle-aged convict who had been sent to prison for bilking investors out of several million dollars through a land-fraud scheme. Just as Bowles had predicted, two D.C. Blacks were arrested by the guards a few days later for trying to extort money from the inmate. They had pushed him down a flight of stairs and threatened to kill him unless he paid them $50 per week. The inmate had rushed to the lieutenant's office and spilled his story to the guards. The two D.C. Blacks were put in the Hole and their victim was moved into a special cellblock over the prison hospital known as the protective-custody unit, where weak inmates, snitches, and sexual deviants were housed for their own safety. It was a classic example, Bowles told Little, of how *not* to extort someone.

"Even a mouse is going to fight if you push him into a corner," Bowles lectured. "You got to understand that if a guy is weak, he's always going to take the easiest way out of a situation. This guy ran to the cops."

The trick to orchestrating a successful scam, Bowles continued, was in thinking three moves ahead, like a chess player. "You got to give your mark someplace to run. You got to get him to go where you want him to go."

One day at lunch, Bowles pointed to an unlikely pair of inmates sitting together at a nearby table. One was a bearded, long-haired former biker and convicted killer, the other a thin clean-shaven man in his mid-thirties. Bowles explained that the biker was being paid to be the thin inmate's bodyguard. It seems the two men had arrived at Leavenworth a few months earlier aboard the same bus, and while they were being held on the fish tier, they became friends. Most nights, the biker stopped by the other man's cell just to chat. A short time after both were released into the main prison population, two thugs burst into the thin inmate's cell, knocked him to the floor, put a knife to his throat, and told him they were going to rape him. As they were pulling off his pants, the biker came along for one of his nightly visits and scared off the thugs. The terrified younger man realized that he needed someone to protect him, so he hired the biker. Each week, the thin inmate's brother, who owned a small manufacturing plant in the Midwest, deposited a check into a savings account for the biker.

What few inmates knew was that the biker, whom Bowles had known off and on for years, had paid the two thugs to terrorize the other man. During one of their first conversations, the thin inmate had foolishly mentioned that his brother was a successful businessman, and from that moment on, the biker had looked for a way to extort money from him.

"You see, he gave the mark someplace to run, a way out of the corner, and the mark did exactly what he was supposed to do," Bowles explained.

When Little first met Bowles, the seasoned convict promised to tell him the secret of being able to walk around in the Hot House without being victimized. This is what Bowles said: "You got to learn how to draw a line. If some guy insults you every time you step out of your cell, first you got to ask yourself, 'Is it me? Have I done something to deserve this disrespect?' If you haven't done anything, then you know he is trying to run over you and you must take it to him immediately. Get right in his face. 'Hey, what the hell is going on here? Are you trying to fuck me? What is your problem, man? Look, we both got numbers in here, and hey, I'm willing to move halfway for you, but you have to move halfway for me. Now if you ain't willing to do that, motherfucker, then you won't be on this tier much longer.'

"That is all you have to do because that is what is reasonable. You gave him an out. You said you'd move halfway. But you drew a line, and if you aren't willing to draw that line and tell that motherfucker that you will make him pay if he crosses it, then you got no principles, you got no standing in here, you got no word, and you got no credibility."

Bowles had never read any books by Wall Street tycoons on the art of deal-making, but he understood raw power. "The only time a guy is going to pull up," he explained, "is if he thinks fucking with you is going to cost him more than he will gain.

"I've never had to stab another man in prison," Bowles continued, "and I ain't no beefed-up, big motherfucker. But I've always made it perfectly clear that if you try to hurt me or kill me, I'm not going to hesitate. I'm going to walk into one of those prison factories and I'm going to get myself a big hatchet and I'm going to walk right down center hall and no one, no one at all, is going to try to stop me unless he is a complete idiot. I will cut off your head with that ax and I'll pay whatever consequences society demands, but there should never be the slightest fucking doubt in anyone's mind that I will do that. Ever."

Bowles made it sound simple, and for him, it was.

CHAPTER NINETEEN

THE CUBANS

In late May Cuban informants, paid off with extra packs of cigarettes, told guards in C cellhouse that a riot was being planned. It had been nearly six months since the Cubans had destroyed the prisons in Atlanta and Oakdale, and the detainees now realized that the concessions they had won by agreeing to a peaceful surrender hadn't improved their lot. They were being held under harrowing conditions in the Hot House, the Immigration and Naturalization Service was going ahead with plans to deport them, and Washington bureaucrats had lost interest in their plight as soon as the riots had ended.

The informants claimed their fellow detainees were planning to start trouble sometime during the week of June 12, when the INS was scheduled to announce the names of the first wave of Cubans to be sent home. This riot was going to be different from the December uprisings, the informants warned. A hostage would be executed to draw attention to the Cubans' frustration, anger, and desperation.

Warden Matthews and Associate Warden Connor immediately began planning for the worst. Guards in the Cuban units were ordered to inspect the locks on each cell door and examine the chains that were wrapped through the doors and cell bars to make certain none had been cut. All keys in the two cellhouses, except for those that were absolutely essential, were removed, and the keys that were left were split up among the guards so that the Cubans would have a difficult time collecting all of them.

160

As the week of June 12 approached, the noisy cellhouses grew quieter. Guards noticed that the Cubans cleaned their plates at every meal regardless of what was served. They were obviously hoarding food.

On the morning of June 11, Warden Matthews told his associate wardens that he had decided to implement what he described as a "divide and conquer" plan. The INS had given him a list of the 205 Cubans at the Hot House who were going to be deported. These unlucky inmates represented less than one-third of all the detainees. "I want to move all the Cubans who are going to get their deportation notices into C cellhouse," Matthews said. "We will move the others into D cellhouse."

Obviously, the Cubans scheduled for deportation were the ones most likely to riot. But the others, Matthews explained, still had a chance of being recommended for parole by the INS. They had a lot to lose if they participated in a riot, because the INS would immediately add their names to the list of deportees.

"If my plan works," said Matthews, "we shouldn't have any trouble with the Cubans in D cellhouse, just the ones in C, and that means we will only have to concentrate on one group."

He wanted the Cubans divided that same night. Shortly after four in the afternoon, Lieutenant Monty Watkins began handing out riot gear to the members of the SORT squad. Each man was issued a black helmet that looked like the one worn by Darth Vader in *Star Wars*, a black jumpsuit, and a padded black vest much like those used by baseball umpires. Associate Warden Connor had told Watkins to keep the SORT team in the basement, out of the inmates' sight but ready to respond within seconds if trouble erupted when the detainees were being shuffled between C and D cellhouses.

Shortly after midnight, when most of the American convicts were asleep, a special squad began moving Cuban prisoners one by one. Each detainee was handcuffed before he was taken from his cell and escorted by a covey of guards to a new cell either in C or D cellhouse. None of the Cubans knew at this point why they were being moved, and none of them resisted. By dawn some two hundred had been relocated.

Both prisoners and guards remained edgy throughout the day of June 12. Guards paired up. "Every time you ran down the tier because some Cuban was yelling, in the back of your head you wondered, Well, is this it? Is the shit storm about to kick off?" one guard said. But there were no unusual incidents.

On June 13, INS officials began notifying the 205 Cubans in C cellhouse that their requests for asylum had been denied and they were going to be returned to Cuba. As the INS workers broke the news, guards in D cellhouse went from cell to cell assuring the detainees there that they were not on the deportation list.

Almost immediately, the mood in D cellhouse relaxed. Across the rotunda, however, in C cellhouse the Cubans became sullen. During the next two days, guards worried. "It's weird," said one. "No one is getting slimed. We haven't had to four-point anyone in their cell. It's like there is some kind of lull going on."

On June 16, a Cuban in C cellhouse started a fire in his cell and yelled, *"Vamos a hacerlo!"* (Let's do it!) Guards sounded an alarm and raced down the tier. The fire was quickly extinguished and the Cuban moved into a waiting cell, where he was chained in a four-point position. More than forty employees, an unusually high number, had responded to the alarm. They had expected other Cubans to join in the ruckus, but none did.

The next day, a Friday, Matthews met with his associate wardens and stressed the need to keep the Hot House operating as routinely as possible. "We don't want to take any privileges away from the American convicts or get them upset," he said. "We don't want to be fighting both groups at the same time."

That evening the guards assigned to the prison auditorium reported a record attendance by the U.S. inmates at the nightly movie. The film was *Friday the 13th—The Final Chapter,* and whenever the indestructible villain impaled another teenage victim, the inmates cheered.

On Saturday morning, June 18, Associate Warden Connor received word that a handful of Cubans at the penitentiary in Lompoc, California, had tried to instigate a riot. They were being flown to the Hot House and would be coming that afternoon. Connor had them moved into individual cells in C cellhouse as soon as they arrived. At 10:30 P.M., three of the troublemakers from Lompoc began ripping up the plumbing in their cells. Water gushed across the floor into the tier. They began screaming *"Vamos a hacerlo!"* just like the inmate earlier in the week. But this time, all the detainees joined in. Within seconds, cups, magazines, toilet paper, light bulbs, even clothing, came flying out of the cells. Some Cubans broke the pipes in their cells, others started fires. Matthews and Connor, who had gone home for the night, hurried back to the penitentiary, as did members of the SORT team. Some Cubans had rubbed their plastic toothbrushes against the concrete floor to sharpen the handles. "Watch your eyes," a guard yelled. "Don't let them poke you in the face."

Amid the flooding water, rising smoke, debris, and screams, Connor calmly took charge. He sent Lieutenant Watkins and the SORT team to deal with the Lompoc troublemakers. He ordered the water in cells that were flooding turned off. He sent guards to the basement to collect tear-gas canisters and gas masks. He told other guards to get fire extinguishers and stand ready.

Watkins, a bulky Vietnam combat veteran, led five members of his SORT team down the tier. Urine and feces splashed against the clear plastic facemasks attached to their riot helmets. When they stopped at the cell of a former Lompoc prisoner, Watkins yelled, "Cuff up!"

"Fuck you!" the Cuban replied.

Watkins didn't bother unlocking the padlock that secured the chain wrapped through the cell door. He snipped it with bolt cutters, opened the cell door, and ordered his team to attack. Within seconds, the Cuban was chained to his bed. Watkins and his squad moved on.

During the next half hour, the SORT squad chained twelve prisoners to their beds. When Watkins came to the thirteenth cell and gave the order "Cuff up," the detainee stepped forward and stuck out his wrists. It was over. Two hours later, Matthews, Connor, and the SORT team went home.

When Matthews inspected C cellhouse at 9 A.M., all the debris from the riot had been cleaned up by Cuban orderlies.

"Some of our Spanish-speaking guards heard the Cubans talking," Matthews explained later that day. "They said we were too well prepared. They didn't think we would be ready for them." And then, with pride, he added, "I guess they learned that this is Leavenworth and we do things differently here." A short time later, Matthews called the guards from the Cuban units together in the prison chapel. Some were worried that they were going to be fired because rumors about staff brutality were still circulating through the Hot House. When they arrived at the chapel, they found a table covered with warm apple-filled pastries and coffee. Matthews thanked them for "upholding Leavenworth's reputation as a can-do penitentiary" and made a point of shaking each man's hand.

"Unfortunately," Matthews told them, "I'm afraid this was only the first round."

A Voice: LIEUTENANT BILL KINDIG

(*Recalling the July 31, 1973, riot at Leavenworth, in which Officer Wayne L. Selle was murdered by inmates.*)

I was the first person to reach Selle. I lifted him up, and when I did, my arms squeezed some of the air out of his chest and he made a groaning sound. I thought he was still alive and I started talking to him and yelling to the other officers to help me. When I realized he was dead, I figured he'd died in my arms and it really bothered me.

I kept wondering if there wasn't something I should have done to save his life. I had nightmares about it later, you know, me coming up to him, grabbing him, him being alive and then dying in my arms. I couldn't sleep because I kept seeing his face. They could have killed any one of us. They didn't have anything against Selle. He was just there, so they stabbed him. The prison doctor told me he had been hit so many times there wasn't anything I could have done and that made me feel better, but I still couldn't shake the image of his face.

I had his blood on my pants, and the next day when I got up, I wore those bloody pants even though my wife told me I shouldn't wear them. I walked right into the visiting room wearing those bloody pants and no one said a word to me all day about how I shouldn't have worn them. I had to wear them. Wayne Selle was a good and decent guy, and he was dead. They had killed him, and the next day, it was like everything was back to normal, like nothing even happened the day before. That made me angry. Damn it, something had *happened. A man had been stabbed to death for no reason. He had died and now everyone was acting like nothing even happened. The inmates in the visiting room were laughing and talking to their visitors and the other officers were going about their jobs and no one was saying anything. That's why I wore those pants. I wanted people to know that I knew Selle had died and that everything wasn't normal and that Wayne Selle's death had meant something. It wasn't something I was going to forget.*

When they began remodeling A cellhouse, I went in there just to see what it looked like, you know, after they had gutted it and torn out all of the tiers and cells, and suddenly I found myself going to where I had found Selle's body. This is about fifteen years later, and yet I could see his face and I started hyperventilating and I got so bad they had to get me the hell out of there.

His face was as clear to me that day as it was when I found his body. Even now, I can still see Selle's face and I still get mad because, you know, there was no reason for them to kill him. No reason at all.

CHAPTER
TWENTY

The hiring of a new personnel clerk at the Hot House didn't usually get much attention, but when Brittany Monet got the job, convicts and guards took notice. Blonde, single, twenty-four years old and striking, Monet worked in an office on the second floor of the administration building and only came into the penitentiary area at lunchtime to eat in the officers' cafeteria. No matter. By the end of Monet's first week on the job, convicts had started rearranging their daily routine so they could be near the rotunda when Monet passed through on her way to lunch. They wanted to get a glimpse of her.

The bureau has always been dominated by men, and has remained so even though Norman Carlson was the first director to really open it up to women and minorities. Under his leadership, women were hired as guards for the first time. They did all the jobs that male guards performed, including strip searches, but only in lower-security prisons. The bureau claimed its maximum-security penitentiaries, such as Leavenworth and Marion, were simply too dangerous for women to work in as guards.

This didn't mean that there were no women inside the Hot House walls. Of the forty female employees, ten actually worked in the main penitentiary or in prison industries, often side by side with inmates. Nearly all, however, were relegated to lower-paying secretarial jobs, not to the top-paying positions in the custody department.

While the bureau was careful to avoid sexism in its employee manuals, women were expected to adhere to several unwritten rules at the Hot House. Within the penitentiary it was customary for them either to walk together in groups or to ask a guard to escort them. Most women followed this practice. Monet didn't.

A few days after she began work, Monet noticed that a guard was trailing her and another woman as they went to lunch.

"Is there something we can do for you, Officer?" Monet asked.

"No, I'm just escorting you girls to the officers' mess," the guard replied.

"We don't need an escort," said Monet. The mess was located at the end of center hallway and there were plenty of guards milling about as the women walked there.

"Well, I'm going to escort you anyway," the guard said. "It's for your own good, girls."

These comments irritated Monet, and later that day she complained to her supervisor. "Correctional officers shouldn't be bodyguards for the staff," she said. "I can take care of myself." She later added that the last two times she had been escorted, the guards had used the opportunity to ask her for a date, and one of them had been married. Monet's superior told the guard who had followed the women to lunch to apologize.

Several days later, a different guard spotted Monet in the prison yard, where she had been sent on an errand by her boss. The guard demanded to know what she was doing walking alone in the compound. Monet berated him and continued on her way.

Lieutenant Edward Pierce was working in the lieutenant's office when the guard came in and complained about Monet. "That blonde bitch is going to get herself or some officer killed," Pierce snapped. "One of these shitheads is going to drag her into a closet, rape her, and cut her throat, and we're not going to find out about it until we find her body."

The two other lieutenants in the room agreed, but neither volunteered to say anything to Monet or her supervisor. "Technically she's right," one said. "An employee can walk wherever he or she wants to, and if we demand that she have an escort, some judge will slap us with a fine and we'll be accused of being sexist pigs. What she's doing, though, is simply crazy."

Monet's attitude upset many of her female coworkers as well. "She is making it dangerous for all of us," complained Susan Avila-McGill, who worked down the hall from Monet. Refusing an escort was only part of the reason for resentment.

The close-fitting business suits, dark-hued hose, and high heels that Monet wore would have been acceptable apparel anywhere else, but in the Hot House, most women intentionally "dressed down." Some even wore the same black blazers, white shirts, and gray slacks that the men wore. "None of us wants to walk down center hall after she goes by because the inmates are so riled up," Avila-McGill said. Monet's good looks had also prompted several guards to stop by her desk and ask her for dates. When Monet announced that she never dated her co-workers, the guards got mad. "That bitch thinks she's too good for us," said one.

Soon, Monet was being ostracized by both guards and her female coworkers. A few women felt sorry for her. Phyllis Driscoll later recalled how difficult it was for her to adjust to working in a traditionally all-male environment. When Driscoll's first boss patted her on the buttocks, Driscoll complained to his superior, only to be told, "Oh well, those things will happen when you're a pretty girl."

But even women who felt strongly about equal rights didn't want guards to stop being their escorts, especially those women who had worked at the Hot House long enough to recall what had happened to Peggy Hudson.

A stocky woman in her late thirties, Hudson had grown up on a Kansas farm, married her high school sweetheart, and taken work at the prison simply because it paid better than most clerical jobs. In 1983, she was at her desk in the prison hospital when an inmate came in carrying a prescription slip. Hudson's boss and another man were standing less than ten feet away when the inmate suddenly darted around her desk, pulled a shank from under his shirt, and pressed it against her chest.

"I'll kill her!" he screamed. "Get out!"

The two men backed out of the office and the inmate kicked the door shut and locked it. He pulled the curtains closed, ordered Hudson to sit down in a chair, and tied her hands with a piece of braided cord he had made from his own hair.

When guards began pounding on the door, the convict yelled that he would kill Hudson if anyone tried to break in. He demanded that another female employee be brought to the office to speak to him. She was the only person he would talk to, he screamed. The guards sent for the woman.

While waiting, the inmate ordered Hudson to stand up and then whispered in her ear, "Pull down your pants!"

"I told him 'No!' I wasn't going to do that," she recalled later.

"It's okay," he said. "I'm not going to hurt you."

When Hudson refused again, the inmate grabbed her and jerked her pants down. He took out his knife, forced her onto the floor, and climbed on her. Hudson sobbed, but her tears didn't stop him from raping her.

A few minutes later, the inmate and Hudson heard voices outside the door. The other employee had arrived, and she and the guards were able to convince the inmate to free Hudson and surrender.

The first person Hudson saw was Warden Jerry O'Brien.

"We had sex," she whispered. "He raped me."

"Oh my God!" said O'Brien.

"I couldn't cry," she recalled later. "I couldn't cry for three days, and then I started sobbing and couldn't stop. My husband and I talked for hours and hours about how we wanted to kill that inmate and how we would make him die slowly."

The FBI told her later that the convict had been planning the rape for three days. He had attacked her simply because she worked in an office with a door that could be locked. He had never spoken to her before the attack and Hudson couldn't remember ever noticing him before he came into the office that morning. "I was just convenient." The inmate was sentenced to an additional thirty-five years in prison, but since he already was serving several life terms, the rape sentence was made to run concurrently. As far as Hudson was concerned, he had "gotten off without any punishment at all."

"I kept thinking about what he said, how he told me he wasn't going to hurt me," Hudson recalled. "After he raped me he said, 'See, I didn't hurt you,' and it's true that people don't die from having sex, but being raped scars you inside. He really hurt me and he hurt my husband and he hurt my family, and the thing about it is, he didn't even care."

Hudson thought about quitting. She was afraid to go back inside the penitentiary compound. But she decided that she wasn't going to let the rapist end her career. She worked in the administration building for a year before returning to a job inside the penitentiary that required her to be in contact with inmates. "I am glad that I am doing something to help keep criminals locked up," she said. "Most of these inmates don't have any conscience. They think they can just do whatever they want and then walk away. If it weren't for the bureau and the people who work for it, that would be true."

Peggy Hudson had watched Brittany Monet and had considered telling her about how dangerous the Hot House was and how quickly someone could be attacked. But Hudson decided not to. It was just as well. Monet said later that knowing about the rape wouldn't have changed her mind about asking guards to escort her. "I'm not naive," she said. "I know this is a dangerous place, but I can also take care of myself. I don't need a babysitter."

Norman Bucklew had noticed Monet the first time she came into the officers' cafeteria, where his job was cleaning tables. The thirty-nine-year-old convicted murderer was sure he could seduce her. Most women found Bucklew handsome. He had short, curly salt-and-pepper hair, a mustache, unflinching steel-gray eyes, and a muscleman's build. But it was his confident, even arrogant manner that made him noticeable. Bucklew had the air of a Boston Brahmin. When he was later asked why he had been so certain he could seduce Monet, he laughed. "A young filly," he said, "doesn't chase after a weak or crippled horse. She picks the strongest stallion in the pack and runs after him."

For her part, when she first met Bucklew, Monet had been curious enough to go back to her office and read his prison file.

The next day, Bucklew was standing outside the cafeteria when Monet came to lunch.

"So you're from New York," he said, obviously pleased that he had managed to discover where Monet had grown up.

"So you're from New Jersey," she retorted with equal cockiness.

From that moment on, they began a game of quiet flirtation. Whenever Monet was too busy to come to the cafeteria, Bucklew fixed her a special plate and had one of her coworkers deliver it. On the days that she did make it to the cafeteria, he brought her ice cream for dessert. One afternoon, Monet found rose petals hidden in her napkin.

The attraction growing between them did not go unnoticed by guards. Monet would later note that she had not violated any bureau regulations by talking to Bucklew. But she acknowledged that she found him appealing. "If anything ever happened at work and I needed someone to protect me, I would depend on him, not the officers," she said. "I think they would have been scared and they wouldn't have protected me from being raped or killed. But I honestly believe he wouldn't have let anyone touch me." When asked later about Monet's comments, Bucklew said she had been "halfway" correct. "No one is gonna rape a broad while I'm around," he explained. "I won't permit that to happen. But hey, if there's a riot and all the hacks are being slaughtered, then that would be okay. See, she's a hack, and if all of them is being killed, then it's nothing personal. It's a convict-versus-hack thing. But rape her? No way. I would stop that."

Three months after she began work at the Hot House, Monet was fired. Her termination notice, ironically, came nine days after she received her first pay increase and promotion. Warden Matthews's termination letter said she was being fired because "numerous staff members have complained to your supervisor regarding your uncooperative and/or unreceptive attitude towards them." He told the union president that Monet was "not cut out" for prison work.

Monet appealed her dismissal to the federal board that oversees personnel complaints. She pointed out that she had received superior performance ratings and had not been warned or received any counseling about her "uncooperative" attitude. She also claimed that the real reason she was being fired was because she had refused to have sex with an associate warden at the prison. Just before her complaint was scheduled for a hearing, Monet agreed to drop it in return for an undisclosed cash settlement from the Justice Department. The associate warden named in Monet's complaint later denied her accusation. "The truth is, she should never have been hired here," he said. "She didn't fit in. I think she had a mothering complex, you know; she wanted to be a mother to the convicts. It probably had something to do with her big breasts."

Bucklew was disappointed when he heard that Monet had been fired. "That broad had heart, and if she had stuck around, we would have eventually gotten together," he said. "I know it, and after I had a bit of that pussy, I would have gotten her to bring me a gun or a few hacksaw blades, and you know what?— a broad like that would have done it because she would have been in love, and when a broad's in love, it's only natural for them to want to help. I'm gonna miss her."

CHAPTER
TWENTY-ONE

NORMAN BUCKLEW

Norman Bucklew flipped several sizzling pork chops over on the grill in the officers' cafeteria and checked the big pot of spaghetti boiling nearby. It was Sunday afternoon, two days after Brittany Monet's firing, and Bucklew was fixing his weekly spaghetti feast for his buddies. Within an hour, six inmates would join him at the same yellow Formica tables that Bucklew cleaned during the week for the guards. The inmates would devour plates of pasta covered with Bucklew's special tomato sauce.

No one in the bureau liked to talk about it, but over the years it had become a custom at the Hot House for the inmate cooks to take over the kitchen for themselves on Sundays. There was no way for the bureau to feed 1,200 inmates three times a day during the week without the help of inmate cooks, and most of these men, like Bucklew, could have earned three times their regular $75 per month salaries by working in prison industries. They chose the lower-paying kitchen duty because they wanted to eat well, and on Sundays they did.

Technically, the kitchen was closed. Inmates had to make do on Sunday morning with a brunch of coffee, milk, and pastries, and a dinner of cold cuts and bread. But behind the kitchen's stainless-steel doors, the inmate cooks divided themselves, as always, along ethnic lines and the mammoth kitchen took on the atmosphere of a church bazaar. Black inmates ate fried chicken with thick white gravy in one area; a handful of

Chicanos dined on tortillas and refried beans in another. Bucklew and his crew ate spaghetti and pork chops in the officers' cafeteria. It was the most private of all the unofficial dining spots, a separate room big enough for about thirty people built between the kitchen and the inmate dining hall.

During the week, the cafeteria was off-limits to inmates. It was the guards' private lounge. For $1.25, they could take as much as they wished from a large salad bar, or choose between two hot entrees, soft drinks, tea, coffee, milk, freshly baked rolls, fresh pies, and cakes. But despite the bargain prices and bountiful selection, the cafeteria was rarely crowded. Years ago, an inmate had been caught urinating into a steam kettle filled with beans bound for the staff dining room. There were stories about convicts ejaculating into sandwiches or spitting in them before serving them to guards. To quiet such fears, the bureau had installed a short-order grill in the cafeteria itself so that employees could watch their food as it was cooked. But that wasn't enough for many of them. They stayed away.

As soon as he arrived, Bucklew locked the front entrance to the cafeteria because he didn't want to be bothered by other inmates or the guards on the Sunday shift. There was a certain irony to having an inmate lock guards out of their own cafeteria and that made Bucklew chuckle as he fussed over his spaghetti sauce. The highly seasoned sauce was his specialty, and it was so good that the Mafia honchos in B cellhouse had been known to send wiseguys to the kitchen to ask politely for a plate.

A bank robber from New Jersey named Artie provided the garlic bread; another bank robber made the onion and tomato salad. Sometimes they even had wine.

"I'm a thief," Bucklew boasted as he stirred his sauce. "I don't think robbing a bank is wrong. I will never think it is wrong. If I want to take the money in a bank, then I'm going to take it, and if you catch me and put me in prison, I'm not going to sniffle about being in the pen. But don't try to tell me what I did was wrong and don't tell me I got no integrity. I'll tell you what having no integrity is. It's claiming you're *not* a thief and then coming into this dining room every day, like these hacks do, and eating lunch without paying for it. Beating the pen out of a buck twenty-five—now *that's* having no integrity."

Guards were supposed to put a ticket inside a clear Plexiglas box at the head of the serving line before eating. Bucklew had made a practice of standing in view of the box so he could tell which guards had paid and which had simply passed their hands over it without depositing a ticket. Officials later acknowledged that the cafeteria frequently served more meals than there were tickets for, but they said the amount was insignificant.

Like most other inmates, Bucklew hated guards. "They are my sworn enemy. The lowest form of life," he said, "even worse than cops." When Bucklew was a teenager growing up in New Jersey, he had heard over his car radio one afternoon that a hitchhiker had just shot a state police officer and was on the run not far from where Bucklew lived. Bucklew drove immediately to the area being searched. "I wanted to find that guy and give him a ride," Bucklew said. "Anybody who killed a cop was okay with me."

Bucklew was twenty-five when he went to prison for the first time, in May 1974, to begin serving a life term for the murder of an armored-car guard during a bungled robbery. He was put in one of the oldest prisons in America, the state prison in Trenton that had first opened in 1797. As far as Bucklew was concerned, it hadn't changed much. "It was like a fucking dungeon," he recalled. "It was noisy and dirty and there were cockroaches everywhere and rats and I'm thinking, hmmm, this is it. This is my fucking home for the rest of my life!"

Two days after he arrived, an older inmate invited Bucklew to a meeting of the "Lifers' Club." It began much like a meeting of Alcoholics Anonymous, with each man standing, giving his first name, and then telling how much time he had served.

"The first one says, 'I got twenty-two years down,' and the next says, 'I got twenty-five years in,' and on and on," Bucklew recalled, "and I'm thinking, 'Shit, these guys have done some serious time in this rat hole.' "

When the meeting ended, an inmate stopped Bucklew.

"Hey, ain't you the kid who robbed the armored car?"

"Yeah," Bucklew replied proudly, "that's me."

"I robbed one myself back in 1950. Killed a guard too."

"We talked for a while," Bucklew remembered, "and then it hit me. This dude had done twenty-four calendar years—*twenty-four*—in prison. I thought, 'I'm in trouble. I'm in serious trouble here. They are going to make me stay here for at least twenty-five years,' and then I thought, 'Fuck this, if my legal appeal is rejected, I'm going to escape.' "

Nearly two years later, Bucklew lost his appeal. He immediately went to work planning an escape. It had been fifteen years since anyone had successfully escaped from Trenton, although several had tried. Sitting on his bunk, Bucklew looked at every inch of his cell. There were only two openings: the air vent, which was much too small, and the toilet. When Bucklew walked over to the toilet and got down on his knees, he noticed that the water pipes leading to it passed through a steel plate welded to the back wall of the cell.

The next morning when he was released to the prison yard for exercise, he offered an inmate who worked in the carpentry shop a bag of marijuana in return for a hammer and chisel. He got the tools a few days later. Bucklew then jammed a piece of wood into the lock on his cell door so that it wouldn't work. Later that day, guards sent an inmate orderly to knock off the weld and the bolts on the lock so that a locksmith could fix it. Once again, Bucklew used marijuana as a bargaining chip and convinced the inmate to take his time breaking open the lock. Disconnecting the toilet, Bucklew got out his hammer and chisel and began removing the weld from the plate on the wall. "I timed my licks with my hammer to his, lick for lick, so the guards couldn't hear me." By the time the inmate had sprung open the lock, Bucklew had finished chiseling the weld from the plate. Bucklew had bought several marshmallow-filled candy bars from the prison commissary, and he chewed them and used the goo as putty to replace the weld. He painted the sticky mixture silver so it looked as if the plate was still welded in place, and slid the toilet back in position.

Working in the dark later that night, Bucklew disconnected the pipes that led to his toilet and pulled off the steel plate. Beneath it was a nine-by-seventeen-inch-square hole that led through the concrete wall into an open space between Bucklew's cell and the cell directly behind it. The space was filled with pipes and electrical wires. Bucklew stuck his hand into the hole, but couldn't reach the other side. He stuck his leg in, too, and couldn't touch it. He now knew that the space was big enough for him to crawl into, although he didn't know where it led. "I couldn't fit through the hole, though," Bucklew recalled, "I was too big. I started running, and quit eating. Every day, all I ate were two tins of sardines, a half orange, and four crackers." Bucklew weighed 220 when he started his crash diet. He calculated that he needed to lose at least 30 pounds to make it through the opening in the wall.

One day while dieting, Bucklew was in the prison law library typing a letter when he decided to replace the machine's ribbon. He couldn't free it from the machine, so he decided to break it. Despite his tremendous strength, Bucklew couldn't tear the ribbon. "That sucker was made out of nylon—just like a rope." He began stealing a few typewriter ribbons each week and wove them into rope back in his cell.

When Bucklew's weight reached 190 pounds, he was able to force himself through the hole behind his toilet. He struck a match and discovered the chamber was five feet wide, six stories high, and filled with pipes and wires. Bucklew had worked at his father's television repair shop as a youngster and had spent summers installing antennas. He was used to climbing and he soon found a pipe that was big enough for him to shinny up. It was a difficult climb, but when he reached the top and managed to strike another match, he found the ceiling covered by a row of bars to prevent anyone from cutting through to the roof. He climbed down, slipped back through the hole into his cell, and sealed the entry to his secret passage with marshmallow goo.

The next day, Bucklew traded marijuana for six pieces of a hacksaw blade. That night he squeezed into the chamber again, climbed the pipe, and, hand-over-hand like a child dangling from monkey bars, made his way across the bars on the ceiling until he was hanging directly under an air vent that led out onto the roof. Bucklew tried to use one of the hacksaw blades to cut the ceiling bars, but it was impossible for him to cut with one hand while holding onto a bar with his other. If he lost his grip, he would fall seventy feet. Disappointed, he returned to his cell.

All the next day, Bucklew puzzled over how he could support himself under the air vent long enough to saw through the ceiling bars. By late afternoon, he had a solution. He stole a steel roller from a law library typewriter and took an inch-wide strong canvas belt from a wire gurney that was hanging in his cellblock. He sewed two loops on the end of the belt, tucked the roller in his pants, and crawled through the opening in his cell wall. This time when Bucklew reached the air vent in the ceiling, he flipped the canvas belt over several bars and slipped the steel roller through the loops. The contraption looked like a trapeze. He put one leg through and shifted his weight on the roller. It held. Now, he could cut through the ceiling bars.

Bucklew decided to only cut for thirty minutes each night in case guards happened by his cell during a surprise check. Each morning he marked his progress on a calendar in his cell. "I kept a running total on the calendar in plain sight. I knew the guards wouldn't figure it out."

Bucklew calculated that it would take him one week to cut through the bars, but when he finished, he discovered there was another row of bars inside the air vent itself that he would have to cut, and these were much thicker than the first row. There was another problem. Even after he cut the bars, Bucklew was going to be too big to get through the air vent. He would have to lose even more weight. For more than a month, Bucklew had only been eating sardines, crackers, and half an orange. Now, he cut his diet to the half orange and four crackers per day.

Bucklew figured he could cut through the second set of bars by August 10, 1976, a good night for an escape because there was no moon. By August 8, he had sawed through one bar and half-way through the next. He was right on schedule. All he needed was two more days, but on August 9, Hurricane Belle hit Trenton, knocking out the spotlights in the prison yard. Bucklew decided to take advantage of the hurricane and leave early. He put a papier-mâché face partway under the covers on his bunk, bunched them up to simulate a body beneath them, and then slid the toilet out of the way. Just as he was about to crawl out of his cell, Bucklew stopped, went over to the calendar on his wall, and wrote "Goodbye!"

He slipped into the chamber, climbed the pipe, made his way to the air vent, and began sawing the final bar. Rain pelted against the vent, and wind made its louvers chatter like hands clapping. Bucklew cut for several minutes and then began pushing against the bar trying to break it, but it refused to budge. He sawed some more and was able to bend the bar this time, but it still wouldn't crack. He tried to push himself through the opening, but he was too big. He began pulling down on the bar with

Triple-murderer Carl Bowles first got into trouble when he was eight years old, and his prison record filled two thick files. Yet after spending nearly twenty-three years in various prisons, he insisted that all he wanted was a friend.

As a teenager Thomas Little thought being a criminal was glamorous. After he was arrested and three inmates in a county jail tried to rape him, he learned otherwise. And then the novice bank robber's luck got even worse. Little was sent to Leavenworth.

Thomas Silverstein had never killed anyone until he found himself in a federal prison, and was quickly accused of three inmate murders. After he stabbed a prison guard to death, he was put in a basement cell where the lights were never dimmed and all he could hear was the buzz of the fluorescent bulbs.

William Post's scruffy appearance and eccentricity made inmates and guards regard him as wacky. But Post had a superior IQ and came from a stable middle-class family, which made psychologists wonder: Why had he been drawn into a life of crime?

Dallas Scott had only been convicted of two bank robberies, but guards considered the tattooed convict to be one of the most dangerous men in Leavenworth because of his suspected membership in the Aryan Brotherhood, the most feared white gang there.

Aerial view of Leavenworth. The first federal penitentiary ever built, it was designed to resemble the U.S. Capitol in Washington, D.C., with a grand silver dome that dominates the Kansas landscape. (*AP/Wide World Photos*)

Warden Robert Matthews was the youngest warden ever put in charge of Leavenworth. He was also the first black warden there. Matthews said it didn't matter. He soon discovered that it did. (*J. J. Zeman*)

Warden Matthews talking with an inmate. Whether "standing mainline" in the dining hall or walking from cell to cell, Matthews made it a priority to be available to the prisoners. (*J. J. Zeman*)

During his seventeen years as director, Norman Carlson made the federal Bureau of Prisons into the most modern prison system in the world. (*Bureau of Prisons photo*)

J. Michael Quinlan, who was Carlson's choice to succeed him, was only the fifth director to run the Bureau of Prisons. He inherited an agency that was on the brink of doubling in size. (*Bureau of Prisons photo*)

Inside the prison industries building an inmate performs his job. In 1986 Leavenworth prisoners produced $27 million worth of goods, netting a $5 million profit. (*Debra Bates-Lamborn*)

In the penitentiary yard convicts play handball against thirty-foot brick walls. The gun tower at the right is one of six, manned at all times by watchers under orders to "shoot to maim" if necessary. (*UPI/Bettmann*)

When Cuban refugees seized control of the Atlanta penitentiary on November 23, 1987, they took hostages and set fires. Firefighters used long ladders to spray water over the prison wall. (*UPI/Bettmann*)

FBI SWAT teams entered the Atlanta penitentiary early on November 24. When the riots in the Atlanta and the Oakdale, Louisiana, prisons finally ended, 719 Cubans were transferred to the C and D cellhouses in Leavenworth. (*UPI/Bettmann*)

D cellhouse in Leavenworth, in which many of the Cubans were housed. It had been set for renovation until the riots intervened. From their cells prisoners could watch television on the sets fixed to the wall on the left, installed at Lt. Bill Slack's request after he was put in charge of the Cubans. Below, on the right, is a recreation cage. (*Debra Bates-Lamborn*)

Steve and Sharon Lacy, now at the U.S. Penitentiary in Marion, Illinois. Both Lacys were Leavenworth employees until they were transferred. Steve sees himself and his friends as society's guardians: "In our world, there are only two sides: them and us, and there's a bunch more of them than us." (*C. A. Maragni*)

Eddie Geouge in the rotunda outside his office. As a marine in Vietnam, he had killed more men than most of the convicted murderers he supervised in Leavenworth. Few prison officials were as tough, and none knew the scams, players, and dangers of prison life as well as Geouge. (*Debra Bates-Lamborn*)

After the Cubans in Leavenworth rioted, Bill Slack was told to bring them under control. Everyone else had used brute force to manage the unruly Cubans. Much to the other guards' horror, Slack offered them more freedom and decent food. (*Russ Kennedy*)

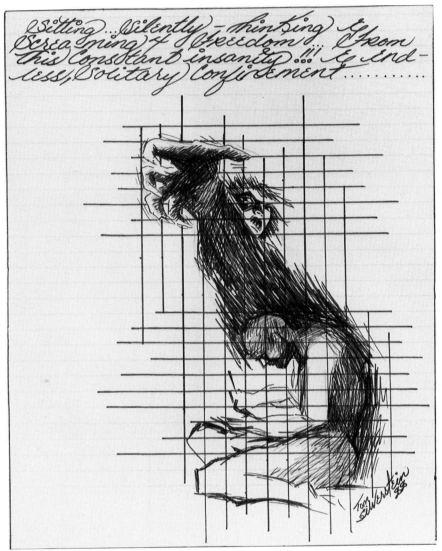

A pen-and-ink drawing by Thomas Silverstein. Drawing and painting were his only outlet in his isolation cell in the Hot House basement, and when he was deprived of drawing materials for three months, he besieged the Bureau of Prisons with formal appeals. When Warden Matthews finally ordered pencils and sketch pads restored to him, the flood of paper abated though his anger did not.

all his weight and strength and it broke suddenly, causing Buck-lew to fall. Luckily, his leg caught the canvas belt on his trapeze, leaving him hanging upside down like a circus performer. Buck-lew swung himself upright and began crawling into the air vent. His head passed through without difficulty, but his shoulders and chest were too big for the opening. "I had to go," he recalled. "It was too late to turn back." With a great push, he forced his chest through the vent, scraping the skin, and within minutes he was on the slate roof in the rain. As he started across, he slipped on the slate and almost slid off. He removed his shoes for better traction and proceeded slowly to the edge, where he used his typewriter ribbon rope, woven of thirty-eight ribbons each fifty feet long, to lower himself to the prison yard.

Bucklew assumed correctly that the guards had organized foot patrols to compensate for the blacked-out spotlight. He slipped a shank from his pants. "I would have killed anyone who tried to stop me," he said, "and I'm certain they would have killed me just as quickly."

Bucklew raced across the yard to the "Death House," so called because it was where convicts were executed. It was a one-story structure built close to the stone wall that circled the prison. Once he climbed onto the Death House roof, there would only be a seven-foot wall between him and freedom. But there was still an obstacle in his way. A guard tower loomed directly over the Death House, and when Bucklew reached the top of the prison wall, he would be on the same eye level as the guard inside the tower. The guard would have to be blind not to see him. "I figured I had a fifty-fifty chance of killing this guy first," Bucklew said. "I figured this guy was trained to reach for his shotgun, and if he did that, he'd be mine because I could crash into the tower and grab the gun as he was swinging it around. But if this hack was smart enough to pull out his pistol, he'd kill me first."

As Bucklew climbed onto the Death House roof and started up the outer wall, he suddenly realized that it was raining so hard that he couldn't see the tower guard. He couldn't even tell if a guard was in the tower. "I snapped. If I couldn't see him, he couldn't see me."

Bucklew jumped down from the wall and ran as fast as he could across the wet grass outside the penitentiary. It was several hours before anyone knew he had escaped, and he wasn't recaptured for a full year.

"I swear to Christ, I have never felt like I did when I hit that ground," Bucklew said, as he added a few more onions to his spaghetti sauce in the officers' mess. "Give me a motorcycle and I will go as fast as it can possibly go. I've flown airplanes that way too. I like the feeling and sensation of speed. I like the feeling of making it with a woman who is right on that same point with you, so you come together. And there is no feeling like having a big pile of money, or listening to a hard rock band after doing two or three tabs of good acid.

"But none of those feelings or even all of them combined can touch the feeling of real live freedom. It's something you only understand when they have taken it and suddenly you reclaim it. I felt like I suddenly got my whole life back."

Bucklew's escape was so ingenious that even the prison officials in Trenton whom he embarrassed paid him a certain amount of grudging respect. They also wondered what Bucklew could have accomplished had he chosen to be law-abiding. The judge who sentenced him had made a similar observation in Bucklew's record. Bucklew appeared to be a natural leader, the judge wrote, yet he had chosen to squander his abilities. Bucklew didn't see it that way.

"I don't respect the law," he explained, "because laws are for people who are weak and need them. If someone comes into my house and takes something, I'm not going to call a cop, I'm going to deal with it, and if I'm not man enough to get it back, then that guy has a right to take whatever he wants because I don't really deserve to own it. That's how society should be. If justice needs to be applied, I will apply it, and the reason that I have a right to apply it is because I have the power to do it. Having the power gives me permission."

Bucklew paused and then said, "When I was little, I was taught to question authority, and I always have. I'm not about to accept what you tell me unless I want to. When you're a kid, everyone thinks that's great, but when you grow up, you are supposed to become a sheep and follow blindly. Now if a psychologist was sitting here, he'd tell you I'm immature and my development isn't right. He'd say I had grasped something as a child and never risen above it. Well, excuse me, but as a child I was taught not to be a stool pigeon. Don't tattletale on other kids. I was taught if someone hits you, you hit them back, and if they even think about hitting you again, you make them never want to see you again. That is what John Wayne always did and everyone in the country thought John Wayne was right. So you tell me—what changed? Who switched the rules? When did these things I was taught as a kid suddenly become the wrong thing to do? I might die in prison, but I'm not going to become an upstanding member of your society, because in order to do that I would have to become a stool pigeon and always run to the cops, a coward afraid to settle my own problems without hiring a lawyer, and a shitbag who blindly follows every goofy guy who gets elected to the White House."

Six other inmates joined Bucklew at this Sunday spaghetti dinner. The conversation centered on guards and how much they hated them. As I listened, I realized that it was not much different from the conversations that I had heard among guards at Benny's, only the guards had talked about how loathsome the convicts were.

"You gotta understand most of these hacks were the guys in high school who everyone picked on—you know, the buttheads who got a jock put on their head in gym class," one inmate explained. "That's why they're hacks, because they are still trying to prove their manhood, and they think by coming in here and acting tough they are real men. Most would shit if you got in their face."

Someone mentioned that Carl Bowles had been fired as the hospital gardener and, just as quickly, an inmate made a crack about "Mrs. Bowles," but no one laughed and the room was quiet for several seconds. It wasn't smart to talk about another convict behind his back, especially Bowles.

By three o'clock, everyone except Bucklew had gone into the auditorium to watch a rock concert taped the night before off MTV.

"When I was little, maybe four or five," Bucklew said as he cleaned the tables, "I would wait at the door for Pops to come home. I had my cowboy hat on, my boots on, and my gun on, and he'd come in and I'd give him a gun and this guy would say, 'Draw!' Now, obviously a twenty-five- or twenty-six-year-old man is going to beat this five-year-old kid to the draw, but what amazed me was that every day, every single day, when he beat me to the draw, he made me put my hands up and turn around and face the wall. Then he would shoot me in the back. Every single fucking day we'd do this, and one day, I reared up on him and I said, 'What's the sense of facing the wall? You are going to shoot me anyway.' And he says, 'Well, maybe today I won't.' So I turned around and he shot me in the back and he did that every day after that. Never once did he not shoot me.

"I thought about it a long time," Bucklew said, "and finally I decided there was a message there. When he came home from work, I shouldn't have been waiting for him. I should have been hiding behind the door or behind the couch. I should have shot him as soon as he came in. Fuck giving him a gun and fuck giving him a chance. You see, I think Pops was trying to teach me something. In life, you can play by someone else's rules or you can play by your own, and if you play by someone else's rules you are going to get fucked every time because they were designed for them, not you. Yeah, that's what old Pops was saying, and it may sound like a stupid point, but I think he was right."

CHAPTER
TWENTY-TWO

THE LIEUTENANT'S OFFICE

The sound of a woman's voice singing about the love of Jesus Christ drifted through center hall early one Sunday morning. Lieutenant Michael Sandels decided to leave the operations desk in the lieutenant's office and see how many inmates were attending the eight A.M. service in the prison chapel. He found about fifty convicts sitting in the wooden pews listening to the lead female vocalist for a Mexican evangelical band from Texas that was touring several prisons. Fifty was a big crowd for Sunday morning. The only religious services that attracted more were the followers of Islam and members of the Moorish Science Temple. They sometimes had as many as one hundred when they met during the week. Most guards didn't consider the Moors, as they were known, a religious sect even though its members were officially recognized as such by the bureau. Nearly all the Moors at Leavenworth were members of the D.C. Blacks gang, and most officials saw the church as a front for gang activity despite protests from its members.

There were other denominations at the Hot House besides the Moors, the Muslims, and the Protestants inside the Chapel. A Roman Catholic mass had been held Saturday night. There were a handful of Jews, Rastafarians, and Native Americans at Leavenworth too. Two chaplains, one a Protestant, the other a Muslim, were in charge of religious programs, but both had only been there a few months and hadn't settled in yet.

While attendance on Sunday was usually small, there was a

group of about ten men who met regularly for Bible school in the chapel's back room. They addressed each other as "Brother" and spent an hour studying scripture under the tutelage of a Native American inmate from the Black Hills of South Dakota who had converted to Christianity. There was one black, another Native American, and six or seven white inmates in the group. These Christians were conspicuous because they were the only men of different races in Leavenworth who ate their meals together, always first bowing their heads in prayer.

Other inmates always segregated themselves in the huge dining room. Blacks ate at the tables along the south wall, dividing themselves according to whether they came from Washington, D.C., California, New York, or somewhere else. The Aryan Brotherhood and various neo-Nazi groups sat along the west wall, as far away as possible from the front doors, located on the east side of the dining room, where prison officials stood mainline. The north half of the room was for other whites and five tables in the far northeastern corner were for the prison's outcasts. This is where the dozen or so Native Americans at Leavenworth sat, along with the blatant homosexuals, inmates who were mentally disturbed, and the Christian Brothers. No one paid much attention to the Christians at the Hot House and it was rare that one of them got into trouble. "I think our fellow prisoners leave us alone because we mind our own business," said one. "Most men get into trouble because they smoke dope, get drunk, chase whores, or gamble. It's like in the outside world. If you hang out in church, you're a lot less likely to get mugged than if you are getting stoned at three A.M. in a biker bar in the red-light district." Then, he offered another comment. "Just because you are a Christian doesn't mean you aren't going to defend yourself or stick up for someone. There is lots of bloodshed in the Bible. Of course that is something most of us try to avoid."

The parole board used to look favorably on inmates who had "found the Lord," Lieutenant Sandels explained, particularly at the time the bureau was following the medical-model rehabilitation program. But that has now changed, and the board doesn't give religious commitment as much weight. As soon as the board modified the way it evaluated inmates, attendance at religious services plummeted, as did enrollments in the educational and vocational classes and therapy groups at the prison.

Less than one hundred men were enrolled in educational and vocational classes now. Only about twenty attended therapy sessions regularly.

"It's hard not to get discouraged in here," said a teacher who had been at the Hot House for two years. "Occasionally you will find someone whom you think you can help and you will try to get close to them, change their life for the better, and when that happens, the other inmates will put pressure on that person to quit coming. You see, most of these men hate correctional officers, and any inmates who get too close to staff members are going to feel the same sort of pressure that we get from guards when we get too close to an inmate. The guards don't trust us if we get too close to inmates. The inmates don't trust inmates who are too friendly with us. It's really difficult to try to help someone under circumstances like this. How can you change a guy without getting personal? Most guys come in here idealistic like me, but after a while, you just show up for a check and that's not good."

Professional criminals such as Carl Bowles, Norman Bucklew, and Dallas Scott saw no use to the prison's programs. Those who participated in rap sessions or attended church were considered naive and weak. "They're looking for a crutch," said Bucklew.

The guards proved as cynical as hardened criminals. "You hope the guy is on the level, but some are just looking for a way to impress the parole board," Sandels explained as he watched the Sunday morning service. "Once they hit the streets, they revert."

By this time, the lead singer had finished and the band was playing its closing hymn. The band's leader, an evangelical preacher, was asking the congregation to pray with him. About half the heads in the room bowed.

"Please, sweet Jesus, touch these men, heal these men, let your mercy and forgiveness flow through them." And then he asked, "Who will come forward and dedicate their life to Jesus? Who will come forward?"

No one in the congregation stirred, even though the preacher continued to plead as the band played. Almost desperate now, he asked, "Who will stand for Jesus? Come, brothers, who will stand up with Jesus today?"

One man stood, followed by another and another, until a total of four were standing.

"Who wants Jesus to touch them, heal them, who wants Jesus to be with them? Raise your hands, brothers, raise your hands!"

The four men who were standing raised their hands, as did two men sitting down.

"Praise the Lord!" said the preacher in triumph. "Now who will come forward?" he repeated. "Who will step up here to the front and receive forgiveness? Who will come forward and dedicate his life to Jesus?"

No one moved, and after a few more minutes of trying, the minister ended the service. Still, he had gotten four men to stand up and two others to raise their hands. He seemed happy as he greeted each inmate as he left the service. "God works in mysterious ways," he said. "I know in my heart that some men's lives were touched today."

CHAPTER
TWENTY-THREE

WILLIAM POST

The Catman had a secret. While the guards and Norman Bucklew fussed about Brittany Monet, William Post had quietly been having an affair with a part-time employee at the Hot House. Now she was getting ready to quit her job and move from Leavenworth, and Post had a favor to ask. He wanted his clandestine lover to bring him a gun.

Post had seduced her nearly two months earlier. They had met when he gave her one of his kittens. The Catman was always looking for good homes for them, and when he heard that there was a prison employee who didn't have a pet, he went directly to her office with the most adorable kitten of the litter. Neither the guards nor the woman's coworkers were suspicious when he did this. Nor did anyone become alarmed when Post started stopping by her desk regularly to ask how the kitten was doing. It was during these conversations that Post and the woman developed a friendship that led to something more.

Later, when he recalled the romance, Post said he had felt confident that the woman would bring him a gun on her last day at work. By that time, they had talked about it several times and Post had assured her that he didn't want the pistol in order to hurt anyone. He intended to turn the gun over to the lieutenant's office and claim he found it hidden in the prison yard. The parole board had rejected his appeal because, in the words of its letter, his institutional achievements were not "deemed sufficient to warrant a more lenient decision." But if the board heard that he

187

had turned in a handgun, Post figured it would have no choice but to grant him an early release. At least, that is what he told the woman. She promised to consider his request but acknowledged she was afraid; if caught, she could be sent to prison. It was her choice, he assured her. He would simply wait until her last day at work to learn whether or not she loved him enough to bring him a gun.

Post had always had a way with women. The employee was not the first one he had seduced while in prison. But of all the women he had known, only Glenda Thomas had been, as he later put it, "my perfect criminal soulmate."

Glenda Thomas was nineteen when she first met Post in Glendale, California, in early 1972. She had a slender figure, a sad face, and a heavy heroin habit. Post, then twenty-six, had just been paroled from San Quentin and was also using drugs. A mutual friend had introduced them, and one day when Post stopped by Thomas's apartment, he found her naked in bed with three men who had given her amphetamines in return for sex. Post pulled a gun and ordered them to leave. Later, when Thomas asked Post why he had kicked them out, he said, "I think there is more to you than being a doped-up whore."

"She was like a wounded animal," Post said of her later. "Her mother had been an alcoholic hooker who used to bring her tricks home and then pass out. Some of the johns had crawled into bed with Glenda. Can you imagine—she was only eight years old. No one had ever given her a break. I thought maybe she'd be different if anyone just let up a little bit."

Post began stopping by to check on Thomas and one afternoon he found her unconscious from a drug overdose. He forced her to walk the floor, made her drink coffee, put her under a cold shower. "She wanted to die," he recalled. When she recovered, he took her to his apartment.

"You eat here, you sleep here, but you don't fuck no one here," he explained to her, "and you don't have to fuck for your rent. You are just here. There's the bathroom, there's the kitchen, there's the food, rent is free, just kick back and take a break for a while."

Post had been supporting himself by robbing banks, and he

and another ex-convict, Robert Butler, left the apartment a few hours later to pull a robbery. Before they reached their target, the car developed mechanical trouble, forcing them to turn back to Post's apartment. Glenda was gone. She had left behind a suicide note written in mascara. Post hurried to her apartment and found her unconscious and lying in her own vomit, a bag of amphetamines nearby. A neighbor called an ambulance while Post gave Glenda mouth-to-mouth resuscitation. Later, at the hospital, doctors told Post that he had saved her life.

Post returned to his apartment and found Butler waiting, drunk and angry. Butler suggested that they rob an all-night market a few blocks away. "You're nuts," said Post. "We'd be lucky to get twenty bucks from that place." He was wrong. They got sixty-five dollars. They also were seen by a customer as they ran from the store. He followed them and took down the license number of their car. Within minutes, a Glendale police car was giving chase. Post pulled his still crippled car to the curb and Butler flung open the passenger door and ran. "I had planned on running," recalled Post, "but as I opened the door I thought, 'You coward. You have been dogging people, waving a pistol in their faces, taking their money, and the first time a guy with a gun comes at you, you want to run and surrender. What kind of punk are you?' That's why I decided to shoot it out."

Post emptied the clip in his .45 automatic, shattering the police car's windshield and hitting the front tire, spotlight, radiator and grille. Racing into a nearby apartment building, he dashed up a stairwell and paused to reload. Just then a tenant opened the door to her apartment to see what was happening. Post pushed his way inside, waving the handgun in her face. For the next eight hours, he hid in the apartment. He kept the woman and her husband, ironically an off-duty policeman, as hostages while police searched the area. By morning, Post felt it was safe for him to escape. He tied up the couple, stole their car, and fled. "I decided not to kill them, because they had done everything I asked."

Post drove to Detroit, Michigan, where he and another ex-convict, Gary Tanksley, began robbing banks. Several weeks later, Post telephoned Glenda.

"I want to be with you," she said, so he arranged to meet her in Las Vegas, Nevada, where they celebrated their reunion by spending and gambling away $12,000 that Post had gotten in his last bank heist.

In need of cash, they drove to Oregon intending to rob a bank. They stopped at a roadside cafe and Post robbed the cashier of $900, but as he bolted outside, the cafe's owner grabbed a shotgun and went after him. Post jumped into the backseat of his car and Glenda hit the accelerator just as the owner fired his first blast. It shattered the rear window. "I'm shaking real bad 'cause there is glass everywhere and this nut is pumping rounds at us, but Glenda is just as serene and as happy as could be."

Post and Glenda returned to Las Vegas and found an easier way to get money.

"Glenda was incredibly sexy, so we decided she would hang out in this hotel bar and when some john hit on her, she would take him upstairs where I would be waiting." At first Post jumped out of the hotel bathroom and robbed the men, who were so embarrassed many of them never reported the robberies. Later, Post gave Thomas a gun and she robbed the johns herself. "We didn't even bother renting a room because Glenda was jamming them right on the elevator. I'd be waiting in a hallway and the elevator door would open and out would fly some guy with a knot on his head. She began really getting off on the power. She started making them drop their pants and bend over and grab their ankles while she got away. She'd stick the gun up in their face and threaten to kill them."

Post said he noticed a change in her. "All Glenda's life, she'd been fucked over by men. She was nothing but a cunt, the slut, a worthless piece of flesh, but now she had a gun and these fat bastards had to admit that this little girl was making them bend over, with their butts naked. She was getting off on the power, so much so that we talked about her killing someone just to see what it was like. We talked about forcing some guy into the car and taking him out to the desert somewhere and having her shoot him just for the experience of it, and I think she could have done it. She was starting to get a thirst for the kill.

"She realized when you have that kind of power you are a shark, and when a shark comes out, all the little minnows put their heads down and hide."

Post had never considered Thomas his equal, nor did he think any woman was. "Prisons ruin your relationships with women because all of your close associates are males," he explained. "Women are dirty-legs, cunts, weaklings. Part of it has to do with guys who get fucked in prison. Everyone calls them 'girls' or 'punks' and that carries over into the outside world. Anyone without a dick is weak, and you might fuck weak people but you don't really respect them. But Glenda was becoming different. It wasn't just the sex between us. It was the mutual thrill of the kill. I remember the first time she jammed a guy. I was hiding in the closet, and after we got the money we went to another room in the hotel and we ripped each other's clothes off and went after each other like fucking animals because of the incredible power that we had over someone else. We had fucking robbed this guy and scared him shitless and that was an unbelievable high."

For six months, Post and Thomas worked Las Vegas as a modern Bonnie and Clyde. But Post got worried that their luck was going to end and Thomas would end up trying to rob an undercover vice cop, so they packed up and drove to Michigan where Post met up once again with Tanksley, his ex-con, bank-robbing buddy.

"For the first time in my life I felt actual fear when I robbed a bank," Post recalled. "I didn't used to care, but I was afraid now because I didn't want to be separated from Glenda."

Post and Tanksley hit several banks together, and Glenda always drove the getaway car. The bank in Dearborn, Michigan, that they intended to rob didn't seem any different from others that the trio had successfully robbed earlier. But it was during that 1973 robbery that Tanksley was killed by the bank guard and Post and Glenda were arrested a few hours later while driving out of town. Post agreed to plead guilty to the Dearborn robbery and several others in return for Thomas's getting a suspended sentence. "It was a good deal, except they required her to stay in the Detroit area for two years of probation, and she didn't know a fucking person there except some sleazy dope fiend that she met in the county jail," Post recalled.

He was sent to the federal prison in Marion, and one month later he received two letters on the same day. He recognized Thomas's writing and opened her letter first. "It was a birthday card and a love letter telling me that she'd wait for me. It really made me feel good," he said. The other letter was from someone in Detroit whom Post didn't know. The letter was dated the day after Thomas had mailed Post his birthday card and the writer identified herself as a friend of hers. It said Glenda had died from an overdose of heroin. This time, there hadn't been anyone around to save her.

Post was waiting when the part-time employee at the Hot House reported for her last day at work. As soon as he saw her face, he knew she hadn't brought him the pistol that he had wanted. She avoided eye contact until he told her that it was okay. He wasn't angry.

"If I'd pushed her more, really pushed hard, I think I could have gotten her to do it," he said later. "But we had a good time together, and you always run a risk when you push someone to do something they really don't want to do.

"It was better just to let her go," he recalled. "We just said good-bye and that was it."

A Voice: BANK ROBBER, AGE 39

When I first came in back in '78, I was always in the free world when I dreamed at night, but recently I stopped dreaming about being outside. Now, even in my dreams, I'm in the penitentiary.

I've been dreaming a lot lately and having this same dream a lot. I'm coming up the tier and there is a riot and guys are sticking all the snitches and burning the prison. In my dream, I go into this room where there are four or five of these little turd guards. You know, the ones that always act so tough and always give you a hard time by messing with your mail. Super cops.

These pigs are crying and moaning and begging for their lives and I walk up and down looking at them, and suddenly I grab one of the fat hacks by his curly hair and I jerk him out in front of everybody and I tell him to pull down his pants and he is begging me not to kill him and he is crying about his wife and kids and telling me how he is sorry for everything he has done.

After he drops his pants, I order him to turn around and

bend over, and when he does, I rip off his shorts and I start fucking him . . . and then out of nowhere I suddenly have a knife and I start stabbing him in the back over and over and over again.

What's wild about this dream is, it's black-and-white until I start sticking this pig and then everything shoots to Technicolor. Brilliant colors, man. Bright reds, yellows, greens.

I used to dream about fucking women—beautiful women with great big tits. I used to dream about being on the street or in the backyard with my old lady and kids. But this is what I dream about now. I dream about fucking a fat prison guard and stabbing him in the back.

It's scary, man.

I wonder what I'll be dreaming a year from now, you know, or maybe five years from now. I wonder what I'll be dreaming when I finally get back on the streets.

CHAPTER
TWENTY-FOUR

THOMAS SILVERSTEIN

While Warden Matthews didn't like the stark conditions in the Cuban units, keeping Thomas Silverstein in even harsher circumstances didn't bother him at all. "This inmate has killed four people in prison," said Matthews, "and has little to lose by killing again." Had Silverstein been found guilty of committing a murder in a state prison, in a state that allowed capital punishment, he would probably have been sentenced to death. But Congress has given federal judges permission to impose the death penalty in only a limited number of cases, and at the time Silverstein committed his murders, the killing of an inmate or a prison guard wasn't one of them. No matter how much the bureau wanted to execute Silverstein, federal law prohibited it.

Matthews defended the isolation that the bureau imposed on him. "Our intent is not to punish or persecute Silverstein. Our intent is simply to keep him away from inmates and staff so he will never have the opportunity to kill again."

While this was true, the bureau kept Silverstein under "no human contact" status for another reason as well. "When an inmate kills a guard, he must be punished," explained a bureau official. "We can't execute Silverstein, so we have no choice but to make his life a living hell. Otherwise other inmates will kill guards too. There has to be some supreme punishment. Every convict knows what Silverstein is going through. We want them to realize that if they cross the same line that he did, they will pay a heavy price."

Matthews had ordered his staff to install two video cameras outside Silverstein's cell so that he could be watched twenty-four hours a day. The cameras couldn't operate in the dark, so the fluorescent bulbs in the cell were left on all the time. Matthews also decided to take away Silverstein's drawing and painting supplies until the bureau had a chance to review his behavior during the Cuban riots. This was the worst punishment that the bureau could inflict on him, because he had considerable artistic talent and was constantly sketching.

Once a week, Matthews visited Silverstein to see if he had any complaints. Silverstein always asked when he was going to be given drawing materials. But one day in August 1988, he raised a different issue. Silverstein held a piece of paper against the bars and complained, "I can't read my mail."

The Hot House guards were under orders to photocopy all letters sent to Silverstein to make certain they didn't contain "secret messages from the Aryan Brotherhood." The copies given to him were so badly reproduced that they weren't legible.

"I'll look into it," said Matthews, jotting down a note on his ever-present pad.

"Sure," Silverstein replied. He didn't believe him, and after the warden left, Silverstein recited a litany of the ways in which guards were harassing him. "These guys are on a bunch of sick little trips," he complained. One guard rattled the bars on his cell at night after he fell asleep. Others would dial the number of the telephone located just outside his cell, letting it ring for as long as fifteen minutes at a time.

"They are trying to drive me crazy," Silverstein charged. Suddenly he put his finger to his mouth and told me to be completely silent. "Do you hear that?" he asked. "Do you hear the hum? It is the buzz of those damn lights. Everyone knows that one of the ways you torture someone is to keep them locked up with the lights on twenty-four hours a day. That's what they are doing here.

"I know what all of this is about," he continued. "It's not security, it's payback time because I killed a guard. It's nothing but revenge, man."

Silverstein was sent to the penitentiary at Marion in 1980 after he was found guilty of killing Danny Atwell in the Hot House. At the time, Marion was an institution in turmoil. Although it was built in 1963 to replace the notorious Alcatraz, it did not actually begin receiving the bureau's so-called "worst of the worst" inmates until 1979, when it was designated as the system's only level-six penitentiary. Before that, it had housed younger inmates, and even after it began accepting tougher prisoners, the bureau continued to run it as an open penitentiary, allowing inmates to roam the compound unrestricted. Pooling all the troublemakers in one prison without instituting any special precautions proved to be a fatal mistake.

"Every warden in the entire system suddenly had an opportunity to get rid of his worst inmates by sending them to us, and that is exactly what they did," a veteran Marion guard recalled. "I'm not certain that anyone in Washington really understood just how many bad apples we had streaming in here."

From the outside, Marion has always looked peaceful. It is built inside a national refuge and is surrounded by pristine lakes, forests, and wildlife. There are no towering cellhouses, no stone walls, only a cluster of low-level, flat-roofed buildings set amid acres of manicured lawns. Except for the guard towers and two chain-link fences with thirteen rolls of razor wire dumped between, the prison might pass for a manufacturing plant.

But in 1980 inside Marion, there was no such serenity. The guards were steadily losing control. Prison logs would later show that between January 1980 and October 1983, there were more serious disturbances at Marion than at any other prison, including fourteen escape attempts, ten group uprisings, fifty-eight serious inmate-on-inmate assaults, thirty-three attacks on staff, and nine murders. Silverstein proved to be in the thick of things.

Because Silverstein had been convicted of killing Atwell, he was assigned a cell in the "control unit" when he first arrived. The unit was a self-contained wing of the prison with seventy-two cells, and it was operated much like a small prison inside the larger prison. At the time, it was the only long-term facility in which prisoners were locked in single-man cells all day and allowed out only to shower or to exercise.

On November 22, 1981, at 7:15 P.M., guards discovered the body of Robert M. Chappelle, a convicted killer and member of the D.C. Blacks prison gang, sprawled under his bed in his locked cell. FBI agents later theorized that Chappelle had been murdered while lying on his bunk, with his head on a pillow propped against the bars of the cell. An autopsy report showed that he had been strangled by a wire slipped around his neck. Based on the bruises, the coroner later testified that two men, each holding one end of the wire, had done the job.

When FBI agents checked prison records, they found that the only inmates who had been let out of their cells simultaneously on that day to exercise by running up and down the tier were Thomas Silverstein and Clayton Fountain, twenty-eight, another convicted murderer.

As in the Danny Atwell murder case, federal prosecutors based their case against Silverstein on testimony given by inmate informants who had cut deals with them. But this time, the chief witness was David Owens, a former pal of Silverstein and an actual member of the Aryan Brotherhood. He claimed Silverstein belonged to the three-man commission that ruled the gang in Marion, and he testified that Fountain was an "AB associate" anxious to "earn his bones." They had killed Chappelle as a favor to the Mexican Mafia, which Owens said was an ally of the AB.

Silverstein and Fountain both claimed they were innocent, but jurors ruled otherwise and both got additional life sentences for the murder.

Chappelle's death worried some bureau officials, who feared that it might spark a war between the AB and the D.C. Blacks gang. But apparently it did not worry them enough to separate gang members at Marion. In fact, while Silverstein and Fountain were on trial for Chappelle's murder, the bureau transferred Raymond "Cadillac" Smith, the national leader of the D.C. Blacks prison gang, from another prison into the control unit in Marion and put him in a cell near Silverstein's. The bureau would later insist it had nowhere else within the entire system secure enough to place Smith, even though guards knew that Chappelle had been a close friend of Smith's and that Smith had vowed to avenge his death.

From the moment that Smith arrived in the control unit, prison logs show that he began trying to kill Silverstein. On September 6, 1982, guards opened Smith's cell electronically so that he could walk down the narrow tier to the shower stall. En route, he stopped in front of Silverstein's cell, pulled a knife from under his towel, and swung at him through the bars. When guards saw what was happening, they sounded an alarm and ran down the tier, but by the time they reached the two men, the knife had vanished and both lied about what had happened.

"I told this hack, 'Hey, we were talking about a football game and he was out there waving his hands around,' " Silverstein recalled. "I hated Smith, but I'm no rat and I wasn't going to tell on him. I was going to take care of it myself."

A few days later, guards caught Smith trying to shoot Silverstein with a zip gun, made from a piece of pipe crammed with sulfur match-heads that worked like gunpowder when lit. Smith was taken to an isolation cell as punishment, but he was returned to his old cell a week later.

"I tried to tell Cadillac that I didn't kill Chappelle, but he didn't believe me and he bragged that he was going to kill me," Silverstein recalled. "Everyone knew what was going on and no one did anything to keep us apart. The guards wanted one of us to kill the other."

Now it was Silverstein's turn. At 7:30 P.M. on September 27, he put his plan in action by asking the guards for permission to exercise with his buddy, Clayton Fountain. Both men were let out of their cells and placed inside a screened recreation cage that ran alongside the tier. Ten minutes later, guards opened the door to Cadillac Smith's cell because it was his turn to walk down the tier and take a shower.

While Smith was showering, Fountain and Silverstein used a piece of hacksaw blade to cut through the wire screen on the exercise cage, and as Smith stepped out of the shower Fountain slipped through the hole in the screen and ran down the tier, shank in hand. Silverstein crawled out of the cage too and was close behind, although he didn't have a knife.

Cadillac Smith had his own knife, hidden under his towel, and as Fountain approached him, he pulled it out and lunged forward, stabbing Fountain in the chest. The impact threw Fountain backward but didn't kill him. Silverstein tackled Smith, knocking him over, and the two men wrestled for control of Smith's knife. Back on his feet, Fountain joined the fight, and he and Silverstein quickly overpowered Smith. Both began stabbing him. The guards on duty sounded an alarm, but no one would open the steel gate that separated them from the inmates. They were not going onto the tier as long as Silverstein and Fountain were armed.

An autopsy would later show that Cadillac Smith had been stabbed sixty-seven times. When Silverstein and Fountain finished, they grabbed his arms and dragged him up and down the tier so that the other inmates, still locked in their cells, could see the bloody corpse. A few white inmates cheered and yelled racial slurs. Then, the two killers surrendered.

The control unit was supposed to be the most secure cellblock in the bureau, yet Silverstein and Fountain had managed to kill two inmates in a matter of months. These deaths, plus the multitude of problems among inmates in the general population of Marion, prompted bureau officials to wonder if it wasn't time to begin cracking down. Some within the bureau urged Director Norman Carlson to lock down the institution, which meant that every inmate would be locked in his cell twenty-three hours a day and only released for one hour of exercise. But others, including the warden at Marion, Harold Miller, argued against such harsh restrictions. They pointed out that inmates in the control unit already were locked in their cells all day long, but that it hadn't stopped Silverstein or Fountain from killing other inmates. Carlson sided with Miller.

No single incident in the bureau's history is as controversial as what happened next. Over the years, guards have made Officer Merle Eugene Clutts into a martyr and inmates have done the same with Silverstein. The men locked horns almost from the moment that they met.

By 1983, Clutts had worked for the bureau for nearly nineteen years, always as a guard at Marion. He had grown up in southern Illinois, had never left the area except for a short stint in the military, and wouldn't have flinched at being described as a redneck cowboy. At age fifty-one, he had a watermelon belly, white hair cropped short, and the weathered looks of a man used to working outdoors on a farm. He didn't talk much, preferred the company of the horses he raised on a few acres outside Marion to most people, and didn't take guff from anyone, whether from an inmate or a fellow guard.

Part of the reason Clutts was moved into the control unit in 1981 was because he wasn't afraid of the inmates. Many other guards were. According to a special task force sent in afterward to investigate his death, most inmates in the control unit, including Silverstein and Fountain, lifted weights during the one hour when they were out of their cells. They also exercised in their cells by doing several hours of calisthenics each day, including hundreds of push-ups and sit-ups, until they became so strong that they could "virtually not be physically controlled by staff." The inmates' strength and violent backgrounds made many of the guards "reluctant to carry out their duties because of fear of personal liability," the panel wrote.

Of all the inmates in the unit, Silverstein was perhaps the most notorious, particularly after he killed Cadillac Smith. Other convicts saw him as a defiant leader, unafraid of guards and the bureau. On the other side was Clutts, one of Marion's tougher guards.

Convicted killer John Greschner, another member of the Aryan Brotherhood and Silverstein's best friend in Marion at the time, had tangled with Clutts before Silverstein arrived at the control unit. "We'd bang heads, back up, and bang heads again, [but] I eventually backed up. I tried to figure out a way to navigate around Clutts. After I backed up, everything was cool; in fact, Clutts even did me some favors. But only after *I* backed up," Greschner recalled. "When Tommy and Clutts started bumping heads, I told Tommy 'You got to back up from this guy or it'll get way beyond a "cop versus convict thing." It will get personal.' And that's what happened. It got personal—real fast."

To this day, Silverstein claims that Clutts set out to break him by harassing him in a dozen petty ways that most guards learn early in their careers. According to Silverstein, Clutts passed him by when it was his turn to be the first to go into the recreation cage. He searched his cell more often than those of other prisoners and left it in a shambles each time. He would hang on to Silverstein's mail and deliver a big bundle of it all at once after several days. At night, he would shine his flashlight in Silverstein's eyes during the inmate counts. Worst of all, according to Silverstein, Clutts would intentionally smudge his artwork, later teasing him by saying, "I did a bit of work on your painting."

Whether or not Clutts actually did these things is impossible to verify. The bureau denies it, of course, while Greschner and other inmates claim Silverstein is telling the truth.

"I remember hearing Clutts tell Tommy, 'Hey, I'm running this shit. You ain't running it. You're a fucking prisoner! I'm the cop, who the fuck you think you are?'" Greschner recalled.

What isn't disputed is that Clutts and Silverstein clearly disliked each other, and regardless of the cause, this dislike turned to a personal hatred—at least on Silverstein's side.

"That guy was torturing me," Silverstein said. "It was like I was a little kid again walking home from school and that bully [Gary] was picking on me. I've always attracted bullies, and I don't know why, but I hate 'em and I hated Clutts. Everyone knew that Clutts and I had a thing. . . . Everyone always says how mean and nasty and rotten I am for killing him. They say he was just doing his job, blah, blah, blah—you know, because he put on a badge he's somehow a saint. But it wasn't like that. When someone starts to poke at you, after a while nothing matters anymore. All you think about is getting revenge, striking out. With me, it was Clutts."

Inside the isolated Marion penitentiary, deeper still within the control unit, the so-called prison within a prison, Silverstein began to fixate on Clutts.

"From the time I'd hear his voice or see him come to work, I'd be pacing my cell," Silverstein recalled. "My whole day would be ruined."

Silverstein became so frazzled that he couldn't draw. When other convicts yelled to him, he didn't answer. At night, he couldn't sleep. All he could think about was Clutts—and getting revenge.

"It just kept building and building, and pretty soon, killing him was all I could think about. Every day, every night, every moment that I was awake, I just thought about how much I wanted to kill him. How much I wanted him dead."

His fellow prisoners noticed that Silverstein had become obsessed. They couldn't talk to him without his turning the conversation to Clutts. No matter what happened, if it was something bad, he accused Clutts of being behind it—even when some other guard was involved.

"I told Tommy, 'Hey, man, when you kill a cop, you know it's over. Your life is gone. You got to get some perspective here,'" recalled Ronnie Bruscino, a convicted murderer who was in a cell near Silverstein's at the time. "Twenty years from now, every new guard will still know you are the one who killed a cop, because that's something the guards never, never forget."

Greschner said he, too, tried to discourage Silverstein. "If you do a cop, you are going to go on Birdman status," he told him, a reference to the Birdman of Alcatraz, who killed a Leavenworth guard and was never released from prison.

But by this time it had reached the point where nothing else mattered to Silverstein except striking out at Clutts. "I knew that I had to do it. I had to kill him."

Sometime in early October, Clutts removed the mattress in Silverstein's cell and replaced it with another one. It is not clear why the mattresses were switched, but Silverstein saw the change as yet another attempt to torture him. Silverstein began plotting a way to kill the guard, and he found plenty of help in carrying out his plan.

After Cadillac Smith was murdered, the bureau decided to handcuff prisoners in the control unit whenever they were taken out of their cells. The inmates would then be escorted by three guards to the shower stall or recreation cage.

The obvious time for Silverstein to attack Clutts was when guards released him from his cell. But he still would have to get out of the handcuffs, find a knife, and make certain that Clutts was trapped on the tier, or else Clutts would simply run off the tier to safety. Whispering to other convicts through the air vents in the back of their cells, Silverstein and his fellow gang members came up with a plan.

On Saturday, October 22, at 8:40 A.M., guards took John Campbell, a reputed member of the Aryan Brotherhood, outside the control unit so he could exercise out-of-doors. A few minutes later, Campbell complained that he was cold and wanted to exercise in the inside cage that ran parallel to the tier. Guards moved him back indoors. From his cell, Silverstein shot Campbell a knowing smile. Step one of the murder plan had been accomplished.

At 9:30, Silverstein was ordered to cuff up so that he could be escorted to the stall for his weekly shower. He stuck out his hands without protest and a pair of handcuffs was snapped over his wrists. He was frisked as he stepped from his cell, no weapons were found, and three guards took him to the shower. As Silverstein walked down the tier, he continued to smile. Step two was going as planned.

Forty minutes later, Silverstein finished his shower. He had been hyped up, nervous, but like most other inmates in the unit he had always taken lengthy showers and he had kept to his routine today to avoid suspicion. Still wet, he called to the guards and was secretly pleased when he saw three of them coming down the tier to open the locked shower door and escort him back to his cell. Clutts was one of the three. The third step had been accomplished.

Silverstein put out his hands to be handcuffed, and turned to walk down the tier. Officers William McClellan and John Mahan were on either side of him. Clutts would follow behind Silverstein. But as the four men began to walk down the tier, they heard a voice.

"Hey, Clutts, I need to talk to you." It was John Campbell, the gang member in the indoor exercise cage.

Clutts turned and walked to the rear of the tier. Without knowing it, he had just completed step four of Silverstein's plan. Clutts had been drawn away from the other two guards and was now standing at the end of the tier, as far away as possible from the exit and steel gate that separated the tier from the guards' office.

As Officers McClellan and Mahan escorted Silverstein back to his cell, he stopped to chat with Randy Gometz, another gang member. Allowing Silverstein to stop at Gometz's cell was against bureau regulations, but these encounters had become common practice in the control unit because guards were afraid to tell the inmates that they couldn't stop to visit.

In a flash, Gometz reached through the bars and used a key to unlock Silverstein's handcuffs. Then he lifted his shirt and Silverstein grabbed a shank tucked in the waistband of Gometz's pants. Step five.

"Look out! He's got a knife!" McClellan yelled as Silverstein spun around.

"This is between me and Clutts!" Silverstein screamed, and shot past the two guards.

"Clutts saw me coming and he froze for a second," Silverstein said. "He knew I had him cornered."

Clutts raised his arms to protect himself, but Silverstein's knife jammed deep into his belly.

"I just went off," Silverstein later recalled. "I just started stabbing him over and over and over again. Clutts tried to hit me, but I didn't even feel it. I'm not hearing nothing. I'm not feeling nothing. I don't know what is going on around me. All I know is that I got a knife and I am jabbing it as fast as I can into Clutts. All I see is his hands moving and me stabbing him and everything else is blank."

Despite his wounds Clutts managed to push Silverstein to one side during the attack, and struggled down the tier. Officer McClellan hurried forward, grabbed him, and helped him toward the steel gate at the front of the tier where they would be safe. Just as they were about to go through it, Silverstein caught up with them, grabbed Clutts's shoulder, jerked him down onto the floor, and began punching him again with the knife.

Officer Mahan, who was standing on the other side of the gate, reached through the bars and smashed a nightstick against Silverstein's head. Silverstein staggered back, and McClellan and Mahan pulled Clutts off the tier and slammed the steel gate shut. Clutts's chest was covered with blood. He had been stabbed forty times.

"This ain't against cops!" Silverstein yelled, the knife still in his hand.

"Drop the shank," ordered a lieutenant who had just arrived at the cellblock.

Silverstein refused. "I honestly believed that they were going to kill me, and I was not going to give up without a fight."

For several minutes the lieutenant talked to Silverstein, finally convincing him to put down the shank and lock himself in his cell.

"I felt that a huge weight had been lifted off me," said Silverstein. "I was so happy Clutts was finally dead."

Unpardonable though the killing of a guard was, at this point Clutts's murder remained an isolated incident, but that quickly changed. Prison officials decided against sweeping the entire control unit for weapons. Instead, they moved Silverstein into an isolation cell and decided to continue operating the control unit as usual.

Eight hours later, Officers Robert L. Hoffman, Sr., Jerry L. Powles, and Roger D. Ditterline were taking Silverstein's friend, Clayton Fountain, back to his cell from the recreation cage when Fountain stopped to talk to another inmate, who repeated the earlier process by unlocking Fountain's handcuffs and giving him a shank.

Fountain spun around and yelled, "You motherfuckers want a piece of this? Come on!"

He then attacked all three guards, stabbing Ditterline first. Powles was second in line. Fountain knocked him to the floor. In a courageous act, Hoffman helped Ditterline off the tier and then went back inside, unarmed, to rescue Powles. Hoffman grabbed his fellow officer and began pulling him to safety as Fountain continued to stab both of them. As soon as the two guards were on the other side of the steel gate, out of Fountain's reach, Hoffman collapsed. He died a few minutes later in the arms of his son, who also worked as a guard at the prison. Because of Hoffman's valor, Ditterline and Powles both survived. Fountain, meanwhile, danced up and down the tier. He later was overheard telling other inmates that he wasn't going to let Silverstein get ahead when it came to "dead bodies."

Never in the history of the bureau had two guards been slain on the same day in the same prison. Director Carlson was outraged. "The murder of an officer can never be justified," he recalled. "Even if Clutts was harassing Silverstein, and I don't believe that he was and there was never any proof that he was, that still didn't give Silverstein the right to murder him."

Marion was clearly slipping further out of control.

Even though the murders had taken place in the control unit, Warden Miller ordered inmates throughout the prison locked in their cells until further notice. Then, two days later, he lifted the order. He still believed that Marion could be operated as an open institution. Within a few days, an inmate was murdered, this time in the general prison population, and four inmates attacked a group of guards. Miller declared a state of emergency, every prisoner was locked in his cell, and Leavenworth's SORT team was sent to Marion to help restore order.

John Greschner, Ronnie Bruscino, and other inmates at Marion would later claim in a class-action lawsuit filed against the bureau that Marion's guards and the SORT team from the

Hot House beat and tortured them in retaliation for the murders of Clutts and Hoffman. After listening to testimony from ninety witnesses and reviewing 150 pieces of evidence during twenty-eight days of trial, a federal magistrate would later conclude that there was "no credible evidence" to prove inmates had been abused. "This is not to say that there may not have been isolated incidents of excessive force," Magistrate Kenneth J. Meyers wrote, but given the circumstances at Marion after the murders, "an extra push or shove would be understandable." He noted that guards were being attacked, doused with feces and urine, fires were being set by inmates, cells were being destroyed, and officers were being told that they would be killed. The magistrate also specifically criticized Greschner and Bruscino, whom he described as "not credible witnesses." He wrote: "This litigation was conceived by a small group of hard-core inmates who are bent on the disruption of the prison system. . . ."

Carlson decided that Marion would remain permanently locked down after the guards and SORT teams restored order. He was not going to let the prison slip out of control again. Inmates remained confined in their cells twenty-three hours per day. Fountain was sent to a prison in Springfield, Missouri. Silverstein went to Atlanta. Both were put under "no human contact."

Five years after the murder, as he sat in the basement of the Hot House recalling how he had stabbed Clutts, Silverstein said that he still thinks about the guard every day. "Even when I dream, Clutts is there. I thought killing him would put an end to it," Silverstein explained, "but it hasn't. He still haunts me. I think about him a lot and I hate him because of what he made me do. He is responsible for me being locked like a wild animal in this cage. He made me give up my life. I didn't know until after I killed him that there are a thousand Cluttses out there and all of them have a stick and all of them want to poke it at me."

Silverstein refused to sleep on a mattress at Leavenworth, he said, because it had been his anger over the mattress that Clutts took from him in Marion that had finally driven him to kill the guard.

Upstairs in the warden's office at the Hot House, a few hours after I finished talking to Silverstein, I watched as Robert Matthews pulled his notepad from his coat pocket during his regular four P.M. meeting with his executive staff and told them that Silverstein's mail was being poorly copied.

"He is the only special inmate we have here and I don't want him sending copies of his letters to some judge or court and getting us in trouble," Matthews said. "Regardless of what he has done, we must accommodate him."

The next day, Silverstein's mail arrived on time and he was able to read each photocopy.

CHAPTER
TWENTY-FIVE

DALLAS SCOTT

Within sixty days after his arrest on drug-smuggling charges, Dallas Scott was taken before the disciplinary-hearing officer at the Hot House. It was the officer's job to decide whether Scott had violated any bureau regulations and, if so, to dispense punishment. Scott arrived with his hands handcuffed behind him. The hearing lasted less than five minutes.

"You are accused of attempting to smuggle heroin into a penal institution," the officer explained. "How do you plead?"

"Not guilty," said Scott. "I don't know nothing about any heroin."

The officer quietly read some papers in front of him and then announced, "I find you guilty."

"Based on what?" Scott asked.

"Statements from people who know you did it," the officer said.

"Can I see them?"

"No."

"Why not?"

"I don't think it would be in the best interest of the people involved, the confidential informants who have given statements about what you did."

"Shit, you don't have no evidence against me," Scott declared. "This is a bum beef. You can't prove anything."

"If you don't have anything further to say," the hearing officer replied, "then I will pronounce sentence."

Scott laughed.

He was sentenced to 65 days in the Hole, stripped of 485 "good days" that had been previously deducted from his prison sentence because of good behavior, and was told that he would be transferred to Marion.

Scott hated the transfer the most. "I'm not sniveling," he said later. "I'll do my time anywhere these bastards put me, but I'd hoped to stay in Leavenworth."

A few hours after the hearing, Scott sat in the Hole and talked about the last time he had been in Marion. He was paroled from the prison in October 1983—the day before Silverstein and Fountain murdered Officers Clutts and Hoffman. Scott was a friend of Silverstein, Fountain, Greschner, Gometz, and Bruscino. As a member of the Aryan Brotherhood, he would have been in the middle of the trouble between the inmates and guards that followed the murders if he hadn't been released the day before. As it turned out, after a series of farcical mishaps Scott got dragged into the Marion mess anyway.

The bureau gave Scott a one-way airplane ticket to Sacramento and $150 in cash on the Friday afternoon he was released. He didn't get far, however, before he was in trouble. It started innocently enough when Scott's flight made a layover stop at the Dallas–Fort Worth airport. "I got a brother, sister, and brother-in-law there I hadn't seen in years, so I gave them a call." He had such a good time visiting with them that he decided to spend Friday night in Dallas and resume his trip the next morning, but when he showed up at the American Airlines ticket counter on Saturday, he was told his original ticket wasn't any good. He had spent too much time in Dallas.

"I started getting real vocal and loud," Scott recalled. "Customers are starting to gather around and I figured the agent will give me a ticket to shut me up, but she didn't back down an inch."

Scott's brother-in-law, standing next to him, was embarrassed and he offered to buy Scott a new ticket. On his way to the gate, Scott stopped to telephone his wife in Sacramento so she'd know he was on his way.

"I finish the call and hustle to the gate and there are two guys in American Airlines blazers standing by the door watching me, and when I get about ten feet away, they shut the door in my face. I said, 'Boy, am I glad to get on this plane,' and this guy says, 'We are through boarding, sir.' I can't believe it, but these sons of bitches won't let me pass. Now, I'm wondering, 'What the hell is it with these people?' I think maybe that bitch at the counter told them to shut the door in my face.''

Irritated, Scott walked back to the public telephones and called his house to tell his wife that he'd missed the flight. Then he returned to the ticket counter and squared off with the same agent with whom he had argued before. Once again, they exchanged angry words, but the agent booked Scott for a later flight. Scott called home with the new flight information and then wandered into an airport lounge, swallowed a few drinks, and lost track of time. When he realized his flight was about to leave, he dashed to the same gate where he had been earlier and slipped onto the airplane. As he was fastening his seat belt, he heard the crew announce that the airplane was bound for Atlanta, Georgia. As the passengers laughed, he rushed down the aisle and off the airplane. Scott had not flown much and had incorrectly assumed that all flights for Sacramento left from the same gate. Again, he found himself across from the ticket agent.

"I've been out of prison for less than forty-eight hours, and I'll admit I was paranoid, but by this time, I'm convinced this bitch is screwing with me," Scott said. "I figure she'd changed that gate on purpose. I am angry. I mean, I got steam coming out of my ears.''

Scott unleashed a string of profanity that only ended when the agent gave him another new ticket. He marched to a pay telephone and called his house. Thomas Silverstein's girlfriend, who happened to be staying with Scott's wife at the time, answered, but before he could give her his new flight information, Scott felt a tap on his shoulder.

"I turn around and see this little bitty guy in a seersucker suit," Scott recalled. "I look at him—and he comes to my shoulders—and he tells me to hang up the telephone. I couldn't believe it.''

"Who the hell are you?'' Scott demanded.

"Airport security,'' the man replied, pulling a badge from his pocket.

"Hey, look, pal,'' Scott said, jabbing the air with a finger in front of the man's face, "the best thing that you can do right now is get the fuck away from me. I've just about had it with you fools!"

Scott turned around. "I don't know what the fuck is going on here," he said in the telephone, but before he could finish the sentence, the security guard grabbed the receiver and tried to take it away. Scott backhanded the guard, knocking him across the corridor.

"Get the fuck away from me!" Scott yelled.

Four other security guards who had been standing by jumped Scott, and the fight was on. It wasn't until two Dallas policemen arrived that he was finally subdued.

"I called my sister from jail, and by this time I am so embarrassed. It's like I'm forty-some years old and I'm thinking, my brother and sister got to be wondering, 'God, we leave this guy by himself for one half hour and he is in jail again!' I figure they're thinking I'm some sort of nut."

Scott's sister pleaded with police to release Scott, and after she paid his fine, he was escorted to the airport and accompanied by two security guards on the Sunday afternoon flight to Sacramento.

Meanwhile, Scott's wife had not gotten word that her husband was spending Saturday night in a Dallas jail, so she had been waiting all night at the airport. When Scott disembarked, he discovered that she had taken a number of amphetamines to stay awake and was in no condition to drive. Even so, they drove off from the airport, and soon were hopelessly lost. "We musta made seven hundred U-turns and I'm a nervous wreck. Cars are zipping by and I am holding on the dash for dear life." That was when he first saw the police car. He told his wife to slow down. "I can't believe what she does. She decides we're going the wrong way and makes a U-turn right in front of this cop. She damn near hits him. I think, 'Shit, I haven't even made it home yet and I'm about to get arrested for the second time!'" The police pulled them over, but Scott managed to talk his way out of the mess and they were both released on the condition that they take a taxi home and leave their truck by the freeway.

By the time the cab got Scott home, it was Monday morning and he was supposed to report to his parole officer. Scott called an outlaw biker friend to give him a ride, and as they were going downtown, they got into an accident and Scott's left foot was injured. But he managed to make his first appointment, limping

into the parole office. Only then did he hear that Silverstein and
Fountain had murdered two guards in Marion and the prison
had been locked down.

"You are going to be under surveillance for a while," his
parole officer warned him. Both the FBI and a special California
prison-gang unit had decided to monitor him because of the
events at Marion and his membership in the Aryan Brotherhood.

Back home, Scott began getting collect calls from gang
members in various prisons asking about Silverstein, Fountain,
and others at Marion. Some callers claimed that guards from
Leavenworth's SORT team were beating inmates. Amid the
hubbub, Silverstein himself telephoned Scott.

"Now Tommy knows that he is being bugged and he knows
a lot of people are getting a lot of heat about what he did in
Marion," Scott recalled. "Tommy wants to take the heat off of
them, so he is trying to explain that it was an independent act
between him and that guard he killed, Clutts. He killed the guy
for specific reasons and it wasn't any gang thing, it was personal,
just between the two of them. Well, I can't just leave this alone,
you know. I got to open my big mouth, 'cause I figure they are
still going to kill him, so I tell Tommy, 'Yeah, everybody understands that it was a personal thing between you and Clutts,' and
then I say, 'And those folks better understand too that you are
not suicidal, meaning that if anything happens to you, then it's
not going to be a personal thing anymore. I'm out here in the
street where I can move around and you're my brother, man,
you know what I mean?' As soon as I hung up, I got to thinking,
'What the hell did I just say?' I mean, it's not like I don't have
enough problems of my own."

Bureau officials would later cite that telephone call as evidence that Scott intended to seek revenge on behalf of the Aryan
Brotherhood for the way inmates were treated at Marion.

At about this time, an ex-convict whom Scott had met in
Folsom State Prison years earlier arrived at Scott's house looking for a place to stay. He and Scott quickly struck a deal. Since
it was now November, the convict, who was in failing health and
in his sixties, could sleep on the sofa in return for stealing
Christmas presents for Scott's family. "He was a pretty good
booster," Scott recalled. "I'd drive him to a shopping center and
he'd come out every so often with whatever I ordered."

One morning, Scott walked into the living room around

eleven o'clock and noticed the old man was still lying on the couch even though the room was filled with noisy kids and three women. An argument broke out between two of the women and one of them threw a telephone at the other, but it missed its target and hit the old man in the head. He still didn't budge. Scott walked over to the couch and checked the old man's pulse.

"Hey, this guy's dead!" Scott announced.

"He ain't dead," Scott's wife said. "You're playing a trick."

One of the women in the room picked up the man's arm. "Shit! He *is* dead!" she said.

Scott asked if anyone had killed him. "Hell no, we didn't kill him," one of the women replied.

"Well," Scott explained, "if he died of natural causes, all we have to do is call the fire department and tell them to come get the body."

No one volunteered to make the call. Meanwhile, one of the women started searching the corpse's pants looking for money. "This gal is trying to get a ring off this guy's hand and I couldn't believe it," Scott recalled. "I mean, this ring is something out of a bubble-gum machine, that's how cheap it is, and this nut is going to break his finger to get it off this old coot."

"You're gonna make it look like someone killed him," Scott complained. "Leave him alone."

Scott finally convinced his teenage son to call the fire department.

The elderly man's death made Scott even more nervous about the police. Everywhere he went that day, he felt he was being followed. "I couldn't conduct any business," he said. Police later claimed that Scott was selling drugs.

The next morning, Scott and his wife put a suitcase in their truck and headed toward Texas, although he wasn't supposed to leave Sacramento without first clearing it with his probation officer. "I was just going to disappear."

They had gotten as far as Southern California that night, when Scott began spitting up blood and his wife rushed him to the University of California at Irvine Medical Center, where he registered under an assumed name. He was given a blood transfusion and listed in critical condition for six days. A blood vessel that led to the liver had burst, causing the internal bleeding. When doctors opened up Scott to repair it, they found that he had chronic hepatitis caused by severe cirrhosis of the liver. At best, they told him, he had ten years to live.

As soon as he could walk, he slipped out of the hospital without paying and continued with his wife to Texas. He checked into a motel in a Dallas suburb, where he later said he had gone to be closer to his relatives. A few days later police burst through his motel door with their weapons drawn. Scott had a pistol, but he didn't reach for it. The bureau later claimed that Scott had driven to Dallas to kill Jim Graham, who worked at a prison camp just outside the city. Graham was the lieutenant who had been in charge of Leavenworth's SORT team just before it was sent to Marion to quell the trouble there. The bureau claimed that the AB had put out a contract on Graham because of the way the SORT team had acted in Marion.

"There was no murder plot," said Scott. "All of it was a bunch of nonsense." The bureau had no proof that he had been plotting to kill Graham, but Scott had violated his parole by leaving Sacramento without permission, and that was sufficient grounds to have his parole revoked. He was sent back to Marion.

Scott saw a certain irony to his story. "I can walk into any prison in this country, any prison, and know immediately what's happening. I can deal with this crazy prison environment, with the so-called worst of the worst convicts in Marion and the so-called prison predators and all that baloney," he explained. "But in the outside world, I'm always getting tripped up. Every time I mess with a Square John, I end up getting fucked because you people have no concept of jailhouse respect and absolutely no honor.

"Take that woman in Dallas at the airport. In prison, she wouldn't have dared talk to me like she did, because I would have grabbed her by the neck and demanded a price for such shitty treatment. But I knew I couldn't do that in your world. You just can't go around out there and grab every fool by the neck when they do something stupid.

"You see," he continued, "in here, I know how to play all the games and play them well, but out on the streets, the deck always seems to be stacked against me."

A few weeks later, Scott was taken from the Leavenworth Hole to Marion.

CHAPTER
TWENTY-SIX

THE CUBANS

Lieutenant Torres Germany had eased off his investigation of brutality in the Cuban units after Shoats's death. The guards in the units had closed ranks and Germany's probe had hit a dead end. But when he arrived at work one morning in the summer of 1988, Germany found a counselor from the Cuban units waiting to speak to him. Besides a case manager, each inmate, including the Cubans, had a specific counselor assigned to him when he first entered the Hot House. It was his job to help the inmate with any personal problems that might arise. The counselor claimed that Cubans in C cellhouse were being physically abused by guards. Germany handed him a legal pad and pen, and asked him to write down every incident of abuse that he knew about. Without hesitating, the counselor began scribbling and had soon filled up several pages. He not only wrote down incidents that he had personally seen, but also stories that he had heard. Among his most serious charges were that Lieutenant Shoats had hit Cuban inmates while they were in handcuffs, and that other guards had chained inmates onto mattresses soaked with feces and urine, dragged handcuffed inmates from their cells, and denied Cuban prisoners food. Guards had even planted knives in some of the Cubans' cells, he charged.

When the counselor finished writing his statement, Germany interrogated him, and the counselor admitted that he had personally despised Shoats. "I was glad when I heard Shoats had been killed," the counselor said. "It was one of the happiest days in my life."

Germany took the counselor's statement to the warden's office. Matthews didn't believe a single one of the accusations. "I felt they simply weren't true, because I had been in that cellhouse too many times to have missed all these things," Matthews explained later. "You must remember, I talked to Cuban prisoners once a week during my rounds and none of them had ever complained about the sort of charges that were being made. Not one single complaint."

Even so, Matthews notified the bureau's Office of Inspections in Washington, D.C., the equivalent of a police department's internal-affairs office, and asked that they send an investigative team to Leavenworth.

Calling in a group of outsiders to investigate the Cuban units was not going to help Matthews's already sagging popularity with the Hot House guards. But the warden wasn't about to have his career ruined or the bureau embarrassed by ignoring the counselor, only to discover too late that he had leaked his charges to the media or notified some congressional subcommittee. Besides, Matthews said, if any of the accusations did turn out to be true, he wanted the guards caught and punished.

Besides notifying the Office of Inspections, Matthews decided to change the leadership inside the Cuban units. As Matthews looked at his list of lieutenants, he focused on one name—Lieutenant William "Bill" Slack, Jr., the operations lieutenant.

"What I liked most about Slack was his maturity," Matthews said later. "He had lots of experience and he was low-key and patient, yet he was tough enough to get the job done."

Matthews knew, however, that putting Slack in charge of the Cubans was going to make some bureau officials nervous. No one had ever said anything publicly to Matthews, but the bureau was still a small enough agency for most employees to know or know of one another, and nearly everyone in the bureau understood that the name Slack had a dark cloud hanging over it.

Warden Matthews didn't like to take chances, but he wanted the best man for the job, and that was Slack. He buzzed his secretary and told her to ask Associate Warden for Custody

Lee Connor to come to the warden's office. Matthews had two announcements: an investigative team was coming in to probe the counselor's charges of brutality and Lieutenant Bill Slack was being put in charge of the Cubans.

As he waited for Connor, Matthews hoped he was making the right choices.

CHAPTER
TWENTY-SEVEN

THE LIEUTENANT'S OFFICE

Thomas Little was about to take a bite of his lunch when Carl Bowles nudged him with his elbow and nodded toward a white convict walking past their table in the prison dining room. The inmate lived on the same tier as Little and Bowles.

"He's got a shank," whispered Bowles. "Gonna be a sticking."

The white inmate was carrying a towel over his right hand, as if he were a waiter, as he walked past the tables in the white section of the dining room and moved toward the serving line by the entrance. Little suddenly understood what was happening.

The night before, the white inmate had gotten into a fistfight with a black convict a few cells down from the cell in A cellhouse that Little and Bowles shared. Everyone but the guards at the end of the tier, who were busy talking, had heard the scuffle, and as soon as the other convicts saw that a black and white were fighting, the inmates on the tier automatically segregated themselves. A dozen whites stood in one corner and a similar number of blacks formed a group across from them. It was an instinctive move. Neither race was going to allow the other to step into the fray.

The fistfight had not been an even match. The more skillful black quickly got the better of his opponent. At one point, he held the white convict in a headlock and the watching blacks began to laugh as the white inmate threw wild punches and gasped for air. When he finally broke free, he stumbled away.

"C'mon, white boy," the black inmate jeered, dancing before him with raised fists.

"Fuck this, I'm gonna kill you, motherfucker," the white inmate replied. He headed down the tier, apparently in search of a knife.

Darting into a nearby laundry room, the black snapped off the metal handle from a mop wringer and then returned to the tier. He dropped the weapon inside a trash can and stood next to it with his arms folded across his chest, waiting for the white inmate to return. Bowles and Little had watched the fistfight, as had Norman Bucklew, and each of them had expected to see a stabbing. But the white inmate didn't return, and his opponent eventually went to his cell for the ten o'clock lock-down.

The next morning, several whites confronted the white inmate and demanded to know what he intended to do. He had embarrassed all of them by fighting so poorly and then disappearing. Now, as he walked across the dining hall, Little realized that the inmate was about to show everyone that he was not scared.

Prison officials were so busy standing mainline that they didn't notice the white inmate as he moved within a few yards of them. His target, facing the other way, hadn't noticed his approach either. He was standing in line talking to a friend when the white inmate suddenly dropped the towel, revealing a seventeen-inch knife. He lunged forward, driving the knife directly into the center of the black man's back. He had tried to sever his victim's spinal cord, but the long blade slid off the backbone and thrust all the way through the man's body, poking through the front of his white shirt. He gasped and fell forward. The white convict pulled out the bloody knife and started to swing again. But Jacob Tyler, a guard who had only worked for the bureau for six months, tackled the knife-wielding convict, knocking him to the floor. Other guards quickly overpowered him.

"You got me, you got me!" he yelled as he was being handcuffed and jerked to his feet. Other guards were standing over the black inmate, who lay clutching his chest. Blood poured from the wound.

"We have to live with these black motherfuckers, but we don't have to take their shit!" the white convict yelled as he was being led from the room. "I'm feeling fine! Why don't you ask that fucking nigger how he feels?"

Little turned back to his salad, Bowles took a drink of coffee, and prison officials resumed standing mainline. Over the years, the bureau had learned that it was better to continue on as if nothing had happened after such incidents rather than send everyone to their cells. None of the convicts who watched the stabbing had taken part in it; therefore locking them up would seem unjust punishment to them and only spark more violence. The attack would be handled through the normal procedures. No special searches for weapons would be done.

Within ten minutes of the stabbing, orderlies had mopped the blood off the floor and everything in the mess hall was back to normal.

PART THREE

The first year, a guard can't do enough for an inmate.
The second year, a guard can't do enough to a convict.

AN OLD PRISON SAYING

CHAPTER
TWENTY-EIGHT

THE LIEUTENANT'S OFFICE

"Let's do it, gentlemen," Steve Lacy, the head of the Hot House's shakedown crew, said as he opened the door to a cell in B cellhouse and led two of his men inside. Two inmates lived in the cell, but only one was there, asleep in the bottom bunk.

"Shakedown," Lacy announced.

"Oh man," the inmate grumbled, still groggy. "Why you always picking on us? We ain't got nothin'."

"Take a walk," Lacy ordered.

The inmate got out of bed, slipped on some pants, and shuffled outside.

Lacy and his crew, two guards whom he had nicknamed Foreskin and Peckerhead, began searching under the bunk bed, looking through books on the cell's only shelf, peering underneath the sink and behind the mirror. It was their job to search cells at random every day for contraband.

"They don't allow these in here anymore," said Foreskin, who had discovered several photographs of a woman clad only in panties in one of the inmate's photo albums. He slipped one of the pictures from its plastic cover.

"Hey, check this out," he said, holding up the photograph.

Lacy and Peckerhead glanced at the snapshot, which showed a woman with her hands cupped under her breasts.

" 'My tits miss your lips!' Honest to God, that's what she's written on the back," Foreskin said.

"Must be his girlfriend," said Peckerhead.

"Yeah," quipped Foreskin, "his wife's probably the fat broad with clothes on in these other pictures." The two guards laughed.

"The bureau doesn't allow naked pictures like that anymore," Foreskin repeated, "but since he got them before the rule change, we won't take them."

"Here's something," Peckerhead said, tossing Lacy a playing card with numbers written on the edge. "Got another," he added, this time producing a matchbook with numbers written inside.

"Here's the best," Peckerhead said a few minutes later, handing Lacy a printed form about four inches long and one inch wide. The words "Medication—Saturdays" were printed at the top of it.

"Gambling slips," Lacy explained. "The printed one was done by some shithead known by the nickname Medication. He pays off on Saturdays. Inmates print these slips in the print shop when they're supposed to be printing government forms."

"Wanta bust him?" Peckerhead asked.

"Naw, but we'll let him know we found his toys," Lacy replied, tossing the slips onto the inmate's locker in plain sight.

Lacy took a pencil-size screwdriver from his shirt pocket and ran the tip over the metal lip above the cell door. "Never wanna put your fingers anywhere you can't see when searching," he explained. Some inmates set booby traps. They tape razor blades along the edge of a doorframe hoping that a guard will run his fingers along the edge. "Never taste anything, either," he advised. Once a guard found a small packet of white powder, suspected narcotics, and tasted some. It was caustic toilet-bowl cleaner.

The two inmates who lived in the cell had collected several clear plastic squeeze bottles, each shaped like a bear wearing a pointed dunce hat. They had contained honey and were sold by the prison commissary, but they were empty now.

"Some shitheads fill these bottles with water and then stick 'em in their dicks," Lacy said. "They figure they can beat a urine test if they squirt water up into their bladders. That way, they think all they're gonna pee is water. But it don't work. They can't get all traces of the drugs out and we still catch 'em.

"I hope no one tells the shitheads that, though," Lacy added.

He tossed the bottles into the trash after cutting holes in each with his pocketknife so it couldn't be used.

Just then Lacy got a call on his portable radio telling him that a telephone call was being transferred to the shakedown office. Lacy hurried there. An FBI agent in Louisiana wanted information about an inmate who had been paroled from Leavenworth a few weeks earlier and was now a suspect in several bank robberies.

"That shithead ran with the Georgia Boys in here," Lacy said, but the agent didn't understand Lacy's prison lingo and Lacy had to explain that the Georgia Boys were a prison gang.

"Let me see what I can find for you," he told him. Then Lacy headed for a cell in A cellhouse.

"I got maybe ten minutes before the shithead who lives here gets off work in prison industries and comes back to his cell," he explained. "He's a member of the Georgia Boys."

Lacy pulled a cardboard box from under the bunk, thumbed through several papers, and spotted an address book. He opened his shirt and slipped the book inside. Searching further, he examined the inmate's photograph album.

"Well, my oh my, what do we have here?" he said, removing a five-by-seven-inch picture that showed several inmates standing with their arms on one another's shoulders. It had been taken in the prison recreation room, where convicts often posed with their buddies for souvenir photographs. "I do believe this one shithead," Lacy said, pointing to one of the inmates in the picture, "is the bank robber the FBI is looking for." He slipped the picture inside his shirt next to the address book, shoved the cardboard box back under the bunk, and hurried out of the cell to a copying machine located in the hallway near the lieutenant's office. By the time he had copied half of the address book, he could hear the noise of convicts filing into center hallway from prison industries. Their workday was over and they were returning to their cells for the four o'clock count. Lacy was running out of time. There was nothing illegal in copying the address book and photograph, he said, but he didn't want the inmate to know what he was doing. Lacy figured the guy would tip off his bank-robbing pal.

As soon as the copying machine spewed out the last page, he tucked the book and photograph back into his shirt and walked briskly back to A cellhouse. The Georgia Boy had not yet returned, but other inmates standing on the tier saw Lacy go into the cell and he knew that they would tell its occupant as soon as he entered the cellblock. Lacy returned the address book and photograph to the cardboard box and slid it under the bunk. He bent over the desk in the cell and began rearranging the items on it so the convict would think he had searched the desk, not the box under the bed.

Lacy stepped from the cell just as the inmate came walking up the tier. They passed without speaking or making eye contact. Neither acknowledged the other's existence.

Back in the shakedown office, Lacy read the photocopied pages of the address book and then reached for his telephone. The robbery suspect's home address wasn't listed in the book, he told the Louisiana FBI agent, but there was a woman's name and address and she was identified in parentheses as the bank robbery suspect's girlfriend. "Find her and you'll probably find him," he said, reading off the street address. Lacy also told the agent that he would mail him a copy of the photograph taken from the cell.

"This is all a big game," Lacy said as he put down the receiver. "They try to beat us and we try to beat them. Sometimes the shitheads win and sometimes the good guys win." Looking down at his copy of the address book, Lacy added, "Today, the good guys won."

CHAPTER
TWENTY-NINE

WILLIAM SLACK, JR.

Lieutenant Bill Slack, Jr., didn't want to be placed in charge of the Cuban units. He liked working as operations lieutenant, and everyone knew that overseeing the Cubans was a thankless and nerve-racking job. Word had also spread through the prison that Warden Matthews had called for an investigation of suspected brutality in the Cuban cellhouse, which made the job even less appealing, particularly to Slack. The last thing he needed was to be linked to a messy brutality case.

Slack couldn't prove it, but he was certain that he had been blacklisted by the bureau for the last five years. Slack had advanced quickly when he joined the bureau as a guard in 1971, but the promotions had stopped in 1983, and Slack knew why. It was his father.

William D. Slack, Sr., had been a lieutenant at the federal prison in Petersburg, Virginia, just south of Washington, D.C., when black gangs from New York City and Washington clashed in the prison dining room on Christmas Day in 1982. Gregory J. Gunter, a thirty-one-year-old guard, had been trapped between the warring gangs and stabbed to death. Two days later, the senior Slack was responsible for getting the gang members out of their cells and ready to be moved to other prisons. Two guards under his command began manhandling inmates in retaliation for the murder of Gunter. One sprayed tear gas on a shirt and stuffed it into a belligerent inmate's mouth; another kicked a naked inmate in the chest.

Over the years, there had always been an understanding that if an inmate attacked a guard, that inmate would later receive "an ass-whipping." But Bureau Director Norman Carlson didn't believe in vigilante justice. "If staff used appropriate force, I backed them to the hilt," he said later, "but if they used it inappropriately and simply thumped inmates, I did the best I could to get them fired and prosecuted. I felt the message had to get out loud and clear that this was not the way we were going to operate."

When Carlson heard about the brutality at Petersburg, he asked the FBI to investigate and encouraged the Justice Department to prosecute. Two guards, and Slack as their supervisor, were indicted.

The senior Slack had worked at the Hot House before moving to Petersburg, and his friends were outraged when they heard that he was going to be tried for permitting what many guards considered had been the proper thing to do. "My God," a veteran Leavenworth guard recalled, "this wasn't some case of a guard beating up an inmate on a whim. These bastards had killed a guard, and in the old days they would have been thankful just to get off with having their asses whipped."

The fact that Carlson investigated the Petersburg incident so infuriated some old-time guards that one year later, when Silverstein and Fountain murdered Officers Clutts and Hoffman in Marion, they unfairly blamed Carlson for the deaths. "Thanks to Carlson, every inmate knew there wasn't a damn thing we could do if they attacked us," said one disgruntled veteran. "He made it so the inmates had more rights than we did."

A U.S. district court judge found the senior Slack guilty of violating the inmates' civil rights by taking part in a conspiracy to punish inmates for the murder of Officer Gunter. The judge said Slack also attempted to keep the brutality from being exposed. Slack was sentenced to five years in prison, but all but four months were suspended.

Bill Slack, Jr., had been devastated by his father's conviction and prison sentence. "My dad always did everything the bureau asked of him," he recalled. "The bureau was his life, and then suddenly, because of that one incident, all those years of service and dedication didn't seem to matter. It didn't seem fair."

When Slack was first indicted, the staff at the Hot House rallied around his family and raised money for his defense. But after he was found guilty, the support waned. Bill Slack wanted to resign, but his father talked him out of it. "My dad told me, 'This has ruined my life; if it ruins yours, that will hurt me even more,' so I stayed on."

On the day his father was taken to prison, a fellow guard brought Slack a teletype that showed which camp his father had been sent to. "I was furious," Bill Slack recalled. "I couldn't believe that my father was an inmate."

Slack began looking at convicts at the Hot House differently. "I'd see how an officer treats an inmate and I'd ask myself, 'If that were my father, would I want him treated that way?' I began to realize that sometimes there were better ways to solve a problem than by simply sending an inmate to the Hole."

Slack soon found himself being passed over for promotions and being viewed by some coworkers with suspicion. At one point, he called a friend in the bureau's headquarters and asked why the promotions had stopped. The Slack name, he was told, was synonymous with the Petersburg incident. Over the years, other guards had been fired for brutality and a handful had even been prosecuted, but his father was the first lieutenant ever sent to prison for *not* stopping brutality done in retaliation for the *murder* of a guard. His father's case had become an unofficial watershed within the bureau. From that point on, guards knew that brutality was illegal regardless of the provocation. Carlson had made his point, but in the process the Slack name had been permanently linked with misconduct. "No one wanted to risk promoting a Slack," Bill Slack recalled. "I was a reminder, an embarrassment."

Once again Slack thought about quitting, but decided against it. Later, he would jokingly recall that one of his relatives had once boxed an exhibition match in the Boston Garden against heavyweight champion John L. Sullivan to raise money for a charity. "He wasn't a good enough boxer to tie Sullivan's shoes," Slack recalled, "but he considered it an honor to step into that ring and he never did let Sullivan knock him down. He just took the licking and kept coming back for more." The comparison, Slack decided, fit.

Born and raised in Worcester, Massachusetts, Slack had

grown up tough. When he was seven, he joined a local gang of white Catholic boys. "In our neighborhood, you either joined a gang or everyone wanted to fight you," he recalled. He was frequently in fights, and whenever he came home with a black eye, his father marched him into the basement and they put on the gloves. "He'd really lay it on me. 'I know what you did wrong,' he'd say, and then *pow*, he'd hit me with his left," Slack recalled. "He would really whip me good, but I don't believe he did it out of anger. He had grown up in the same type of neighborhood, and he didn't want me to go out there and be a bad-ass, but he knew that if a boy in our neighborhood didn't defend himself, everyone would pick on him and beat him up, and he didn't want that for his son."

Slack joined the Marine Corps after high school and was sent to Vietnam as a radioman. When he was discharged in October 1970, he returned to Lewisburg, Pennsylvania, where his father had gone to work as a prison guard. The younger Slack joined the bureau too and discovered that the fact his father was a guard didn't mean he was treated any better than other new hires. "In those days, no one trusted you until you proved that you weren't a coward or a snitch," said Slack. "The older officers used to send you down to ask the captain for a piece of equipment that didn't exist. After the captain chewed your ass for being so stupid, he'd casually ask, 'Hey, who put you up to this?' and if you told, everyone knew you were a rat and couldn't be trusted."

Like most other penitentiaries, Lewisburg had its own version of what is known in the bureau as the "acid test." Whenever an inmate refused to come out of his cell, the old-timers would make certain that a new guard went through the door first. The older guards would wait for a few minutes before coming to the rescue. They wanted to see how the new guard reacted to violence.

"There was a sense of brotherhood among the staff, and they didn't let just anyone into their group because they knew that someday their life might depend on you and they didn't want anyone behind them who was going to run away or was going to rat on them," said Slack.

Slack was finally accepted after he grabbed an inmate who was swinging a knife at another convict. Another guard tackled the convict's unarmed opponent. But when the operations lieutenant wrote up his report, the guards' roles were reversed. "The report said this other guy had grabbed the inmate with the knife, not me. He had seven years' experience and the lieutenant wanted him to get the promotion." Slack didn't complain.

"When new officers come into prison they are given a rule book, but they are really educated by their peers," said Slack, "and the same is true for inmates. Most hook up with someone and find out the unwritten rules—where to eat in the dining room, who's a snitch, who they can trust. We are both caught in the same world where there are rules and then there are *rules*."

What Slack tried to do, especially after his father's conviction, was not to worry about which set of rules to adhere to, but to treat inmates with compassion and common sense.

"I am almost ashamed to say it in public, but the key to being a good correctional officer is having a caring attitude. Now that sounds to most staff here as being weak and not very macho," Slack said. "It sounds like you are giving in to the inmates—or at least, that is how the staff interprets it, anyway—but it is not the same at all.

"Our job is to be professional and get the job done, and the best way to do that is by letting your conscience be your guide, not by always following this regulation or that procedure. If an inmate hasn't had a change of underwear in two weeks, you should care enough to get him a change of underwear. If he hasn't had a shower in a week, you should care enough to get him a shower. You shouldn't have to wait for someone to tell you to do that or have some regulation tell you."

Slack's attitude was not always appreciated by others, particularly those who were sticklers for regulations. Once while escorting an inmate to a federal courthouse for a trial outside Leavenworth, Slack drove through the drive-in lane of a fast-food restaurant and told the prisoner to order whatever he wanted.

"I told him that I'd treat him to Burger King if he didn't give us any shit," Slack explained to the guard with him. But the guard later complained, because bureau regulations only allowed inmates to have something to eat if they were being transported during regular mealtimes and were traveling a specific number of miles outside the prison. When Slack was asked by his superiors why he had bought the inmate lunch, Slack replied, "Because the inmate was hungry."

"To you and me, eating at Burger King isn't a big deal," Slack said, recalling the incident. "But to a guy who's been locked up for ten or fifteen years, it's a real treat. It makes them feel like they are still part of the outside world."

Slack also wanted to make a point. "Some U.S. marshals and other lieutenants pull a cheap trick on inmates during these outside trips by telling an inmate that he'll get fed when he gets to prison. Only when the inmate finally gets there, he finds that the kitchen is closed and he's out a meal. Meanwhile, the marshal pockets the money that he should have spent feeding the inmate. It's not right, and I want inmates to know I don't play that game." Slack's supervisors decided to forget about the Burger King incident.

Neither Warden Matthews nor Associate Warden Connor gave Slack a choice about overseeing the Cuban units. Lieutenant Monty Watkins would be his second-in-command. They told Slack that he would take charge of the Cubans on September 20.

Slack knew that the guards' morale in the Cuban cellblocks was miserable and that the detainees were more raucous than ever. He didn't know how much time he would have to familiarize himself with the Cubans and figure out how to improve things. As it turned out, he didn't get any time. Late in the afternoon that Slack took charge, the Cubans in C cellhouse rioted.

CHAPTER THIRTY

THE CUBANS

The riot in C cellhouse began shortly after five P.M. as guards served the Cubans their evening meal. Each white Styrofoam container pushed through the cell bars contained a sandwich made of two pieces of white bread with a mixture of chopped ham and mayonnaise inside. There were potato chips and a piece of fruit. One of the Cubans complained about the meal. Another joined him, and soon it seemed as if all 257 Cubans in the cellhouse were screaming and throwing their food out onto the tier. Ham spread, bread, chips, and fruit were splattered against the floor and walls.

"When they ran out of food to throw, they began throwing feces and urine," the Hot House's newly arrived captain, David Ham, explained, "and when they made it so we couldn't do our job, it was time for a show of force and we moved in."

Associate Warden Lee Connor ordered Lieutenant Monty Watkins and his SORT team to go from cell to cell and handcuff every Cuban in the cellhouse. Anyone who refused to cuff up would be chained in a four-point position to a bed. There would be no exceptions, and Watkins was told to ask each inmate only once to comply. SORT began a methodical march through the cellblock. The Cubans had seen SORT back in June when they had first attempted to riot. The team's actions now didn't intimidate them—at first. But as the SORT team moved along the tier, the detainees saw the guards were carrying a new piece of equipment—black riot batons. The clubs were three feet long and had a shiny chrome ball the size of a marble attached to their ends. These metal balls had a humane purpose, according to the manufacturer. If a guard jabbed an inmate in the rib cage, the ball would slide off the rib without breaking the bone and would instead tear the intercostal muscle, causing intense pain but no permanent damage. The clubs were something new for the Cubans to think about.

By the time the SORT team had put six Cubans into the four-point position, the cellhouse began to quiet down. By midnight, Cuban orderlies had cleaned the tiers, and the only sign that there had been trouble was the fact that six inmates were still chained to their beds.

Lieutenant Bill Slack had watched the disturbance, but it had been Connor who had called the shots. The next morning, Warden Matthews toured the cellblock with Slack and told the lieutenant he could have all the manpower and whatever extra supplies that he needed to keep the Cubans under control. Matthews was as determined as he had been when the Cubans first arrived to make certain they did not riot. After Matthews left, Slack went on another tour of his own. With an interpreter at his side, Slack stopped at each cell, introduced himself as the new lieutenant in charge, and then, as his guards watched in amazement, asked the Cubans for their help.

"I need you to be patient and give me a chance to improve things," Slack said. "You got to give me some time. You got to realize if you as an individual or a member of a group set fire or tear this place up, then our money and time will go toward repairs rather than increasing things I want to do for you."

No other lieutenant had ever introduced himself to the Cubans or asked for their cooperation. Most of the Cubans didn't respond, but a few demanded to know what Slack planned to do for them.

"Better food and more of it," Slack told two Cubans in one cell. "I got some ideas about televisions too, but I can't do any of it if you don't give me some time." And then Slack said something that both his own guards and the Cubans found astounding.

"You got to trust me," he told the Cubans. "I'll never lie to you. My word is good, and I expect you to keep your word, too."

Several hours later, after he finished talking to every Cuban in the cellhouse Slack left for a meeting with Connor. "We got to have a special meal tonight for the Cubans," he explained. "I gave them my word." Slack had been forced to take the Cuban-unit job. He had been promised whatever manpower and money he needed to keep the Cubans in line. But he didn't want more guards or more money. He wanted better food, and by personally promising the Cubans that they would get better food, Slack had put his bosses—as they say in prison—"on front street." If Matthews and Connor wanted Slack to succeed, it was up to them to cajole the food administrator into bettering his performance. When the guards delivered the evening meal that night, it arrived in the same Styrofoam containers as always, but when the Cubans opened them, they found two sandwiches, crackers, a candy bar, a piece of chicken, and an apple. There was nearly twice as much to eat as the meal served the day before, and all of it was fresh. The next morning, Slack once again went by each cell personally and asked about the meal. "I kept my word," he told each Cuban. "Now you keep yours. I need more time. You need to be patient and things will get better." In a single day, Bill Slack managed to accomplish what no other lieutenant had been able to do during the entire ten months that the Cubans had been at the Hot House. He got the detainees to cooperate with him. While there would be isolated incidents during the next few weeks, there were no group demonstrations and for the first time the mood within C cellhouse began to improve. The Cubans couldn't quite figure out Slack, and neither could many of the guards.

Slack knew that one meal wasn't going to appease the Cubans for long or make them trust him. He had to move quickly or his negotiated truce would collapse. He continued to push for better food. "If all a guy has to look forward to every day is a meal," Slack explained, "he gets really upset when it is not good or it's not served on time." Slack did some checking and discovered that the Cubans were generally fed meals made from whatever food was left over from the meals served the main prison population. If the American convicts ate hamburgers on Wednesday, the Cubans got meat loaf on Thursday. Slack also discovered that most of the meals were served late, and that when the Cubans did get food prepared especially for them, it was generally something the American prisoners would have refused. An example: sauerkraut, a dish that few Cubans had tasted and fewer ate. Slack began to complain—a move that outraged the food administrator. But Slack didn't care. He pressured his bosses for better food and he got it. For the next several weeks, Slack personally tasted each meal, and he called the kitchen every day, half an hour before it was time for the Cubans to be fed, just to make certain that everything was on schedule. Only once did Slack catch the kitchen trying to serve the Cubans a meal that didn't meet his standards. Slack rejected it and Connor and Matthews backed him up.

Once the food situation was improved, Slack turned his attention to finding ways to keep the Cubans busy. He asked Matthews for permission to buy several color televisions. The cellhouse already had a few television sets, but they were in the recreation cages where the Cubans were allowed one hour of exercise per day. Most of them never got to watch television for a full hour, because they were being moved to and from their cells during that period. The hour limit also made it impossible for them to watch a complete movie or sports program. Slack suggested that additional television sets be purchased and mounted on the cellhouse walls in strategic positions so that the Cubans could watch them from their cells. He asked for money to buy several video players so he could show Spanish-language movies rather than English ones. Matthews approved the requests.

Next Slack turned his attention to personal telephone calls. An inmate never knew when he would be able to make his once-a-month telephone call, because he couldn't be certain when a telephone would be brought to his cell. It depended on how busy the guards were and how many other inmates were waiting. When the inmate finally got the phone, he was given time to dial only one number. If no one answered, he was out of luck. Slack set up a schedule and kept a list of inmates whose calls didn't get through, so that they could place a second call.

What Slack was doing was not extraordinary. Improving the meals, buying televisions, making certain each inmate got a telephone call were simple ideas. Still, no one before him had tried them. He came up with the changes, he said, by simply putting himself in the Cubans' shoes. "If I were a detainee, I'd be pissed off too," Slack said. "Some of these men have been locked up for eight or nine years for small things they did in Miami and they are caught in a bunch of red tape and politics." This didn't mean that the detainees weren't dangerous. Slack considered the Cuban units to be the most threatening cellblocks in the prison for guards. But in one sense, what the Cubans had done on the streets, and whether or not they rioted in Oakdale and Atlanta, didn't matter. "The bottom line is that if you treat these men like animals, they will definitely act like animals and we will all pay the price. If you treat them like men, maybe, just maybe, they will respond like men."

Slack soon discovered that Cubans in C cellhouse were telling Cubans in D cellhouse about him, but he wasn't certain how, because detainees were prohibited from corresponding with one another. He found out that the Cubans were beating the prohibition by putting a fictitious address on the envelope and writing the name of the person that they actually wanted the letter sent to in the space reserved for the return address. When the post office returned the letter to Leavenworth marked ADDRESS UNKNOWN, it was automatically delivered to the Cuban in D cellhouse.

Slack began improving working conditions for the guards too. Some had been inside the Cuban units ever since the detainees arrived. This included several who had worked for Shoats and who were now under suspicion of brutality. Slack suggested that one third of the guard force be replaced immediately, another third be moved out in three months, and the final third in six months. He suggested that no guard be allowed to work longer than one year in the Cuban units, including himself. "This is simply too intense and stressful."

After a few weeks, Slack made his most controversial decision. In the past, the Cubans had been placed in cells at random. No one had ever asked or cared whether they liked their cellmates. Each day as Slack walked the tiers, Cubans asked him for permission to move to different cells. Many of the Cubans were homosexuals, and Slack knew that some of the men were interested in changing cells because they wanted to be with their lovers. Others wanted to move in with their cousins, brothers, and friends. Slack decided to allow the Cubans to pick their own cellmates, but he required them to maintain several weeks of good conduct before he agreed to any changes and he then made both men promise that they would not fight if he put them together. Slack's decision to allow Cubans who were flagrant homosexuals to cell together outraged some guards. Behind his back, they called him a weak sister, and accused him of ignoring the bureau's regulations against homosexuality. Slack claimed he was being pragmatic, simply trying to make the Cubans understand that they were responsible for how they would be treated. If a Cuban followed the rules, he got extra privileges. If he didn't, he got nothing special.

An incident on September 24, four days after Slack took charge, dramatized the new attitude that Slack brought to C cellhouse. A guard asked him for permission to chain a Cuban to his bed because the detainee had refused a direct order. Slack decided to investigate. According to the guard, the Cuban had refused to cuff up and leave his cell so it could be searched for contraband. But the Cuban told Slack that he had been saving the granola bars served at mealtime and didn't want them taken away. He had thirteen bars, and he knew the guard would confiscate all but five of them, the maximum a detainee was supposed to keep in his cell. Slack looked at the Cuban. The detainee knew that if he disobeyed an order, he could be put in a four-point position, yet the granola bars meant so much to him that he was willing to risk it.

"Ask him if his cellmate has any granola bars," Slack told the interpreter.

"No," the interpreter replied. "His cellmate ate all of his granola bars when they were served with the meals."

"Okay," Slack said, "tell him to give five of the bars to his cellmate. Tell him he can keep five bars for himself. The other three he has to give away to another inmate or eat right now."

The interpreter relayed the suggestion to the anxious Cuban, who quickly agreed and began eating granola bars. The Cuban then stuck out his hands to be handcuffed, and thanked Slack. It seemed like a good compromise to Slack. But after he left, the guard who shackled the prisoner was irritated. "He shouldn't have negotiated. We should've four-pointed this prick. He let that Cuban beat us."

Sitting in his office later, after working fifteen straight hours, Slack wearily defended his solution. He was exhausted. For the past hour either the telephone or guards had been interrupting him repeatedly as he tried to complete a two-inch-high stack of paperwork before going home. "A few granola bars aren't worth a confrontation, at least not to me," he said. "It's not worth risking either the inmate or an officer getting hurt."

Lighting yet another cigarette, he continued: "Technically, yeah, we could have gone in there and chained him down. And sure, I'm certain his cellmate gave him back the five bars after we left, so he's still got too many granola bars in his cell. But what I did made sense, and it worked, and no one got hurt—and that's worth something, or at least, it should be worth something too."

CHAPTER
THIRTY-ONE

DALLAS SCOTT

As soon as Dallas Scott was assigned a cell at Marion, he began searching for some legal loophole that would help him overturn his 1976 conviction for bank robbery. He really didn't think he had much of a chance. He wasn't a lawyer, didn't have much education, and the trial had taken place more than a decade earlier. But none of that mattered. Scott needed to find something to occupy his time at Marion, something to give him some hope. Otherwise he would slowly go crazy being locked all day in a cell.

Life at Marion was designed to be monotonous, and it was. Scott's world consisted of fifty-one square feet of living space that came equipped with a mattress, toilet, locker, sink, mirror, small black-and-white television, and radio.

Scott got up each morning at six A.M. when breakfast was slipped through the bars. He ate, watched the morning news, and went back to bed until ten o'clock, when he did an hour of exercise and then ate lunch. He'd watch the afternoon movie shown on the prison's closed-circuit channel, and then turn off the television and work on his legal appeal. He refused to watch soap operas.

"Guys in here are crazy about their soap operas," Scott explained. "Some guys have watched them for years, and they get so caught up in them they won't come out of their cells when it's time for recreation 'cause they don't want to miss them."

Scott liked having a television, but he also considered it a trap. "It's a tool that they use to pacify you," he said. "You got to learn how to turn off that television or else you will sit all day in front of it and forget what prison is all about. You become a lamb, which is exactly what the administration wants."

Scott would turn the set on around dinnertime and watch the national news. He used to watch a game show before the news, but he stopped in protest when a black man appeared as a contestant.

At some point during the day, Scott would be released with seven other inmates to exercise outside his cell. On nice days, the group played basketball outdoors in a wire-enclosed cage. But sometimes Scott would use the time to take a shower or walk along the tier talking to other inmates through the bars of their cells.

Scott's return to Marion had been a family reunion of sorts. Gang members John Greschner and Ronnie Bruscino were still there, as were other inmates whom Scott had known for more than a decade. None of these inmates was well-known outside the bureau, certainly not like some of Marion's notorious prisoners such as John A. Walker, Jr., the head of a family spy ring that sold secrets for eighteen years to the KGB; Edwin Wilson, the CIA "Death Merchant" who supplied plastic explosives to Libyan terrorists; or Joseph Franklin, the Ku Klux Klansman convicted of killing two black men and suspected of at least thirteen other racist murders. Within the bureau, however, Scott and his crowd were considered much more trouble.

"Most inmates come into prison, follow the rules, do their time, get something out of it, and never come back," explained Marion's warden, Gary L. Henman. "But some inmates come in and actually form their own prison culture. These men refuse to conform or follow rules. They want to conduct business in here just like when they are on the streets. They want to steal, sell drugs, whatever, and they are very disruptive."

For some convicts, in a twisted sense, being housed in Marion was an honor. "When you're a kid," explained Greschner, who was sent to a reformatory when he was nine, "you got to have some sort of role model, and the baddest motherfuckers at the reformatory—the guys who tried to escape and didn't take any shit—those were the people I admired." When he was nineteen, Greschner was considered to be such a sophisticated criminal that he was sent by Minnesota officials to a state prison even though he was under twenty-one and therefore eligible for a youth facility. "I liked it. I felt totally comfortable in the environment. I was around older guys who I'd heard about for years and years, and they were like heroes to me." Now at age thirty-eight, Greschner was the convict that younger thugs looked up to.

Scott saw himself much the same way. "I know it sounds silly that some guy like me locked in a cell is a role model, but the reason these youngsters see me or Tommy Silverstein as a role model is because we stick by certain principles. I always tell these youngsters about Tommy and try to make them understand that Tommy did something he had to do and we don't feel like he was wrong to do it. It's important for us and these younger kids to remember Tommy, because he's gonna be down a long, long time, and it's important that we keep him in our thoughts."

Each man had to find his own way to beat the drudgery of Marion. Some simply slept as many as twenty hours per day. As the years inched by, it became harder and harder for long-term inmates to recall what being on the streets was like. The highest suicide rate in the bureau was among white men in their early twenties, and Scott was convinced that one reason was that they hadn't learned how to "do time." In order to survive Marion, a man had to learn this. Scott knew how and so did Greschner, who had spent a cumulative total of thirteen years locked in various Holes or in a cell at Marion. "To be healthy, you need to interact with other people, and when you lose that, when you are in isolation or locked up by yourself day after day, all you got is what you are carrying around in your own head," Greschner explained. "After a while you start losing the extra baggage. You learn you don't need all the things that society says you need to survive and be happy. Your world starts shrinking. The memories get old and you start losing your identity. Eventually you hit rock bottom, where it is just you and your own demons, and the isolation forces you to examine yourself, your fundamental foundation of who you really are.

"Some people get to that point and find there is nothing there, so they string themselves up. Others break and bail out. They flip over because they are weak and can't take it anymore. But some get down to rock bottom and discover who they are.

"For me," Greschner continued, "what I found was a hard, cold ball. I discovered that all I really needed to survive in this world is the will to live and a knife."

The best way to "do time," Scott and Greschner explained, was by "beating the man." Pour breakfast cereal in the sink in your cell, add water, and let it curdle for several days. It will become potent enough to get you drunk. You've just beat the man. Remove the thin steel wire from inside an eyeglass case and rub it against the bars. It will saw through them. You've just beat the man. Take the plastic wrap covering your food and roll it tight around a toothbrush. Heat it with matches until it becomes hard, and then spend several hours rubbing it against the floor, making its edges sharp. You've just made yourself a plastic knife and beat the man. All of these things had been done at Marion at one time or another, and just when guards were certain they had seen it all, convicts like Scott and Greschner would come up with proof that they hadn't. Greschner recently hid a piece of hacksaw blade up his nose. "This is the best fucking thing you have done in a long time, Greschner," a guard marveled when the blade was removed.

Beating the man was lesson number one. Lesson two was to feed off the hate. "Anything they do that doesn't kill you in prison, should make you stronger," Scott explained. "The more they try to break you, the more you want to beat them." Pure, unadulterated hate could sustain a man for years. Hate gave a convict a thirst for revenge and a will to survive, if for no other reason than simply to deny his captors the satisfaction of beating him. This was why the convicts were constantly belittling guards, Scott said. Even in prison, they had found someone to look down on. Every day was a contest of wills, a game of "them versus us," a challenge.

"I don't care what your track record is for the last twenty or thirty years, a man can wake up in the morning and, for whatever reason, throw in the towel and give up," said Scott. The opposite was just as true. Every day that an inmate survived in prison without breaking, he had won a silent victory. He had beat the man.

Armed with a dictionary, Scott began plowing through the yellowed transcript of his trial, reading each word, studying every objection made by the lawyers and the judge's rulings. Each morning, afternoon, and night, Scott scoured lawbooks.

Because much of what he read was lawyer gibberish, Scott frequently would look up each word's definition. He spent weeks going over and over his trial transcript, and when he finished, he was disheartened. He hadn't found any glaring errors.

And then Scott made an amazing discovery. One of the documents that he had obtained was the pre-sentence report prepared for the judge who had sentenced him. The report was written by a parole officer who had routinely outlined Scott's family history, cited his previous crimes, and recommended that Scott receive the maximum eighteen-year sentence. But buried in the report was a bit of information that Scott had never known. It was about the gun that was introduced at his trial as the weapon used during the crime.

Scott had been charged with robbing a bank on December 12, 1975, near his home in Sacramento. A lone gunman had walked into the bank, fired a pistol into the ceiling, and scooped the cash out of the tellers' cages. The police had stopped Scott a short time later while he was driving his truck, and had found a black-and-white shirt and .38 caliber revolver underneath the driver's seat. The bank robber had worn a black-and-white shirt, and a ballistics check showed that Scott's pistol was the same caliber as the one fired into the bank ceiling. Those two pieces of evidence had been enough to convince the jury at his March 1976 trial that he was guilty.

What Scott learned for the first time as he sat in his prison cell at Marion was that the Sacramento police had found someone else's fingerprints on the pistol.

Scott quickly realized that his attorney had made a critical error during the trial. The attorney had asked the police whether Scott's fingerprints were found on the gun, and the detective who testified said they were not. But the attorney had *not* asked whether someone else's fingerprints were found, and neither the detective nor the U.S. attorney had volunteered that information.

The pre-sentence report also revealed that the police had found several fingerprints inside the bank that they believed belonged to the gunman, yet "no similarities were found between these latent prints and fingerprints of Dallas Scott."

The fact that someone else's fingerprints were found on the gun was significant, Scott claimed, because he frequently loaned his truck to his friends, most of whom had criminal records. Had his attorney known about the fingerprints, he could have argued that someone besides Scott had borrowed the pickup, found the pistol under the front seat, and used it to rob the bank.

There was another tidbit of information in the record that Scott found interesting. The black-and-white shirt that was discovered in his truck had short sleeves. None of the bank tellers who testified at the trial had described the gunman as having tattoos, yet Scott's arms were covered with them, and in a short-sleeved shirt, they would have been easy to spot.

The trial transcript provided Scott with one more discovery. After the U.S. attorney introduced the gun as evidence, Scott's attorney had objected. He claimed the gun and shirt had been seized illegally because the police had searched the truck without a warrant. The judge heard the complaint, overruled it, and then adjourned the trial for the day because it was getting late. When Scott reached page 431 of the trial transcript, he realized that the court reporter had not transcribed his attorney's objection and the judge's ruling on it. That meant the official transcript was incomplete. "This was crucial," Scott claimed later, "because my appeal was handled by a different attorney, who had not been at my trial."

Scott felt optimistic. He believed he had found two reasons for a judge to set aside his conviction and order a new trial. If that happened, Scott figured the robbery case would most likely be dismissed. After all, the robbery had taken place in 1975 and Scott was certain that most of the witnesses wouldn't remember enough to testify against him at a new trial.

Scott began writing a "request for relief." In it, he claimed that federal prosecutors had failed to disclose evidence favorable to him (the fingerprints on the gun), that the official court transcript was incomplete (since his attorney's objection and the judge's ruling were missing), and that his attorneys had done an inadequate job of representing him.

Scott buttressed his request by painstakingly listing other legal precedents. "*See Brady v. Maryland, 373 U.S. 83,*" Scott wrote, and "*Bauman v. U.S. Ca (Ariz.) 1982, F2d. 565.*" To make certain that he hadn't missed any applicable cases, Scott added, "*See also the fourth and eighth amendments to the United States*

Constitution!" Before mailing his petition, Scott added a final
personal note to the judge. He didn't have any money, he explained, nor did he have the "experence to muddy clear waters
with wiley tricks." His only experience inside a courtroom was
as a defendant, but he had spent twenty-two years in prison
because he had been found guilty of breaking "the law." Now,
for the first time, he said, "the law" was on his side.

> My complaints here are serious and legitimate and
> are easily verifiable through any effort at all on the
> courts part. The petitioner is painfully aware that any
> court in the land could easly find a dozen way to subvert
> this petition, but trusts and prays this honorable court
> to weigh and judge these issues honestly, fairly and
> strickly on their own merits, then render a fair and
> honest decision.

Scott mailed his request to the appropriate court. If the
judge ruled in his favor, it would be the ultimate irony: a convict
legitimately beating the man at his own game with his own
rules.

CHAPTER
THIRTY-TWO

THE LIEUTENANT'S OFFICE

"Knife fight! Kitchen!"

Lieutenants Edward Pierce and Tracy Johns ran toward the kitchen when the alarm came over their portable radios. Johns had only been at the Hot House for a short time, replacing Shoats, and even though he came from Marion, Pierce wasn't certain how the novice lieutenant would react to a knife fight. Some staff members were reluctant to step in between two fighting inmates, especially if they had knives.

As the two lieutenants burst through the kitchen doors, Pierce noticed that there were at least six prison employees watching the fight and none had done anything to stop it. The onlookers were food stewards, not guards, which meant they were paid to supervise inmate cooks and help prepare the meals. But that didn't matter. Every male employee who worked inside the penitentiary was required by bureau regulations to react to emergencies and had been trained in how to stop fights. Every one of them. Later, when one of the stewards was asked why he hadn't tried to stop the brawl, he said, "Most of us have wives and kids or grandkids. You tell me: Are you going to risk your life by stepping in front of a knife when you have one lousy piece of shit trying to kill another lousy piece of shit?"

Lieutenant Pierce didn't feel that way. "It's my job to keep these assholes from killing each other, and I'll be damned if I'm going to end up in some federal court somewhere trying to

247

explain to a judge why I watched two inmates stab one another and didn't do anything to stop them."

Pierce had noticed something else as he entered the kitchen. Lieutenant Johns, longer-legged than Pierce, had passed him when they were racing to the fight, but when they reached the kitchen's double doors, Johns had slowed down.

"We hit the door at the same time," Pierce said, "and I wondered to myself, 'Hey, what's happening here?' So I put Johns to a test. I said to myself, 'Okay, let's see what you are made of,' and I intentionally went for the victim. That left the guy with the knife for Johns. I wanted to see if Johns had enough guts to do what was necessary."

Pierce knew both inmates. Drew McCabe, a stocky bank robber from Oklahoma, was swinging a large knife at a New Jersey crook named Nick Funicelli, who was unarmed and trying to block the blows with his arms. Blood spurted from at least a dozen cuts on Funicelli's hands, forearms, face, and chest.

"Put the weapon down!" Pierce screamed as he dashed past McCabe and tackled Funicelli, knocking him to the floor. Pierce shielded the inmate's body with his own.

McCabe lunged forward. Johns didn't hesitate. He grabbed McCabe from behind, wrapped his arms around his chest, and jerked them up, forcing McCabe to raise his hands over his head. Johns locked his hands behind McCabe's neck and fell to the floor, taking McCabe with him. As soon as they hit, the knife fell free and the food stewards rushed forward to help subdue McCabe.

McCabe was not injured and was taken to the Hole. But Funicelli was spitting up blood.

"I'm bleeding!" Funicelli screamed. "Why am I bleeding so much?"

"Hey, the medical staff is the only one who can tell you that!" replied Pierce, as he led Funicelli to the hospital.

"This guy had blood squirting out of every hole in his body," Pierce recalled. "I got his blood all over my ears, shirt, pants, forehead, tie, tie tack, I mean, he was cut from asshole to appetite."

A few hours later when Pierce was typing his report about the fight, he glanced at McCabe's record and noticed that he only had four more months of his six-year prison sentence to serve.

"This asshole was practically out the front door," Pierce said. Why had McCabe risked getting more time in prison when he was about to be released?

Over in the Hole, McCabe later explained that he had been forced to stab Funicelli. The trouble began three days earlier, he said, when an inmate rushed into his cell and said, "Hey, Funicelli says you're a rat. He says you snitch to the cops to keep from going to the Hole. What are you gonna do about it?"

"What the fuck business is it of yours?" McCabe replied. "Keep your fucking nose out of it."

But he was worried. "If I don't do nothing, Funicelli is gonna keep telling everyone I'm a rat, and guys are gonna believe him, 'cause they're gonna say, 'McCabe must be a snitch or else he'd do something to shut Funicelli up.' "

McCabe said he tried to resolve the problem by asking a mutual friend to talk to Funicelli. "I wanted to know if Funicelli was willing to apologize. He was drunk when he said it, you know, and probably just shooting off his mouth. I figured it won't be no big deal this way, if he apologizes. But no, when my friend asks Funicelli, the dumb motherfucker repeats it. He calls me a snitch again.

"I couldn't believe the son of a bitch was doing this," McCabe continued, "putting me in this sort of spot, 'cause I'm about to go home. But I got no choice now. You gotta understand that in here, you can't let nothing slide. It don't matter if you are ten years or ten minutes away from going home. If I let Funicelli get over on me, let him call me a rat, then all sorts of guys would've moved on me. I'd have guys telling me to bring 'em back ice cream cones from the commissary, telling me to do their laundry, and then bending me over and fucking me, 'cause word would go out: 'Hey, McCabe won't fight 'cause he's about to go home.'

"I know these guys in here, and a lot of them is okay, but some are animals, and I mean dirty, stinking, rotten, filthy scum of the earth, and they'll make your life one fucking long nightmare if you ain't willing to draw blood. So you see, I didn't really have a choice. I had to stab him."

McCabe's explanation and rationalization was of no concern to Pierce. "It's an FBI matter now," he said. Besides typing his report, Pierce filled out another piece of paper. It was a recommendation to the bureau's regional office that Johns receive a $500 cash bonus for risking his life while on duty.

"Johns, why, he did me proud," Pierce explained. "He showed he had what it takes to be a Leavenworth lieutenant."

CHAPTER
THIRTY-THREE

CARL BOWLES AND THOMAS LITTLE

Norman Bucklew was drunk and itching for a fight when he slid into a metal folding chair in the television room on the fifth floor of A cellhouse. It was seven P.M., and Thomas Little had just turned the channel to *America's Most Wanted*, a weekly program that reenacted actual crimes and asked viewers to call a toll-free number if they could help solve them.

Little had asked the other ten convicts in the room if they objected to his tuning in the show. None had—but that was before Bucklew came in.

"This is a fucking snitch program," Bucklew bellowed.

No one in the room reacted.

"Oh, looky, looky, there's the rat number on the screen to call," Bucklew continued. "Everyone grab a pencil and write down the rat number."

Two or three inmates, sensing trouble, left.

"Fucking show is turning everyone into goddamn snitches. Shouldn't be watching this motherfucker."

An inmate sitting near Bucklew turned toward him. "You calling me a rat?" he asked angrily. " 'Cause if you are, then we need to deal with it."

"I'm saying this is a fucking rat program," Bucklew replied, not backing down. "And we shouldn't be watching it. I'm not going to watch it."

Bucklew left the room.

The next morning, Carl Bowles woke up angry.

251

"What fucking right does Bucklew have to tell me what I can and can't watch on television?" he asked Little.

"C'mon, Carl, he was drunk and this ain't worth the trouble," Little replied.

For the rest of that morning, Bowles and Little avoided Bucklew, but that afternoon it was Little's turn to get upset. He and a few other inmates went into the television room to watch the afternoon movie, but Bucklew had turned the channel to MTV, and even though he wasn't in the room, no one wanted to risk changing the channel. They were afraid of him.

Each floor of A cellhouse had two television rooms and each was large enough to accommodate forty inmates. According to bureau policy, inmates were supposed to select programs based on a vote of the men who wanted to watch television. But this democratic process simply didn't work. All the television rooms in the cellhouse were controlled by blacks except for the one on the fifth floor used by Bowles, Little, and Bucklew. No votes were taken in it; instead inmates wrote down their preferences on a sheet of paper hanging near the television. On this particular afternoon, Bucklew had claimed the afternoon time slot as his.

After several minutes of grumbling, Little marched up to the sign-up list and wrote the word VOTE across the entire page.

"Anyone who thinks they are running this television room is wrong," he declared. "You can tell 'em to stick it in their ass. This is a public room." Then he went to tell Bowles what he had done.

Within the hour, Bucklew confronted Little and Bowles in the television room.

"Carl," Bucklew began, "I've known you for years and I got all the respect in the world for you and I don't disrespect you and I don't mean to ever disrespect you."

Then he turned and faced Little. "But you," Bucklew said, his voice rising in anger, "you I don't know, and you're a fucking asshole."

Having "disrespected" Little to his face, Bucklew stepped outside the television room and waited for Little to join him. But it was Carl Bowles who came through the door.

"Why did you call Tom an asshole?" Bowles asked calmly.

"Because he spoke behind my back," Bucklew replied.

"As long as I've been around Tom, and as much as I've been

around him, I've never heard Tom say nothing behind your back," said Bowles, "and he won't say nothing behind your back that he won't say to your face."

"Then why ain't he out here right now?" Bucklew demanded.

"'Cause I told him not to come out."

"Well, the only reason, and I mean the only reason why I'm letting this ride is out of respect to you," Bucklew said. "The kid I don't respect."

This is how Bowles later recalled his reaction. "I told him, 'Hey, don't cut Tom any room because of me. Tom catches what he catches. If he disrespects you, then you take it to him and deal with it. I got no problem with an ass-kicking, but I ain't gonna stand by and let you kill my friend over a fucking television show. That's stupid for both of you. It's not a killing offense. An ass-whipping, sure, but a killing over a television show? It don't call for no killing.'"

Both men went to their cells.

Although Bowles had promised that he wouldn't interfere, both he and Bucklew knew that Bowles probably would have no choice but to step in if Bucklew attacked Little. This was because of the nature of the Hot House. While Bowles and Little insisted that they were only friends, other inmates looked upon Bowles as Little's guardian. If Bowles stood by and watched Bucklew beat Little, other inmates would think that Bowles was afraid of Bucklew. They would begin insulting him as well as Little. The code required that Bowles would have to kill Bucklew if he raised his hand against Little. Bucklew understood all these consequences. He would have to kill Bowles before he could touch Little.

A few hours after the confrontation in the television room, Little knocked on Bucklew's cell door and quietly asked to come inside. He had come, he said, because Bowles had sent him to deal with the problem.

This is how Bucklew later recalled the conversation. "Listen, kid," Bucklew began, "you got no respect coming from me, 'cause you're riding on Carl. If it weren't for Carl, you'd have thirty niggers lining up to fuck you."

Little tried to turn the conversation to the television room, but Bucklew refused.

"You're a punk," said Bucklew. "I talk to Carl, not you."

He then dismissed Little.

For the next several days, Bucklew and Bowles watched each other. Each was waiting for the other to make a move. In the Hot House, no one fought by the Queensberry Rules, especially convicted killers such as Bucklew and Bowles. "In here, there's no 'Put up your dukes' bullshit," an inmate explained. "When guys like a Bucklew or a Bowles get into a fight with another inmate, it only lasts a few seconds, 'cause they are going to rip out a guy's windpipe with their first blow and rip off his nuts with their second."

For his part, Little stayed close to Bowles. In fact, he never left his sight. All of this was going on, of course, without the guards having any idea that the two murderers were facing off against each other.

And then fate intervened. Late one night, a guard caught Bucklew's winemaking partner drinking in his cell. As Bucklew watched, the guard hustled the inmate down the tier toward the Hole. Bucklew knew that his friend had hidden a large plastic container of hooch in his cell and he wanted to get it before the guard came back. But Bucklew needed a "jigger," someone to watch for the guard. The only white inmates available were Bowles and Little. Bucklew asked them to help and they agreed.

"Helping him had nothing to do with our disagreement," Little later recalled. "I hoped he'd drop dead, but this was a convict-versus-police thing with the wine and I wasn't going to do anything to get him busted."

No one mentioned the television-room incident again. Years earlier, such a peaceful standoff would have been unlikely. But neither Bowles nor Bucklew wanted to be sent to Marion, and both realized that a fight between them could only end with one of them dead.

But Bowles also understood that Little's trouble with Bucklew was a prologue to what was to come, and in a sense, it was his fault. He had taught Little that the only way a convict got respect in prison was by being willing to kill. Like a child taking his first step, Little was now beginning to test Bowles's theory. He emulated Bowles. But there was a major difference between the teacher and student: no one questioned that Bowles was a killer, but Little had never killed anyone and the other inmates still saw him as Bowles's sissy.

"Tom ain't no coward and he ain't no sissy," Bowles said. "People are misjudging him, but I don't want him put in a situation where he is going to have to grab a mop wringer and kill someone in here just to prove himself. He don't need to get himself a life beef to show he's a man. The best thing to do is get Tom transferred."

By the fall of 1988, Bowles had received replies from the jailers, attorneys, and the judge in Florida familiar with Little's case. All of the letters showed that Little had never been charged with or convicted of escaping from jail. Clearly, the bureau had made a mistake sending him to the Hot House. Bowles had taken the evidence to Little's case manager and to his prison counselor, and both had agreed to recommend that Little be transferred to a lower-security prison. Every ninety days, inmates were reviewed by a unit team that noted their progress or lack of it. Little's team consisted of his case manager, his prison counselor, and the A cellhouse manager, Eddie Geouge. Bowles figured the deck was stacked in Little's favor and he would get his transfer. But when Little came out of the five-minute session, he was upset. Geouge had nixed the move.

Originally, Little had been told that he would have to spend five years in Leavenworth. After studying the letters that Bowles had collected for Little, Geouge was willing to reduce Little's stay to two years. But that was it. No immediate transfer.

Geouge later explained that he didn't like the way Bowles was orchestrating Little's affairs. "It's dangerous to allow one inmate to run another inmate's life in here," Geouge said, "and that was what Bowles was doing." Geouge said that Bowles was making Little into a replica of himself. "If that's what Little wants, to be a miniature Carl Bowles, then he belongs here, not a lower-level prison."

Part of the reason why Geouge was irritated at Bowles was because a few weeks earlier, Bowles had asked for permission to meet Little's mother. "This woman was coming to visit her son, and she wanted to know why her son was living in a cell with a convicted murderer who had spent twenty-three years in prison," Geouge recalled, "and Bowles wanted to be the one to explain it to her. We don't let inmates explain things." Geouge had rejected Bowles's request.

Little's mother wasn't the only person curious about her

son's relationship with Bowles. Other convicts were grumbling, particularly homosexuals who were not allowed to share the same cells as their lovers. "Carl Bowles is dangerous, so the bureau is buying him off—letting him have a sissy to keep him entertained and out of trouble," one complained.

Warden Matthews had heard similar comments and he wasn't happy either. "The reason Bowles and Little are allowed to cell together is because I believe in putting people into cells who are compatible, not because they are homosexual lovers," he said. "Homosexuality is a product of this environment, but the bureau does not condone it and neither do I.

"In this case," Matthews continued, "I think we've let this situation go too far. It does look like we are promoting homosexuality, especially when we assigned Bowles and his sissy to the same job outside the hospital. It would have been better if one worked in industry and the other somewhere else, but for some reason someone decided to put them together. Maybe it was to keep Bowles happy. I don't know. But the point is that we are treating them differently from other inmates and I really don't believe in doing that and I plan to look into it."

Carl Bowles knew that he and Little were running out of time. Even though Connor had fired them as caretakers of the hospital grounds, they were still working as a team, collecting trash in another section of the compound. If Matthews and Associate Warden Connor decided to split them up by reassigning Little to a job in prison industries, Little would be tested by other inmates.

"These dumb motherfuckers are going to put Thomas in a situation where he's not going to have any choice but to stab someone, and then they're gonna say, 'See, we knew he belonged in a penitentiary all along,' " Bowles complained.

The problem was Eddie Geouge, Bowles decided. He had to figure out a way around him.

CHAPTER
THIRTY-FOUR

EDWARD GEOUGE

A New Jersey bank robber nicknamed Lumpy, who had a history of attacking guards, woke up one morning and decided to kill Eddie Geouge. Lumpy had had a tough week. He had been fired from his job in the kitchen for arguing with his boss, a guard had assigned him extra work around the cellhouse as punishment for not keeping his cell clean, and his mother had died and Geouge had denied his request to attend her funeral. (The bureau sometimes allowed inmates to attend funerals if their families paid the cost of having guards accompany them.) Lumpy would later recall that when he got out of his bunk, he had simply said to himself, "Fuck this! I don't care anymore. I'm going to kill Geouge."

When Lumpy didn't show up for work at his new prison job that morning, his boss notified the lieutenant's office, and at 9:35, Lieutenant Tracy Johns spotted Lumpy sitting in the bleachers in the prison yard with two other inmates.

"Need to talk to you in the lieutenant's office," said Johns as he approached the trio.

"I ain't going," Lumpy replied.

"C'mon," Johns ordered.

"I got a knife," Lumpy blurted. "I'm gonna kill Geouge!"

Johns froze. "I didn't know exactly what he had in mind," Johns recalled later, "but if he had a knife and his buddies were backing him, I figured I was in trouble."

As Johns stood silent, Lumpy suddenly covered his face with

257

his hands and began to sob. "He just broke down right there," Johns recalled. He frisked Lumpy and found nothing. During questioning, Lumpy said he had gotten a knife that morning and had waited for an hour for Geouge to arrive at his office in the cellhouse. Geouge never came, so Lumpy got rid of the knife and went into the yard to think.

It turned out that Geouge had been delayed at home. "I don't mean to belittle this," he said, when he was told that Lumpy had been stalking him, "but in this business this sort of thing happens, and you can't worry about it or you'd never come to work."

Better than most, Geouge knew death. As a soldier in Vietnam, Geouge had killed for the first time when he was eighteen. By the time he ended his combat tour two years later, he had received four Purple Hearts, two Bronze Stars, a Silver Star, and had stopped counting the number of enemy he had killed. His specialty was setting up ambushes.

"I slept with the first one I killed for a long time," he recalled. "Knowing that I'd killed another human being bothered me. But although I hate to admit it, killing is no different from anything else. It's like walking. After you take that first step, it becomes easy. You get used to it, and it got so it wasn't difficult at all for me."

During a particularly fierce firefight in December 1968 in the A Shau Valley, all but two of Geouge's men were killed. They were badly outnumbered, so Geouge ordered both men to retreat while he—in what the army later described as an extraordinary act of valor—fired an M-60 machine gun at the enemy troops until all its ammunition was spent. He then fired all the rounds in his M-16. Only after that did Geouge retreat. "I didn't want to die. I wasn't one of those guys who felt he was born to fight and die in Vietnam, and I remember thinking, 'Goddamn, Geouge, what the hell are you doing? You are going to die. They are going to kill you. Why didn't you fall back with those other two guys?' And I honestly didn't know why I stayed. I really didn't. I just felt someone had to do it." He managed to elude the attacking enemy troops and was later rescued by a helicopter.

Geouge had never turned away from a fight, nor did he understand men who shrank from blood. The son of a prison guard at the federal penitentiary in Lompoc, California, Geouge had been a self-described "hell-raiser" as a teenager. He quit school at age sixteen to work. Two years later, he married Pistol, who was two weeks shy of her fifteenth birthday. They were poor. She hoed weeds with migrant workers to help support them. He was drafted less than one month after their wedding.

The army made Geouge a drill sergeant when his tour in Vietnam ended, but Geouge didn't reenlist. A friend gave him a job working in a bar. "I didn't have any skills," he recalled. "I was going nowhere and sure to become an alcoholic."

When the bureau hired him in 1970 as a guard at Lompoc, where his father still worked, he and Pistol were elated. "We felt rich," remembered Pistol. Geouge was paid $6,200 per year. "I felt very grateful to the bureau," she added.

On his first day at work, a beefy inmate walked up to the much shorter and bone-thin Geouge and said, "I hear you're Geouge's kid. On the best day in your life, you couldn't whip me." Replied Geouge, "I never said I could, but just before you get me whipped, you're gonna wonder if you'll get it done. Now you want to fight or talk?" The inmate walked away.

In the early 1970s, the bureau didn't have specially trained and outfitted SORT teams. Instead they operated "riot squads," made up of volunteers who did whatever was necessary to stop an inmate from hurting other inmates or staff. Geouge became the "first man," which meant that when a cell door was opened, he was the first to scramble inside and confront an inmate. He enjoyed it.

Geouge earned the rank of senior lieutenant in only five years, an amazing feat at the time. He was one of the bureau's most promising young officers and he was proving to be especially good at investigating prison murders.

From Lompoc, Geouge was sent to the penitentiary in Atlanta, and on December 4, 1979, he solved one of the most gruesome murders in the prison's history. A twenty-two-year-old dietician, who joined the bureau directly from college and had only worked at the prison for a few weeks, was found dead in the library at the prison hospital. Geouge discovered a package of Pall Mall cigarettes lying under her skirt, which had been jerked down around her ankles. The pack had apparently fallen out of an inmate's pocket while he was raping her. Geouge also found a coffee cup on a shelf near the door. Armed with those two clues, Geouge checked the sheet that inmates were required to sign when they first came into the hospital. One of the patients listed on it was Robert E. Lee Hogan, Jr., a convicted rapist. The name Hogan sounded familiar to Geouge, and when he looked at the coffee cup, he remembered why. The letter *H* was scratched on the bottom. Geouge went immediately to Hogan's cell and found a freshly opened carton of Pall Mall cigarettes next to the bunk. It was missing one pack. Geouge called the FBI, and when agents interviewed Hogan, he admitted that he had raped and murdered the woman.

Over the coming years, friends and neighbors would ask Geouge if he ever felt sorry for the inmates he guarded. People unfamiliar with prisons frequently talked sympathetically about convicts, as if they really didn't deserve to be locked up. Whenever this happened, Geouge would remember the afternoon that he spent with two FBI agents listening to Hogan confess. Geouge's investigation showed that Hogan had actually gone to the hospital to kill a psychiatrist who had been treating him, but she had gone to lunch, so Hogan walked the halls aimlessly until he came upon the dietician. In a voice that was chilling because it was so calm, Hogan described what had happened.

> I just took the knife out of my pants and I held it there for a second and she was gonna scream or something, 'cause she took a big breath, and I told her that was the worst thing that she could do. . . . I asked her to take off her dress and remove her panty hose. . . . I couldn't achieve an erection. She said she had never had sex before and was a virgin, and I told her to quit lying. . . . I got on top of her . . . somewhere during that time I achieved ejaculation, but sex wasn't the major thing on my mind. I said, "I'm going to let you go." She said, "I won't tell anybody, just don't hurt me." I said, "All right, but I'm going to have to tie you up." I took her panties and put them in her mouth and took her panty hose and tied them across her mouth. . . . I laid her back down on the floor and tried to choke her, but it just seemed the more I choked the more, you know, her eyes wouldn't close, like she wasn't going to

die. So I told her to close her eyes and she did, and when she did I knew this choking deal wasn't doing no good. So I took the knife and tilted her head back. . . . When I first stuck it in her throat, it just didn't seem like it was working. She still had her eyes open looking at me. I told her again to close her eyes and she did, so I used both hands and I tried to force it in, then I took a dust broom and I held the knife with my left hand and hammered it in with my right hand using the dust broom . . . I pulled the knife all the way to the left and then all the way to the right and I knew, I knew that would kill her 'cause that would cut everything on the inside of her neck.

Recalling his feelings that day, Geouge said, "I looked at him and I thought, 'You are a total piece of worthless shit.'"

Geouge was still in Atlanta in 1980 when the bureau decided to change it into a prison for Cuban detainees. As always, Geouge was put in charge of the troublemakers.

"He worked twelve to sixteen hours, seven days a week," recalled Pistol Geouge. "The bureau pushed and pushed, and had pushed him as far as it could, but whenever I started to complain, I stopped myself, because the bureau had been so good for us— providing us with a house, a good salary. I was loyal to it, even though I knew Eddie was at the point where he was both mentally and psychologically exhausted . . . and then it happened."

Geouge was talking to a contentious Cuban when the detainee suddenly flinched. "I honestly thought he was taking a swing at me, so I backhanded him and the blow knocked him down," Geouge recalled. Geouge's boss, a captain, was standing nearby and he slugged and kicked the Cuban while he was on the floor.

When the Cuban later complained about brutality, Director Carlson sent Jerry O'Brien to investigate. "The real story is, they just smacked this inmate around a little bit because he was mouthy," O'Brien said. "They weren't trying to hurt him. It was more slapping him to get his attention."

Before O'Brien filed a written report, he briefed Carlson. "Norm looked at me and said, 'Fire 'em both.' That was it." O'Brien waited a day and went back in to see Carlson. "I told him more about the situation," O'Brien recalled, "but he didn't change his mind. Norm was totally against brutality." Still, O'Brien waited. "Finally, I went in for a third time and just blurted it out. I said, 'Norm, that place is wild. The frustration level among staff is high. It demands some compassion.' He listened to me for a while and said, 'Okay.' So we demoted the captain, and Eddie Geouge was suspended for two weeks and transferred to the penitentiary at Terre Haute [Indiana]. It was really a shame because Geouge was on the rise. He had been destined to move up the ladder."

The Geouges felt victimized. "I am convinced the bureau really was trying to force me out," said Geouge. "I think Carlson and the others expected me to quit or crawl into the woodwork and simply lay down."

At Terre Haute, Geouge earned the highest job-performance evaluations possible, but did not receive a single promotion. "I felt very betrayed and very bitter for a long, long time," said Pistol Geouge. "The bureau had always treated us as family, and then, because of this one mistake, everyone turned against us."

Four years later, Geouge was sent to an even less desirable assignment, the prison in Oxford, Wisconsin. On January 29, 1984, the mutilated body of Boyd H. Spikerman, a guard who had worked at the prison less than six months, was discovered. Once again, Geouge put his investigative skills to work. Geouge quickly identified the murderer as Matthew Granger, a convicted killer and braggart who had killed Spikerman because he wanted to gain admittance to the Aryan Brotherhood.

Granger had hoped that by killing a guard—just as Silverstein and Fountain had done in Marion less than three months earlier—he would be accepted by the AB.

Like the dietician murdered in Atlanta, the guard had been chosen simply because he was convenient. Granger later bragged about the killing to a television reporter. "I killed him about four different ways. I stabbed him, cut his eyes out, cut his throat out, strangled him, beat him with a fire extinguisher and flashlight, and stuck a ring of keys down his mouth." And then Granger looked directly into the camera and said, "This has just begun for me. I'm only thirty-one years old. I got a lot of bodies to collect yet."

Geouge received a special citation from the bureau for his

investigation of the Granger murder. Ironically, it was Carlson who awarded it to him. When Carlson retired in July 1987, Geouge was promoted to the Hot House. A few weeks after he arrived, he found a bullet dangling from a piece of string tied to his mailbox outside his new home. Officers in Oxford called him later that day to tell him an informant had revealed that several inmates had put out a contract on Geouge and his family. The bullet was meant as a warning that the inmates knew where he lived. Geouge and his family took what precautions they could, but there was little to do but wait. Nothing happened.

Sometimes, Geouge said, when he thought about the long hours, low pay, danger, the lack of respect that guards received in most communities, and the daily grind of dealing with society's violent psychotics, he wondered why he stayed on. But those moments never lasted long.

"Not everyone can do this kind of work," he said, "but it's always come easy to me and I enjoy it. Quite frankly, I think the traits that you need to be a good officer and the traits you need to be a good convict are very, very similar.

"I think I would make a good convict. I have the qualities you need—toughness, not being afraid of violence. I can handle that. But there is one big difference that separates us. Convicts are predators. They hurt other people. They take advantage of other people. They really only care about themselves. They don't attack the strong, they prey off the weak and helpless in our society and they destroy lives.

"I can be violent, just as violent as any inmate in here, if the situation demands that. I can even kill. I have killed many men. But I am not a predator, and that is what separates us from them. We don't cross that line."

CHAPTER
THIRTY-FIVE

THE LIEUTENANT'S OFFICE

"What's happening?" Lieutenant Monty Watkins asked as Lieutenant Edward Pierce bolted past him in center hall toward the east yard.

"Deuces!" Pierce yelled, and Watkins immediately fell in behind him.

Whenever someone dialed the numbers 2–2–2 on an internal telephone, an alarm sounded in the control center. "Triple deuces" was only supposed to be dialed when an officer was in trouble. Every staff member was supposed to run to the phone that had been used to sound the alarm. The only guards exempted were those at posts considered too critical to be abandoned. As the two lieutenants exited from the main penitentiary and entered the east yard, they were joined by Lieutenant Tracy Johns.

Someone in the prison industries building had sounded the alarm at 10:50 A.M., and as the three men bolted toward the building, they ran into a wave of convicts who just had been released from their jobs in the textile shop for lunch. Johns ordered the men to clear a path, and as they did, he yelled to the guard stationed at the metal detector in the east yard:

"Hold 'em here."

An immediate groan rose from the inmates as they realized they were going to have to wait in the yard until the emergency was resolved. They were ordered to stop at the metal detector, which was located halfway between the industries building and the main penitentiary. Most sat down on the sidewalk and grass, a few pulled out smokes.

Shortly after the three lieutenants disappeared into the industries building, another thirty employees came running into the yard in response to the alarm. It is about fifty yards from the main penitentiary to prison industries, and the staff members had to pass the waiting inmates to get there.

"Here comes the cavalry!" one inmate cracked.

"Please, God! O-o-o-h-h-h, God, p-l-e-a-s-e let there be a body this time!" another convict said.

The guard at the metal detector, who was not supposed to leave his post when an alarm was sounded, acted as if he hadn't heard the wisecracks.

About one minute later, a group of about twenty more staff members came into the yard, but they were moving much more slowly. These were stragglers; many were older men, some were fat and simply couldn't keep up with the first group. But there were a few guards in this group who were young and in good condition. Some worked in remote areas of the prison and were late because they had come from far away, but one or two were always among the last to respond.

"Cowards!" one of the inmates said.

"Better hurry," said another sarcastically. "Gonna miss the fun!"

"Run, fat boys, run," heckled a third.

Once this group disappeared, there was nothing for the inmates to do but continue waiting. As always, the whites had grouped themselves away from the blacks. Earl Coleman-Bey, a burly black convicted murderer, drug dealer, and head of the D.C. Blacks gang, sat on the grass near the detector. "If you ever wanted some hostages," he said, "all you gotta do is sound deuces. These dummies will run right to you."

"Shit, Earl," another inmate volunteered. "Sound them deuces three or four times, and these fat motherfuckers will be running around so much they'll all be dead of heart attacks."

The group surrounding Coleman-Bey laughed. The whites didn't react.

Every inmate was expected to work unless he had a medical disability. The convicts waiting near the detector were among the six hundred inmates at the Hot House who had jobs in prison industries. They earned an average of $250 per month working eight hours a day at the print shop, textile shop, or furniture plant. They could earn incentive pay too, and vacation days, normally spent lounging around their cells.

Any inmate who didn't want to work in UNICOR was assigned a job somewhere else in the prison. At best, he earned $75 a month painting the cellblocks, waxing and buffing floors, helping in the kitchen, or doing other odd jobs. Most of these men only worked about four hours a day, and about one third of them were assigned to what the convicts called "make work"—jobs created just to give them something to do.

The industries building at the Hot House was a four-story brick structure with three wings. The print shop was on the lower floors of the first wing, textile work was done on the upper floors, and the furniture factory was in the other two wings, together with a storage area and administrative offices.

Unlike jobs in the outside world, work assignments at UNI-COR were often based on the length of an inmate's sentence rather than on his educational background or skills. Men serving several life sentences with little chance of parole were taught the most complicated tasks and were often trained as equipment repairmen. Short-termers were given easily learned, routine work. It was not unusual for older convicts, who had been in Leavenworth for years, to know more about the various presses, sewing machines, and assembly-line operations than the associate warden for industries who served on the warden's executive staff.

None of the products made by convicts at Leavenworth could be sold to the public. That was one of the conditions Congress placed on the bureau when UNICOR was created. The politicians wanted to make certain that convicts wouldn't take jobs away from the local community or compete with private industry. Inmates in the textile plant sewed together T-shirts for the army and canvas bags for the postal service. The print shop made nearly all the forms and stationery used by the bureau. Chairs, desks, and bookcases made by the furniture factory went to the cadet quarters at West Point or to other military installations.

Seventy staff members worked at UNICOR. Many of them had started out as guards but had switched because they could earn better pay at UNICOR and work regular hours. The fact that UNICOR supervisors made more money and worked better hours irked most guards, and some didn't associate with them. But what really caused tension between the guards and the supervisors was the atmosphere in prison industries. It was not uncommon for inmates to call their supervisors by their first names or join them for coffee breaks. No self-respecting guard ever allowed an inmate to get that friendly. The reason such familiarity was tolerated in UNICOR was because its staff needed the inmates' cooperation in order to meet production deadlines. Whenever inmates felt they were being abused by a manager, they slowed down.

Technically, the UNICOR employees were responsible for guarding the inmates as well as supervising them, but there was little need for tight security inside the building even though many of the inmates worked with tools that could have easily been used as weapons. This was because the inmates genuinely wanted to earn money for themselves or their families and they didn't want to do anything on the job that might shut down the program or get them fired. The bureau had closed UNICOR operations in the past when it felt the inmates were too rebellious or when there were repeated problems in a factory.

In appearance, the three plants at the Hot House looked no different from any print, textile, or furniture-manufacturing operation outside the walls. But there were subtle reminders of where they were located.

"We were sewing together T-shirts," an inmate recalled, "and I had just about filled my basket. I was going to turn it in to my boss. We were way behind, so we were getting a bonus for every basket we did over our normal quota. Anyway, I got up to take a piss, and when I come back my basket is empty. I mean, as soon as I turned my back, these shitheads I worked with stole every one of my T-shirts for their baskets."

The triple-deuces alarm that had brought Lieutenants Pierce, Watkins, and Johns running into the building to help rescue a staff member was another reminder. But when the men burst into the textile shop, they didn't find an emergency. The room was empty except for rows of industrial sewing machines and yards of canvas ready to be cut into mailbags. Obviously, one of the convicts now sitting outside the building by the metal detector had sneaked into the floor supervisor's office and dialed the alarm moments before he and the other men had been released to go to lunch. It was impossible to guess why. It was against the rules for inmates to use any telephones without permission except for the pay phones in the cellhouses. The inmate might have been playing a prank, responding to another inmate's dare, or he might have had some other reason. Perhaps a friend of his had wanted to move some drugs or hooch in one of the cellhouses and had asked the inmate to set off the alarm in the industries building to distract the guards. The three lieutenants could only guess.

They returned to the prison yard and Johns told the guard manning the metal detector to let the inmates proceed to lunch in the mess hall. As Johns watched them file through the detector, another call came through on his radio. An inmate had cut himself with a knife in the kitchen and was hurrying out into the yard on his way to the prison hospital. Johns was told to make certain that the wound was an accident.

The bleeding inmate had run through center hall and had left a trail of red drops on the white tile floor. Two women employees who worked in the administration building were on their way to lunch at the officers' mess when they noticed the blood. An inmate coming down the hall in the opposite direction had seen it too and he bent down, touched his index finger to one of the spots, and swirled it into a larger circle on the floor. He glanced at the two approaching women and stood up so that he was facing them. He raised his blood-smudged index finger, making an obscene gesture, and then slowly licked the blood from it with his tongue.

Grimacing, the two women hurried past him.

The inmate laughed, and continued his walk down center hall.

CHAPTER THIRTY-SIX

Putting Slack in charge of the Cubans had proved to be a good decision. Warden Matthews was pleased. In fact, he felt things were going well overall. The penitentiary floors were shiny, all the cellblocks had been painted, inmates were talking to him, and he had his own crew of associate wardens in place. So there was really no reason for him to overreact when he learned that Bureau Director J. Michael Quinlan was coming to visit on September 27. But he did. As soon as Matthews heard about the visit, he called his associate wardens together and they started planning for the event with such intensity that guards began to joke that "Jesus Christ himself" was coming.

On the day before the visit, Matthews huddled with Associate Warden Connor to go over last-minute details. Quinlan would be met at the airport Tuesday night and driven to the warden's house for a dinner with the penitentiary's top staff. The next morning, he would be taken on a tour of the Hot House before being driven to Kansas City, where he was scheduled to speak at a Justice Department conference for U.S. attorneys.

Matthews wanted the prison tour to appear unplanned, but he and Connor had actually compiled a detailed account of where Quinlan and his entourage would go and what they would see. No detail had been left to chance. Special cleaning crews had already been sent down the corridors that the group would walk along. Every floor had been scrubbed and polished, every wall freshly painted. Connor had assumed that sometime during

269

the tour someone would ask to see the inside of a cell. He had decided to take the group through B cellhouse, where the cells were made of concrete blocks and had solid steel doors, not bars. Connor had selected several cells along the route and ordered them cleaned, painted, and stripped of any embarrassing nude photographs. Guards would make certain before the tour that the beds in each of these cells were made in military fashion.

Maintenance crews had been busy outside the penitentiary too. The front lawn had been mowed and was scheduled to be mowed again a few hours before Quinlan arrived. It would be cut twice, in different directions, to disguise any telltale mowing marks. New flowers had been planted. All the bushes had been trimmed. The yellow lines in the parking lot had been repainted, as had the wood trim in the lobby. There was so much painting being done that guards complained: anyone who stood still for longer than a minute risked being dabbed with enamel.

Matthews and Connor had also taken precautions when it came to inmates. Any inmate who guards thought might pose a threat, embarrass Quinlan, or cause any sort of demonstration during the tour was to be locked in the Hole during the visit. Just to be on the safe side, Connor told Matthews that five guards would walk well ahead of the tour group, out of sight. They would ensure that there were no large groups of convicts milling around or lying in wait to interrupt the tour. This advance group of guards would also alert staff members that the tour was coming, so no one would be surprised when the director appeared. Lieutenant Charlie Hill, the only Native American at the penitentiary, would walk a few feet ahead of the tour group with two other officers to open all gates so Quinlan and the others wouldn't have to wait. Connor had personally gone over the list of guards who would be on duty and within sight of the tour. Each would wear a clean white shirt and a black Bureau blazer. Any guards who were grossly overweight or consistently sloppy had been temporarily reassigned to areas out of view. The guards along the tour route were going to be young, athletically built, sharply dressed. Some would be blacks and Hispanics.

After the tour, Quinlan and his guests would eat lunch in the officers' cafeteria. The room would be cleared of all but one or two guards before the dignitaries arrived, Connor explained, so they wouldn't have to wait in line. The three inmate cooks, including Norman Bucklew, would be dressed in clean, white, pressed uniforms and would be wearing plastic gloves and chef's hats, which they normally never wore. The tables would be covered with red-and-white checked tablecloths with fresh-cut flowers as centerpieces, rather than the ashtrays, metal napkin holders, and plastic ketchup and mustard squirt bottles that usually sat on the tabletops. Lunch would be sirloin steak.

After lunch, Quinlan would be escorted to the front lawn, where he would stand on a wooden platform built especially for his visit and answer questions from reporters, who would be fed pastries and coffee before Quinlan appeared.

As soon as the press conference was over, Matthews and the associate wardens would drive Quinlan and his guests to Kansas City in washed and waxed bureau cars. Over the weekend, Matthews and his top managers had made a practice run from the prison to the hotel where Quinlan was speaking to make certain that everyone knew the route.

After going over the arrangements with Connor, Matthews felt confident that his staff was ready. The following day, during his regular Tuesday meeting with department heads, Matthews gave final instructions. "Nothing has a higher priority than this visit," he said. "There is no reason for any of you to be talking on the telephone or doing anything else except standing at attention when Mr. Quinlan enters your area."

The warden reminded the group that each of them was to bring a main dish to his house that night for the potluck dinner in Quinlan's honor. "This is an opportunity for you to meet Mike socially," he said. "It will be good for your careers."

All during Tuesday, various guards were pulled from their jobs and sent to Kansas City International Airport to ferry U.S. attorneys to their downtown hotels. That night at Benny's, several guards complained about being used as chauffeurs. They had heard stories about the extremes that other wardens had gone to when a director visited. One warden at a prison in the Northeast had poured flour over the dirty snow by the prison entrance so that it would look nice when the director visited. But the Hot House staff had always prided itself on being above such antics. They groused that asking guards to serve as drivers was certainly something that former warden Jerry O'Brien would not have done.

Then, after all the planning, Quinlan missed his flight Tuesday night and couldn't come to the warden's house for dinner. Matthews was disappointed. He had planned the dinner as a favor to his top managers, but when they arrived at his house and heard the news, most of them didn't seem to mind. Jackets came off, ties were loosened, everyone ate and then gathered around the bar in the large family room downstairs. One associate warden's wife got tipsy. Through the patio doors, the group watched as a terrific thunderstorm lit up the sky, giving them a panoramic view of the Hot House situated directly below the hill where Matthews lived. Five times during the storm, bolts struck lightning rods on the penitentiary's dome, but none of the charges did any damage. Nothing, it seemed, could faze the old penitentiary.

Quinlan arrived at Leavenworth promptly the next morning, accompanied by a high-ranking Justice Department official, Frank Keating, as well as two U.S. attorneys from Missouri and Kansas. They were hustled into Matthews's office where a table of fruit, pastries, juice, and coffee was waiting. Matthews gave each visitor a gold-plated key from the prison attached to a mahogany plaque inscribed with his name.

The tour went just as Matthews and Connor had planned. When one of the U.S. attorneys asked to see the inside of a cell, Connor quickly volunteered, "Let's look in this one," and the door to one of the previously prepared cells was opened.

There was only one incident that hadn't been choreographed. As the group walked past a television room in B cellhouse, one of the attorneys looked at the movie being shown.

"I didn't know they watched movies like that!" he said.

The cable-television show was R-rated and showed a couple engaged in sex.

"Well, sir, they can watch whatever is on cable," an embarrassed guard replied.

Matthews sat with Quinlan during lunch. Norman Bucklew eyed them from behind the food serving line. He had overheard guards talking about Quinlan's visit weeks earlier, and he had decided on the morning of the director's visit that he would make a point of talking to Quinlan at lunchtime. Bucklew wanted to know why inmates in Leavenworth couldn't buy portable televisions for their cells. "I know of at least three or four murders that have happened while I've been in the joint because of fights over televisions," Bucklew had explained earlier. "They let us buy radios, why not small televisions? I decided to jam him about them that day."

Bucklew had rehearsed his speech several times and was ready when Quinlan came through the serving line, but Quinlan had been talking and Bucklew didn't want to rudely interrupt. Bucklew kept waiting and waiting but there never seemed to be an opportune moment to approach the director while he was eating.

As soon as he finished, Bucklew started toward him. But Quinlan was already standing and starting to leave, and Bucklew didn't want to chase after him. And then it happened. Without explanation, Quinlan stopped, turned around, and walked directly over to Bucklew.

"Excellent meal," Quinlan said. "Thank you."

Bucklew was less than a foot away. The director had spoken to him first. There wasn't any reason why Bucklew couldn't ask about the televisions. But as he stood there dressed in his paper chef's hat and plastic gloves, he simply nodded and looked embarrassed. Quinlan turned and walked away.

A few minutes later in Matthews's office, Quinlan, the two U.S. attorneys, and Frank Keating briefly discussed what each of them intended to say to the media at the press conference that Matthews had set up.

Quinlan said he wanted a discussion about a new bureau program that forced convicts to pay their court fines. In the past, he explained, no one ever checked to make certain that convicts paid up. But recently the bureau had started warning inmates that they might jeopardize their chances at parole if they didn't pay their fines, and, so far, more than $12 million had been collected.

Even though the program was the bureau's idea and had nothing to do with Frank Keating's office in the Justice Department, Quinlan bowed to political protocol and urged that Keating be the first to explain the program and its success.

"I think I'll say something like 'Crime doesn't pay, but criminals do,' " Keating said.

"That's really great," Quinlan replied.

Now ready, the group started to walk outside, but Matthews

stopped them. The only reporter waiting was Connie Parish from *The Leavenworth Times*. No one else had shown up. She was invited inside the warden's office.

"This is the brainchild of one of Mike's wardens. . . ." Keating said, recalling the history of the program as it had been explained to him minutes before. Keating paused and then added, "It proves, I guess, that crime still doesn't pay, but criminals do."

Everyone chuckled.

Matthews was exuberant a few hours later, after Quinlan was gone. "This proves Leavenworth really rises to the occasion," he said. "I think Mike was impressed, particularly since not many inmates ran up to him with complaints."

CHAPTER THIRTY-SEVEN

ROBERT MATTHEWS

"Some people can't understand why anyone would choose to work in a prison," Warden Matthews explained one afternoon. "They just figure we can't get jobs anywhere else, but I believe it takes a certain calling just like the ministry takes a certain calling. In fact, I think this *is* my calling. I've always believed that deep down, I am doing exactly what I was supposed to do. My profession is also my ministry."

It was not odd for Matthews to describe his job as a ministry. His grandparents had raised him, and Matthews's grandfather was a self-trained Baptist preacher. During the day, the old man worked as a foreman in the Florida citrus groves. At night, he preached. Most nights, his grandson was with him.

"Many times I was the only kid in church. Sometimes I was the usher, other times I would recite verses from the Bible," Matthews recalled. But as he got older, Matthews began to resent being dragged to church. "I promised myself that I'd never force my children to attend church," he said. Still, he and his family were regular members of a Baptist congregation in Leavenworth. "I feel I'm missing something if I don't go to church each Sunday. I feel guilty."

As a child growing up in segregated Fort Pierce, Florida, the only white man that Matthews ever spoke to was an insurance agent who came by each week to personally collect a few dollars in premiums. At one point, Matthews told his grandmother that he wanted to be a state policeman when he grew up because he liked their uniforms. She laughed. "Honey, only white people can be state policemen," she told him. Matthews immediately put the idea out of his mind.

Later, in the 1960s when Martin Luther King, Jr., was being jailed, civil-rights workers were being slain, and Southern white sheriffs were unleashing attack dogs and firing water hoses at blacks as they demonstrated against segregation, Matthews told his grandparents that whites seemed more like devils than human beings. They corrected him. It was just as wrong to judge white people by the color of their skin as it was for whites to judge blacks, he was told. In his grandparents' house, people were judged according to whether they were good or evil, moral or immoral. Race had nothing to do with it.

Matthews enlisted in the air force after high school because he couldn't afford college. Four years later, with help from the GI bill, he enrolled at Florida A & M University, a predominantly black school in Tallahassee. He didn't have any idea what he wanted to major in, but when he was a sophomore, an event at the Attica State Correctional Facility in New York changed that.

On September 9, 1971, inmates at Attica rioted. Four days later, the racially motivated uprising ended when 1,500 state police and other law-enforcement officers staged an air and ground attack on the inmate-controlled prison. Nine guards being held hostage and twenty-eight prisoners were killed during the melee. Although Attica was a state prison, Bureau Director Norman Carlson would later describe it as a "watershed" in the corrections field. "Suddenly, the entire country became interested in prison reform and started demanding changes."

Attica had exploded, in part, because nearly all of the guards were white and many of its prisoners were black. The bureau, Carlson realized, was also largely white. In 1970, 93 percent of its employees were white, while 65 percent of its inmates were white, and 35 percent were minorities. Carlson launched an aggressive minority-recruitment campaign and Gerald M. Farkas, an associate warden at a minimum-security prison in Tallahassee, turned to Florida A & M University for recruits. Matthews was the first student Farkas went after.

"Farkas was a smooth, sophisticated, articulate guy," Matthews recalled. "He dressed sharp, spoke well, and was intelligent. He changed my image, because before that I figured prison guards were a bunch of knuckle-draggers." Matthews went to work at the prison as a summer intern and became hooked.

Years later Matthews would describe Farkas as his mentor when he first joined the bureau. At the time, Farkas was an oddity. The son of a prominent, well-to-do Jewish family from Pittsburgh, Pennsylvania, Farkas had set out to study medicine in college, but had become fascinated with the criminal mind and the growing belief that convicts could be cured. The idea didn't seem far-fetched in the idealistic 1950s. After all, Jonas Salk had developed a vaccine for polio, the space age was dawning, and everything seemed possible. Farkas abandoned his medical studies, earned a master's degree in the new field of "correctional management," and, much to his family's dismay, went to work in a state prison as a guard. Farkas was convinced that communication, not brute force, was the key to prison management, but he found few prison officials willing to listen. "No one saw much value in communication when I first started out," Farkas recalled. "Most prisons operated under the Rule of Silence, which meant convicts couldn't speak unless a guard asked them a direct question."

Farkas joined the bureau because it paid more than state prisons did, and when Carlson became director in 1970, he brought Farkas to Washington for a two-year stint as his executive assistant. Carlson then sent Farkas to Tallahassee, and later as warden to the penitentiary in Lompoc before bringing him back to Washington to oversee UNICOR, the prison industries program. Until he retired in late 1988, the liberal Farkas remained an eccentric in the ultra-conservative bureau. He never tired of advocating communication rather than force in dealing with inmates. The notepad for inmate complaints that Matthews always carried was a testament to Farkas's teaching.

After Matthews graduated from college, he moved to Terre Haute, Indiana, to attend graduate school. Farkas made certain that the penitentiary there hired Matthews full-time as soon as he finished his degree. At Terre Haute, Matthews was confronted for the first time with accusations from black inmates of "selling out to whitey."

"At first, it bothered me, but I just didn't buy it," he

recalled. "I've always believed there should be a consequence to your actions. You shouldn't be able to weasel your way out of something simply because of your race or by claiming that you were poor or that you had a lousy home. I've always believed in following the law."

Farkas had told Carlson about Matthews, and the director made certain Matthews was on a fast track. "The thing I liked about Bob Matthews was that he never tried to use the fact that he was black to get ahead," Carlson recalled later. "But I knew our minority-recruitment program wouldn't work unless blacks and other minorities saw that they had a future in the bureau, and the best way to show that was by promoting minorities as fast as possible into top jobs. Bob was one of the best minorities we had, so I promoted him quickly."

Matthews was named the warden at the prison in Ashland, Kentucky, in 1981, after being in the bureau only eight years. His meteoric rise outraged some older whites who were passed over. Matthews reacted by working harder than ever.

In February 1983, Carlson told Matthews that the Reagan administration, smarting from ongoing charges of racism, wanted to appoint a black as the U.S. marshal in Washington, D.C., the largest marshal's office in the country. The White House had asked for Carlson's help because it knew that he had actively recruited and trained minorities in the bureau. Carlson had recommended Matthews. But he cautioned the young warden about taking the job. The U.S. marshal and his deputies were supposed to provide security in the district's courtrooms, take care of prisoners awaiting trial, track down anyone who had escaped or not shown up for trial, and serve eviction notices for landlords. But the office was in disarray. The previous U.S. marshal had lasted only two weeks before being fired by the White House, federal judges claimed the deputy marshals frequently brought the wrong defendants to court or mistakenly freed prisoners, and a ten-month probe by the FBI had revealed that some deputies had accepted bribes from landlords in return for short-cutting the eviction process.

Matthews agreed to accept the appointment, even though it meant transferring from the bureau to another agency within the Justice Department.

"Robert Matthews was walking into a lion's den," recalled

Roger Ray, now the U.S. marshal in the eastern district of Virginia, who was brought in to serve as Matthews's top deputy. "Can you imagine how the staff felt when they were told that someone from the Bureau of Prisons was coming in to clean up a federal marshal's office? Who the hell did he think he was?"

On the first day, nearly all 106 employees called in sick. Ray telephoned deputies in Virginia for help. Matthews was unfazed.

"Bob called all of us in top management into his office one day and told us to write out our goals. Everyone just looked at each other and wondered what the hell this guy was talking about, because none of us had ever been asked to do that before," said Ray. The next afternoon, Matthews asked each of them what he had done to meet those objectives. Every day after that, in his afternoon close-out sessions, he asked them for an accounting of that day's activities and how they had met their goals. He was applying the identical techniques to the marshal's office that he had learned as a warden, the same procedures that he would later use at Leavenworth. "Bob wanted action. He wanted progress, and he demanded perfection, and if you didn't want to give one hundred percent, he got rid of you," Ray said.

After several turbulent months, the marshal's office started operating smoothly. Morale was good. The office was performing its various jobs well. Even the old, dirty cells where prisoners were held by marshals before trials had been cleaned and painted. "He was an absolute stickler for sanitation and renovation," recalled Ray.

Despite the improvements, Matthews was still not satisfied. He decided to reduce the office's five-year backlog of unserved eviction notices. Thousands of D.C. residents were living in apartments and houses without paying their rent because their landlords couldn't get the federal marshals to serve eviction papers. It was an unpleasant, sometimes dangerous task and it had always had a low priority in the office. During the spring of 1984, Matthews devised a plan to serve notices on three thousand tenants. The office had been serving less than one eviction notice per week, and he intended to average three hundred. A special crew of heavily armed U.S. marshals wearing bulletproof vests marched up to the doors of the rental properties and began serving notices to stunned tenants. As the marshals stood by, crews hired by the landlords dragged the tenants' personal belongings into the street. One tenant was so upset that he fired a shotgun through the locked door of his apartment, killing a landlord. The murder made front-page news, and tenant groups protested to the mayor, but Matthews refused to budge.

"The worst evictions," recalled Matthews, who watched several of them, "were the ones that involved small kids. Sometimes the kids were home alone and we had to move them and their stuff outside. Other times the kids would come home from school and find their stuff piled by the street curb. That was hard for me to handle."

Still, he continued his campaign. "I had raised my right hand and pledged to follow the law, and what I was doing was the law. I was acting in my official capacity. I had to get those notices served and that's what I did."

Once tenants realized that they might be evicted, hundreds flocked to pay their overdue bills. The media attention subsided and the five-year backlog was eliminated in four months.

In January 1985, Matthews voluntarily resigned as marshal and returned to the bureau. The White House, stunned by his performance, awarded him the highest honor given by the Justice Department for public service.

At the Hot House, Matthews knew that guards didn't like his focus on sanitation and inmate communication. But he had dealt with disgruntled employees before, especially in the U.S. marshal's office. "There is always anxiety during my first year, because I have specific goals that I want to accomplish, and while it is not my intent, some of the staff aren't going to like or understand those goals," he explained. "But I am certain that over time they will see that what I am doing is in the best interests of everyone."

At Benny's the guards weren't so sure.

CHAPTER
THIRTY-EIGHT

At Warden Matthews's request the Office of Inspections sent two investigators, Phil Potter and Jim Schenkenberg, from Washington, D.C., to the Hot House in late 1988 to determine whether Cuban prisoners had been brutalized by Lieutenant Phillip Shoats, Jr., and his men. When they arrived, both investigators appeared to be sympathetic.

"We realized it was going to be frustrating to the officers to have us come in and second-guess them," said Schenkenberg, "so we tried to be sensitive." Potter, a former lieutenant who had dealt with Cubans in Atlanta in 1984, told guards that he understood how difficult these prisoners could be. "I knew where these officers were coming from. But I told them, you don't cover up if someone's crossed the line. You admit you made a mistake and people will understand. It's the people who try to hide errors who get into trouble."

Despite these assurances, the guards who had worked with Shoats considered both inspectors to be "headhunters" and didn't trust them. While Potter and Schenkenberg conducted their probe, these guards launched an investigation of their own. Word had leaked out that someone had given Warden Matthews a written account of brutality in the Cuban units, as well as the names of guards who were allegedly involved. This was true, of course. The prison counselor who had first raised the charges had written such a statement. But that counselor no longer worked for the bureau. He had transferred to the Immigration

and Naturalization Service, another branch of the Justice Department, and had left the prison several weeks before the inspectors arrived. Because the counselor was gone, none of the
guards suspected him as the informant. Instead, they looked for
someone within their own ranks who they figured had, in their
words, "snitched." It didn't take long for them to find a suspect.
Officer Juan Torres, a quiet man in his early thirties, had worked
at Leavenworth for only six months and had barely known
Shoats, but Torres had never been accepted by the other guards.
He was a loner who didn't stop at Benny's after work for a beer
with other guards. He spoke Spanish and had been seen joking
and chatting with Cuban prisoners. He wasn't from the Leavenworth area; he had been recruited in Arizona, where the bureau
had gone to hire Hispanics. Most important of all, Torres was
viewed as a do-gooder because he was a devout Roman Catholic
and a guard who went by the rule book.

"We all figured he was the weak link," said a guard, "but we
weren't certain until he was interviewed by the headhunters."

Without realizing it, Schenkenberg and Potter had inadver-
tently aided the guards in their search for the snitch. Schenkenberg had conducted his interviews in an upstairs office of the
administration building while Potter had done his in an office
next to the warden's. It was impossible for a guard to enter
either room without first being seen by the men working in the
prison control center, and each time Potter or Schenkenberg
called someone in for questioning, the guards in the center wrote
down that man's name and timed the interview.

Torres held the record—ninety minutes with Potter.

Each night after work, the guards who had worked for
Shoats gathered at Benny's to review the names on the control-
center list. Nearly all, they decided, could be trusted to follow
the so-called "blue code," an unwritten pact between law enforcement officers that requires them to never say anything
incriminating against a fellow officer. Everyone, that is, except
for Torres.

As soon as Potter and Schenkenberg completed their investigation and left Leavenworth, the guards decided to test their
theory, but rather than ask Torres point-blank about what he
had told Potter, they decided to take a subtle approach.

"I was eating lunch with some guys," Torres recalled later,

"when one of them asked if we would tell on someone if we saw him thump a Cuban. Everyone else said they wouldn't, but I didn't say nothing. This guy pressed me and I said, 'Hey, I ain't losing my job or going to prison because of someone else.' After that, people began calling me a snitch."

Torres soon found himself being shunned by his peers. No one wanted to work on the same tier as he did. Most avoided speaking to him. One morning when he went to his mailbox outside the lieutenant's office, he found the word SNITCH written over his name. He tore the name tag off and replaced it with TORRES, but an hour later the word SNITCH was back. That night, he got the first of several obscene phone calls. "Guys would call and say, 'Hey, snitch, how'd you like to suck my dick?' and then hang up."

One of the guards who claimed Torres was a snitch was unapologetic when asked later at Benny's why he was harassing him. "We want that son of a bitch gone and he'll eventually get the message," he explained. "The guy's a rat. He tried to get us fired and put in prison."

Lieutenant Slack saw what was happening and he knew that Torres was being falsely accused. "I began putting out word that the rumor about him wasn't true," said Slack. "I put it out to people who I knew would pass it on down, but it was really up to Torres to prove he wasn't a snitch, and that was going to take time. You see, there wasn't much I could do. If he didn't give any indication that he was a snitch, the other guards would accept him. But if he came running to me or Connor for help, then he would be marked forever as a snitch."

The guards were not only angry at Torres but at Matthews for notifying the Office of Inspections to begin with, rather than handling the charges himself, especially after Matthews made it clear that he didn't believe any brutality had taken place. "Why in the hell did he put us through all this if he didn't believe anything happened?" complained one.

An incident shortly after the two investigators left town further alienated the guards. Associate Warden Lee Connor decided to discipline a popular veteran guard who was in charge of the metal detector in the east prison yard, between the main penitentiary and prison industries. Each inmate was required to walk through the metal detector when he went to work each day, again at noon when he came back inside the main penitentiary for lunch, and later that afternoon when the work day ended. The detector was supposed to help the guard find knives, but it was so sensitive that it beeped whenever an inmate with a metal belt buckle or steel-tipped work boots walked through it. Frisking each inmate didn't seem practical to the guard, so he simply waved most inmates through even if the machine beeped.

Connor thought the guard was being lazy, but rather than lecturing him, he sent Lieutenant Tracy Johns to watch him for two days. Stationed at a window in the prison hospital, Johns faithfully recorded the number of inmates the guard actually frisked, and turned the data over to Connor. There weren't many, so Connor began the bureaucratic procedure to fire the guard. The guard protested and claimed that he knew based on his experience who needed to be frisked and who didn't. He notified his union representative, who immediately complained to Warden Matthews. According to the union contract, an employee was supposed to be told immediately if he had done something wrong. He was supposed to be given a chance to correct his behavior. He wasn't supposed to be spied on for two days and then fired. Matthews agreed, and Connor was forced to keep the guard on, although he was moved to a different job.

Although Matthews had ruled in favor of the guard, the incident was damaging. "All he and Connor care about is getting a promotion, and if they can do it by catching one of us screwing up, they'll do it," a guard complained. Connor further hurt his credibility by assigning an inexperienced guard to the metal detector. This officer decided to search *every* inmate, causing the line of inmates trying to get to work to back up like rush-hour traffic. When the line at the detector was stalled for fifteen minutes one morning, nearly one hundred frustrated inmates protested by returning to their cells instead of going to work. Connor quickly switched guards at the detector, this time putting a veteran in charge. Like the original officer, the new man picked inmates at random to frisk.

The confusion at the metal detector and the Cuban investigation had caused morale to sink to such a degree that one of the lieutenants decided on his own to find out what was wrong. "Why is morale so low?" he asked in a questionnaire slipped in each guard's mailbox.

Connor was furious when he heard about the questionnaire and immediately demanded that it be collected and destroyed. "Of course they'll say morale is low when you phrase a question that way," he explained.

"There is a feeling that Matthews and Connor don't really know what they are doing," a veteran guard said later, "and that means one of these days we'll either have an escape or a riot and someone's going to get hurt."

As was his nature, Matthews remained upbeat and positive as 1988 came to a close, but it was clear that he and Connor both needed a success.

Eddie Geouge gave them one.

As the unit manager in A cellhouse, Geouge was supposed to spend his time conducting unit team sessions and filing paperwork. But he was still an investigator at heart, and when an inmate was found badly beaten in a recreation room in A cellhouse in early November, Geouge decided to find out why. He had known for months that a group of strong-arm white convicts operated a poker game in the room, and he suspected that they were involved in drug dealing and extortion as well. He began monitoring their telephone conversations, and after listening to hours and hours of tape-recorded calls, he was able to identify the three inmates involved in the drug, gambling, and extortion ring. Each had foolishly bragged about making money while in prison. Two of the inmates were the muscle behind the game, the third was the brains. Geouge decided to check each of their prison accounts. Inmates were only allowed to have twenty dollars in cash. Any more than that had to be deposited in an account at the prison, from which the inmates could draw to buy goods at the commissary. Besides keeping track of how much money each inmate had, the accounting office kept a log that identified the names of family members or friends who sent money to the prison to be deposited in an inmate's account.

Geouge noticed that the inmate with the "brains" had only one contact who regularly sent him money. It was a woman in New Jersey. Geouge jotted down her name and address and checked the records of the other two inmates in the ring. The same woman was making regular deposits in their accounts too. Geouge asked the FBI to examine the woman's bank records. Based on his experience, Geouge figured that the woman was working as a "bank" for the prisoners. Whenever an inmate got into debt by playing poker or buying dope or being the victim of extortion, he contacted relatives or friends outside the prison and asked them to send a check or money order to the woman in New Jersey. It wasn't uncommon for inmates to maintain bank accounts outside Leavenworth, particularly drug dealers and Mafia figures. Sometimes the accounts were in the inmates' names, but often they were under the names of their relatives or girlfriends. Either way, money that was withdrawn from these accounts could not be tracked by the bureau. After the woman in New Jersey received an inmate's check, she deposited it in her account and then sent the three inmates in Leavenworth money orders that were automatically deposited into their prison accounts.

A few weeks after Geouge notified the FBI, an agent telephoned and told him that the woman in New Jersey was depositing as much as $10,000 per month into her checking account even though she was unemployed and didn't have any visible source of income.

Geouge wasn't surprised by what the FBI had discovered, but he was shocked at the amount that the ring in A cellhouse was collecting. The woman was taking in as much as $120,000 per year—all of it apparently from illegal activities inside the Hot House. Obviously, since the bureau limited the amount an inmate could receive in prison to $105 per month, the woman was only depositing a small portion of what the ring was getting into Leavenworth inmates' accounts. Geouge figured the woman put the rest of the money into other bank accounts that the inmates controlled. The funds were probably used to buy drugs, which were then smuggled into prison by other outsiders.

Even though Geouge now understood what was happening, he didn't have enough evidence to make a case. He couldn't do anything but watch and wait. Then one afternoon an inmate asked to see Geouge in private. He explained that he wanted a transfer to a less secure prison closer to his home. Geouge knew the inmate was a gambler and he suspected that he had played in the high-stakes game on the fourth tier.

"I don't give nothing if I don't get nothing," Geouge later recalled saying.

"What do you want?" the inmate asked.

"The poker game on four gallery."

It was a formidable request, because the white convicts running the game would probably kill anyone who turned them in. But the inmate agreed after Geouge assured him that he would be transferred from the Hot House before any arrests were made. The inmate not only gave Geouge all the information that he needed, but also disclosed that the poker game was rigged.

As soon as the informant was transferred, Geouge turned the case over to Lieutenant Torres Germany, who promptly took the three inmates to the Hole. The fact that they were arrested by Germany, not Geouge, made it even more difficult for the inmates to figure out how they had been caught. All of them were sent to Marion.

It was the biggest bust since Matthews became warden, and he and Connor were thrilled. Even Santa Claus couldn't have brought them a better present.

CHAPTER
THIRTY-NINE

THOMAS SILVERSTEIN

Thomas Silverstein missed his art supplies. Alone in his isolation cell in the Hot House basement where the lights burned twenty-four hours a day, Silverstein needed something to keep his mind occupied, and drawing had always been his escape. Matthews and Connor came downstairs once a week to see him, and every time they opened the door and looked at him through the two rows of bars, Silverstein asked them for art supplies. Each week, they refused. Finally, Silverstein decided to, as he later put it, "play their stupid paperwork game."

Any inmate who felt he was being treated unfairly by the bureau could complain by filing an administrative remedy appeal, commonly called a BP-9 form. It went directly to the warden, who had fifteen days to respond. If the inmate was unsatisfied with the warden's answer, he could appeal it to the warden's boss by filing a BP-10 form with the regional director. If the inmate felt the regional director's answer was inadequate, he could file yet another form, a BP-11, with bureau headquarters.

Silverstein had never bothered filing written complaints because he suspected the process was a waste of time. But after he killed Officer Merle Clutts in Marion, the bureau had pointed out that there was absolutely no proof that Clutts had been harassing Silverstein as he had claimed; Silverstein had never filed any formal complaint against Clutts, so therefore the bureau could find no logical reason for Silverstein's attack.

This time, Silverstein filed a BP-9.

I've been in prison thirteen years and have never been denied drawing materials. I'm an artist and this is how I occupy my endless hours in a cage and express my love and appreciation to my loved ones who have stood by me all these years . . . I promise not to harm, hurt, or threaten, etc., anyone with my drawings or cause any undue concern to those who have denied me them.

Matthews replied on the same day that Silverstein gave him the complaint.

Your status at USP Leavenworth will remain as indicated upon your arrival to include a denial of art material in your cell. Your activity during the riot at USP Atlanta is being investigated and a final determination will be made upon the termination of the investigation. Your request is denied.

Silverstein appealed to the regional director by filing a BP-10.

With just a pencil and regular writing paper, I've stretched my imagination to the max and it's beyond me what my drawings have to do with an investigation in Atlanta. It seems denying me this innocent-enuf pastime puts the cart before the mule in that I'm being punished before a case has even been brought against me.

Regional Director Larry DuBois had thirty days to reply, but answered the complaint within a week:

A review of this matter reveals that the warden's response to your request for administrative remedy (BP-9) fully addressed the issues you have raised. . . . Your regional administrative remedy appeal (BP-10) is denied.

Silverstein immediately sent a BP-11 to bureau headquarters. He pointed out in the appeal that he had been given art supplies while a prisoner in Atlanta and had never gotten into any trouble there. The answer from bureau headquarters was brief. It said:

> The warden and regional director have responded
> to your concern and we affirm their responses. . . . Your
> appeal is denied.

Silverstein hadn't really expected that anyone in the bureau would come to his aid, but he wanted to document the inconsistent way in which the bureau was treating him. In Atlanta, he had been given paints, brushes, even canvas.

"Why do they have to do this to me?" he asked. "They got my ass behind bars and they're never letting me out. Isn't that enough? Why do they have to pull this other shit?"

Silverstein claimed he was being punished by guards in other ways. Letters from his friends outside prison were delivered weeks after they had been written and some were never delivered at all. Photographs enclosed in letters from his relatives were missing when the letters were brought to his cell. One week dessert was missing from his dinner tray. When Silverstein asked about this, the guard who slipped the tray through the bars simply grinned. Silverstein accused him of eating the desserts and the guard denied it, but after the accusation, the desserts reappeared.

Each time Silverstein felt he was being treated unfairly, he filed a written complaint. Warden Matthews rejected every one of them, as did the regional office and bureau headquarters. Before long, Silverstein had a file folder stuffed with more than a dozen rejected complaints.

Matthews insisted there was nothing unfair in how Silverstein was treated. "We should be able to explain everything we do in regard to Silverstein, and I think we can and have done exactly that in our BP-nines."

Although Silverstein was losing his paper war in Leavenworth, he was able to obtain through the federal Freedom of Information Act a copy of a bureau investigative report confirming that guards in Marion had harassed him after Merle Clutts was murdered. In December 1983 he had been moved from Atlanta to Marion for a short period, to stand trial for Clutts's death; and his claim that guards there had tormented him was later substantiated by an investigator sent to Marion by Director Carlson. According to the investigator's report, guards played a radio outside Silverstein's cell nonstop for two days as loudly as possible, beat on his cell door with wooden clubs, told Silverstein that they were going to kill him, and sprinkled salt, pepper, and "unknown foreign particles" on his food. As soon as Silverstein received a copy of that report, he filed a $1.75 million lawsuit against the bureau.

Because Silverstein was being kept in total isolation, the bureau required prison psychologist Dr. Thomas White to examine him once a month and file a report on his mental health. White normally spoke to him for only a few minutes. "It is not necessary to talk to him for a long time to determine whether or not he is suffering from mental distress," said White.

"What kind of sick trip are you on?" Silverstein asked the psychologist one afternoon during his monthly visit. "If I killed myself down here and people came in here to investigate, I mean normal-thinking people, not the sick ones you hire to work here, if normal people saw what you are doing to me—with the lights on twenty-four hours a day, not letting me have any visitors, never letting me go outdoors in the sunshine, and all this shit— they'd say, 'Why'd you leave him down there locked up alone so long? Why didn't you see this coming? Aren't you the shrink? Don't you know keeping a man in a cage all day with the lights on and without any other people around is really sick?' What are you going to tell them, Doc? How you going to justify this?"

White left the cell without replying. Later, in his office, he said that he thought some of the security measures that had been put into place for Silverstein were excessive, but the bureau had been so outraged by the murder of Clutts that it was impossible for anyone to change them.

In his monthly report, White wrote:

> Silverstein voiced no problems or complaints of a psychological nature.... He is well organized in his thought content and appears to be doing well, showing no sign of debilitating emotional distress which would warrant a change in his housing at this time. He appears to be in relatively good spirits. His hygiene and

general attitude appeared to reflect a satisfactory level of adjustment to his status . . . He is not viewed as a threat to himself at this time.

A short time after Silverstein confronted White, guards noticed that he had printed the word FREEDOM in big letters on the wall of his stainless-steel shower stall. He had formed the letters by rubbing his fingers against the grime that had built up on the wall. The guards ordered Silverstein to clean the shower and remove the word.

"Can't," he replied. "I don't have any hot water to use to clean it." The guards said later that they were genuinely shocked. For six months, Silverstein had been taking cold showers because no one had turned on the hot water valve into his cell. The guards claimed that this was an accident. When Silverstein was asked why he hadn't complained about not having any hot water, he said, "I just figured it was one of their sick little trips."

After three months of denying Silverstein drawing materials, Matthews finally told the guards to give him colored pencils and a sketch pad. A few months later, he was given paints and brushes. They arrived without explanation.

Now that he could work on his art, Silverstein stopped bickering with Matthews, Connor, and White. But his silence didn't mean that he wasn't angry. "I'm supposed to walk around like everything is cool and act like it ain't personal, you know, like Matthews is just doing his job by keeping the lights on twenty-four hours, and Connor doesn't really mean anything by not letting me go out into the sunshine. I'm not supposed to have hard feelings against them. Well, fuck that. It's personal."

Silverstein spent most of December 1988 painting an oil portrait that showed a prisoner whose shirt had been ripped off. The prisoner was alone in a cell, bent down with his face touching the floor as if he had just been beaten. Silverstein called it "Solitary Confinement."

"I hate these guards," he said, "and what they are doing to me."

When I told this to Matthews, he was not surprised, but he strongly disagreed when I suggested that the guards also hated Silverstein. "We are professionals doing our job. None of us likes what Silverstein did, but hate is too strong."

Eddie Geouge was not nearly as diplomatic. "If I could, I would execute that piece of shit and I would not lose a second of sleep. I would kill him because he is nothing but an animal, and as far as I'm concerned, he gave up the right to live in our society by believing he had a license to kill whoever he wanted. Who gave him the right to destroy so many? Murder is forever, and a person should have to pay the consequences for murder. They shouldn't be allowed to come in here for a few years and then be released to kill again."

In the lieutenant's office, David Ham, the new captain at Leavenworth, was passing around a Christmas card that someone had made as a joke on the bureau's computer. It had a large, ornate cross on the cover along with a stained-glass church window. It was supposed to be for Silverstein. The cover said:

"FOR YOU TOMMY! A CHRISTMAS CARD. *JESUS LOVES YOU!*"

Inside, the card read: "EVERYONE ELSE THINKS YOU'RE AN ASSHOLE!"

CHAPTER FORTY

When the disciplinary-hearing officer at Leavenworth retired in late 1988, Warden Matthews recommended Eddie Geouge for the job and the bureau's Regional Director DuBois agreed. Geouge was happy with the promotion. In his mind, it meant the reprimand that he had received eight years earlier for backhanding a Cuban prisoner had finally been forgiven.

Carl Bowles and Thomas Little were also exuberant at the news that Geouge was no longer going to be in charge of A cellhouse. They were even more pleased when Matthews appointed Lieutenant Torres Germany as the new cellhouse manager. They had always gotten along well with Germany and felt he would be more receptive than Geouge to Little's plea for a transfer. They were right. Little walked out of his next unit team review smiling. With Geouge gone, the team had recommended Little for a transfer. Warden Matthews quickly approved it. He was eager to see Bowles and Little separated. Within a week, the bureau notified Little that he soon would be moved to a new medium-security prison opening in Marianna, Florida.

Little had spent eighteen months in the Hot House. From the day that he first arrived at Leavenworth, all he had wanted was to get out. Yet now that he was finally being transferred, he was depressed.

"Carl and I stayed up talking on the night before I was scheduled to go," Little said. "It was so emotional. We talked about everything he had taught me, about how I should carry myself, about all the things we had been through together, and I told him, I said, 'Carl, you are my father now.' I said, 'My real father never cared about me, but you do, so I am making you my father and I am your son.' "

The next morning, Bowles gave Little some parting advice. "When you get to Marianna," he said, "be careful, keep your mouth shut, and don't trust anyone."

Both men laughed. It was the same advice that he had given Little when they first met.

As Little told Bowles good-bye, the young inmate couldn't help but notice that the convicted killer, one of the most dangerous inmates in the entire federal system, had tears in his eyes.

A few hours later, Little walked down the front of the penitentiary to a bus that took him to the U.S. marshal's jet at the Kansas City airport. Guards ordered Little and several other inmates to wait on the runway as several fish were escorted off the airplane and into the bus for its return trip to Leavenworth. Little watched each one pass by and enter the bus just as he had done a year and a half before.

Little said later that he wasn't certain that he was actually leaving Leavenworth until the plane was in the air. "I kept waiting for someone to say they had made a mistake and I was going back."

As he stared out the window, Little realized that the pilot was swinging northwest of the airport and was about to fly over Leavenworth. He looked down. Far beneath him, the penitentiary's silver dome reflected the morning sunshine.

CHAPTER
FORTY-ONE

DALLAS SCOTT

Dallas Scott was reading a western novel in his cell at Marion when he received a packet of legal documents from Sacramento. The papers were a response to the motion he had filed to overturn his 1976 bank-robbery conviction. U.S. Magistrate John Moulds had read Scott's petition and ruled that the legal issues he raised were worthy of investigation. Moulds had ordered the U.S. attorney's office and Scott to prepare for a special hearing in Sacramento at which both sides would present their arguments.

Scott was thrilled. Most petitions filed by convicts are quickly rejected by the courts. Moulds's decision showed that the issues Scott raised were important enough to make the possibility of overturning his conviction real. But there was one bit of information in the packet that Scott didn't like. Moulds had told Scott to hire an attorney to represent him at the hearing because the court was not willing to bring Scott there. Scott had planned on representing himself. He didn't trust lawyers, especially any whom he could afford.

A few days later, a guard stopped outside his cell with another packet. A grand jury in Topeka, Kansas, had issued a sixteen-count indictment against Scott, charging him with attempting to smuggle 2.75 grams of heroin worth $500 into Leavenworth. Under the new drug-trafficking laws that Congress had recently passed, Scott faced up to sixty years in prison and four million dollars in fines.

"Get your stuff packed," a guard told him. "You're going back to Leavenworth for the trial."

Scott quickly scribbled a note to his daughter, Star, telling her that he was being transferred. He had not seen Star, who was in her early twenties, for five years, but they corresponded regularly, and in his last letter Scott had been optimistic about his chances of eventually being released.

"I sure hated to tell her that the old man was back in a jackpot again," he recalled later. "I reckon she knows by now, though, that if there are any sinking ships anywhere around, I will find one and jump aboard."

By the time Scott finished the letter, a group of guards had assembled outside his cell to escort him down to a waiting van. His pals, John Greschner and Ronnie Bruscino, wished him luck as he walked past their cells.

He was going to need it.

CHAPTER
FORTY-TWO

WILLIAM POST

For reasons that no one at Leavenworth quite understood, inmates rarely had trouble finding women willing to correspond or visit them. Surprisingly often, these relationships led to marriage. The third Thursday of each month was reserved for weddings in the prison visiting room and there were at least two every month, sometimes more. Many of the brides had never known their husbands outside prison. Some of them married inmates who had no chance of parole. Because the bureau did not permit conjugal visits, many of the marriages were never consummated. But it didn't matter. Every morning just before eight o'clock, a steady stream of women, often dressed in their Sunday best and with children in tow, congregated outside the prison entrance waiting to visit inmates.

William Post had gotten married while in prison, and he still wore his wedding ring although the marriage had been dissolved. He met his bride in 1979, six years after he went to prison in Marion for bank robbery and learned that Glenda Thomas had died from a drug overdose. By that time, Post had managed to move from Marion to the state prison in Folsom, California, where he was serving time for the robbery of the all-night market and his shootout with Glendale police. Post had been corresponding with his niece while at Folsom, and in August she convinced her best friend, Priscilla Kane, to go with her to visit "Uncle Bill."

Kane was twenty-five, had been married eleven years, and

lived in Stockton with her husband and two small children, Carey and Kimberly. From the moment she met Post, she was intrigued. He looked much different from the way he was to appear years later in Leavenworth. While in Folsom, Post was meticulous about his appearance. "You could have cut bread with the creases in his pants," Kane recalled. "He even ironed his T-shirts."

The two women had to visit with Post via a telephone in a booth in which inmates were separated from visitors by a Plexiglas window. When Kane asked Post why he was not permitted to meet visitors in person like other convicts, he explained that he was being punished because a woman had been caught smuggling him a handcuff key a few days before.

When she returned to her home, Kane began receiving daily letters from Post. Her husband thought it was funny that she was corresponding with a bank robber, but Kane soon found herself sharing the most intimate details of her life with her new pen pal. "A man in prison can focus completely on you, and Bill did just that," Kane recalled. "I used to get long, beautiful letters. I'd never met a man I could talk to on such a high intellectual level. He challenged my mind. It used to take me an hour just to look up the words in the dictionary that I wanted to use to answer his letters."

Years later Kane would look back upon those days when she first met Post and describe herself as "perfect prey." She had had a miserable childhood. Her father had sexually abused her older sister and then had abandoned the family when the police were notified. Kane's sister developed anorexia and died. Kane married at age fifteen to escape from home, only to have her marriage turn sour. She and her husband still lived together, but slept in separate bedrooms.

Shortly after Kane met Post, doctors discovered that she had cancer of the uterus, and performed a hysterectomy. "Bill had flowers sent to me and called me on the phone every day I was in the hospital," she recalled. "He always had time to listen to me and he told me exactly what I wanted and needed to hear. He said I was beautiful, that I was still sexy and desirable after the operation. He told me I was extremely important to him."

In 1980, Kane divorced her husband. She was in love with Post. Twice each week, she and her children drove to Folsom to be with him. A guard took her aside one afternoon. "You're not like most women who come here," he said. "You got a nice family, well-mannered kids. Do yourself a favor and stay away from Post." The advice irritated Kane. "Bill was so gentle and loving, especially with my children," she recalled. "They adored him. They loved him as if he were their real father, and he really was helping me discover who I was and gain self-confidence. I was sure he was different from other inmates."

One day while Kane was waiting for Post to be brought into the visiting room, she overheard a guard talking to a woman. "Today's not your day to visit inmate Post," the guard said, turning the woman away.

As soon as Post came into the room, Kane described what she had heard and Post confessed. The visitor was Cynthia Post. He had known her for more than one year. They had met each other through an advertisement in a white-supremacy magazine, he said. The woman had fallen in love with him, quit her job, sold her home in Tennessee, moved to California to be near him, and changed her last name to his. She had been visiting Post on the days that Kane and her children stayed at home.

"He told me it was over between them," she recalled, "and that he loved me and my children. I was so head over heels in love, I just accepted that."

Cynthia Post confronted Kane and her children when they came out of prison that same day.

"I want you to know you are getting into more than you think," Cynthia Post said.

"You don't know what you're talking about," Kane replied, expecting an angry exchange.

Instead, Cynthia Post burst into tears, and Kane felt so sorry for her that she embraced her. "You don't know what you are getting into," Cynthia Post repeated. "He'll use you and then just throw you away."

Kane refused to think the worst of Post. "I really believed that Bill loved me, really, really and truly loved me, so I just ignored everything that would normally make a person suspicious," she said. "I finally had found someone who loved me for who I was. Who accepted me and encouraged me."

Kane was thrilled when Post asked her to marry him. But

when she told Post's niece, who had introduced them, the woman was outraged. "She came to see me at my house carrying a stack of love letters from Bill," Kane said. "He had been courting her too." Kane drove to Folsom and demanded an explanation. But Post was again persuasive enough to convince her that he loved only her and on February 5, 1982, they were married at Folsom Prison.

Post had told Kane that the parole board considered married convicts a much better parole risk than those without families, and Kane quickly became a relentless advocate for her husband. Six years later, officials at Folsom would still remember Priscilla Kane Post as the woman who "drove us all nuts about getting her husband a parole."

Post was paroled from the state prison a short time later, but was immediately turned over to the bureau to finish his sentence for bank robbery, and was transferred to Leavenworth.

Kane wanted to follow him, but she became ill, was bedridden for several months, lost her job, and spent what savings she had. Despite those problems, Kane felt confident that she would be able to rebuild her life with her husband after the federal Parole Commission considered his appeal in June 1983. She was sure that Post would be paroled.

Kane had spent months preparing for the June parole meeting. She had found two employers who promised to hire Post if he were released. She had solicited dozens of letters of recommendation for him. She had even cajoled her ex-husband into writing a favorable letter in Post's defense. Despite her illness, Kane continued to make calls to various public officials on Post's behalf.

The most touching pleas presented to the parole commission, however, came from Kane herself and her two children, particularly her daughter, Kimberly. Written in the large scrawl of a seven-year-old, Kimberly's letter to the commission said:

> I need my daddy. I love my daddy. I know he has done wrong but he has been good now. I beg you to let him come home so he can hold me in his arms without having to always leave me alone. He cries when I leave and I cry too. I love him.

Priscilla Kane's four-page handwritten note was equally poignant:

> I don't trust easily especially where my life or the lives of my children are concerned. But after knowing Bill for over three years and being his wife for over sixteen months, I have found that no one could be a better husband or father than Bill. He has never had a family of his own before, it does make a difference. Our children need him, I need him too. Kimberly has brought his picture to the table at meal time many times and announced 'Daddy is having dinner at home tonight.' This baby has vowed not to cut her hair until her daddy is home. Her hair is well below her waist now! Please let Bill go!

It was during this period that Post had attempted various therapy groups, gotten his college degree, and won the accolades of the teachers who taught in prison. He had kept out of trouble, too. In short, he seemed to be the perfect candidate for parole.

"I was so convinced that he was going to be released that I didn't even consider what would happen if the commission said no," Kane said.

It did.

Kane and Post were dumbstruck. "We had worked so hard and it seemed so unfair. There just didn't seem like there was any reason for him not to be set free," said Kane. "I was furious and my children were crushed."

Kane wanted to visit him, but she couldn't afford the trip. A friend telephoned Prison Fellowship Ministries, the national organization founded by former White House Special Counsel Charles W. Colson, who had served time in prison for his role in the Watergate scandal. Colson's organization paid to send Kane and her children to Leavenworth. "It was a miracle," Kane recalled, "a true miracle."

The first day of the visit was wonderful. "I was so happy just to be with him." But the second day turned ugly. Post began arguing with Kane's children, at one point threatening to spank Kimberly. "He no longer had any patience with them." Even more disturbing to Kane was the fact that Post asked her to help him escape. "He asked me to bring him a handcuff key," she said. "I couldn't believe it. I told him, 'Look, I'm not a gun moll. You had that with Glenda Thomas, but I'm no Bonnie and Clyde. I love you. I will stick with you, but I'm not going to do anything illegal.''

Kane thought Post would be happy when she told him on the third and final day of their visit that she had found an apartment in Leavenworth and was planning to move to Kansas. But he suddenly became cold, and when she returned to Stockton, he telephoned her. "I want to put the marriage on hold," he said.

During the next few weeks, Kane received a number of strange telephone calls from him. "I'm not a prude, but he wanted me to do things that I wouldn't do, sexual things over the telephone that I wouldn't do." He also sent her letters that included the numbers of stolen credit cards and asked her to use them to buy things for him.

"I didn't know what was happening. It was like this was a different man from the one I married and loved."

Overnight, Post stopped writing and calling. Her letters went unanswered. Even her children couldn't get Post to reply. A few months later, Kane received a copy of divorce papers from Post in the mail. "We always had promised if we ever parted, we'd tell each other face-to-face," she said. "Then these papers arrived with no explanation, nothing."

Several years later, when Post was asked about Kane and her children, he said that he had loved them, but had intentionally ended the relationship after his parole was denied.

"It was hard to cut it off, particularly because of the little girl," Post said. "She [Priscilla Kane] was really special, but when I realized that I wasn't getting out, I knew I had to end it. She was such a loving person that she would have stuck with me and would still be here today if I hadn't driven her away, but what was the point? What kind of life could she and those kids have had waiting for me? I decided to drive her away. I had to do it, if not for her, then for my own sanity. It is much harder to do time if you are looking to the future, particularly if you know there isn't any future out there.

"I don't know how she feels about me, but the truth is that ending the relationship was probably the only decent thing I have done in my life."

For three years Kane grieved over Post. "I felt so stupid,"

she said. "I used to look in the mirror and say, 'You were a straight-A student, you are intelligent, how did you let someone do this to you?' " During her five-year relationship with Post, she had given him nearly $10,000. But it was the emotional toll on herself and her children that hurt the most, she said. "My son and daughter idolized this man. *He was their father!* And then he just walked away. They couldn't understand how anyone could be so cold, and neither could I.

"Most women I met at prison were abused, mistreated, and misunderstood in the outside world," Kane explained. "All they wanted was someone to love them, and then they fell into that trap where the man that they loved used them. . . . I thought we were different—I *knew* we were different. But after all these years, I honestly don't know if Bill really ever loved me or was simply using me to get a parole.

"Can you believe it?" she asked. "I loved this man, married this man, planned to build my future with this man, and believed in this man, and today I still don't know whether he loved me or was simply using me."

PART FOUR

Cain said to Abel his brother, "Let us go out to the field." And when they were in the field, Cain rose up against his brother Abel, and killed him. Then the LORD said to Cain, "Where is Abel your brother?" He said, "I do not know; am I my brother's keeper?"

THE FIRST MURDER
Genesis, chapter 4, verses 8–9
The Holy Bible

CHAPTER
FORTY-THREE

THE LIEUTENANT'S OFFICE

Lieutenant Monty Watkins was typing a report early Sunday morning when the control center sounded an alarm. Watkins dashed down center hall, through the rotunda and steel gates, and into the lobby of the administration building where an elderly, heavyset woman was lying on the floor. She had collapsed while waiting to go into the prison visiting room. Vandell Racy, the guard stationed in the lobby, was administering CPR.

The woman had come to visit her son, a bank robber. She had thin silver hair, cut short, and was dressed in a baggy and badly faded paisley-print dress. When she collapsed, her skirt had pulled up above her knees, revealing pale, flabby skin and numerous varicose veins. A woman in her forties, later identified as her daughter, was kneeling next to the woman.

"Oh, Mama! Mama!" the daughter wailed. "Is she gonna be all right? Is she gonna make it? Oh, Mama, Mama! Do something! Did you call an ambulance? Is a doctor coming? Oh, Mama, Mama, please don't die. Is the ambulance coming?"

No one answered her questions nor did she wait for answers. As Racy continued to push on the woman's chest, her daughter continued screaming, "Oh, Mama, don't die! Don't die!"

Standing at the feet of the old woman was a little girl with Down's syndrome. She was about the size of an eight-year-old and clutched a well-worn doll in her left hand. The doll was

307

wearing a dress made from the same paisley fabric as the elderly woman's. The child spotted Watkins and stared at the huge black lieutenant as he lifted his portable radio to his mouth and asked if an ambulance was en route.

As soon as the shrieking daughter heard Watkins talk into the radio, she turned on him. "It's all your fault. The chair outside don't work. I told her not to climb them steps today. Yesterday, she felt dizzy all morning and sick, but she's got to see her son. We drove three days to see him. Why didn't you fix that chair? I'm telling you, it's your fault."

The woman was referring to an electrically driven chair outside the penitentiary that was supposed to carry elderly and handicapped visitors up the forty-three front steps. The chair ran along a track beside the handrail, but it never had worked well and had been inoperative for some time.

"Oh my God! Is she breathing? I don't see her breath!" the daughter cried.

"She's breathing," Racy replied calmly.

An ambulance pulled in front of the penitentiary and two paramedics ran into the lobby. "I got a pulse," said one, as they lifted the old woman onto a stretcher and carried her out the glass front doors. The daughter grabbed the little girl's hand and pulled her toward the exit. Before they left, the daughter turned and again yelled at Watkins: "It's your fault."

The little girl, still clutching her doll, smiled at him.

Watkins looked at his watch: 8:52 A.M. When he returned to the lieutenant's office, the phone rang. It was the control center calling.

"What time?" Watkins asked, scribbling a note. "9:04. Okay, got it. How old? Eighty-four. Is the chaplain around? Well, someone needs to tell the inmate that she's dead. Okay. Thanks."

The old woman had died before reaching the Leavenworth hospital. She had suffered a heart attack. Watkins slipped a sheet of paper into the typewriter and began writing a report about the incident.

"If her son hadn't been in prison, she wouldn't have had to walk up the steps to visit him," he said. "Don't see how she can blame me."

The next day a maintenance crew fixed the chair.

CHAPTER
FORTY-FOUR

EDWARD GEOUGE

"My name is Geouge. I'm the disciplinary-hearing officer," Eddie Geouge explained to an inmate who sat, hands cuffed behind his back, on the edge of a metal chair across the table from Geouge. They were in an office in the Hole. The prisoner had been accused of assaulting a guard and had been brought before Geouge for a hearing. His was one of ten cases that Geouge was scheduled to resolve on a Tuesday in late December 1988, in his new role as the DHO at Leavenworth. As such, Geouge would determine whether the man was guilty and then recommend a punishment. Geouge's report would be sent to his boss, Regional Director DuBois, for approval. A copy would go to Warden Matthews. In the bureau's eyes, the fact that Geouge worked for the regional office rather than directly for the warden insured the DHO a certain independence.

"You are accused of—" Geouge continued, but the convict interrupted him.

"This is a joke," the convict declared. "I didn't do a damn thing!"

"Now listen," Geouge said sternly, looking straight at him. "I'm going to read you this charge. Then I'm going to ask you how you plead. You will get—"

"Didn't do a damn thing. Ain't fucking right," the convict interrupted again, louder this time, totally ignoring Geouge. "I ain't gonna sit here and—"

"You're right about that," Geouge interjected, "because I'll have you removed if you can't control—"

"Shit, all this is—"

"Look," snapped Geouge, "I'm trying to read this charge. Now, you aren't going to run this hearing, *I* am going—"

"Fuck those papers!" the inmate yelled, lunging forward from the chair. A guard standing behind him grabbed his left shoulder and pulled him back. Another guard stepped forward to help.

Geouge tried again. "You are not going to run this hearing," he repeated. "Now, let's start this again, and this time you let me finish and then I'll be polite and let you say what's on your mind. The charge against you is—"

"Fuck the charge," the inmate declared. "And fuck you."

"Get him out of here," Geouge ordered. The guards took the inmate's arms and escorted him out the door and down the tier to his cell. He continued yelling profanities at Geouge as he was taken past other cells.

"You tell 'em, brother," an inmate shouted.

"Fuck 'em," called another.

Back inside the conference room, Geouge turned to his secretary: "Be sure to note that I told him three times to be quiet, but he refused and lunged forward." Geouge examined the inmate's thick prison record and read several written statements the guards had filed about the alleged assault. "I find this inmate guilty and sentence him to thirty days in the Hole and recommend a transfer to Marion," Geouge said. The secretary noted his decision. Only the regional director could approve a transfer to Marion, but most were automatically granted if they were recommended by a DHO.

The confrontation annoyed Geouge. As he walked over to a stainless-steel coffeepot that looked as if it had never been cleaned and filled his cup, he said, "Most of these guys hate the police when they're on the street, so why would anyone think they'd change when they come in here? There's not much I can do when one of them wants to be a shit but haul his ass out of here."

According to bureau regulations, Geouge was the only official at Leavenworth with the authority to sentence an inmate to the Hole. Guards, lieutenants, and Warden Matthews could send an inmate there temporarily, but after sixty days he either had to be released or formally charged and taken before Geouge for a hearing. These internal sessions were much different from court hearings and were intentionally stacked in the guards' favor. Statements by staff members were automatically considered more credible than those by inmates, and while inmates could call witnesses to speak in their defense, they were not allowed to question the guards. If an inmate wished, he could ask to be represented by a staff member who could ask questions on his behalf, but the bureau did not permit inmates to interrogate a guard directly, nor did it allow convicts to hide behind legal technicalities and other niceties afforded them in a regular court. If a guard said an inmate was guilty, that was good enough for the bureau. Because the process was so skewed in favor of the guards, inmates often claimed that the hearing process was a sham. They complained that nearly everyone who was brought before a hearing officer was found guilty. In the bureau's defense, nearly all of the inmates arrested *were* guilty and the cases against them so blatant that it would have been impossible for a hearing officer to rule any other way.

But unlike his predecessor, who had a reputation for rubber-stamping cases, Geouge grilled the accused and the guards to make certain each was telling the truth. Although he had only been the hearing officer for a few months, he had managed to irritate some guards by rejecting their incident reports, commonly called "shots," which outlined the charges against the inmate.

When Geouge saw the next inmate being brought into the room, he figured his day was going from bad to worse. This prisoner had been accused of making a bomb out of thousands of sulfur match-heads he had hoarded, packed into a can, and then wrapped with roofing nails. Guards claimed he planned to attach the bomb to the light socket in another inmate's cell so that when the man flipped the switch, the electric current would ignite the match-heads, causing an explosion that would shoot the nails across the cell like shrapnel. Geouge read the charge and the statements by four guards who claimed the inmate had started running when a guard decided to frisk him. During the chase that followed, the inmate stripped off his pea-green jacket and threw it to the floor. Officer Bill Terrell looked through the pockets and found the bomb, which he cautiously carried outside the prison. The device was later destroyed by the Leavenworth bomb squad.

"This charge is a bunch of shit," the inmate said after

Geouge finished reciting the details of the case. "I wasn't wearing a coat and I can prove it." He had three eyewitnesses, he said, who were willing to testify that he was being framed by a guard who didn't like him. Geouge called the witnesses into the room one by one and listened to their statements.

"Did you see him throw down his jacket?" Geouge asked the first one.

"No, sir," came the reply. "Why, he wasn't wearing a jacket."

Geouge rephrased his question when quizzing the second.

"What color jacket was the inmate wearing?" he asked. But the witness saw through the trick.

"I don't remember him wearing a jacket," he testified. "No, sir, I'm sure he wasn't."

When the third witness was brought in, Geouge tried a new tactic. He asked him to describe what the inmate was wearing, beginning with the color of his shoes.

"He was wearing black shoes, green pants . . ." the inmate said.

"Wait, you said black pants and green shoes?"

"No, green pants and black shoes."

"Black shoes?"

"That's right."

"And green pants?" asked Geouge. "Okay, I got it. Now, was his jacket black or green?"

"Oh, it was green, pea green, you know," the convict blurted out before realizing his blunder. "I mean, uh, it wasn't green, it was, uh, well, he didn't have no jacket on."

Geouge dismissed the man and quickly turned to the accused. "Do you go by the nickname 'The Hated One'?" Geouge asked.

"Never heard that before. Man, that's really cold. Who'd go by something like that?" he replied cockily.

"Your prison record says you have used that nickname for several years."

"That's a lie."

"Four officers said they saw you throw down the jacket."

"They're lying, all of them."

"You know what was written in the jacket?"

"How could I?" the inmate asked. "It wasn't mine."

"Inside someone had written 'Property of The Hated One.' "
The inmate shrugged, unmoved.

Geouge found him guilty, sentenced him to 120 days in the Hole, and recommended a transfer to Marion.

For the next four hours, Geouge dispensed prison justice. Several convicts had been caught drinking homemade hooch, one had disobeyed an order, another had put a knife to an inmate's throat and demanded sex. Besides those cases, Geouge had two others held over from a hearing a week before. One involved a bulky white inmate covered with tattoos, serving several life terms for murder. Guards had found a shank hidden in the bed in his cell, but he had told Geouge that the bed had been moved into his cell only a few hours before the knife was discovered. It was a replacement brought in because his bed was broken.

"I never seen that knife before," the inmate had claimed.

The story seemed plausible, so Geouge had postponed making a decision until he had a chance to investigate the inmate's story. He discovered that the bed had just been moved into the inmate's cell as he had claimed.

"I checked out your story," Geouge said when the inmate was brought into the room.

"Okay," the inmate snarled.

"Well, what you told me is the truth, so I'm expunging this charge and turning you loose."

The inmate was shocked. "Well, this is a first," he said.

"I figure you've been a shithead in other areas, but not this time," Geouge replied.

"Hell, Geouge," the inmate said with a grin. "You know me. If I have a weapon, I'm going to use it."

"Get out of here," Geouge said, "and don't come back."

Geouge had conducted a second investigation on his own since the hearings last week. This case involved a convicted murderer who had demanded that he be moved into one of the cells above the prison hospital, where inmates who needed to be protected from other convicts were housed for their own safety. The inmate claimed he owed several thousand dollars in gambling debts and was going to be murdered unless he was moved to "PC"—protective custody.

Geouge had been suspicious because the convict had been in

various prisons for more than twenty years and clearly knew
how to take care of himself. In fact, his prison file showed that he
had been accused of shaking down weaker inmates and it listed
him as a reputed hit man for a California motorcycle gang.

Geouge had discovered that the inmate's real motive in
wanting to move into a cell above the hospital was money. He
had reportedly accepted a contract to kill an inmate housed
there who had disclosed a drug-smuggling operation in B cellhouse. Had Geouge agreed to the move, the inmate would have
been able to complete the murder-for-hire.

"I don't believe your story," said Geouge when the inmate
was brought before him. "But if you're really in danger, you'll be
safer here in the Hole, so we'll just take this one day at a time."

The inmate was angry. "Hey, I demand you move me to PC."

"Hey," Geouge replied in the identical tone of voice. "You
don't demand anything here. You'll be safe in the Hole." (A few
days later, the inmate asked to be returned to the general population.)

Geouge worked through lunch without taking a break. By
late afternoon, he was ready to hear his final case of the day. It
involved a twenty-nine-year-old black inmate from Washington,
D.C., accused of gambling on Sunday football games.

"I'm guilty," the inmate replied when Geouge asked how he
wished to plead.

The case seemed rather simple. It had been a long day.
Geouge's secretary and the guards in the room were anxious to
leave, but there was something about the convict's docility that
made Geouge decide to ask a few more questions.

"Like to gamble?" Geouge asked.

"I got nothing else to do to pass the time, man."

"Who'd you bet on last Sunday?"

"Chicago. I always bet Chicago Bears."

"Then you lost?"

"Yeah, fifteen bucks, and I only get sixteen a month working
in industry."

"Well, we did you a favor by locking your butt up and
keeping you from wasting any more money," said Geouge.

The convict chuckled. "I've been saving up for the Super
Bowl," he said candidly. "I love watching that Super Bowl especially if my Bears are in it."

"Jesus!" Geouge said as he read through the inmate's record. "You've been busted for gambling several times and once for having more than the twenty-dollar cash limit in your cell."

"Yeah," said the inmate. "That's the only weekend I won."

Everyone in the room laughed. The convict's honesty was a refreshing change. Geouge continued reading the file. "I see why you gamble," he said. The inmate was serving a 125-year sentence for robbery, rape, and assaulting a police officer. He had already served seven years.

"What else am I going to do in here?" the inmate asked. "I don't have a chance to party like you do."

"Do I look to you like someone who likes to party?" Geouge replied gruffly.

"No, uh, no sir, I mean, you look like you got something to go home to, sir. What the hell do I have to do to enjoy my time? I bet, but I don't get over my head and I always pay up. My reputation is good, you ask anyone, I always pay and never cause trouble."

"Listen," said Geouge, "we're trying to tighten up on gambling because some guys are getting in over their heads, but I'm going to suspend this and turn you loose. The catch is, you got to maintain clean conduct for six months. If you're caught gambling, you're coming back to the Hole to serve time on this charge and any new charges. You understand?"

"Thank you," the inmate said. He stood to leave, but before he reached the door, Geouge stopped him.

"Hey, I want you to do me a favor," Geouge said. "Before you place your bet on the Super Bowl, come find me and tell me which team you're backing, because with your record I want to bet on the other team."

The inmate appeared confused. He turned toward the door, then stopped and turned around as if he wanted to speak, only to turn toward the door once again and stop. And then he finally understood. Geouge was giving him a break. The veteran officer knew that the inmate wasn't going to stop gambling, particularly with the Super Bowl coming up. But Geouge also understood, he said later, that sometimes a twenty-nine-year-old inmate facing another 118 years in prison deserved a bit of compassion, particularly when he had told the truth at his hearing and was willing to take his punishment without complaint.

"Hey, Geouge," the inmate said as he stood in the doorway of the hearing room.

"Yeah?" Geouge replied.

"For a cop, you're all right."

CHAPTER
FORTY-FIVE

WILLIAM SLACK

On Christmas Day, Warden Matthews decided to pay a surprise visit to the Cuban units. As he and Bill Slack walked from cell to cell wishing the detainees a Merry Christmas, one of them began to applaud. He said in broken English that he was showing his appreciation to Slack. Two weeks earlier, Slack had brought a Polaroid camera, white shirt, black tie, and sport jacket into the cellhouse. He told the detainees that they could each put on the clothes and have their picture taken in an area of the cellhouse where the cells and bars wouldn't be visible. They could mail the pictures to their wives, friends, and family enclosed with Christmas cards that were being donated to them by a local card manufacturer. The Cuban said he had been in prison for seven years and this was the first photograph that he had been able to send home to his children.

Slack grinned sheepishly, told the Cuban in awkward Spanish *"Felices Navidad,"* and continued down the tier with Matthews. Then the man in the next cell also applauded and suddenly the entire tier began clapping for Slack.

As he and Matthews walked up and down the five levels, inmates stood at the front of their cells cheering and applauding. Matthews was exuberant when he left the unit. Slack beamed with pride. Five days later, guards found a Cuban hanging from his cell. He had committed suicide.

"This place is a roller coaster," Slack said. "Highs and lows, highs and lows."

317

Because the suicide was the first by a Cuban detainee in Leavenworth since the Atlanta and Oakdale riots, nearly all the major newspapers and national television networks carried the story. Most claimed the Cubans being housed in the penitentiary were despondent. *The Kansas City Star* reported that Warden Matthews had ordered his staff to perform a "psychological autopsy" to determine why the Cuban had killed himself. But "to others, there was no mystery," the newspaper wrote. It quoted George Crossland, cofounder of the Mariel Assistance Program, a support group for detainees and their families, saying, "These people have told me over and over and over they'd rather die than go back to Cuba."

Reporters assumed that the Cuban had killed himself because of the conditions at the penitentiary. It made for a powerful story, but it was not true. He had left a note, and in it he explained that he was committing suicide because he had just learned that he had the AIDS virus and his homosexual lover had left him.

Fred Fry, the prison's spokesman, knew the reason for the suicide, but he was prohibited by federal privacy laws from releasing the inmate's medical records, so there was no way for him to correct the inaccurate news accounts.

The incident disturbed Slack, not because of the media's faulty assumptions, but because he realized that the bureau hadn't taken any special precautions to prevent AIDS from spreading inside the Cuban units. Whenever an American inmate was diagnosed as having AIDS, he was transferred to the bureau's medical center in Springfield, Missouri. But Cubans with AIDS were being kept in the same cellhouses as those not infected. Slack knew that homosexual activity among Cubans was rampant. He also knew that most Cubans didn't know who had the disease. Yet, when Slack mentioned the potential danger of keeping all the Cubans with AIDS in the units, he was told that the bureau had no choice. Because of the riots, all Cubans who were considered to be troublemakers were to remain in the Hot House.

Slack began to worry about his guards. Whenever a Cuban was diagnosed as having AIDS, a notation was made in his prison file, though the acronym AIDS was never mentioned. Instead, the bureau wrote "body fluid precaution." Guards working in the Cuban units were supposed to be familiar with the inmates' files, but Slack knew that many of them never checked the records.

After the suicide, Slack made a point of reminding his guards about the threat of AIDS, particularly when they were responding to emergencies that involved a Cuban who was bleeding. Each guard was told to carry plastic surgical gloves with him and put them on when he came in contact with blood, but despite Slack's warnings, few ever did.

A few weeks after the suicide in C cellhouse, the guards who had worked with the Cubans received good news. The bureau's Office of Inspections finally announced that it could not substantiate any of the brutality charges filed by the former prison counselor at Leavenworth. The investigators, who had never spoken to any Cubans at the Hot House, said their probe had documented some isolated incidents which indicated Cubans were treated in ways "inconsistent with bureau policy," but there was no evidence that Cubans had been systematically brutalized.

"This wasn't really a surprise," Warden Matthews said nonchalantly when he heard the announcement. "I knew all along that the charges were exaggerated."

But at Benny's that night, the guards who had been under suspicion held a spontaneous celebration. More than one had been afraid that he would be reprimanded. "If I followed the best officer in Leavenworth around for a month, I could gather enough evidence on him to get him fired," said one guard. "It's not that you set out to screw up. It's just that all of us are bound to make mistakes in this business, and that includes losing your temper and reacting sometimes in violation of bureau regulations."

Another guard admitted that he had been one of the officers who had violated regulations. "I had a real loudmouth yelling and screaming on my tier and I couldn't get him to shut up. He kept trying to start trouble. Finally, I sent my number-two officer to get something from the office downstairs so I could be alone. I ran down to the Cuban's cell and called him up to the bars, and when he got there, I grabbed his throat and pulled his face up against the bars so he cracked his forehead real good. I said, 'You dumb motherfucker, shut the fuck up,' and, you know, after that he always kept quiet on my shift." When asked if he had told the investigators that story, the guard laughed.

Someone suggested a toast to the late Phillip Shoats, Jr., and after a few seconds of embarrassed silence, several of Shoats's defenders raised their beer cans.

"I don't care what he did at home," said one. "He was okay at work."

A few minutes later, a guard mentioned Juan Torres, the suspected snitch.

"It's payback time," said one.

"We should jump that prick in the parking lot and whip his ass."

"Don't worry. He'll get his. It's just a matter of time. Everyone knows he's a snitch, and someday he'll get into a situation where he's going to need someone backing him up, and when that happens, he'll discover there's no one there—just like when we needed him to back us up and he wasn't there."

None of the guards thought that Torres was innocent. "It doesn't matter how the investigation turned out. That fuck betrayed us all by talking."

Another guard added, "These headhunters will ruin your career, just like they did Geouge because he slapped a Cuban. Well, if an inmate even looks like he's gonna take a shot at me, I'm getting in the first lick. No one pays us to be punching bags."

The next day Slack happened to see Torres, and the lieutenant asked him if the pressure was off now that Internal Affairs had cleared the Cuban units. Torres said that someone was still writing the name SNITCH on his mailbox. When it came time for the quarterly staff rotation, Slack recommended that Torres be assigned to a guard tower rather than put into a cellhouse, where he would have to depend on other guards if there were a fight or stabbing. Connor agreed.

"I'm not going to let anyone drive me away," Torres said later. "I'm not a coward, but this treatment really gets to you after a while." Most guards, he said, refused to speak to him.

Despite Slack's progress in the Cuban units, he still found the pressure frustrating. "This place swallows you up," he explained. "Just communicating a simple request becomes a major task." The stress of eighteen-hour days was beginning to show. At his wife's urging, he decided to take a weekend off and go fishing. But as he was leaving one Friday afternoon, a guard nicknamed Beans because of his Boston accent came into Slack's office with a "shot" that he wanted Slack to take action on. Beans claimed that a Cuban had refused an order and he wanted the inmate locked in an isolation cell as punishment.

Slack recognized the Cuban's name and he knew that the detainee was not a troublemaker. He also knew that Beans was. Slack took the shot and slipped it in his desk drawer. He would take care of it on Monday, he decided, when he had time to hear the inmate's version. Beans looked angry when he left Slack's office that afternoon.

Although the fish weren't biting over the weekend, Slack returned on Monday relaxed. He had only been at his desk for a few minutes when guard Jacob Tyler came in carrying a knife.

"Hey, boss, I found this shank," he said.

Slack picked up the weapon and examined it. It looked familiar.

"Where'd you find it?" Slack asked.

"Cell one-eighteen," said Tyler.

Suddenly Slack remembered where he had seen the knife before, and he recalled the name of the Cuban assigned to cell 118. Slack knew that Tyler was lying.

"Want me to put the Cuban in isolation?" Tyler asked.

"No," said Slack.

As soon as Tyler left, Slack called in Beans.

"What's up, boss?" Beans asked.

"You planting shanks nowadays?" Slack replied, tossing the knife across his desk. Beans looked puzzled. "You need to tell your buddy that if he's going to plant a shank, he shouldn't pick one that's already been turned in before."

The knife that Tyler claimed to have discovered in the Cuban's cell had been turned in to the lieutenant's office several months earlier. By chance, Slack had been there when it was found. He remembered it because of its peculiar shape.

Beans seemed surprised. "I don't know nothing, I swear," he stammered. Then why had Tyler claimed that he had found the knife in the cell of the very same Cuban that Beans had reported on Friday?

Slack was ready to recommend that both guards be reprimanded, but first he sent Beans to talk to Tyler and find out what was happening. A short while later, Beans returned. He admitted that he had been angry Friday and had complained to Tyler. At that point, Tyler had said, "I'll fix that Cuban," but Beans swore he hadn't helped Tyler plant the knife.

Tyler came to Slack's house that night and admitted taking the knife from the lieutenant's office and lying about finding it in cell 118. He was trying to "help out" Beans, he said, and pleaded with Slack not to report him. All he had ever wanted to be was a guard. His grandfather had worked at the penitentiary and Tyler wanted to make the old man proud. As he talked, Tyler began to cry.

"It's my life," he said. "Don't fire me."

But Slack had done some checking on Tyler, and had learned that other lieutenants suspected him of planting knives in the past. Most guards consider themselves lucky if they find one knife every six months, but during one 6-week period, Tyler had turned in more than a dozen knives. Slack didn't mind bending rules when it came to allowing a Cuban to keep extra granola bars, but he didn't like a liar and he didn't like anyone who planted evidence. He suggested that Tyler resign to avoid an investigation that would embarrass him and the bureau.

The next day Tyler quit without giving the personnel office an explanation.

CHAPTER FORTY-SIX

WILLIAM POST

The inmate informant's hand was shaking as he lit a cigarette, took a deep drag, and slowly blew the smoke out, calming his nerves.

"They moved the date up," he said. "They're gonna bust out this Friday."

Lieutenant Bill Thomas could tell the man was frightened. He had reason to be. For the past several days, he had been providing Thomas with information about what he claimed was a major prison breakout being plotted jointly by two groups, the Black Liberation Army, a militant black gang, and The Order, a neo-Nazi white-supremacy group. The unlikely alliance planned to smuggle in several handguns, which they would use in an attack on the rear gate of the penitentiary where deliveries were made. When the inmates began shooting inside the compound, two vans carrying armed men were supposed to rush up to the back gate after a sniper had killed the tower guard there. They would scale the tower, where the controls for the double rear gates were located. Once inside, they would free the inmates and escape.

It was a wild story, but Thomas, an eighteen-year bureau veteran, was convinced the informant was telling him the truth. He had always given reliable information in the past, and Thomas knew enough about the BLA and The Order to know neither would hesitate to launch such a bloody assault. But Thomas had no hard evidence and there was no time for him to get any. The escape was originally scheduled to take place in several weeks, but the inmate had just learned that the guns were being smuggled inside in two days, on January 5, with the escape now scheduled for Friday, January 6.

"You got to move now," the inmate told Thomas.

"How are they bringing in the guns?"

The snitch whispered, "The Catman."

William Post was sleeping when six guards rushed into his cell. At first, he thought he was dreaming.

"Wake up!" one yelled.

Post, who slept with his wristwatch on, looked at the dial. It was ten minutes after twelve, January 4, 1989. "I thought I'd overslept and it was noontime and I'd missed work," he said later. "But when we walked out on the tier, there was no one else around, and it hit me that it was midnight—not noon—and I was being arrested."

"Where we going?" Post asked.

"You know where you're going," Lieutenant Monty Watkins replied.

"Why you guys doing this?"

"You know why," Watkins answered.

Irritated, Post snapped, "Okay, sure—I know where and I know why."

He was taken to the Hole without any further exchange and within the next few hours, six more inmates joined him. A special squad of guards also hustled two inmates to an airstrip, where they were flown on a private plane to Marion. By noon, everyone in the Hot House knew about the arrests and that Bruce Carroll Pierce, age 30, and Richard Scutari, age 38, had been transferred to Marion during the night as punishment for being the alleged masterminds of the escape plot.

When Thomas had learned the escape had been moved up, he had met immediately with Associate Warden Connor and Warden Matthews, who gave their approval for the arrests of Post and the six others, and the emergency trip for Pierce and Scutari. The informant had been moved to another prison for his own safety.

Pierce and Scutari were members of The Order and both were serving long sentences for the murder of radio talk-show host Alan Berg. Pierce had fired the machine-gun burst that killed Berg on June 18, 1984, as he returned to his home in Denver, Colorado, after his nightly radio show. Scutari had been the lookout. Berg's murder was supposed to be the first in a series of assassinations by members of The Order in their self-declared war against ZOG, an acronym for the "Zionist Occupational Government," the catchall term The Order used to describe Jews, blacks, liberals, and anyone else its members didn't like. They had killed Berg because he was a "liberal Jew."

Besides murder, Pierce and Scutari had also been found guilty of stealing $3.6 million during the robbery of a Brinks truck in northern California. Scutari had read the Ninety-first Psalm aloud to The Order members before the heist; Pierce had jumped onto the hood of the armored truck when it was forced off Highway 20 near Ukiah and had sprayed the windshield with bullets. Only half of the money had ever been recovered.

Three of the inmates taken to the Hole with Post were members of the Black Liberation Army, a sworn enemy of all whites. But necessity had made the two groups join forces, Thomas said. "They had a common bond. All of the inmates were doing heavy, heavy time, and they all wanted out."

The informant had told Thomas that the BLA was responsible for smuggling the guns in and that Pierce and Scutari were in charge of arranging the outside attack on the rear tower. That assault was going to be made by members of various white hate groups who considered Pierce and Scutari political prisoners and heroes. Post belonged to neither the BLA or The Order, but he had been recruited because he helped load trash from the prison kitchen into a truck that came into the penitentiary compound three times a week to remove refuse. The guns for the escape were supposed to be smuggled in on that truck and it was Post's job to get them off and hide them.

"Post was a pivotal player in the escape," Thomas said. "He was in it as deep as you can get."

Thanks to the informant's tip, Thomas was confident that all the inmates involved in the plot had been arrested before they were able to smuggle in any guns. But there was no way to tell if their friends outside the prison had heard about the arrests. As far as Thomas knew, they could still be planning to kill the rear tower guard at a predetermined time on Friday, January 6, and race up to the gate in their two vans. Not wishing to take any chances, Connor decided on January 5 that all guards in the gun towers were to wear bulletproof vests until further notice. The next morning, four guards dressed in military flak jackets and carrying automatic rifles sat in an unmarked car parked in front of the penitentiary. The engine was kept running so that they could respond within moments if there were an emergency. All day Friday, tower guards used binoculars to scan visitors and their vehicles as they arrived at the penitentiary. Inside the prison, guards used hand-held metal detectors to check inmates for weapons. One convict later complained that he had been searched seventeen times in less than three hours.

By nightfall, Thomas and the guards began to relax. Nothing unusual had happened. The guards in the tower wore bulletproof vests over the weekend, but the four guards stationed in the car were ordered back to their regular posts. By Monday, the vests were back in storage.

Post sat in the Hole for seven days before officials told him and the other six inmates why they had been arrested. Each was offered a deal. If any inmate was willing to testify in court against the others, he would not be charged with escape and would be dealt with more leniently.

"We really don't have sufficient evidence to prove what Pierce, Scutari, and Post were up to," Thomas acknowledged, "at least not in a court of law." Unless one of the inmates agreed to be a witness, none of the convicts could be charged with attempted escape in the federal courthouse in Topeka. "The only way we could have gotten enough proof to prosecute these inmates in a federal court," Warden Matthews said, "is by letting them actually go ahead with their plan, letting them smuggle guns in here and attack the rear gate. Obviously, I am not going to jeopardize my people or inmates in order to make a case."

Post and the other inmates knew what was going on and they were suspicious whenever one of them was taken out of the Hole for questioning, worried that he might talk. When guards told Post that I wanted to speak with him and he agreed, one inmate yelled, "Hey, Post, why you talking to some writer?"

"Because I want to," Post replied.

"Maybe you're thinking of snitching."

"Maybe I am," Post replied calmly, "and maybe I'm going

to slip into your cell tonight and slit your throat, stupid mother-fucker."

Other inmates laughed. Most had seen the two of us talking numerous times before.

Post was led into an isolation cell near the front door of the Hole for our interview. Lieutenant Edward Pierce ordered guards to leave his hands cuffed behind his back even though we were separated by bars. That irked Post. "A few days ago, you and I were walking around the prison and no one thought any-thing of it," he complained. "Now, I'm such a dangerous convict, I have to be handcuffed and kept in a cage when we talk. This is all part of the macho bullshit around here. They're showing me they are in charge—as if I needed to be reminded."

Post said the escape plot was a hoax. "Some snitch made up the entire thing and they have fallen for it. Now, they've locked up everyone who they think might know something, and they are waiting to see who is going to be the first to snitch. They're hoping someone will come in and tell them what they want to hear, and the really sick part is that someone will, because it'll help him get a parole. They'll just make something up."

As far as Post was concerned, he was a victim of circum-stance. Because he worked at the trash dumpster and had struck up a friendship with Pierce, he had been included in the "escape fantasy."

"Some snitch saw us talking, and thought, 'Hey, why would a so-called nigger lover'—me—'be talking to an Order guy, a white supremacist?' We're supposed to hate each other. Then he makes up this elaborate escape plot all because Pierce and I just like to debate one another."

Several days passed, yet no inmate came forward to testify against his peers. Post had always hated prison. He wanted to be free. But like the others, he refused to rat. Since none of the inmates had confessed, federal prosecutors couldn't file crimi-nal charges against anyone, but the bureau had enough evidence to bring Post and the others before Eddie Geouge for a DHO hearing, and all of them were found guilty based on statements by Lieutenant Thomas and the informant. Post was told that he was being transferred to the penitentiary at Lompoc, California.

"I don't really care anymore," Post said. "I mean, after the Parole Commission turned me down the last time, it became clear to me that they are going to make me do twenty or twenty-five years in prison for bank robbery. It doesn't matter what I do or don't do, whether I am good or bad, I am going to spend twenty-five years in prison.

"Let's be real frank here. If society had wanted me to make it, the parole board should've cut me loose when I was married [to Priscilla Kane], but they didn't, so now, in my mind, I've been cutting the streets loose. They are no longer part of my life."

His only regret about leaving was the cats. "I was outside in the exercise area yesterday and I saw Tiger, and they say cats forget you and don't miss you, but I saw Tiger and he runs over, so I reached out and petted him and he purred like he was saying, 'Hey, where you been?' " Shortly after he was arrested, Post had sent word to Carl Bowles and asked him to feed the cats. Bowles, who worked in the west yard near the trash dumpster where Post kept his cat supplies, had agreed. "I know Carl will take care of Tiger for me," Post said. "He'll be okay. I'm weaning myself from Tiger too now. I have to."

A short time later, he was ordered to pack his personal belongings. We talked for a final time in the Hole about his life.

"If I could keep only one memory or moment in my life and that was it—all the rest would be erased—I think the one moment that I would keep is the shootout with the police in Glendale. The experience of shooting it out with that cop was absolutely, totally, the most beautiful experience in my life. I'm not crazy. *It was beautiful!*

"Do you know what happens in moments of extreme peril? Time slows down. Things seem to be in slow motion. You get tunnel vision. You get audio collapse and can't hear things. Perhaps it is because I'm such a spin-out and have eighteen things going around in my mind at once. Maybe that focusing was good, but again, this is not an exaggeration, that moment of pure terror and peril was the absolute best. It was like they say when someone goes to the gallows. Every color is that much brighter, every smell that much stronger. It was that absolute shitty scariness of knowing that you could be killed at any second, that your life could be suddenly taken away, that made it so exhilarating.

"The truth is, I've always liked living on the edge of madness, being the one out there—the one that they are trying to catch—the lone warrior who does his own thing, who answers only to himself."

By this time, the guards were ready to take Post.

"There is an old prison saying," Post said before leaving. "Whenever a guard gives you an order, a convict quietly thinks to himself, 'Okay, boss, I understand. I know the rules. This is your prison, but they are my streets.' In here, they got the keys. They can do what they want with me. The Parole Commission can continue to reject my appeals. But someday I'll be out, someday I'll be free, and they will be my streets again."

Post left. I later heard that the first thing he did when he arrived at Lompoc was ask if there were any cats around.

CHAPTER FORTY-SEVEN

THE LIEUTENANT'S OFFICE

During the four o'clock count, when inmates were locked in their cells, three guards escorted a tall, muscular black inmate from the Hole, across the yard into the penitentiary, and down center hall. Two guards were standing on each side of the prisoner holding him by the arms; the third walked behind them. As the group reached the rotunda, several guards talking there became quiet. The inmate's head fell forward and flopped from side to side. A string of drool hung from his mouth.

One of the guards explained what was going on. The night before, the inmate had thrown his dinner tray at Ray Moore, the senior guard assigned to the Hole. That morning, he burned the mattress in his cell. When guards moved him to another cell in the Hole, he stripped and somehow set his own clothes on fire. Guards called one of the prison's three psychologists, who examined the inmate, said he was clearly "mentally unstable," and recommended that he be moved to the bureau's psychiatric ward at the medical center in Springfield, Missouri. It was where all mentally disturbed convicts were housed. Just before the four o'clock count, a team of guards went into the inmate's cell and held him down so a physician's assistant could give him "the juice." Most inmates feared this more than any other action. The first shot contained three hundred milligrams of the antipsychotic drug Thorazine, but that wasn't enough to knock out the bulky convict. The second pop contained a slightly larger dose and it had done the trick.

"He ain't feeling no pain now," said James Luongo, one of the escorting guards, as he passed us in the rotunda.

"Hey, maybe I should get some juice," another guard joked. "It looks like good shit."

The convict was led outside into the afternoon sunshine and down the front steps of the prison, his feet dragging helplessly a step or two behind him. His eyes were open but unfocused. The guards lifted him into the backseat of a waiting van. His cuffed hands fell loosely into his lap, his head fell forward, and his mouth continued to drool.

"I hope he don't shit his pants," said one of the guards assigned to ride in the van with the prisoner to Springfield. "They sometimes do that, you know. They just lose it after they get the juice, and you have to ride all the way to Springfield smelling that shit."

"At least he ain't gonna cause us any trouble," said another guard.

They all laughed.

CHAPTER
FORTY-EIGHT

ROBERT MATTHEWS

Word that Warden Matthews had prevented an escape by The Order and the Black Liberation Army spread through the bureau, and within days there were rumors around Leavenworth that he was going to be promoted. It wasn't only the escape attempt. Matthews had heard from various officials that Director Quinlan had been pleased with his visit. By mid-January the speculation that Matthews would soon be named to a regional director's post was so widespread that most employees accepted it as fact. Larry Munger, the penitentiary's personnel director, confidently predicted one day at lunch that Quinlan would make the announcement about Matthews "within a week."

At the bureau's headquarters in Washington, however, there was no such certainty about Matthews. Some there thought that his dismissal of Jerry O'Brien's associate wardens had been poorly handled. Others had heard that morale among the guards was terrible. In the past, neither of these complaints would have caused much of a fuss. Former director Norman Carlson ran the bureau along military lines when he was director. Employees followed orders like foot soldiers. Wardens were expected to be dynamic leaders unafraid of occasional grumbling by the troops. At least that is what Matthews had been taught.

But J. Michael Quinlan had a somewhat different view. After he became director on July 1, 1987, he announced that his top priority was improving the working conditions for employees. Almost immediately, he proved he was serious by giving them the right to list their job preferences when it came time for transfers. Nearly one third of all bureau employees were required to move from one prison to another on an average of once every two years. In the past, they had never been asked if they had a preference. Carlson believed that some jobs within the bureau, especially those at prisons in desolate areas, were so unappealing that no staff members would ever volunteer for them, so transfers were based on what was best for the bureau, not individuals. Quinlan himself had quietly resented never being asked his preference.

There was a good reason why Quinlan had made keeping employees happy such a priority. As had been predicted during Carlson's last year as director, the bureau was expanding, and Quinlan understood that it needed to make itself attractive if it wanted to recruit first-rate employees.

"We have to be careful in the sort of staff members we choose," Quinlan explained. "The problem is that a lot of people come into this business because they have always wanted to have power over another human being for whatever reason— early childhood development problems or whatever—and that requires retraining and a heavy emphasis on what is and what is not acceptable."

One way to make certain that poor employees were weeded out was by having good supervisors. The Hot House had always been a training ground for lieutenants and other midlevel managers, so the fact that guards there were disgruntled took on new significance.

The speculation about Matthews's being promoted ended abruptly in February when Quinlan chose R. Calvin Edwards, the warden at the penitentiary in Terre Haute, Indiana, to fill the regional directorship that was open. Edwards was black, and his selection was seen in the Hot House as a double strike against Matthews. Not only had he not gotten the promotion, but Quinlan had chosen another black manager before him.

For his part, Matthews quickly voiced approval of Quinlan's choice. "Edwards is a good man. I'm not disappointed. There will be other openings."

But later he acknowledged some self-doubt. "Sometimes I

feel I missed something by not working as a correctional officer on a tier," he explained. "I came directly in as a caseworker, and I think that makes it harder sometimes for officers to relate to me and me to them. I think some of the old-time guards here have trouble accepting me."

At Benny's, the grunt guards celebrated when Matthews was passed over. "People are telling Quinlan what is really going on here, not just what Matthews wants him to hear," said one.

"Matthews worries too much about inmates, not enough about staff," added another guard. "That wasn't a big deal under Carlson, but it is now. Times are changing."

A Voice: *DAVID HAM, LEAVENWORTH'S CAPTAIN*

Let me tell you about Slim. He was a big black inmate who was so well hung he could suck his own dick or screw his own butt. Hey, I'm serious now. I mean, this guy really could. Anyway, this white boy comes in to see me. He's afraid of Slim because Slim is going to fuck him, so I tell this kid he's got three choices—he can lock up [go into protective custody], get raped, or protect his manhood.

Well, he starts crying. I mean, he's got tears coming down his cheeks and he's blubbering about how he don't want to get raped, and how he's afraid, and how I got to protect him from Slim.

I pulled his jacket and read it and this puke is in prison because he kidnapped two boys, ages three and five, and took them up to a cabin and tortured them, repeatedly sexually raped and tortured them, and then killed them both.

Now you tell me: how much sympathy do you think I'm going to have for some punk who does that to two innocent kids? I got children of my own, you know. How much would you have? And now this puke wants me to protect him from Slim.

Can you imagine what it's like to be put in a position where you have to make decisions like this every day? You get cynical. When you see how people act and what they do in here, you get callous. That's why I've always believed that people in the corrections business really have a lot of love for human beings.

I'm not joking now. You have to have a real love for your fellow man to put up with having shit thrown in your face and punks like that kid coming to you asking for your help. You have to have a lot of love in your heart to act professionally and do the right thing no matter what you feel.

CHAPTER
FORTY-NINE

While everyone in Leavenworth speculated about Warden Matthews's future, Steve Lacy was promoted to the rank of lieutenant and notified that he was being transferred to a medium-security prison in Phoenix, Arizona. Lacy was well-known because he was head of the prison's shakedown crew, had worked at the prison eight years, and was married to Sharon Lacy, another prison employee. Lacy's life centered around the Hot House. The tall Texas native couldn't remember a time when he didn't want to be, as he put it, "a cop." Even as a schoolboy, he had thought of himself as a policeman. "You can look at some kids and say, 'Yeah, little Johnny is going to grow up and be a thug 'cause he acts like one,' and sure enough, he ends up in a penitentiary," Lacy explained. "And then there are guys who grow up and get into it with the Johnnies of this world. They say, 'No, you are not going to pick on this guy and you are not going to take his lunch money because *I'm* not going to let you do it. You just don't do those things.' I was one of them. I don't like bullies and there have been times when I've seen someone who won't stand up for himself and I have stepped in and stopped Johnny, because I knew I could.

"Guys like me," Lacy said, "grow up to be cops."

On January 14, a going-away party was held for the Lacys at the Officers Training Center, a meeting hall across from the penitentiary. It was a beer-and-potato-chips affair, with the men clustered around a silvery keg in a corner by the front door while the women sat at folding tables. Both Lacys wore blue denim jeans, cowboy boots, and western shirts. The crowd was diverse. Roy Moore, a wiry, balding, gray-bearded guard who rode a Harley Davidson motorcycle, arrived wearing a black Harley Davidson T-shirt and matching hat, with a knife hanging from his belt. Moore was a tough-talking, beer-guzzling, popular thirty-nine-year-old guard who had embarrassed Matthews when he first arrived and was giving a tour to a regional director. At the time, Moore was assigned to the rear gate and was not supposed to allow anyone to pass unless the person showed him a bureau identification card or he recognized his face. When Matthews and Larry DuBois appeared at the gate, Moore didn't recognize the regional director, so he asked to see his identification card. DuBois didn't have it, but Matthews jokingly offered to vouch for his boss. Moore wasn't impressed. "Sorry, bureau policy says I can't let you through. You might be holding the warden hostage." Matthews was not amused, though he persuaded Moore to open the gate. The story had endeared Moore to his fellow guards, particularly at Benny's where it became a legend.

Moore was one of fifty-seven employees who came to the party. All were white except for one older black guard who stopped by for a few minutes to congratulate Lacy but didn't stay or mingle. Warden Matthews didn't attend. Instead, he sent Connor to say a few words. No one was surprised. Lacy was one of O'Brien's old guard and he didn't think much of Matthews's management style. As far as Lacy was concerned, the bureau was too soft and it was managers like Matthews who were responsible. "Jesus Christ, these inmates get to see first-run movies, have HBO and Las Vegas–style entertainment. It's bullshit. If I want to go to college, I have to pay for it, but these assholes can go to college free and my tax dollars pay for it. It's bullshit," he repeated.

The Lacys' going-away party was run by Wayne Smith, who now worked in the regional office in Kansas City but had been the captain at the Hot House under O'Brien. Sharon Lacy had worked as Smith's secretary. "We're here tonight to say goodbye to Pee-Wee and Pumpkin," Smith began. Pumpkin was clearly Sharon, but he wasn't certain why Steve Lacy was called Pee-Wee. Smith then turned the platform over to one of Lacy's friends, who recounted a raucous and fictitious story about Lacy's pre-marriage days that ended with a woman describing his potency in "pee-wee" terms. That speaker was followed by other friends who roasted the couple with more stories filled with sexual innuendo. There were gag gifts and the standard employee farewell gift for every Leavenworth guard—a huge brass ball, as in "It takes brass balls to work at Leavenworth." Sharon Lacy's boss in the business office recalled how she had tricked him, as part of an office prank, into believing that he was being sued for sexual discrimination. In retelling the story, the speaker made a racist slur, but the crowd enjoyed the tale, and when it came time for Sharon and Steve to react to the hour's worth of barbs, they gave as many one-liners as they had taken.

And then Steve Lacy turned serious. "I just want you all to realize the good old days, they'll come back," he said. "You can count on it." Lacy was referring to a time in the bureau's history, he explained later, "when officers had more rights than inmates" and the Hot House was "really a penitentiary, not a nursery school." It was a time when you didn't have "inmates crawling up on Daddy's knee at meals to snivel," a slap at Warden Matthews's practice of jotting down inmate complaints during mainline.

After the formal program, most of the men gathered around Ralph Seever, the legendary lieutenant who had spent his career at Leavenworth and was revered by guards as the best there ever was. As it so often did, the talk turned to Thomas Silverstein, and Seever recalled the first time that he had met Silverstein and how, in his view, he was not much different from other murderers. Inmates, Seever explained, expect guards always to tell them no and to punish them when they violate the rules. It's all part of the game. "But you never want the relationship to get personal," he warned. Whenever an inmate believes for some reason that the natural conflict between convicts and officers is personal, his ego is at stake, and in a penitentiary, image is a thousand times more important than reality. The fact that Seever attended the Lacys' party was a tribute. If Seever thought highly of Lacy, then the veteran guards in Leavenworth knew he was all right.

It had been the U.S. Air Force that first sent Steve Lacy to Leavenworth. His father was a U.S. Customs agent and Lacy was anxious to emulate him. "I was taught that there is right and there is wrong," Lacy recalled. "There is no gray and I believe that, and if I am fortunate enough to have children, they will be raised the same way. You learn the rules and you play by those rules and it doesn't matter if you like them or not. There is only 'Yes sir' and 'No sir' and that's how things should be." Lacy joined the military after high school graduation and was sent to Korea as a military policeman. He earned a reputation there for being a tough, streetwise cop and made a series of sensational drug busts, but he was always cynical about his job and his bosses, and this so irritated his commanding officer that Lacy was eventually reassigned to guard duty at the disciplinary barracks at Fort Leavenworth. Most would have hated the job. He loved it. After he was discharged, Lacy worked for the town of Leavenworth as a police officer until there was an opening at the federal penitentiary. He reported to work in July 1983.

Just as in the military, Steve Lacy's frequently acid tongue made some supervisors cringe. "I'm not prejudiced when it comes to inmates," Lacy liked to say. "I hate all of them the same." Another favorite: "If you don't like what I'm doing, then fuck you, and if you have any friends, then fuck them too." Lacy prided himself on "telling things just like they are, not how some big shot wants them." While his personality often was annoying, none of his bosses questioned his dedication. He was the first to volunteer, the first to accept risky assignments. When he wasn't at work, he was at Benny's with other off-duty guards. "My work comes first," he said. "It comes before family, wife, everyone, and it has to be that way, because in this business, every officer's life depends on his fellow officer being there to back him up. If the telephone rings, then I'm on my way to the penitentiary no matter what time or what I am doing."

Lacy married for the first time shortly after he went to work at the Hot House. It didn't last. "My wife would want me to talk about what had happened at work when I got home, but that was the last thing I wanted to do," Lacy recalled. "She really didn't understand all the shit that goes on in here and I got tired of trying to explain it. I got so I just wouldn't say nothing because I didn't want to yap to her about it." How could Lacy explain over pork chops and green beans at dinner what it felt like to surprise a convict in his cell who was "sucking his own

dick''? How could he tell her about the inmate who raped another inmate with a broom handle and then beat him unconscious? How could he describe how it felt to carry an inmate to
the prison hospital after he had been stabbed and had blood
squirting out of his chest all over your hands and chest? Worse,
how could Lacy explain to her how much he loved working in
the prison and how he'd much rather be there than sitting at
home with her watching television at night?

"I stood at work one day and watched John Greschner and
another inmate kill this snitch. They had waited seven years—
seven years—to get him and they were stabbing him right in
front of me in center hall," Lacy said. "They had shanks so big
they looked like swords." Lacy had tried to tell his wife about the
stabbing. "I was sitting at the dinner table and I said, 'I saw a
man lose his life today. I watched the whole thing,' but she really
didn't understand." Angry, Lacy had gone to Benny's to be with
his buddies. They understood.

When Lacy decided to get a divorce, it was Lou, a fellow
guard, who offered him his spare bedroom. When Lacy needed
someone to talk to, it was his buddies at Benny's who sat by his
side, got him drunk, took him home. And when Lacy began
dating again, it was these same friends who organized the "hog"
contest, a monthly competition in which each guard tried to find
the ugliest woman he could to ask out on a date. They would
bring her to Benny's for everyone to see and then afterward
return to Benny's and vote on who had the worst-looking date.
The winner got to drink all night for free. Steve Lacy couldn't
think of a single friend he had who didn't work at the Hot House.
"The reason we tend to socialize together is because no one else
really understands what we do," he said. "Civilians look down
on us, but when they need someone to protect them, they come
running. When I was a cop on the streets, I waited and counted
once to see how long it would take someone to say thank you. It
was six months. Six months before someone actually thanked
me for putting my butt on the line." Lacy and his friends were
society's guardians, he said. "In our world, there are only two
sides: them and us, and there's a bunch more of them than us."

After his divorce, Lacy secretly began dating Sharon, who
was then working as Captain Smith's secretary in the lieutenant's office. She was in her early twenties and had grown up in

the Leavenworth area. She was extremely popular. She was outgoing and, as a coworker later put it, perky, with long brown hair, ivory skin, and an attractive figure. She was smart, too.

When other employees discovered that Lacy was dating her, there were problems. "Some of the lieutenants began writing negative reviews of Steve, because they didn't like him crossing that staff/management line," Sharon Lacy recalled. "That stopped when we decided to get married." In order to avoid possible conflicts, Sharon transferred out of the lieutenant's office—management—to a job in prison industries. She had worked in industries before, when she first came to work at the prison in September 1984, but she had trouble adjusting to the work environment this time. The fact that convicts were looked upon as coworkers and called supervisers by their first names bothered her. "I had read reports and these inmates' jackets. I'd sat through disciplinary hearings," she recalled. "I was surprised some of those inmates were still alive after reading what they had done. I still thought like a cop, and the staff in industries got upset with me. They'd tell me, 'Hey, you got to get along with these inmates or else they won't work. You got to treat them better.' They tried to deprogram me, but I refused to go back to their level because I had seen the real side of these men and most were monsters."

Sharon Lacy told inmates not to call her by her first name and when one did, even though she was a secretary she saw to it that he was fired from his job. She also became the first woman in the prison's history to write a shot that resulted in an inmate's being taken to the Hole. She eventually became so uncomfortable working in industries that she moved to a new job in the administrative building away from inmates. She would have a similar job when she and Steve moved to Phoenix.

The fact that neither she nor Lacy had any friends other than their coworkers didn't bother him, but it did Sharon. "It worries me because Steve's dad was like that. All his life, all he did was work, work, work. He gave his life to the Customs Service, and suddenly it was over and he was retired and out of it. I ask Steve, 'What happens when we retire? What happens when we are not part of the bureau family anymore?' But, so far, he doesn't want anything else."

She thought a lot about the "bureau family." "People don't

understand bureau people, not at all. You can absolutely hate
someone in the bureau, but if you go to Benny's and there is a
fight, everyone in the bureau will stand behind that person, even
if they hate his guts. It doesn't matter, because he's one of them
and everyone else is an outsider. And you should hear these guys
talk. These guys thrive on violence. You should hear them talk
about a killing and how the prison needs a good inmate stabbing. They are all like that. It's addicting to them."

Benny's had a disc jockey playing records when the Lacys
and a dozen of their friends arrived from the training center to
continue the farewell celebration. The disc jockey had streaked
blonde hair and wore a gold earring. Some guards joked about
getting the earring for Steve Lacy to wear. One of Lacy's pals
told the DJ about the Lacys' promotion and asked him to play a
song just for Steve and Sharon to dance to. "Don't make it any of
that nigger music," he warned, referring to rap songs. The DJ,
somewhat intimidated, asked for a suggestion. Minutes later,
the couple took the floor to the country-western sounds of "The
South is Going to Rise Again."

One of Lacy's best friends had driven up from Texas to
attend the party. He had been a guard at the Hot House, but had
been promoted to lieutenant and transferred to a medium-
security prison. Over a beer, he explained that going from a
penitentiary to a kiddie joint hadn't been easy. "I hope Steve
does better than me," he said. He had been accused of brutality
five times. The last charge was filed after he ripped off an inmate's shirt because the inmate had refused to strip for a search
as ordered. "In Leavenworth, inmates are thankful to get steak,"
he complained. "Where I'm working now, they take it back to
the cook and tell him they want it medium-rare." (A few months
later, the lieutenant was demoted and returned to Leavenworth
as a guard.)

Lacy knew the transition was going to be difficult, especially since he had felt that Leavenworth was too easy on inmates. He was also aware of Sharon's concerns about their lack
of friends outside prison. But tonight was no time to dwell on
problems. They planned to dance all night and then have breakfast at a local diner. "Not everyone is meant to do prison work,"
Lacy said, and then, putting his arms around Lou, the guard
who had taken him in when he first got his divorce, and the pal

who had driven up from Texas to be with him, he added, "but if you stick around, you get addicted, you can't stop and it takes over your life, and I can tell you right now, if I were asked, I'd follow these two guys into a group of inmates any time, any place, and I'd never have to worry about my back as long as they were with me, and they would do the same thing for me."

"Damn right," one said. The other nodded.

"I'd give my life for these guys," he concluded, "and they would give up their life for me. And that isn't something that many people can say."

CHAPTER
FIFTY

Shortly after lunchtime on March 10, a dark-haired man wearing a freshly ironed white shirt, pressed slacks, and a blue nylon jacket walked up to the guard who was working inside the prison rotunda and introduced himself.

"I'm a safety inspector from bureau headquarters," the stranger explained. "Just finished checking B cellhouse."

Visits by various federal inspectors were common at the Hot House and this stranger looked no different from any other inspector. He carried a folder filled with various official forms and he seemed friendly enough. For several minutes, the two men talked, and then the inspector asked the guard to unlock the door that led into the prison visiting room. The guard didn't have a key but he called another guard who did. Once the inspector went through the steel door, the rotunda guard called the officers stationed inside the visiting room.

"Hey," he warned, "you got a safety inspector from Washington coming your way."

The inspector had to walk down a hallway in order to reach the visiting room. A guard was waiting to let him inside. The inspector examined the portable fire extinguishers hanging on the walls, asked the guards a few questions, jotted some notes in his folder, and then announced that he was finished. He asked the guards to let him out the room's front door, the same one that visitors used, and they obliged. Moments later, the inspector walked down the prison's front steps to a waiting taxi.

It wasn't until a few hours later that guards discovered the safety inspector was not a bureau employee from Washington. Robert A. Litchfield, a forty-two-year-old bank robber serving a 145-year sentence, had fooled them. He had literally talked his way out of prison. It was the first successful escape from the Hot House in twelve years.

Associate Warden Lee Connor was the first to hear that Litchfield was missing. Warden Matthews was in Kansas City getting a haircut and couldn't be reached by telephone, so the guards in the control center called Connor when they discovered that the daily four o'clock count was one inmate short. At that point they hadn't yet identified the missing inmate, and Connor's first thought was that it was Norman Bucklew. When he found it was Litchfield, he was irritated but somewhat relieved. "When I heard the name, I knew this was the real thing and I felt sick," said Connor. "But I also knew that Litchfield wasn't going to leave a trail of dead bodies behind like a Carl Bowles or a Norman Bucklew would."

Robert Litchfield was somewhat of a legend among law-enforcement agencies because of his ability to talk himself out of trouble. In February 1986, he had escaped from the bureau's prison in Talladega, Alabama, by posing as a federal parole officer. There too he had walked out the front door.

After that escape, Litchfield robbed more than a dozen banks in Michigan, Georgia, and Florida, most of the time posing as a U.S. Treasury agent. Although he sometimes carried a BB gun during his robberies, he had never harmed anyone. He told police that one reason he was so successful at convincing people that he was a Treasury agent was because he wore a miniature American flag in the lapel of his coat and a tie clasp made to look like a pair of tiny handcuffs. "That's how all of those Treasury guys dress," he said with a grin.

Litchfield proved just as talented at fooling the FBI as he was at tricking bank managers. Once during a robbery in Boise, Idaho, he looked outside and noticed that the building was being surrounded by FBI agents and the local police. Litchfield had locked the bank's employees in a room but someone had sounded a silent alarm. When the FBI demanded over a bullhorn that the robber inside surrender, Litchfield calmly stepped out the front door. Agents grabbed him, but during the next few minutes, Litchfield convinced them that he was the bank's security officer, not the robber. He volunteered to help them apprehend the real crook, who he said was still inside the bank. Litchfield drew a diagram of the bank for the FBI, described the robber, and even offered tips on how to sneak inside and free the hostages. As soon as the FBI turned its attention back to the bank, he slipped into his car and drove away.

That incident had so outraged the FBI that it put Litchfield on its Ten Most Wanted list, and the quick-talking robber was captured in May 1987 and sent to Leavenworth. There he had deliberately kept out of trouble and done his best to blend into the crowd. He wanted to remain faceless.

Most of the guards who worked in the prison had never heard of Litchfield, and few recognized his photograph when Connor posted it a few hours after the escape. By the time Warden Matthews returned to the penitentiary that night, Connor had figured out how Litchfield had gotten away. "He was smart enough to use us," Connor told Matthews, "and we played right into his hands."

No one was supposed to enter or leave the main penitentiary without the permission of the control center. The guards inside it were responsible for identifying everyone who passed through the prison's steel gates. But Litchfield bypassed the center by getting the rotunda guard to let him into the visiting room. Those who came and went inside the visiting room were the responsibility of the guards stationed in it, and they never bothered to ask Litchfield for identification because the rotunda guard had already telephoned and identified him as a safety inspector.

"We actually helped Litchfield escape," Connor explained, "because we had one staff member in the rotunda telling another staff member in the visiting room that Litchfield was a safety inspector. We vouched for him."

"Connor was under incredible pressure," recalled Dan McCauley, an officer who worked with Connor the night of the escape. "He was taking the escape hard. He was angry and embarrassed. He blamed himself. But Matthews was amazingly calm and diplomatic. 'Name me a penitentiary where someone hasn't escaped,' he said. He was really cool about the entire thing and his composure calmed people down."

Fourteen days later, Litchfield robbed a bank in Tucker, Georgia, by posing as a gas company inspector and convincing the employees that there was a dangerous gas leak in the building. He hustled them into a conference room, locked them inside, and stole $38,000 from the vault.

Two weeks after that robbery, U.S. marshals surprised him as he stepped off an elevator at an exclusive condominium in Pensacola Beach, Florida. His face was swollen and bruised from plastic surgery that he had undergone only a few days earlier. The surgery had so changed his appearance that a deputy from Kansas had to be flown to Florida to identify him. The plastic surgeon was later quoted as saying that Litchfield asked to look like the movie star Robert De Niro. Litchfield received an additional thirty-five-year sentence for the escape and the Tucker bank robbery. This time, the bureau put him in Marion.

"If the officers had followed proper procedures, Litchfield would not have escaped," Matthews said later, "but I think things were running so smoothly that our people were lulled to sleep. It's been twelve years since an escape, two and a half years since a murder. We were simply too relaxed, and that's partly my fault because I want things around here to be laid back."

After that incident, Connor wrote himself a note that he kept in the top drawer of his desk. It was a list of his priorities as associate warden. It read, *1. NO ESCAPES! 2. No staff members hurt! 3. No convicts hurt . . .* He wrote another note the next day and slipped it next to the first one. It read, *1,200 ASSHOLES.* Connor decided he had spent too much time worrying about the Cuban units, not enough thinking about the American prisoners. "It's a reminder to me that I got twelve hundred assholes besides the Cubans to watch."

Staff morale was affected for weeks. Normally friendly guards avoided speaking to inmates. Any violation of prison rules, no matter how slight, was dealt with harshly. At Benny's, guards drank their beers in uncharacteristic silence. "Leavenworth's pride was really, really hurt," Connor said. "Everyone felt bad." Matthews agreed. "I think the way Litchfield escaped made it worse. He just walked out the front door and really rubbed our faces in it. In some ways, it would have been better for staff morale if he'd gone over the wall in a blaze of gunfire."

Matthews and Connor instituted an array of new security

precautions. But Matthews didn't dwell on the escape. Instead, he went to work rebuilding staff confidence and morale. With the enthusiasm of a high school coach giving a pregame pep talk, he made a point of stopping to talk to guards as he made his rounds, bragging about the great job that each was doing, reciting the merits of the Leavenworth staff. No one liked the fact that Litchfield had gulled them, Matthews preached, but every so often the inmates were going to get away with something. "It's unfortunate but inevitable."

"I didn't want the staff to get so down on themselves that they began doubting their abilities," he later explained, "because that would only result in more problems."

By the beginning of April, most of the gloom had dissipated, and Matthews had gained a new popularity. Even his harshest critics were complimentary about the way he had handled the Litchfield escape, and they felt the sort of kinship with him that develops whenever people share a harrowing experience. Warden Matthews had been passed over for a promotion and so had most of the Hot House guards at some point during their careers. Matthews had been badly embarrassed by the escape, but instead of using the guards as scapegoats, he had accepted full responsibility. Most importantly, he had defended Leavenworth. It was still the best institution in the federal system, he bragged, with the finest staff in the bureau. And he had said this over and over again, with the conviction and enthusiasm of a man who seemed genuinely to believe what he was saying.

An incident at Benny's a few weeks after the escape illustrated the newfound respect for Matthews. Two guards from Marion, who had brought a prisoner to Leavenworth earlier that day, joined three Hot House guards for drinks after work. At one point during the conversation one of the outsiders asked, "Hey, what's it like working for a nigger warden?"

The remark was not the first racial slur made around the table that evening, although it was the first reference to Matthews. Unlike the other racial epithets, however, this one was challenged.

"The man you're referring to happens to be warden of the best penitentiary in this fucking system," a Hot House guard replied coldly, "and around here, we call him Warden Matthews or Mr. Matthews."

Thinking the statement was a joke, the two outsiders began to laugh, but when they realized the others were serious they stopped, and for several seconds there was a strained silence at the table. The subject was dropped. What made the exchange noteworthy was that the guard who defended Matthews had only a few weeks earlier used the same racist terminology to describe the warden. Later, when he was reminded of this in private, the guard said, without the slightest touch of embarrassment or shame, "Hey, Matthews may be a nigger, but he's our nigger now, and I'm gonna back him. He's earned my respect."

CHAPTER
FIFTY-ONE

DALLAS SCOTT

Shortly after Dallas Scott was taken from Marion to the Hole in Leavenworth, he felt sharp pains in his stomach. When he tried to get out of his bunk, his legs went out from under him and he had to crawl to the toilet. There was blood in his vomit. At first he figured he had food poisoning, but when no one else in the Hole became ill, he knew that it was his chronic hepatitis flaring up.

Scott had been sick like this before. Two years earlier, his legs, ankles, and feet had swollen to nearly double their normal size and he had become so ill that doctors sent him to the bureau's medical center in Springfield, where he was bedridden for three months. As Scott lay shivering in his bunk in the Hole, he decided that he was about to die. Years of drug and alcohol abuse were finally about to kill him. Yet, even though he continued to vomit and shake, he refused to let the guards take him to the hospital. The only professionals that Scott trusted less than lawyers were doctors, especially those who worked for the bureau. He sipped water to prevent dehydration, and stubbornly remained in his cell.

One afternoon, a guard brought him a certified letter from the U.S. magistrate in Sacramento who had agreed to review Scott's motion for a new trial on his 1976 bank robbery conviction. Inside was a ten-page ruling, but Scott only got through the first paragraph before he was swearing.

His appeal had been rejected. His claim that he had been

denied a fair trial because prosecutors had never told him about the mysterious fingerprints on the robbery weapon and because part of his trial transcript had not been recorded were "unfortunate" mistakes, the magistrate wrote. But they were also "harmless."

The unidentified fingerprints found on the pistol could have belonged to Scott's wife, since Scott had testified earlier that the gun belonged to her. The fingerprints at the bank thought to be the robber's could have belonged to customers. "Although this court does not condone the prosecution's failure to disclose the fingerprint information . . . it is unlikely that the fingerprint evidence would have made any difference in Scott's ultimate conviction," said the ruling. There was other evidence that pointed to Scott. Several witnesses had testified that the robber talked in a "funny way," and Scott had a unique Texas accent. The most common denomination of money stolen from the bank was one-dollar bills, and two hours after the robbery, Scott had redeemed a citizen's-band radio from a pawn shop by paying $45 in one-dollar bills. The magistrate acknowledged that such evidence was circumstantial, but when it was added together it "pointed towards Scott as the robber." There was no comment about why none of the witnesses had mentioned Scott's prison tattoos when they described the robber. Apparently, the magistrate had thought this unimportant.

The fact that part of the court transcript was missing also wasn't sufficient grounds for a new trial, the ruling stated, because the material wasn't that relevant to the trial.

"I had been stretched out flat on my back for four days, about half-expecting 'Old Scratch' to come knocking at the door," Scott recalled, "but when they hit me with the deal from California, I shot straight up off the bunk, cussed, stomped around the cell for a while, then hit the shower and spent sixteen hours digging through my trial transcripts, briefs, case law, notes, et cetera. Suddenly, I felt pretty good. You see, I knew this asshole was wrong. I had them beat at their own game and I wasn't going to die before I proved them wrong."

Scott went to work on an appeal of the magistrate's ruling. He also sent an angry letter to the attorney whom the magistrate had forced him to hire. Scott had borrowed $5,000 from friends outside the prison in order to comply with the order that he be represented at the court hearing. The attorney had filed all the proper court documents and had represented Scott before the magistrate, but Scott was unsatisfied with his performance and he wanted him to know it. "You are a spineless coward and lying piece of shit," Scott wrote, in a letter firing the lawyer. These were some of the nicer terms he used.

By the time Scott had finished mailing the proper forms to appeal the magistrate's ruling, it was time for him to be tried in Topeka on the drug-smuggling charges. He wanted to act as his own attorney in the case, but this judge wouldn't allow it either, and Mark Works, a twenty-seven-year-old lawyer fresh out of a Topeka law school, was assigned to the case. Works, who had never before represented an inmate and had little experience in criminal cases, didn't have much to work with, especially after federal prosecutors played the tape recording of Scott's telephone call threatening Bill Hutchinson's girlfriend.

Scott had always denied that it was his voice on the tape, but there was no mistaking his accent when prosecutors played the tape for the jurors. By the second day of the trial, he realized he was losing and he asked that Works be fired as his attorney. The judge denied his request. Scott then announced that he wanted to call several inmates from Marion to testify on his behalf, as well as some from Leavenworth. Federal prosecutors immediately claimed that Scott was simply trying to give his buddies a chance to get away from Marion so they could attempt an escape. When the judge denied the request, Scott threw down his pencil and shouted, "This is bullshit! This motherfucker is denying all my witnesses." Two U.S. marshals scrambled to the defense table. The next day, the judge permitted Scott to call several inmates, but only from Leavenworth.

The jury found Scott guilty and the judge sentenced him to 210 months (17.5 years) and a fine of $750 for attempting to smuggle $500 worth of heroin into the prison. Under the new drug-sentencing laws, Scott had to serve at least fifteen years of the sentence, and it wouldn't start until he had completed the six years that were still hanging over his head from his conviction for his 1976 bank robbery.

Back in the Hole at the Hot House, Scott was incredulous. The trial was "a railroad job," he complained, not because he was innocent (evidence at the trial proved otherwise), but be-

cause he didn't feel the judge and prosecutors had played fair.
"If I'd have been able to defend myself or could've afforded an
expensive lawyer, I'd have gotten off," Scott complained. "This
is what sucks about this bullshit system of ours. I should get to
play by the same rules as everyone else, but because I don't have
the money and am tagged as a prison gang member, I don't.
When you're in a supermarket with a ham in your arms and
there are six people in front of you each with a ham, and the
clerk says, 'That will be five dollars,' to each of them and then
she comes to you and says, 'That will be fifteen dollars,' that is
not fair. You should have to pay the same price as everyone else.
But everyone always wants me to pay more."

A few days after his conviction, guards told Scott that he
had a visitor. He assumed it was Mark Works coming to say
good-bye. Despite the fact that Scott had wanted the young
attorney fired, he liked Works. But waiting in the visiting room
were Scott's daughter, Star, and his two granddaughters, ages
two and three. It was the first time that Scott had seen his
grandchildren and he spent the entire day bouncing the two
girls on his knees, playing games with them, and fetching them
treats from the candy machine. "I looked like I had been through
a war by the time I got back to the cell," he said later, proudly.

The visit had caused a flood of memories. "When I was in
prison in Lompoc, my wife came to see me with my son, who was
then fourteen," Scott recalled. "I remember looking at that kid,
and he looked just like me and I could hear my voice in his voice
and he was a pretty hep kid, a sharp kid, and we were bullshitting, and all of a sudden, I looked at him and thought, 'Damn, I
was fourteen the first time I went into the Dallas County Jail.'
I'm looking at my kid and I think, he has got to be similar to
what I looked like and he looks like a baby to me. It set me back,
'cause I wondered, 'How in the hell did I survive back then? How
did I make it all those years?'

"It also made me sad because I realized that I've spent my
entire fucking life behind bars. I've been convicted of two lousy
bank robberies, yet I've never really gotten out of prison. I really
have missed everything a normal person gets to do, like raise
kids and just walk the streets."

There was a sadness to his voice. "This gets so old. You get
tired of all the silly-ass games—the young bucks who come in

here thinking they've discovered something new by being tough, the fucking guards, the bureau always fucking with you.

"But after all these years, what else do I got? If I were to get out tomorrow, do you actually think I could change? You think the government is going to give me Social Security? You think I'm going to be happy working at some fast-food joint flipping burgers with teenage kids? Fuck, no. I went down a path a long time ago and all them doors have been closed, but I never thought it'd end up this way. I never thought I'd spend my life in prison."

Scott knew that he was going to be sent back to Marion. He also knew that even if he did somehow prevail and get his 1976 bank robbery conviction overturned, he still faced another 17.5 years in jail, and that was equivalent to a death sentence. His recent bout with hepatitis had reminded him of his own frailty. He recalled the doctors' estimate of his life expectancy back in 1983 when they had first diagnosed his liver problem. Ten more years at most. He was going to die in prison, probably Marion.

"I'm going to keep fighting them," he said. "I ain't dying on someone else's schedule. I know I may not ever get out of here. It don't look like it now. The rest of my life, I am probably going to spend in a cell locked up twenty-three hours each day by myself. But with all my failures by society's standards, I'm not a failure to me—in my own eyes—and that's what really counts. Have I robbed banks? Yeah, fuck yes. Am I an outlaw? Yeah, fuck yes. But so what? You think I invented stealing?

"When I'm laying down sucking that last breath of air, I'll be doing it alone, and I'm the only one that I got to answer to, and when that time comes and I'm thinking about my life, the robberies and this and that, I'll be able to say, 'Hey, I can live with that.' I never harmed anyone, never stole from anyone poorer than me, never went out of my way to fuck with anybody, and I never let the man beat me. I never ratted on anybody, never kissed a guard's ass. I stuck with my principles. They sure as hell aren't society's principles, but I stuck with them, and that means I can die with a clear conscience."

A few days later, Scott was transferred to Marion.

CHAPTER
FIFTY-TWO

NORMAN BUCKLEW

Few inmates enjoyed Robert Litchfield's escape more than Norman Bucklew. The fact that Litchfield had made a fool out of the Hot House guards tickled him. The only thing better, he said, would have been if he had been the one who escaped. "I know I would have stayed out longer than he did," Bucklew remarked.

Bucklew had lived two separate lives. He had grown up in New Jersey, married his neighborhood sweetheart, fathered a son, used drugs, killed an armored-car guard during a bungled robbery, and been sent to Trenton State Prison. But as soon as Bucklew crawled over the prison wall during Hurricane Belle in August 1976, he had started a new life. He assumed the police would expect him to go home to his wife and son—then five years old—or to contact his parents. Instead, he took on a new identity, headed west, and never looked back.

Bucklew was twenty-seven and, if he had decided to go straight, he might have succeeded in disappearing. But as soon as he reached St. Louis, Missouri, he began robbing banks. He also fell in love, got married, adopted one daughter, fathered another, and eventually got caught.

In the spring of 1988, Bucklew learned that his two daughters from St. Louis were coming to visit him in Leavenworth. He had not seen Heather and Sarah, now ages eighteen and nine respectively, for three years, and on the night before the visit he was as excited as a child on Christmas Eve.

Most Friday nights Bucklew got drunk, but not tonight. He

355

sat at the metal desk in his cell and made notes about what he wanted to say to his daughters. "Most kids get to know their parents by being with them every day," he explained. "I don't got that luxury. I want to give them some understanding about who I am and what I believe."

He especially wanted to explain himself to Sarah, who had only been three weeks old when he was recaptured. Heather was eight, so she could remember a few things about the year that he spent with her and her mother, Laura Ashmore, before he was sent back to prison.

As he sat in his cell, Bucklew recalled how he had met Ashmore only one week after he escaped from Trenton. He was in a bar when he saw her, then a twenty-three-year-old bleached-blonde beauty, sitting at a table with her girlfriend. Strutting over to the two women, Bucklew asked, "Which one of you girls wants to pick me up?"

Ashmore had laughed and invited him to sit down. "We were both intimidated by Norman's size," she recalled. "He was so big and strong." She and Bucklew spent the next few hours talking. It got so late they decided to have breakfast together at a diner and then Ashmore agreed to go with him to the trailer he had rented.

"I don't know you and I'm not going to have sex with you," she said. "I just want to get some rest." Bucklew rubbed her back while she fell asleep. "He didn't pressure me or come on strong and we didn't have sex," she said later. "He just wanted me next to him."

Ashmore had grown up in St. Louis, married when she was sixteen, and later divorced. She was raising Heather, then five years old, and living on welfare checks. Bucklew wanted to meet the child, so the three of them got together at a public park. "My daughter was hyperactive and most guys couldn't stand being around her, but he loved all her energy. He wore her out running around the park with her," Ashmore recalled.

At one point, Bucklew put his arm around Ashmore and she reciprocated by reaching her arm around his waist, but she jerked her hand away when she felt the grip of a gun sticking out of his belt under his bulky sweatshirt. She didn't ask why he was carrying it, but Bucklew volunteered an explanation. "I'm afraid someone might hurt me," he told her with a smirk.

Bucklew sent her flowers, bought her clothes, and spent hours playing with Heather. Ashmore was happy, but she knew there was something odd about her new boyfriend. One afternoon she introduced him to a girlfriend, and after he left, the woman asked her if Bucklew had been in prison.

"I don't know," Ashmore replied. "Why?"

"Because my brother was in prison and they walk the same way. You know, like animals looking to pounce on someone or have someone pounce on them. Haven't you noticed?"

Ashmore began watching Bucklew more closely. He did walk funny, she noticed. He also ate with his arm resting on the table beside his plate, as if he were guarding it. Whenever he saw a police car, he always made some profane comment about it.

Despite all this, Ashmore moved into an apartment with him three weeks after they met. "Months later, after Norman was arrested, people asked me how I could live with a bank robber," Ashmore recalled. "It made me mad. Hey, this bank robber took care of my daughter. He fed her and clothed her and loved her and that was more than her father had ever done for her. Everyone thought my first husband was great because he came from a religious family, but he was a drunk and he used to beat me up. His mother would come over to our house, and he'd smack me around, and she'd just sit there and say it was my duty to take it. He gave me two black eyes once and this woman blamed me for not being a good enough wife. She said the Bible said I should obey him."

In Ashmore's eyes, Bucklew treated her like a princess. "I know what broads are for, okay?" Bucklew explained later. "They are for taking care of and being used. I know there are a lot of little girls out there who want to run the world and I just stay away from them. I want a woman who is worried about whether I am going to like what she is wearing, is worried about fixing her fingernails and hair because I like the fingernails and hair fixed. I like to take them shopping and I like to watch them trying on clothes, and I particularly like how they feel after you are done buying them.

"Now, this broad is a fucking dingbat. She is real good in giving pussy. I'd give her four and a half stars on that. She's real good at cooking and cleaning house and is the best mother ever to live, but give her a job, even something simple like sitting

down and taking tickets at a movie theater, and she is going to
be sick on the second or third day. That's okay with me, though,
'cause I don't want no broad of mine working. I'll take care of all
that. All she has to do is keep me happy.''

Ashmore was not allowed to speak to any other men unless
it was okay with Bucklew. When the two of them went into a
restaurant, he walked ahead, she followed. He also ordered for
her, told her what to wear, how to fix her hair.

Ashmore loved it.

"When I was little, I was sick a lot, and my daddy took care
of me because Mama worked nights. I was always Daddy's little
girl and I liked having someone take care of me," she said. "I felt
secure. I knew he wouldn't let anyone harm me."

One night, Ashmore and Bucklew were out with some
friends when Ashmore said something that one of the men didn't
like. "Mind your own business," he snapped.

Ashmore began to cry.

Bucklew had been out of the room when this exchange took
place, but when he found Ashmore in tears, he grabbed the man
by the throat.

"You apologize to my old lady or I'll rip out your windpipe!" he yelled. The man quickly complied. Bucklew told Ashmore later that he was going to kill the man but she talked him
out of it.

A similar incident happened months later after Bucklew
was recaptured and put in Marion. "I was waiting to visit with
him," Ashmore said, "and an inmate walked past me and said,
'Hey, lady, nice ass.' I never told Norman, but another convict
mentioned it to him, and the next week when I visited him,
Norman said, 'Hey, I heard some guy said you had a nice ass last
week,' and I said, 'Yeah,' and he said, 'I hear that guy got hurt
this week. Someone beat him up real bad.' I said, 'Is he dead?'
And he said, 'Naw, but he probably wishes he was.' I said, 'Did
you do that?' and he laughed. He was proud of the fact that he
had beaten this guy up for offending me. And you know, so was I.
I'd never had anyone care enough about me to do something like
that. I was proud."

But Ashmore hadn't been so thrilled when Bucklew became
violent with her when they lived together. "We were driving
down the street once and he suddenly backhanded me," Ash-

more remembered. "I asked him why he hit me and he said because I had been looking at some guy, but the truth was, I was just daydreaming." Bucklew recalled that same incident later. "I cracked her a good one," he explained, "because she had it coming. Now, I don't believe in beating up women, but if my old lady is talking to some man, she's gonna get knocked to the floor every time because I know old ladies are good for three things: giving pussy, cooking, and taking care of kids, and if I see her talking to another man, I know she ain't cooking, I know she ain't taking care of his kids, so she and him must be talking about pussy."

The entire time that he and Ashmore were living together, Bucklew was robbing banks. He would spend most days driving around different sections of town noting how close the police stations were to banks. He kept two police scanners in his car, and maps marked with potential getaway routes. He always used the same method for each robbery. He would drive to a bowling alley the night before the robbery. "A guy gets out of his car wearing a yellow shirt on his back that says 'Mac's Pizza' and you know he is going to be inside for at least two hours bowling in some league," Bucklew explained. "That gives you time to steal his car and get it out of the neighborhood."

Bucklew always stole an older car, preferably a station wagon, which he parked in the lot of an apartment complex or hospital about two miles from the bank that he intended to rob. "No one pays attention if an old station wagon shows up parked in their lot, but if a Lamborghini is there, everyone notices." The following day, Bucklew would drive right up to the bank's front door. "I wanted everyone inside the bank to notice that car, to focus on it, because two minutes after the robbery, I was going to dump it and be in a different one." Bucklew would run into the bank wearing a mask and waving a shotgun. "Open your drawers!" he'd yell as he leaped over the counter. He would grab the cash in the tellers' drawers and run out of the bank. "I had it timed so I could be in and out of a bank within one minute," he bragged. He would drive the stolen car back to the apartment complex and switch cars.

"Robbing banks is easy," said Bucklew. "What other business tells its employees to hand over the money if someone comes in and asks for it?"

Robbing the Boatmen's Bank of Concord Village in St. Louis, on May 27, 1977, proved to be the exception. An off-duty policeman, Ray McDonough, happened to be one of the bank's customers when Bucklew came charging in with his shotgun and jumped up on the counter. McDonough pulled out his .38 caliber revolver and shot Bucklew in the chest. "I heard the bang and then I see this fucking gun bounce out in the middle of the floor and a pair of legs scrambling under a desk," Bucklew recalled. "But I didn't know I'd been shot." The bullet had hit him in the abdomen, but missed his vital organs.

The feet that Bucklew spotted under the desk belonged to McDonough, who had ducked for cover after his bullet failed to kill Bucklew. He thought Bucklew was wearing a bulletproof vest. "I could have ground-swept him with the shotgun," Bucklew recalled, "but there is a broad standing on one side and another broad on the other, and if I pulled that trigger, I would have killed him and definitely one of the broads, and I didn't know I had been hit so I didn't fire. I just grabbed the money and ran." Bucklew escaped with $48,146 and it wasn't until he was driving away from the bank that he realized he was bleeding.

When he got home, he stuck a Tampax into the wound and scribbled a telephone number on a pad for Ashmore.

"If something happens and I die tonight, call this number," Bucklew told her. "Have the guy who answers take me out in the woods and dump me somewhere. Take what money we got and start over."

Ashmore, who was seven months pregnant at the time, was terrified. "I'm madly in love with him," she recalled. "Heather is in the next room asking what is wrong with Daddy, blood is coming out of his side, and he wants me to dump him in the woods somewhere. It was crazy."

The next morning, Bucklew flew to Las Vegas on a commercial flight, rented a car, and drove to Bullhead, Arizona, where he told a doctor that the bullet wound was caused by a ricochet during target practice.

Back in St. Louis, the shooting and robbery had caught the attention of the media, who dubbed the robber "the Bionic Bandit," because he seemed invincible to gunfire. The police claimed the Bionic Bandit had stolen $117,500 from seven banks. All this attention worried Bucklew. He wanted to leave

St. Louis, but Ashmore wanted to wait until after she had their baby.

On June 26, Sarah was born. Bucklew was stopped during a routine traffic check three weeks later and arrested when police spotted several weapons in his car. A fingerprint check showed that he had escaped from Trenton State Prison.

Bucklew was taken to a cell in the St. Clair County Jail in Belleville, Missouri, but when the jailer started to open the cell door, Bucklew stopped him.

"Hey, you put me in a cell with these four niggers, and you're gonna find cold bodies tomorrow," Bucklew said. "I don't cell with niggers."

The jailer didn't know what to do, and neither did the black inmates inside the cell.

"I'm telling you, someone's gonna be killed if I go in there, and it ain't gonna be me," Bucklew repeated.

He was taken to a different cell.

"Most whites fuck up right away when they come into prison, because they try to be friendly," Bucklew said later. "Let's say a white dude is put in a cell with maybe fifteen niggers. If he says hello or even nods to them, then he's already doomed. You see, half of them will think he is just being polite and treating them with respect, but the other half will know he is weak and afraid, because they know that a white man isn't even going to acknowledge them if he's been in prison before, because whites don't speak to niggers in prison. These niggers are going to move on that guy as soon as the hack disappears."

The St. Louis police were able to link Bucklew to five bank robberies. He received the maximum sentence of 125 years. Ashmore was not charged with any crimes. Bucklew was turned over to the bureau and taken to the control unit in Marion because of his history of escape attempts, including several tries while he was awaiting trial. Ashmore followed him to Marion, and one year later, she and Bucklew were married in the prison's visiting room. "I wanted Sarah to know her father," Ashmore explained, "and I still loved this man."

But the marriage didn't last. Bucklew sent all his prison earnings to Ashmore, but it was barely enough to pay the rent and she couldn't keep a job. She divorced him and married a longtime friend. "It wasn't love. I still loved Norman, but I needed someone to support me and the girls," she said. Bucklew stopped talking to Ashmore, although he continued writing and telephoning his daughters.

Bucklew tried to escape from Marion twice. On January 13, 1982, he was caught as he was cutting his way through the prison's wire fence. On September 17, 1984, he was convicted of conspiring with another inmate to hire a group of Puerto Rican terrorists to launch an armed assault on Marion.

Bucklew had mellowed since then, enough so that the bureau had sent him to Leavenworth. Now, as he sat in his cell thinking about his upcoming visit with Heather and Sarah, Bucklew wrote at the top of a notepad:

1. Hacks.

"I got to warn Heather about the hacks around here," he explained. "She might go into a bar, you know, and she's got to understand that these hacks and the police are my sworn enemy. They aren't fooling and neither am I. Someday a hack or cop is going to kill me, and if one of my daughters married one of these bastards, it would be all over. It would be the one thing I couldn't ever forgive."

Next on the pad, Bucklew wrote:

2. The killing.

Sarah, he explained, had asked him on the telephone one day if he had ever killed anyone. He had said yes and promised to tell her about it. "I'm not a bullshitter," Bucklew said. "I'm gonna tell her tomorrow when we visit exactly what I did and let both of them know that, yeah, I am an evil bastard, but I am also their father and I love them."

While Bucklew was making his notes, across town in a Leavenworth motel Heather and Sarah were eating pizza and talking about their father.

"I remember once I was all dressed up in a blue outfit, like my very best dress, and I went to get a drink of milk from the jug and it spilled all over my dress and I had to, like, change and I cried because I wanted my dad to see the dress and see how pretty I looked," remembered Sarah. She had brought a special dress for this visit too. Her mother had helped her pack it, and even though she was only nine and too young to wear nylon hose, she was going to wear the dress with flats and no socks because she wanted to look "sophisticated."

Sarah was a skinny, freckle-faced girl with brown hair cut in a Buster Brown. She had a pixie's grin, made friends quickly, and was always moving about. In contrast, Heather was reserved and naive. She had given birth to a son only a few months earlier, but had decided not to marry the father because she felt he was irresponsible. Even though she was a mother, she seemed like a child herself.

Sarah, Heather, and Heather's baby lived with their mother. Laura Ashmore, who had divorced her third husband after having another baby, collected welfare, and babysat to earn extra money. They rented an old two-story house in a seedy area of St. Louis.

"When my dad was first arrested and it was in all the papers and on television and everything, the kids in school gave me a hard time about it and made fun of me," Heather recalled. "They said he killed people and called me the 'killer's kid.' But I never knew him when he killed anybody. I just knew him as my dad and I always have loved him."

Heather had written Bucklew faithfully, usually two letters a week, since his arrest ten years ago. "Me and Mom fight a lot, really scream at each other, and my dad is really the only person I can talk to, 'cause it's always been easier for me to write on paper what I felt than to really say it," she explained. "I write him long letters and he always writes back."

Sarah interrupted: "My mom told me once, like, they'd had an argument over where my baby bed was going to go because she wanted to put it where he kept his motorcycle."

"That's right," added Heather, giggling. "He had his Harley on one side of the room, a punching bag in the middle, and furniture on the other side. I remember."

"My mother told me, like, he used to do all these exercises," Sarah continued.

"Yeah, he always wanted Mom and me to go running with him and he'd go for miles and miles and miles," interjected Heather.

"And my mom told me, like, he used to make Heather drink carrot juice . . ." Sarah added.

"Worse than that, beet juice . . ." said Heather.

Both girls were quiet. "I think we're both so excited, I don't know if we can sleep at all tonight," said Heather.

Bucklew forgot all about his script the next morning when guards let him inside the visiting room to see his daughters and grandson. Instead, he fussed over the baby, played chess with Sarah, and talked to Heather about her future.

"You got to get out of this welfare world your mother is in," he lectured. "Go to junior college, learn how to talk right. You don't need to be falling in love with a motorcycle-riding dude like I was. You need to find a dude, you know, maybe he's been married once, got a few kids, someone who's responsible, give you some security. A guy like me, hey, he'll give you a good time, a great time, but he'll never give you security."

During the conversation, Heather let slip that her sister was having trouble in school. A bully had been taking Sarah's lunch money from her.

"What ya going to do?" Bucklew asked Sarah.

"I think I'll tell the principal," replied the nine-year-old.

"Whoa there," Bucklew replied. "No daughter of mine is going to be a rat. You got to solve your own problems."

"Well, she's bigger than me," Sarah said.

"You could go get a sock and put a dollar's worth of pennies in it and sneak up behind her and whack her a real good one in the head with it." Bucklew was serious.

"Daddy, they'd put me in reform school."

"Well, maybe they would, maybe they wouldn't, but I'll bet she wouldn't bother you anymore."

Sarah seemed unconvinced and the subject was dropped. The next day went quickly and it was soon time for them to leave. The guards permitted each girl to hug and kiss Bucklew, and then he was taken back inside. Heather started to cry outside the prison. "When I was growing up, I always had the same dream," she explained, "that someday my dad would get out and he and my mom would get married again and we would be a family again. I used to wish it more than anything and think about it night after night. But I'm older now and I don't think it will ever happen. It's too late, at least for me, because I have a son of my own now and will have to move out."

"I don't think my dad would do anything wrong if they let him go," volunteered Sarah.

Heather disagreed. "I asked him once what he'd do if he got out and he said, 'Grab a pillowcase.' Maybe he was joking, but I think he meant he was going to rob banks again. That's just how he is, I mean, he's my dad and I love him, but sometimes he thinks funny, but that don't mean I don't wish he was with us."

When Bucklew was caught in St. Louis, the newspapers had published a story that described the armored-car guard Bucklew had killed in New Jersey. The guard had been married and had a young daughter. When Heather read the story, it upset her. Sometimes she wondered what that girl was like. They had something in common, she decided. Both were growing up without their fathers.

"I don't think my dad is bad, but I wish sometimes he wasn't the way he is," Heather said. "I know he did wrong, but I miss him a lot and it hurts because he's not with us."

Bucklew felt the visit had gone well, even though he'd forgot to mention almost everything on his notepad. When I asked him if he didn't feel guilty about being in prison and not being with his daughters, he said, "No. I'm not here because I deserted them or because I don't love them. Maybe they think I deserted them, but I was a criminal before they was even born, and that's who I am.

"Look," he continued, "I don't want them to think that I'm a fucking nut, but I am compared to everyone else in the world and that's something I can't change."

Can't change or don't really wish to change? I asked. "Can't," replied Bucklew.

A short time after the girls' visit, a fire started in the prison kitchen. When a food steward tried to put out the blaze with a fire extinguisher, the flames shot up as if they had been doused with gasoline. Bucklew and the other inmates burst into laughter. After the fire was out, guards discovered that someone had removed the fire-fighting chemicals from the extinguisher and hidden hooch inside it. Everyone knew it was Bucklew, although there was no proof.

When I asked him about it, he grinned. "Hey, I don't even drink," he deadpanned. And then he added, "Hey, I came into prison a cowboy, and there isn't anything these bastards can do to change me. I'm going out a cowboy too.

"I am who I am."

CHAPTER
FIFTY-THREE

CARL BOWLES AND THOMAS LITTLE

The medium-security prison at Marianna, Florida, was much more relaxed than the Hot House, according to the weekly letters that Thomas Little wrote faithfully to Carl Bowles. "These guys don't know nothing about jailhouse respect," Little complained in one. "Guys in here will snitch right in front of you. They'll walk right up to the man and rat on you while you're watching them do it! Nobody thinks nothing about being a rat in here. It's more like a Sunday school than a prison."

Bowles always replied with the same advice: "Watch your back. Don't trust no man."

Much to everyone's surprise, Bowles had not chosen a new cell partner from the fish tank after Little left Leavenworth. Some younger convicts had arrived, but Bowles didn't pay any attention to them, and other white convicts classified by the bureau as sexual predators took the fish for their own.

One morning in early June, Lee Connor received a telephone call from an excited lieutenant at Marianna.

"We have information that Carl Bowles is planning an escape," the lieutenant announced.

A confidential informant in Marianna had tipped off guards to Bowles's plans. He was supposedly digging a tunnel from the storeroom in the west yard under the prison wall.

Robert Litchfield's escape from Leavenworth was still fresh in Connor's mind and he didn't intend to take any chances. As soon as Connor put down the receiver, he sent guards to arrest Bowles and dispatched a team to search for the tunnel.

"I don't know why I'm in the Hole," Bowles said after his arrest. "They just came and got me . . . But what's really worrying me is Tom. If they are locking me up, they're probably locking up him too and he don't need this. He don't need to be sent back here or sent to some other pen."

Bowles was silent for several minutes and then he said, "I'll guarantee you of one thing. I know Tom didn't say anything to get me in trouble. Connor himself could walk in here and tell me I'm locked up because Little put out a story on me and I'd say, 'Yeah, sure.' But I wouldn't believe it. I wouldn't care if they brought a signed statement to me, because I wouldn't believe them—because I believe in my heart that Tom cares about me. I know he does."

When news of Bowles's arrest spread through the Hot House, several inmates began to chuckle. They figured Little had said something to get Bowles locked up. "That's what these sissies do," explained one inmate. "Once they get away and the convict can't get to them anymore, they get revenge for all those nights they were fucked in the ass."

The day after he was taken to the Hole, Bowles knew that guards were looking for a tunnel. He had heard it through the prison grapevine and seen guards from a window in the Hole as they searched the prison grounds near the storeroom.

"There ain't no tunnel," he complained. "Somebody set me up."

Connor called off the search three days later after guards were unable to find any trace of a tunnel. It was a hoax, he decided. Officials in Marianna had reached the same conclusion. The lieutenant there had been hoodwinked by his confidential informant who, it turned out, had been Little's cell partner. The informant had concocted the entire story in order to get a transfer from Marianna to the prison in Talladega. He had used information that Little had told him during their casual conversations to piece together the story and make it plausible. His ruse had worked. The informant had been transferred shortly after he tipped off the lieutenant.

What no one in Leavenworth knew, except for Connor, was that Little had been arrested on the same night as Bowles and put in the Hole in Marianna. The lieutenant had wanted to scare Little and had figured that he would squeal on Bowles. He had figured wrong. Instead, Little had tried three times to send

Bowles letters warning him about what was happening. The guards had read the letters and then returned them to Little after deciding that they didn't contain any incriminating evidence, but they would not mail them. They were surprised at Little's fierce loyalty to Bowles. They found it alarming.

While Little was still being held in the Hole at Marianna, two FBI agents interrogated him about a series of threatening letters that had been mailed from the prison to a federal judge. The FBI suspected him, but it became clear during their conversation that he wasn't the letter writer. What also became clear to the agents was that Thomas Little was totally absorbed by his friendship with Carl Bowles. "Carl Bowles and me are the best friends ever in the history of mankind," Little bragged. "He has helped me more than any man alive." And then he added, "When I get out, I'm going to do whatever is necessary to help him." Little was scheduled to be released no later than 1994, and the longer he talked to the FBI agents, the more convinced they became that Little intended to someday break Bowles out of the Hot House.

The FBI agents told the bureau about their conversation with Little, and officials decided to forbid the two men from writing to each other. They were told as soon as they were released from their respective Holes. Little protested. "I don't think the bureau realizes Carl helps me with my head and it makes my time easier," he said. "All I want is to be able to stay in contact with my friend."

The bureau claimed Bowles had "brainwashed" Little, and it said that the two men had spent their time in Leavenworth plotting future crimes that they could do together.

"We really underestimated Carl Bowles," a guard in Leavenworth said. "We all sat here and laughed about how Bowles was simply using Little as his sissie, but it seems old Carl was playing a much bigger game. This whole thing wasn't about sex at all. It was about Carl turning that kid into a little Carl Bowles. It wouldn't surprise me if Little did try to break him out of here or died trying to."

Bowles was irritated when he heard the brainwashing accusation.

"Look around here," Bowles said, scanning the cellhouse. "Do you really expect me to believe that in two hundred years of dealing with people, this prison is the best that society can come up with to deal with criminals like me? I don't. Even a cold-blooded killer like me knows that if you want to touch or influence someone, if you want to change them, you got to get down in their life. You want to change me, rehabilitate me, save me? Okay, you got to understand what makes me tick, what I feel, and why I think like I do.

"But that takes putting your ass on the line. That takes actually getting to know another person. It's easier to build a prison than to really get involved in someone's life. It's easier to lock me up than really care about me.

"Have you ever given freely, unselfishly of yourself to another without thoughts of material gain, even if it could mean risking your life?" Bowles continued. "Have you ever felt or shared your life so closely that you eat, sleep, work, and experience the same stimuli day after day? I don't mean passing time like on the streets, with a thousand contacts with people and things. I mean one-to-one communication like in a prison. You know, like when the food gives you heartburn, well, you both eat it, you both feel it. *That's* being the same. Bad weather, well, you both see it, feel it. The same. The lights go out—you're both in the dark together. If the shower water is cold, you both get uncomfortable together. You're gonna speak up for him. Him you. He's gonna cover for you, you him.

"That's how it is with Tom and me. I touched Tom's life like the bureau can never touch it, like society can never touch it, like no one can ever touch it, because I was in here with him and I cared! I mattered, he mattered.

"Do I know Tom, truly know him? Hell, I lived as Tom in here, Tom lived as me. That's something you never forget. He won't, never will. Neither will I. Tom and me, me and Tom—the same. Tom knows what I mean and so do I. That will never change. We are one, and as long as one of us is in chains, we both are. Tom understands that and so do I. That ain't brainwashing. That's love."

A Voice: MURDERER, AGE 39

The first time I was fucked I was sixteen in a county jail. Three of 'em grabbed me, two held me by the arms, the other one pulled down my pants. They took turns. But by the time the first son of a bitch got off of me, it wasn't the getting-fucked part that hurt, it was the fact these fuckers could just do it to me like I was a piece of meat.

The next day I was angry and scared. There wasn't much in this cell, but there was this wire screen over a vent and I noticed a piece of it was loose, so I reached up and bent it back and forth until it busted loose and then I had me a piece of wire about as long as a short pencil. I waited until one of these bastards took a nap after lunch and I took the wire and stabbed him in his face. I was aiming at his eyeball because I wanted to blind this bastard, but I missed and it hit him right by his nose and hit the bone there and bent and came right out the side of his cheek like a fish-hook. He starts screaming and grabs his face and I started smacking him and the guards came and hauled my ass out of there and took him to the hospital.

Maybe six years later, I'm doing some running around and howdy-doody, I get my butt busted in some fucking tiny town in Arizona and these hicks put me in a cell with this kid, probably seventeen or so, and you know what I did? I fucked him. I beat the shit out of him first and then I rolled him over and I fucked his ass.

And you know what, when I was doing it, I thought about how I'd been fucked, I sure did. I kept thinking about how it felt to be fucked in the ass, how much I had hated it, how humiliated I'd been.

You see, I finally understood why those motherfuckers fucked me when I was just a kid.

It really didn't have nothing to do with sex. It had to do with power. All my life, people been fucking me, and when I was fucking that kid, I hated what I was doing, but I loved it too, because it was me on top and there wasn't one fucking thing he could do to stop me. Nothing. I was in charge, complete control.

I could have done whatever the fuck I wanted to him and it is a fucking amazing feeling when you feel that way.

CHAPTER
FIFTY-FOUR

THOMAS SILVERSTEIN

In the basement of the Hot House, Thomas Silverstein resumed filing BP-9, BP-10, and BP-11 complaints with the bureau. He asked for permission to exercise outdoors where he could "breathe fresh air," to be moved to a cell where he could see, hear, and speak with other convicts, to have the lights in his cell turned off or at least dimmed at night when he slept. He complained because he was required to take a urine test each month to determine whether he was using illegal drugs. It was an unnecessary precaution, he argued, "since I'm in total solitary confinement and have no contact with other prisoners or visitors."

Every request that Silverstein made was rejected by Warden Matthews, who always gave the same rationale. In order to "maintain security . . . your request is denied."

Once a month, Silverstein was permitted to place a ten-minute collect telephone call. In the spring of 1989, he asked for permission to telephone a woman friend in London, England. She had promised to pay for the call. Warden Matthews denied the request for "security reasons." Silverstein appealed to the regional director, but this request was also denied. In his final plea to bureau headquarters, Silverstein argued that an overseas call was no more threatening to security than the long-distance call that he was permitted to make. "If she were in New York or California, you would let me call," he wrote. But Assistant Director K. M. Hawk again rejected Silverstein's request.

371

He didn't cite security as a reason: rather he wrote that overseas calls required too much "staff time and supervision." Silverstein was flabbergasted. "I realize the bureau isn't known for hiring brain surgeons, but can someone please tell me why it takes more staff to dial a number in England than it does to dial a number in California?" he asked.

Undeterred, his English pen pal announced that she was coming to the United States for a vacation and wanted to visit Silverstein. He filed an immediate request for permission to see her, but Matthews rejected it. "Our visiting policy requires that inmates have an established relationship with prospective visitors prior to their incarceration," Matthews wrote. "Your request does not meet this requirement."

Based on the bureau's rules, Silverstein could not visit with anyone he met after 1977, when he was first brought to the Hot House.

At about this same time, Matthews told Silverstein that he would not be allowed to enter any paintings in the Leavenworth Art Fair, the one time each year when inmates are allowed to sell their art (at bureau-set prices) to the public. Matthews said he didn't want Silverstein profiting from the notoriety that he received by killing Officer Merle Clutts. "People will buy a picture just because he painted it," Matthews said, "just because it says Silverstein on it, and that isn't right."

Silverstein stopped talking. He ignored Matthews, Connor, and the guards. On June 20, 1989, Matthews noted Silverstein's muteness in a monthly report to the regional office.

> When Silverstein was denied [permission to submit paintings to the art show] he became visibly upset and stopped all conversation with the staff.... He turned his television on, began pacing his cell and avoided all eye contact. Other staff have noted similar behavior recently when he is in a situation where he does not get his way. In the past, when he was placed in a conflict situation, he would intellectualize the issues and attempt to persuade and articulate his position. He has also requested a tape recorder to listen to motivational tapes. This request was also denied and his response was to ignore the person delivering the

information. . . . We will keep you informed of any changes.

I was not at Leavenworth when Silverstein started his silence strike, but he wrote me about it:

> My keepers look and sound human but deep down their actions are totally alien to me. They refuse me a visit with someone I care about because of "security" but Matthews brings tours through here—U.S. attorneys, judges, other BOPers—to see the big bad Silverstein in his cage. These places are just a giant monkey cage where people come to gloat and laugh at the misery of others.

By June of 1989, Silverstein had been under "no human contact" status for nearly six years. It was beginning to take its toll. He was easily depressed. "Most prisoners look forward to the day when they'll be set free," Silverstein explained. "All I can hope for or have left to hope for is that I can hold on to my sanity through it all. This is a nightmare, and it is strange having a nightmare when you're not even asleep, sitting in your very own personalized coffin, watching yourself rot away, day by day, minute by minute, wondering which part of yourself is first to decay. Is it your mind or your body or your soul or do they all die away simultaneously, until one day you look in the mirror and see tombstones in your eyes?"

He hated Matthews, Connor, and the guards now more than ever. "They want me to go crazy. They want to point their fingers at me and say, 'See, see, we told you he is a lunatic.' No one outside prison really understands how sick these people are. It is easier to assume that we deserve what we get. It's easier to believe we are all a bunch of animals, because if people on the streets began seeing us as people, they wouldn't allow the bureau to do what they are doing here.

"I didn't come in here a killer, but in here you learn hate. The insanity in here is cultivated by the guards. They feed the beast that lingers within all of us—just like Matthews and Connor are doing now by denying me even the most simple of requests—a telephone call, a visit, the joy of selling a painting.

"Sometimes, the thought of killing someone brings a smile to my face. It gets real sick when you start to look upon someone else's death as happiness, but I am not alone. How many guards in here have told you that they want to see me dead, and how did they react when they thought I was going to fly over the wall in Atlanta on a hang glider? They wanted to shoot me. They wanted to kill me.

"I find myself smiling at the thought of me killing Clutts each time they deny me a phone call, a visit, or keep the lights on. I find it harder and harder to repent and ask for forgiveness, because deep inside I can feel that hatred and anger growing."

Silverstein captured his feelings on paper. On an ordinary writing tablet, he had started to write a letter, but instead the black ink pen in his hand seemed to move by itself, rapidly sketching its own design. At the bottom of the page was a prisoner, naked, humbled behind bars, and rising out of the prisoner like a phoenix was a vicious, scowling, wild-eyed monster with his hand thrust forward from the cell, more a claw than fingers, reaching out to kill. When he finished the drawing, Silverstein wrote in block letters on the page: "SITTING, SILENTLY, THINKING AND SCREAMING FOR FREEDOM FROM THIS CONSTANT INSANITY AND ENDLESS SOLITARY CONFINE-MENT."

He had considered suicide, he said. "Some days, particularly when I'm blue, I think it would be the best way out of this nightmare. I don't always know why I did what I did, but the pain is there, and in those dark moments, the peace of death is inviting." He would not kill himself, however, because "that's what the BOPers want," and because if he did, his death would send other convicts a signal that "fighting back is useless."

In early July, Silverstein was told that he was going to be moved out of the basement into new quarters designed specifically for him. The bureau had built a new 120-bed special-housing unit in the east prison yard and one end of it contained a special cell just for Silverstein. When it was time for him to be transferred, a group of burly guards gathered outside his cell. Silverstein was ordered to strip, to bend over and spread his buttocks, to open his mouth and stick out his tongue. Convinced he wasn't hiding any weapons, the guards gave him a new set of clothing and ordered him to turn around and stick his hands through a letter-size window in the cell door. They put two pairs of handcuffs on him and then ordered him to move his legs close to the bars so that they could reach through and put two sets of leg irons on his ankles. Once that was completed, they opened the cell door, rushed in, and grabbed him. He didn't resist and was led upstairs to a waiting wheelchair. He was chained into it so he could no longer move his arms or feet, and then pushed through the rotunda and down center hall. It was after ten P.M., so all of the inmates were locked up for the night. At the end of center hall, he was pushed outside. It was the first time that Silverstein had been outdoors since the Cuban riots seventeen months earlier. He stared up at the black Kansas sky and wet his lips as if to taste the night's warm summer breeze. A few minutes later, he was in his new "home," which the guards called "the Silverstein suite." The lights were on. They would never be turned off. The bureau had decided that it cost too much to equip the cell with cameras that could see in the dark. "I'm not certain having the lights on all the time really bothers him," said Connor. "I think after six years he's used to it."

A month later, Silverstein wrote me this letter:

I am worried that my complaints will make it sound as if I am crying and sniveling. This is my cross to bear and as I sit here growing more frustrated by the minute, wondering what tomorrow will bring or next year or five years from now, I have to wonder what the fuck I have accomplished by talking to you. You see things in prison never change for the better. They only get worse by the minute when left unattended year after year after year until convicts finally explode and riot. The bottom line is—who the heck wants to listen to a crybaby? And for those who think I got what I deserve, my complaints just bring glee and laughs. To them this torture—messing with mail, denying visits—is sweet revenge. All I can say is fine and dandy, go ahead and gloat, but they should remember this about prisoners who go through this sick trip. Someday most of us finally get out of this hell and even a rational dog after getting kicked around year after year after year attacks when his cage door is finally opened.

CHAPTER
FIFTY-FIVE

ROBERT MATTHEWS

Warden Matthews couldn't have been happier on the day he celebrated his two-year anniversary at Leavenworth, July 13, 1989. "The other day I was walking down the institution's front steps and I was saying to myself, 'Jeez, I love my job,'" Matthews said. "The sun was shining and I was smiling and it was just a beautiful day and I was really happy with my lot in life. Everything is going so well."

The regional office had just chosen a Leavenworth guard as the outstanding employee of the year, a much-coveted bureau honor. The prison's SORT team had defeated its rival from Marion in a day-long competition that tested each team's skill at rifle and pistol shooting, weight lifting, footraces, rappelling, and a tug-of-war. Warden Matthews had been given a special award by Director Quinlan for instituting a community liaison program that brought civic leaders into the penitentiary once every four months for a tour and lunch.

Matthews was quick to recall other achievements. Lieutenant Bill Slack had arranged for Cubans to study English in small groups outside their cells and he'd put forty of them to work in prison industries. Eddie Geouge was doing well as the disciplinary-hearing officer. The penitentiary looked better than it ever had. It had been painted, repaired, two of its cellhouses had been remodeled, and construction crews were busy working on a third.

But most important of all, Matthews felt that he had finally won the support of the guards. Each year during National Corrections Week, all the penitentiary employees were invited to pose with the warden on the front steps of the Hot House for a group photograph. The pictures were placed in the prison archives where albums that contained similar photos dating back to the year the prison opened were kept. Only a few dozen employees had shown up for the photo session during Matthews's first year. But this time around the front steps had been crowded with close to three hundred employees. Nearly all of the staff at work during the day shift had posed with the warden. Matthews had been so delighted that he had hung copies of the photographs from both years in the warden's office so that everyone could see the enormous difference.

"I finally feel that the Bob Matthews administration is in place totally now," he said. "I do not mean to take anything away from Jerry O'Brien, but I now feel that I am doing the work, that my system is in place, and that the staff is behind me one hundred percent. The transition is complete. This is now my institution."

But despite all that he had accomplished, there was one area where Matthews could not claim any improvement. There was absolutely no evidence that anything he had done as warden during the past two years had helped rehabilitate a single convict.

This did not bother the warden at all. When he was a young caseworker just beginning his career at the penitentiary in Terre Haute, he had believed in rehabilitation. He had taken a personal interest in a young black bank robber from a Chicago ghetto who was the same age as he was. "He was a perfect inmate," Matthews recalled. "He was polite, respectful, and really seemed anxious to want to improve himself." Matthews helped the inmate earn his high school diploma and enroll in college courses. He spent hours talking to the inmate about his future and counseling him. "This inmate had been arrested robbing a bank with his older brothers," Matthews said, "and I was convinced that he was pressured into the robbery by them."

Matthews was so certain that the inmate had been rehabilitated that when it came time for him to go before the parole board, he wrote an impassioned plea on the inmate's behalf. The parole board voted to free the inmate, and over the next few years, Matthews often wondered what had happened to him. "I used to picture him teaching high school or college somewhere, raising a family, paying back his debt to society. If anyone was ever going to make it, he was."

And then one day ten years later, Matthews heard a voice call his name as he walked through a prison in Kentucky. It was the inmate. "He was in a wheelchair," Matthews said. "He had been shot in the back shortly after he was paroled. He had been robbing a bank with his brothers. He was paralyzed from the waist down."

Matthews was quiet after telling the story, and then he said, "There is evil in this world and sometimes you can't do anything to change that. You must accept it and deal with it. There are certain people who are just bad people, and these people are going to do bad things. That is why we need penitentiaries. That is why we need Leavenworth and that is why we will always have penitentiaries like Leavenworth."

It was later than usual when Warden Matthews finished his daily close-out session with his executive staff and left for home. As he walked from the warden's office into the prison lobby, he could hear the muffled sounds of hundreds of inmates inside the great rotunda as they headed toward the dining hall for dinner. The officers in the control center nodded in respect as Matthews stood in front of the penitentiary's steel front grille, waiting for it to open so he could leave. He hurried down the white limestone front steps guarded by two statues of growling lions. Jerry O'Brien had installed the lions. O'Brien thought they gave Leavenworth a certain regal atmosphere. He also hoped they would intimidate inmates when they first arrived. The guard in the tower yelled a cheery "Good night, sir!" to Matthews as he strolled across the asphalt to his car, now shaded from the hot July sun by the trees that lined the circular drive. It had taken him two full years, but he had finally accomplished his goal.

Robert Matthews was the master of the Hot House.

Six months later, he was gone. Director Quinlan sent him to take charge of the penitentiary at Atlanta. On January 1, 1990, Matthews's successor turned his car into the penitentiary's drive, drove past the guard tower, and slipped into the parking spot marked WARDEN. Within minutes he was climbing the Hot House's forty-three front steps.

AUTHOR'S NOTE

This book is a factual account of the activities inside the United States penitentiary in Leavenworth, Kansas, between July 1987 and July 1989. The material is based on interviews, prison and court records, newspaper accounts of various crimes, and personal observations by the author. More than one hundred people were interviewed face-to-face for this book, including several whose names do not appear but whose comments proved helpful in describing prison life. A few names have been changed to protect persons from physical harm or prosecution, but the only major character who was given a pseudonym was Norman Bucklew. All other convicts whose stories are described at length chose to use their actual names.

It would have been impossible to write this book without the cooperation of J. Michael Quinlan, director of the Bureau of Prisons. There is no constitutional guarantee that gives authors the right to enter prisons and interview inmates, yet Director Quinlan permitted me to come and go as I wished. There was never any attempt by guards to monitor my movements or conversations, and, to the best of my knowledge, no inmate or employee was ever coerced to speak to me or punished for doing so. I am grateful to Director Quinlan and to Warden Robert Matthews for their openness. I am also indebted to the employees and inmates at the Hot House who shared their stories with me.

I wish to thank the following persons by name. In Leavenworth: Frederick Thaufeer al-Deen, Terrance Alden, Gary Anderson, Susan Avila-McGill, Alvin Bass, Kirk Binszler, William Blount, Carl Bowles, Sam Callibone, Charles Carter, Barry Chapin, Carl Cheek, Steve Chuning, Earl Coleman-Bey, Lee Connor, Don Denny, H. W. Diamond, Sr., John Dobre, Phyllis Driscoll, Connie Duncan, Jeffrey Duncan, Armando Figueroa, Frank Flying Horse, Leonard Foresta, Yvonne M. Frament, Fred Fry, Burrell Fuller, Edward Gallegos, Daryel Garrison, Edward Geouge, Torres Germany, Richard Green, David Ham, Mike Harris, Jim Henderson, Charles Hill, Mike Janas, Sabrina Johns, Tracy Johns, Bill Kindig, Sharon Lacy, Steve Lacy, Bob Lawrence, Albert Lee III, Thomas Edgar Little, Bill Lucas, James Luongo, Bill Masters, Dan McCauley, Janice McCauley, Steve McGill, Cherre Miller, Eric Mitchell, Ray Moore, Carlos Moran, Osiris Morejon, Daisy Morello, Larry Munger, Kenneth Myer, Steve Myhand, Mark Nash, Bruce Newkirk, Jim Orr, Pat Othic, Craig Ozarowski, Connie Parish, Franklyn Perry, Leonard Peltier, David Phillips, Edward Pierce, William Post, Wade Rabb, Vandell Racy, Randy Ream, Ranldy Reed, Barbara Ricktor, Pamela Rothberger, John Rowe, John Rule, Eddie Sanchez, Mike Sandels, Jim Schroeder, Dallas Scott, Jim Sheeve, Jacquelyn Shivers, Ralph Siever, Dennis Silverberg, Thomas Silverstein, Ron Simpson, LeRoy Skaggs, Bill Slack, Bruce Smith, Clyde Smith, Dick Smith, J. R. Smith, Wayne Smith, Don Stiles, Dan Tedrick, Bill Terrell, Barbara Thomas, Bill Thomas, John Trott, Joe Trustee, Glenn Walters, Monty Watkins, Thomas White, Bill Whited, Ernie Williams, Jerry Wolfe, Mark W. Works.

In Washington: Clair A. Cripe, Gerald Farkas, Lloyd Hooker, John Jackson, Tom Kane, Laura Mecoy, Kathryn L. Morse, Roger Ray, Craig Trout. In Marion: Ronnie Bruscino, Randy J. Davis, John Greschner, Gary Henman, R. A. Litchfield, Mike Sizemore. Others include: Lawrence Y. Bitterman, Norman Carlson, Linda Davis, Maxine Evans, David Freeman, Jerry O'Brien, Jeannie Pellman, Elke Shoats, Doris Smith, Michael Stotts, Lois Wadsworth, Father John Wielebski.

I would particularly wish to thank two fellow writers, Walter Harrington and Patricia Hersch, who gave me excellent editorial guidance and moral support, as well as Ann Harris and Fred Klein, my editors at Bantam Books.

Others whose help I would like to acknowledge include: George and Linda Earley; Stephen J. O'Neil of the Los Angeles law firm of Sheppard, Mullin, Richter & Hampton; Carolyn Hunter; Nelson and Ginny DeMille; Karen Lockwood; Jay Myerson; Keran Harrington; Toni Shaklee; Lynn and LouAnn Smith; Dr. C. T. Shades; Donna and Wayne Wolfersberger; and my friends at United Christian Parish.

Last, I would like to thank my parents, Elmer and Jean Earley, for their loving advice and support; Barbara Hunter Earley, my wife, who put up with my being gone for months at a time while I was in Leavenworth; and Steve, Kev, and Kathy Earley, who were always waiting at home for Daddy with a smile and a hug.

ABOUT
THE
AUTHOR

PETE EARLEY's interest in prisons dates back to the 1970s, when he wrote a series of newspaper articles about the inhumane treatment of mentally ill convicts being held in the Oklahoma state prison system. He is the author of the bestselling *Family of Spies: Inside the John Walker Spy Ring*. A former reporter for *The Washington Post*, he has also written for *The New York Times, The International Herald Tribune*, and several national magazines.